W9-CAA-831

ALSO BY DAN WHITE

The Cactus Eaters

Under the Stars

Under the Stars

HOW AMERICA FELL IN LOVE
WITH CAMPING

DAN WHITE

HENRY HOLT AND COMPANY   NEW YORK

Henry Holt and Company, LLC
Publishers since 1866
175 Fifth Avenue
New York, New York 10010
www.henryholt.com

Henry Holt® and 🏛® are registered trademarks of
Henry Holt and Company, LLC.

Library of Congress Cataloging-in-Publication Data

Names: White, Dan, 1967–
Title: Under the stars : how America fell in love with camping / Dan White.
Description: New York : Henry Holt and Co., 2016. | Includes bibliographical
    references and index.
Identifiers: LCCN 2015042691| ISBN 9781627791953 (hardback) |
    ISBN 9781627791960 (electronic book)
Subjects: LCSH: Camping—United States. | Outdoor life—United States. |
    BISAC: NATURE / General. | TRAVEL / Special Interest / Adventure. | SPORTS
    & RECREATION / Camping.
Classification: LCC GV191.4 .W49 2016 | DDC 796.54—dc23
LC record available at http://lccn.loc.gov/2015042691

ISBN: 978-1-62779-195-3

Our books may be purchased in bulk for promotional, educational, or business use.
Please contact your local bookseller or the Macmillan Corporate and Premium Sales Department at
(800) 221-7945, extension 5442, or by e-mail at MacmillanSpecialMarkets@macmillan.com.

First Edition 2016

Tree graphic image by Edward Topor

Designed by Kelly S. Too

Printed in the United States of America

1 3 5 7 9 10 8 6 4 2

To Julianna and Amy for making this book possible, and to my dear father, Victor White (1926–2016), who died just before the publication of this book. He was my first camping hero and a major influence on my creative life. May his memory be a blessing to everyone who knew him and loved him.

What though? May there not come one glorious day in the weary year when we may cast aside every grief and every separate care and invite the soul to a day of rest? And in the future, when the days of trouble come, as they will come, I shall remember that grand day of rest, and the abundance of trout and bass wherewith I was comforted.

—George Washington Sears, aka "Nessmuk," 1883

I heard two noises coming from two separate areas of space over there. One of them could have been an owl, but the other one sounded like a cackling.

—Joshua Leonard, *The Blair Witch Project*, 1999

CONTENTS

———

Under the Stars

The Euro-Caucasians who started building settlements in North America in the early seventeenth century would have had a hard time recognizing the camping we do today. So would the gold rushers and the pioneers. As Cindy Aron wrote in her book *Working at Play: A History of Vacations in the United States*, "The earliest American 'campers' were not on vacation . . . The wilderness, for most such people, held little charm. It represented hardship, strenuous labor, and danger—a place to be traversed, subdued, and settled." Granted, some forms of camping are closer to the original spirit of survival camping than others, but if we're choosing whether to camp, it still falls into the realm of lifestyle or recreational camping. Just like "pick your own strawberries," pleasure camping is a playful and indulgent twist on something that was not meant to be fun in its original incarnation.

Recreational camping is not an invention like the dynamo or the incandescent lightbulb. It's a product of gradual refinement and much reconsideration, not just of camping practices but also of the animating philosophies behind them. Today's camping is the end result of changing attitudes toward wilderness as a place of mischief, devilry, and derangement in colonial times to a place of release, relaxation, or even worship. An estimated fifty million people camp every year in the United States. When contemplating such gigantic numbers, I had to wonder about the roots of this pastime, about the people who first experimented with voluntary camping, when it became popular, and how it changed or did not change with time. In the course of this journey, I began to notice that campers, including me, tended to dip their buckets into the same reservoir of tropes and traditions, unconsciously acting out the history of camping. A few brilliant, charismatic, and troubled young men with bold ideas and extravagant facial hair, and a few brave women who ventured into the forests and mountains in spite of restrictive clothing, double standards, and widespread prejudices, influenced the camping we practice today.

If you've camped because you wanted a more strenuous life to build up your character and prove something about yourself; or slept in a three-sided "lean-to" facing a cook fire; or spent thousands of dollars to stay in a luxury tent with a parquet floor, kitchen, and bathroom along with an optional "tent butler" who roasted your s'mores for you; or if you've had ecstatic visions in forests, or gone on "value added" camping trips involving yoga, lectures, site restorations, and trash pickups, you owe something to the people who launched recreational camping nearly two centuries ago.

To pay tribute to those men and women, I wanted, as much as possible, to see what they saw and do as they did. My general rule is that I could not write about any period of camping history without living through it as much as possible. In my tribute to a survivalist who camped without any gear or clothing a century ago, I went to a forest and camped with nothing, or as close to nothing as I could manage. To understand the once-standard practice of hiring a backwoods guide to accompany nineteenth-century campers into the Adirondacks of upstate New York, I went out there and hired a backwoods helper myself. As part of my exploration of Leave No Trace camping, I set out to clean up one of America's most popular mountains, using a biohazardous waste receptacle called the Immaculator. I camped in the croc-and-gator-infested Everglades with one of the least-represented groups of people in American campgrounds to explore the thorniest question in outdoor recreation today: What can be done about the blinding whiteness of camping and the diversity gap in the woods?

When safety and logistics permitted, I made sure to bring my wife and, in particular, my young daughter on these campouts, because my parents transmitted their love of the wilderness to me when I was a young child. I wanted to preserve and sustain this value for Julianna so she wouldn't grow up to be a twenty-first-century neurasthenic glued to whichever digital gewgaw will become "a thing" by the time she reaches adolescence. So I hope you've cinched up your Gore-Tex boots, slathered yourself with SPF 100 sunscreen, and updated your life insurance policy. Throw your things in the backseat. It's time to go camping.

1

Help Me, Henry

How many a man has dated a new era in his life from the reading
of a book?

—Henry David Thoreau, *Walden*

Everyone has an overwhelming influence at a tender age. One person or entity rules over them. For some unfortunates, it's Ayn Rand. For others, it's Paulo Coelho, Viktor Frankl, Judas Priest, or Neil Peart, the drummer and lyricist from the rock band Rush. Henry David Thoreau is an influence that must overcome you when you're young or not at all. Otherwise he cannot infect you. You'll develop immunity. If you pick it up when you're too old, his most famous book, *Walden*, tastes funny: a treacle pie with too much vinegar. The odd flavor makes sense, considering Thoreau was young, heartbroken, drifty, and confused when he set out to have the experiences that informed the book. That is one reason *Walden* remains a classic for literary-minded campers, with special appeal to youthful wilderness explorers and aspirants to the simple life. Thoreau speaks to people like my younger self: lumpy, shiftless, bumbling, insecure, unsettled, unfulfilled, and out of step with the times. In proclaiming the woods a refuge, Thoreau, in an offbeat and prickly way, helped generations of nervous Americans fall in love with camping.

In his combative and seductive writings, Thoreau gave Americans their first coherent and persuasive conservation philosophy. But it took a while for the book and its notions to take hold. *Walden*, published in 1854, sold briskly during its first month, but interest soon fell off. For the next fifteen years, it sold an average of three hundred copies annually. Then it got into the hands of long-haired wilderness prophet John Muir, who used it as a template for his rhapsodic and angry writings about woodlands, meadows, and mountains and the need to preserve them from lumber interests and livestock. Robert Frost, another great champion of the book, observed in 1915 that *Walden* "must have a good deal to do with the making of me." The book began its upward tilt in the early twentieth century, when its ecological message caught on. Much has changed since the days when Thoreau looked out from his cabin at a nation that measured woods "in terms of board feet, not in terms of watershed protection, birds and music," Justice William O. Douglas of the U.S. Supreme Court once remarked. *Walden*, with its warnings, tart observations, and detailed instructions for renewal in the wilderness, helped bring about the change.

The book was radical in its time. Even now it is divisive. It was meant to be. Thoreau sometimes acted like a Puritan, a judgmental prig, and a scold—no booze, no fornication—with annoying temperance rants and occasional salvos at his readers. "It is very evident what mean and skulking lives many of you live," he wrote in *Walden*. Yet he ridiculed Puritan ideas about everything, from the importance of daily toil for its own sake to the wickedness of the woods. I see him as a turncoat, old before his time but rebelling against old ways. An agitator and mischief maker, Thoreau had no use for the busybody neighbors who considered him a gadfly and a lazybones. If he acted like a geriatric sourpuss from time to time, we can give him a bit of license, because Thoreau was the nineteenth-century equivalent of the Raging Grannies.

When Thoreau was a young man, taking his first camping and boating trips, his countrymen were still breaking away from the influence of America's Calvinist founders. In 1662 the Puritan poet Michael Wigglesworth wrote that forests were places of "fiends, and brutish men / That devils worshipped." In Puritan speeches and poems, the woods were always "howling," "whooping," "roaring," "screaming," "singing," "ranting," and "insulting." In a cheeky riposte, Thoreau remarked in 1857 that "generally speaking a howling wilderness does not howl; it is the imagination of the traveler that does the howling." By making natural areas seem like places of renewal instead of madness and demons, Thoreau brought America just a little bit closer to today's world of dome tents, grill racks, and self-inflating sleeping pads.

He was a fine backwoodsman and camper, although he did some silly things in the outdoors from time to time. In one campout, he and his brother, perhaps because of bad planning, were forced to eat cocoa and bread for supper after a long day's rowing. In a journey to Maine, he and his campmates set up their tent so close to the fire that it burned to a crisp, forcing them to shelter from the rain beneath their upturned bateau. But Thoreau's appreciative readers value him not so much for his backcountry prowess as for his powers of observation and description. His writing is ecstatic and specific, larded with insight and biting humor, grounded in details about the natural world and his interior landscape. His antimaterialistic and antimodernist passages and promises of moral perfection in the wilderness challenge his readers to disrupt their lives by taking a journey into the trees. Venturing alone in the wild, a wanderer might discover in the first rays of the "morning star" that he or she has the same nobility as pilgrims from the heroic ages.

There lies the promise and the inherent danger of Thoreau's writing. Deep in the forest, we might "settle ourselves, and work and wedge our feet downward through the mud and slush of opinion and prejudice and tradition and delusion . . . till we come to a hard bottom and rocks in place, which we call *reality*." Thoreau tells us that a retreat to the wilderness is no retreat at all; nor is it an interruption. No, it is the life *outside* the woods, the toil and the compromise that intrude. Days and nights among the trees is not time off the books. It is not a subtraction from the days of life but an addition to them. Such advice intoxicates us, but Thoreau's words can be fatal if we take them too far without sufficient preparation; he tells us to go out and do it for ourselves, but sometimes nature does not abide. Nature is freedom and sunshine. Nature is also bears, yellow jackets, rockfall, and vertical exposure. Nature wins. In promising freedom and deliverance in wild places, Thoreau sent more than a few copycats to their doom, and has put many more in perilous situations. *You can do it too*, Thoreau seems to tell us, but sometimes the answer is *No, I can't*. Here I speak from grim experience. On more than one occasion, *Walden*, that beloved, accursed book, nearly cost me my life.

My *Walden*-provoked near-death incidents in the woods are legion—near drownings, tumblings, dehydration, you name it—but the most recent and frightening example took place in one of the worst areas for a man to get lost in the United States: the jungles of eastern Kentucky. I headed out there for the same reason I ever go to the wilderness: because Henry told me that "village life" would make me "stagnate" unless I enjoyed the "tonic" and "compensation" of mists and marshes, pinewoods, high grass, toads, and hickories, the "living and decaying trees, the thunder cloud and the rain" as often as possible.

Before this camping trip took a turn toward the nightmarish, the journey was lovely and elemental.

I was camped alone on the first night with my battered copy of *Walden* beneath some old-growth hemlocks and white oaks in southeastern Kentucky. I was settling into my sleeping spot, nipping from an eighth of frontier whiskey, listening to the night birds of the western Appalachians, close-reading passages at random, and eating cold pumpkin curry straight from the foil pouch. What more could a man ask of his life? My finger settled on a sentence I hoped would inspire me, but it turned out to be a ridiculous tirade about liquor. "I believe that water is the only drink for a wise man. Wine is not so noble a liquor; and think of dashing the hopes of a morning with a cup of warm coffee, or of an evening with a dish of tea!" "Oh, shut up, Henry! Why don't you lighten up?"

Platforms of wrinkled limestone rose above the trees. The nightjars asked the same question all night long: "Whip or wheel? Whip or wheel?" I was having a fine time out there, and my ego was getting the better of me because I was doing a freelance travel writing assignment, involving a hike and overnight campout along a new forty-two-mile section of the Pine Mountain State Scenic Trail. When it's finished, the PMT will be part of a sixteen-hundred-mile-long pathway called the Great Eastern Trail, connecting Alabama with New York. I could hardly believe that someone was paying me to go camping. The thought of this made me more self-confident than I had any reason to be. Somehow I'd disregarded the ominous nickname of the Kentucky backwoods: the Dark and Bloody Ground.

The next day, I packed my scant belongings and headed deeper into the forest to hike the trail through a land of rhododendron tunnels, gorges, and rose pogonia. I'd heard the pathway was well marked with square-shaped blue and yellow blazes on the trees. I thought my seven-dollar drugstore compass, the vague map I'd printed from the Internet, and my one-gallon plastic water jug would get me through.

I followed a narrow path downhill over crispy leaves, past green and lichen-encrusted brown rocks. This land of ancient rock slides, mansion-size boulders, and vertical drops had a dreamlike quality that made it hard to believe I was there. Below me, I saw a natural bridge called Eagle Arch Rock. Framed in the clearing, it looked like a levitating boulder. Blobs of berry-speckled bear scat gummed my boots. "This is your life now," I said as I sucked in my gut and lifted my backpack to press my body through a cleft in a boulder.

My unwarranted self-possession made me careless. After a good while of sauntering, and staring dreamily, into the green, I failed to notice the path and the blue and yellow blazes on the trees were nowhere in sight. Less than two hours after leaving camp, I was lost. I spun around, looking for any signifier that would take me back to the trail. I found none. Now I remembered that even Daniel Boone, one of the most accomplished woodsmen in America, found these Kentucky backwoods confounding. "No, I can't say I was ever lost," the elderly Boone reportedly told the portrait painter Chester Harding in 1820. "But I was bewildered once for three days."

I could not afford to be turned around for half a week like Boone. The day was quite warm, I was sweating profusely, and I had been profligate about my water gulping. Now I had barely enough water to last until afternoon. For another hour, I walked aimlessly, hoping for a miracle reunion with the trail, my hiking boots making burp sounds on the boggy ground. I marched into the bushes, interrupting a pair of amorous toads. A flock of eastern wild turkey crashed through the underbrush, heads bobbing. They looked like upright vultures. Their brains are two thirds bigger than those of domestic "factory" turkeys. As I was finding out for myself, the unwilding process fosters stupidity.

I was starting to panic now, walking in loop-the-loops on boggy ground. The water ticked beneath my feet. Boulders walled me off on one side. On the other side, a ridge plunged into darkness. Far away, the Cumberland Plateau rose out of the mist. Magnolias, maples, and basswoods formed a green barrier. A garter snake flicked its tongue. I tore through some nettles, tripped over pebbles, and found myself on what appeared to be an old abandoned buggy road along a slippery alcove of rocks and hard-packed dirt. The ten-foot-wide path traveled along a ledge above an expanse of black mud with streams branching across it. Between the cliff and path, murky water formed a natural moat. The fear hit me then: *You are in the*

Kentucky backwoods, you've got no GPS, you didn't bring a good map because there were supposed to be blazes, and now you're nowhere.

I ran back and forth on the buggy trail, but I was rushing toward nothing, my old and scratched-up Pacific Crest Trail backpack clunking against me. For the next few hours, I kept on walking in mad circles. Why the hell did I bring *Walden* instead of some end-of-days man-versus-nature tactical survival book? "Help me, Henry," I thought to myself. "Please. You were the one who brought me out here. I'm in a tight spot. *Do something.*"

In the past, I made bad mistakes when panic set in. I vowed not to do that again. Sitting on that eastern Kentucky rock, I took out the copy of *Walden* just to have the weight of it in my hand. I felt an odd mixture of appreciation and resentment. Because of that book, I've had more raptures and catastrophes than I can count; I took it with me on a dozen trips. Now it didn't have a front cover anymore. As I flipped through the pages, I hoped that Henry would tell me something, anything, that would help me get me the hell out of there.

That copy of *Walden* came into my possession under strange circumstances, during the summer after my college graduation. A few of us stragglers were holding on to our undergraduate lives. I had been squatting at Alpha Delta Phi, my eccentric coed frat house in Middletown, Connecticut, dodging phone bills, filching beers from the communal refrigerator, and pining for my only girlfriend ever. We met at a writing class, where we bonded over our love for Edward Hoagland essays and Willa Cather novels. Now she was moving to Seattle to find herself without me. When I walked out of the frat and showed up at a house party near the other side of campus, I was hopped up on self-pity. "The house is red-tagged anyway," the host told me. "Unfit for human occupancy. They're tearing it down." He accepted my cold six-pack and handed me a hammer. "Go crazy," he said. Every room was a scene of destruction. Scared and jobless college kids attacked the house with broomsticks and bats, overturning a cabinet, kicking doors until they splintered on their hinges. The house shook with impact tremors. After some hesitation, I stood on a sofa, jumped up, and knocked a hole in the ceiling. Flakes of plaster settled on my eyelashes.

The next day, without knowing why, I showed up dry-mouthed and hungover at the condemned house, which had a crawl space I hadn't noticed before. Without a flashlight, I slipped into the opening under the floorboards and crawled in the dark until my head banged into a box of books.

I dragged it into the light. Someone had written TO BE DISCARDED on the cardboard in red permanent marker. I stuffed the box in the trunk of my Oldsmobile Cutlass Supreme and drove to the Alpha Delta Phi house. What a trove that box turned out to be: lots of Graham Greene, some J. P. Donleavy novels, a luridly illustrated leather-bound book on spell casting and Satanism that I cherish to this day, and a mint-condition first printing of E. B. White's *The Points of My Compass*, which I read in one gulp.

Every essay in the White book is compelling, but the one that really got to me was "A Slight Sound at Evening," which called my attention to the glories of Thoreau and *Walden*. I'd heard of the latter book, of course, but had avoided it, assuming it was a political screed or survival-in-the-woods polemic. But White cast *Walden* as "the best youth's companion yet written in America," and said that the book was "like an invitation to life's dance, assuring the troubled recipient that no matter what befalls him in the way of success or failure he will always be welcome to the party—that the music is played for him, too, if he will but listen and move his feet."

Alongside the White book was a copy of *Walden* itself, waterlogged, underlined, dog-eared, but readable. It was as if White himself were standing there making introductions. White made *Walden* seem like pure uplift, but for me, in my first explorations, the most catching part of the text was its implicit threat. If I did *not* live deliberately, if I did *not* "front only the essential facts of life," and *not* see what it had to teach, at the end of my days I would "discover that I had not lived." That was quite a lesson for an overprotected, mollycoddled, and risk-averse young man whose ruling principle was fear. The book nagged at me in my postcollegiate years. I disregarded its message, though it reminded me, at all turns, that my life lacked agency. I hadn't seen or done anything worthwhile. "What is called resignation is confirmed desperation," Thoreau said. I could avoid such a fate by consoling myself "with the bravery of minks and muskrats." To front the essential facts, I could commune with the creatures of the forest, or at least commiserate with them. In shielding myself from direct experience, pleasurable or painful, I was half-alive. "No way of thinking or doing, however ancient, can be trusted without proof." In this way, I could address the uncertainty of living: "Life! Who knows what it is and what it does?"

In his late twenties, Thoreau had little to show for his college degree. Maybe he felt guilty that his mom and dad had to scramble to pay the $179 yearly tuition for him to attend Harvard. He was a schoolteacher for a while, but he resigned after whipping his students for no apparent reason after his employers accused him of being too nice to them. His other occupations: surveyor, occasional lecturer, and part-time editor of a literary magazine with a puny circulation. It wasn't that Thoreau lacked skills. He was a better swimmer, boater, walker, and runner than most anyone in his hometown of Concord, Massachusetts. He could shoot a snowball off a post. He was so handy that he built a serviceable boat, the *Musketaquid*, from scratch with his brother in a week. Its mast doubled as a tent pole. The two of them used it to explore the Concord and Merrimack Rivers in 1839. Thoreau was so dexterous he could reach into a pile of pencils at his dad's business and come out with a perfect dozen every time. He once made a pair of gloves to cover the claws of chickens rampaging through the garden of his friend and mentor Ralph Waldo Emerson. Yet he had reason to feel like a washout.

Like my collegiate self until senior year, he was a loser in love. Sometimes he came across as owlish and aloof. He was, in the words of one acquaintance, Nathaniel Hawthorne, "Ugly as sin. . . . He is . . . long-nosed, queer-mouthed, and with uncouth and rustic, though courteous manners, corresponding very well with such an exterior."

Thoreau had a cold fish reputation in Concord, but he fell hard and

Henry David Thoreau: writer, philosopher, conservationist,
simple-life advocate, camper, and alleged "flibbertigibbet."

painfully for a minister's daughter named Ellen Sewall. His brother John loved her, too, but neither one could win her over. She had some affection for Thoreau, but her father considered him a transcendentalist radical and would have none of it. How I'd love to find evidence that Thoreau flattened the burdock with some lovely young Lyceum Circuit groupie, but there is no evidence to suggest he was anything other than a lifelong virgin. After another romantic heartbreak, Thoreau wrote one of the saddest references to fruit in literary history: "Our life without love is . . . like the cocoanut in which the milk is dried up."

Soon, the lovelorn Thoreau would have to contend with profound grief in addition to his romantic frustration. John, his older brother, best friend, and loyal camping partner, caught tetanus by nicking himself so slightly with a shaving razor that the wound barely bled. John contracted lockjaw. He passed away in Thoreau's arms in 1842. Thoreau was so tormented that he developed symptoms that resembled lockjaw. For a while, his family was sure he was going to die next, but the spell broke. His agonies were psychosomatic. Like so many wilderness wayfarers Thoreau has inspired since then, he looked to the woods for healing. But poor Thoreau soon had reason to doubt his prowess as a woodsman.

In April 1844, when he was out on a camping trip with his friend Edward Sherman Hoar, the two of them decided to cook up a fish stew in a rotting stump in a patch of woods between Concord and Fairhaven Bay. The friends failed to notice the dry and brittle ground all around them. This was a colossally stupid move. Thoreau recalled, "That way went the flames with wild delight, and we felt that we had no control over the demonic creature to which we had given birth." Because of this ugly incident, which destroyed three hundred acres of forest, the townspeople of Concord gave this friendly but awkward young man a nasty nickname: Woodsburner. They also called him a "damned rascal" and, worst of all, a "flibbertigibbet." Thoreau, in a bizarre journal entry, later described himself watching the fire with a certain amount of excitement and admiration. This was not a very auspicious beginning for the father of modern environmentalism.

His writing about the incident emphasized the spectacle of the fire. Is it possible that this strange display of enthusiasm belied a secret guilt about the accident that drove him closer to *Walden*? If so, it pushed him toward a destiny that became inevitable for him after he read *Nature*, Emerson's ode to the wild, written in 1836. That elegant and beautiful book-length essay did more than just start transcendentalism. It presented the woods as a house of worship without walls and a place where boyhood never ends.

"In good health, the air is a cordial of incredible virtue," Emerson wrote.

> Crossing a bare common, in snow puddles, at twilight, under a clouded sky, without having in my thoughts any occurrence of special good fortune, I have enjoyed a perfect exhilaration. I am glad to the brink of fear. In the woods too, a man casts off his years, as the snake his slough, and at what period soever of life, is always a child. In the woods, is perpetual youth. . . . In the woods, we return to reason and faith. There I feel that nothing can befall me in life,—no disgrace, no calamity (leaving me my eyes), which nature cannot repair. Standing on the bare ground,—my head bathed by the blithe air, and uplifted into infinite space,—all mean egotism vanishes. I become a transparent eye-ball; I am nothing; I see all; the currents of the Universal Being circulate through me; I am part or particle of God.

Along with another Emerson essay, "Self-Reliance," *Nature* created an instant blueprint for the experience Thoreau craved. All he needed was one more push toward the woods. This came on March 5, 1845, in the form of a letter from his friend Ellery Channing, urging him to begin the grand process of devouring himself alive. Thoreau needed a retreat to reduce his life to its elements. He wanted open time to write and pay tribute to his poor lost John and their times in the woods.

Walden Pond, in Concord, was not Thoreau's first choice for a camping spot. If things had gone differently, his masterwork would have been written somewhere else, which meant the book might have been called *Fairhaven Hill*, or *The Weird Dell*. When a landholder named Flint refused Thoreau's request to build a cabin near Sandy Pond, Thoreau was so enraged that he condemned the man to literary hell in *Walden*, where he called Flint "the unclean and stupid farmer . . . some skin-flint." His choice of Walden Pond was, in part, a matter of convenience because Emerson owned undeveloped land there. Instead of a tent, Thoreau decided to camp out with something sturdier—a cabin, but a basic ten-by-fifteen-foot version, with walls to keep out the elements, but no rodent proofing (mice came and went) and no security; the doors had no locks.

If you're out there camping with borrowed equipment or stuff you've scrounged from the Salvation Army—as I have done many times—take heart in the fact that Thoreau had to borrow his hatchet and make do with recycled shanty boards, "sappy" refuse shingles for roofing and siding, "second-hand windows with glass," and a thousand recovered bricks. The cabin cost him $28.12 to make. The modern-day equivalent would be less than nine hundred dollars. Like today's recreational campsites, his cozy shack on Emerson's lakeside property was never meant to be permanent. It was a temporary life that he would have to leave one day so he could hit the lecture circuit, polish up his notes, and deliver his book to the world. This was camping as a public act that was meant to reverberate beyond the pond.

Walden espouses a form of living that seemed new to Thoreau's contemporaries. But he was not the first to find pleasure, rejuvenation, and freedom by sleeping in the woods.

One early description of a sometimes-pleasurable campout comes from William Byrd II of Westover, a Virginia plantation owner, hobbyist-naturalist, and writer. In 1728, Byrd headed into the forest as part of a group of surveyors, survivalist types, and officials on a 242-mile adventure from the shores of the Atlantic into the heights of the Blue Ridge Mountains. He and his men were trying to fix the disputed boundary line of North Carolina and Virginia, which was in shambles. During their journey, Byrd and his comrades bloodied themselves on wild grape thorns, and fell face-first into piles of sucking mud. They were forced to build trenches around their camp as a rainstorm washed in. "Every thing was so thoroughly soaked," Byrd complained.

In spite of the harsh terrain and wet weather, Byrd and his crew had fun out there sometimes. One day, he and his men arrived in a lovely open field, close to a planter friend's "tolerable good house" with "clean furniture." The planter offered the men lodging, "and yet we could not be tempted." Byrd feared that sleeping inside would make his men grow "too tender." He also liked the idea of camping for pleasure, not out of desperation. The idea of it sounded "so new, so sweet." The evening was pure joy. "A clear sky, spangled with stars, was our canopy, which being the last thing we saw before we fell asleep, gave us magnificent dreams."

If Byrd and Henry David Thoreau lived in the same historical period and in the same town, they would not have been friends. Byrd was a slave owner, a sexual libertine, and a creepy sadist who humiliated his servants.

He was also a snob who could afford to have a romantic view of the land because he had other people toiling in the fields for him. But at least the two men had one thing in common: Byrd's campout, like Thoreau's stay at Walden Pond, was provocative, brash, and even shocking in its time. A North Carolina senator, staying at the planter's house, stumbled into Byrd's camp and was so amazed to see human beings sleeping on the ground by choice that he started jumping around and shouting. Later on, after apologizing for scaring the campers, the senator "swore he was so taken with our lodging, that he would set fire to his house as soon as he got home, and teach his wife and children to lie, like us, in the open field," Byrd reported. In his writings about the camping trip, Byrd mocked the "Losers" who preferred "featherbeds and warm apartments" to slumbering outdoors.

Thoreau's predecessors in the wild also included the mountain men, the scraggly group of long-haired rogues and adventurers who dominated the western frontier in the early nineteenth century, trapping beaver for pelts to feed the fur trade. Their days of glory lasted from the 1820s to the 1840s. Clad in deerskin shirts, and conditioned to hike for days without sleep while eating the most miserable food, these men could shoot with deadly precision and, like Thoreau after them, reveled in the freedom they found in the forest. Unlike Thoreau, they loved to have rowdy good times, especially at their legendary annual camping "rendezvous," where lots of them got blindingly drunk from great big containers of alcohol, including a substance called "tangle leg"—perhaps because it made them lurch around like broken-legged insects—and "tarantula juice," sharper than any spider bite.

Their survival techniques, borrowed, stolen, and adapted from Native Americans, would influence late-nineteenth-century woodcraft campers. But the mountain men were in no sense recreational campers. Their lives were often brutish and short. Many of them were in desperate circumstances and escaping poverty back home. Thoreau shared their wanderlust, but he framed the wilderness in a very different way. At a time when many Americans aligned themselves *against* nature, Thoreau stood with the forest and camped against conformity, boredom, the forces of slavery and mechanization, and America's unprovoked war with Mexico in 1846.

If Thoreau was tone-deaf and flippant when he dared compare the "slavery" of the office worker to that of more than three million African Americans in literal slavery, his message, aimed at the quietly desperate and nature-starved clerks of America, is just as valid now as it was in the mid-nineteenth century. Perhaps there was something prankish, and not just symbolic, in the move to the pond. But if *Walden* is meant to be a joke, it is a deadly serious one. From his pulpit in the cramped cabin, Thoreau took aim at contemporary life, and his aim remains true. "Every aspect of the move to Walden was symbolic or representative," notes Robert Richardson in his acclaimed biography *Henry Thoreau: A Life of the Mind.* "The move itself was an emancipation from town and family, building the cabin was proof of his ability to shelter himself, growing beans showed he could feed himself, and have something left over."

Thoreau also used wilderness as a way to disrupt his life on purpose, to stop himself from settling into stasis, conforming, giving up, surrendering to materialism and easy comforts. No wonder so many modern-day pilgrims, such as Christopher McCandless, have fallen into the book. John Krakauer's nonfiction best seller *Into the Wild*, published in 1996, tells the story of this bright and idealistic young Emory University graduate, who took to heart Thoreau's injunction to pare life down to its essentials. A close and admiring reader of Thoreau, McCandless picked up on the smart-assed, provocateur side of his hero. Before embarking on a fatal path toward self-reliance in the Alaskan bush, McCandless burned his Social Security card and his paper money, and donated his life savings, a sum of twenty-four thousand dollars, to Oxfam America. Perhaps he looked to *Walden* as a model and an impossibly high standard for the transformative American campout.

For 113 days in the backcountry in 1992, the twenty-four-year-old McCandless tried to live like a combination of Henry Thoreau and a hardscrabble survivalist from the pages of Jack London, whom he also idolized. McCandless blended transcendentalist idealism with a desire to "find himself" in a more raw form of nature. A derelict Fairbanks City Transit System bus was his cabin, a raging glacial river his Walden Pond. In September 1992 a moose hunter stumbled upon the bus and McCandless's starved, sixty-seven-pound body. A copy of *Walden*, with a missing cover, was lying near the corpse. McCandless had highlighted a passage:

> Rather than love, than money, than fame, give me truth. I sat at a table where were rich food and wine in abundance, an obsequious attendance, but sincerity and truth were not; and I went away hungry from the inhospitable board. The hospitality was as cold as the ices.

I cannot imagine Thoreau, the practical Yankee who accepted odd jobs during his tenure at Walden Pond, praising McCandless for burning money or going out to live full-time in a landscape he didn't know. Yet I find it hard to dismiss McCandless, who, if he'd survived his adventure, would have had a great deal to say about humility, practicality, and overcoming ignorance. Besides, there is something about *Walden* that challenges us all to go much farther than Thoreau ever dreamed. *Walden* was, and continues to be, a jumping-off point for adventurers seeking to go deeper into the woods. The cabin was a testing ground, a means "to live a primitive and frontier life though in the midst of an outward civilization," Thoreau wrote. In other words, he knew full well that he was not testing himself against true wilderness, "but simulating its conditions in a sort of symbolic or laboratory experiment," Robert Richardson, the Thoreau biographer, wrote.

These days, *Walden* comes in for a certain amount of ridicule. One of the earliest takedowns of the book was printed in 1849, five years before *Walden* was even published. That year, Horace Greeley, the powerful editor of the *New-York Tribune*, and an ardent Thoreau admirer, wrote an editorial about Thoreau's lectures regarding his "Life in the Woods," a series of speeches that served as material for the book-in-progress. It spoke about this strange little man who lived all alone in a cabin, worked hardly ever, and rested much of the time; who communed with woodchucks and scorned those who toiled their days away. That July, a *Tribune* reader sent an angry letter to the editor. Writing on behalf of his shrew of a wife, the respondent called Thoreau "a whimsy or else a good-for-nothing, selfish, crab-like sort of chap" who was leading "a cold and snailish kind of existence . . . both infernal and infernally stupid." Coincidentally enough, the writer of that letter's last name was Thorough.

All these years later, the angry rebuttals continue. Perhaps Thoreau's admirers would not have to defend him against unbelievers, year after tiresome year, if his adventure had been just a wee less rustic and genteel and a touch more extreme. Thoreau's decision to live for a couple of years at Walden Pond was not that daring, even though his mother and sisters worried about him, way out in the lonely forest one and a half miles from town. The book that has kindled so many campfires is about an experience that was not exactly camping, and not much of a trip at all.

While Thoreau was at Walden Pond, from July 4, 1845, to September 6,

1847, where the Fitchburg Railroad passed "about a hundred rods south" of the cabin, Herman Melville embarked on a whaling ship voyage, having the adventures that informed his 1851 literary flop *Moby-Dick*. The Donner Party was heading westward, hoping for better things. Thoreau's stay coincided also with the dangerous journeys of John Charles Frémont, and with Sir John Franklin's attempt to find the Northwest Passage, which ended with the captain and his men entombed in ice and dying from hunger and exposure.

You will find no such episodes of horror in *Walden*. In my first read-through, before the book started to take effect, I kept wondering, "When the hell is something, anything, going to *happen*?" I'd been told it was a survivalist tract, but Thoreau never captures a moose in a deadfall trap or leaps from one side of a crevasse to the other; nor does he gut a pouncing catamount with a sixteen-inch fixed-blade Bowie knife.

What did Thoreau actually do out at Walden? Not a whole hell of a lot from a *Survivor* or Bear Grylls perspective. If you were to take a documentary film crew from one of those sweaty survivalist programs, put them in a time machine, and send them to Walden Pond, they would be poleaxed from boredom. Thoreau hoed a row to plant beans. He bathed daily in the lake. Some jerk named Seeley stole his nails, and then had the gall to stand around, idle and unconcerned, while Thoreau worked on the cabin. Two ladies came over and visited him. They took his drinking dipper and never returned it. "They came to steal," Thoreau fulminated in his diary. "They were a disgrace to their sex and to humanity. Pariahs of the moral world. . . . They will never know peace till they have returned the dipper."

Thoreau dined on simple food, including unleavened raisin bread and roasted horned pout, a sort of fish. Also, Thoreau befriended a wild mouse, which ran up his pantaloons and ate cheese from his hand. When he pulled out his flute and played a solo, the mouse seemed to listen and become his friend. He took long walks and roughed out two books. In solitude, in his patch of forest, Thoreau occupied his "sunny doorway" from sunrise until noon every day, "rapt in a revery, amidst the pines and hickories and sumachs, in undisturbed solitude and stillness, while the birds sang around or flitted noiseless through the house, until by the sun falling in at my west window, or the noise of some traveller's wagon on the distant highway, I was reminded of the lapse of time."

Those who care too much about his stridency and his antisensual aspect ignore his borderline erotic episodes of transport in nature. He listened to the pond freeze up and thaw. He fretted about woodchucks bothering his bean sprouts, and asked a trapper if there was anything to be done about this. "Yes," the trapper replied. "Shoot 'em, you damn fool." As far as plot is concerned, that's about it. I am always astonished when people carp at Thoreau for his "capricious" decision to reduce two years on Walden Pond to just one year in his book. I consider this reduction an editorial act of mercy. *Walden* is a greatest hits version of his limited experiences out there, and for good reason. How many descriptions of rocks and bean fields do we really want?

Walden is not so dramatic on the surface, but then again, not much ever really happens when we camp out. Thoreau, like all the most thoughtful campers, was a miniaturist who writ small moments large. An ever-changing music filled his ears at Walden Pond, and he, like no other camper in American history, was able to capture the sounds on paper and share them with the world: the "squirrels on the roof and under the floor, a whip-poor-will on the ridge-pole, a blue jay screaming beneath the window, a hare or woodchuck under the house, a screech owl or a cat owl behind it, a flock of wild geese or a laughing loon on the pond, . . . a fox to bark in the night," and the "sturdy pitch pines rubbing and creaking against the shingles for want of room, their roots reaching quite under the house." Few other campers have lavished so much attention on frogs and the "hilarious rules of their old festal tables." He took the time to nail down the sound of their particular *tr-r-r-oonk* (*ribbet-ribbet* did not suffice).

I will, however, admit to being disappointed and embarrassed when I found out Thoreau wasn't really the "Hermit of Concord." For most of his days on the pond, he was by himself, but he had binges of conviviality, including parties, with twenty-five to thirty people stuffed in the cabin at one time or spilling into the woods. Thoreau wasn't a drinker and was a little uptight, so I doubt it got that wild, but from the sound of it, he had loads of company, including the family of Bronson Alcott. Ellery Channing hung out at the house and slept on a cot for two weeks.

Thoreau's spirited social life reminds me of certain backcountry and car camps, where instant communities form. Everybody seemed to know where Thoreau was staying. At least he made note of this in *Walden*, without providing details: "I had more visitors while I lived in the woods than at any other period of my life." Another passage implies that he volunteered his cabin as a stop on the Underground Railroad; he described encounters with "runaway slaves with plantation manners, who listened from time to time, like the fox in the fable, as if they heard the hounds a-baying on their track, and looked at me beseechingly, as much as to say,—'O Christian, will you send me back?'" He also wrote about helping one of them on his way to freedom: "One real runaway slave, among the rest, . . . I helped to forward toward the north star."

People barged in on him constantly. Peepers were common; Thoreau had no curtains on the windows. A local alcoholic went to the cabin begging for a drink. "I knew that rum or something like it was the only drink he loved," Thoreau said, "but I gave him a dish of warm pond water, which was all I had, nevertheless, which to my astonishment he drank, being used to drinking." Thoreau, in turn, made no effort to sequester himself from the town. He visited the village of Concord frequently because he hungered for "homeopathic doses" of gossip, which gives lie to the notion that he was a joyless misanthrope.

Aside from being a nonhermit, Thoreau gratefully accepted handouts from his family during his time on the pond. The scolds and skeptics of Concord claimed that Thoreau's mother and sisters brought him fresh pies and baskets of delicious doughnuts and let him raid the cookie jar. According to one often-repeated and perhaps apocryphal account, he came running right back to his parents every time he heard the dinner bell tolling during one of his forest rambles. His alleged behavior makes me wonder if there is such a thing as a "pure" self-sufficient campout that is anything less than a form of physical and mental torture. How often does our solitude and pleasure in camp depend on the largesse of others? How many times did I take handouts (including family-size cans of cling peaches) from horse campers along the Pacific Crest Trail? How many times have other campers saved me by leaving out caches of water on desert crossings, or feeding me cheeseburgers?

He could have hidden himself in a cave or retreated to the western territories. But Thoreau, by choosing a place so close to town, shows us that the best campouts are where you find them, that you don't have to head way "out there"—as I was doing in Kentucky—to lose yourself in nature's power. In praising the wild things on the margins of town, Thoreau gives us a strong antidote to an obnoxious sort of acquisitive, where-no-man-has-gone-before, chest-thumping manifest destiny–tainted strain of camping.

At a time when other men were conquering and charting and exploring the world and risking their lives, he dared to suggest, in his essay "Walking," published posthumously in 1862, that "Two or three hours' walking will carry me to as strange a country as I expect ever to see." In saying such things, he showed us how to appreciate the nature that is all around us, in urban corridors, in suburbs, or right down the block. He became the father of the backyard campout, and the pioneer of the campout as an interior journey. The exterior journey is not all-important. It is possible to be in a forest physically and tied to your office mentally. It was Thoreau who gave Bill Bryson and Cheryl Strayed permission to have complete and fulfilling experiences on the Appalachian and Pacific Crest Trails, respectively, without having to hike the whole goddamn thing. The outward and interior journeys reinforced each other. "Be rather the Mungo Park, the Lewis and Clark and Frobisher, of your own streams and oceans," he wrote.

Still, the purists who ignore the symbolic and satirical aspects of Thoreau's enterprise might carp, "Why listen to this clown? What has he ever done to test his ideas against wild nature?" To them, I can only say that Thoreau appreciated the difference between wildness and wilderness. Just as McCandless may have read *Walden* as an invitation to explore the Alaskan frontier, Thoreau used the cabin as a sort of base camp. During his trip to the Maine wilderness in 1846, when he was taking a respite from his Walden cabin, he built up his spirits with a hearty breakfast and "a dipper of condensed waterspout." Then he left his campmates behind, climbed to the clouds, and felt the strong winds on the summit tablelands of Mount Katahdin, where a "vast, Titanic, inhuman nature" confronted him. Nature spoke to him, and not kindly.

Why came ye here before your time? This ground is not prepared for you. Is it not enough that I smile in the valleys? I have never made this soil for thy feet, this air for thy breathing, these rocks for thy neighbors. I cannot pity nor fondle thee here, but forever relentlessly drive thee hence to where I am kind. Why seek me where I have not called thee, and then complain because you find me but a stepmother? Shouldst thou freeze or starve, or shudder thy life away, here is no shrine, nor altar, nor any access to my ear.

Such threats made Thoreau want to run for his life. Having seen the "real" wild nature, he knew full well that *Walden* was not going to be a survivalist memoir. Like all the best camping stories, it's more of a stand-off between domesticity and the wild. And his decision to leave the cabin was just as important as his decision to move there. The pond was only the beginning. When he left, he kept up his life of mischief, lecturing on the time he spent in jail for tax resistance, in a bold antislavery statement that led to his famous essay "Civil Disobedience." The simplicity of camping stayed with him when he moved back from the woods in 1847. In 1855 his only piece of taxable property was a rowboat, or so he claimed. He continued to study nature, and he made his famous speech about wildness containing the preservation of the world. The spirit did not desert him when he was wasting away from tuberculosis, either. His final mumblings about moose and Indians, shortly before his death at age forty-four, on May 6, 1862, were infused with the spirit of the camp.

Since those early days of poring over *Walden*, I've wondered if I'd have been better off if the book had never entered my life. I guess it depends on what you mean by better off. If not for *Walden*, I would not have sloshed my way through sphagnum bogs in Oregon, or woken under white birches and mist on the Grafton Loop in Maine. I wouldn't have scars on my leg from barbed wire near the California-Mexico border after ditching my job with my then girlfriend and hiking the Pacific Crest Trail in my early twenties. I wouldn't have tried to hike part of the Appalachian Trail in the mud season and lost a boot in the process, which forced me to hop all the way down Killington Peak with a trash bag tied around my dripping sock. I'd never have had frostbite on my fingers and toes from camping in the White Mountains of New Hampshire in late October; nor would I have bad dreams from walking thirty waterless miles near Lassen Volcanic National Park, or from the time in the North Cascades when one of my hiking partners went insane and threatened to cut the throats of everybody in the trail camp, forcing us all to sneak out in the middle of the night, not even lighting our flashlights for fear of waking him up, and leaving notes on the ground to misdirect him.

In those fraught times in the wilderness, when home was far, my return was not guaranteed, all my water was gone, and the path was nowhere to be found, I blamed Thoreau for praising the woods from the comfort of his cozy cabin. I cursed him for starting the fights I had to finish. That trip in Kentucky was one of those times. Lost, confused, feeling thirsty, down to my last sip of water, running my index finger down the spine of that ratty paperback, I could not decide whether *Walden* was a boon or a liability. It had led me into the deep woods and given me no direction home.

When I stood searching through the book, all I found were instructions on the art of getting lost, which did me little good: ". . . if we go beyond our usual course we still carry in our minds the bearing of some neighboring cape; and not till we are completely lost, or turned round—for a man needs only to be turned round once with his eyes shut in this world to be lost— do we appreciate the vastness and strangeness of nature. Every man has to learn the points of compass again as often as he awakes, whether from sleep or any abstraction."

"Gee, thanks, Henry," I said out loud.

Lacking any other recourse, I tried it out. Embrace the strangeness when you're lost. I looked toward a distant gap and flat-top mountains in the distance, rising over pools of fog. Falling leaves swirled, reversing their course before touching ground, falling upward. The leaves were black-and-blue spicebush swallowtail butterflies—felty, with orange glow dots, and pointy appendages on their wings.

The butterfly cloud directed me toward a knife-drop ridge. My almost worthless trail map had few details. It seemed to be printed on two-ply toilet paper and had barely legible letters smeared across it. What now, Henry? The land was a mad tangle of ridges and mountains. My map showed a highway due west of here. To get there, I would have to cross hellacious terrain—near-vertical drops and ledges leading to valleys full of invasive rosebushes. The grade was too steep to walk but fine for sliding. I cinched my backpack, sat on it, and launched myself off the cliff. "Arrrrgggghh!" I shouted. My backpack was a toboggan, bouncing down the mountain. On the way down, I could hear the *huffa-huffa-squonk* sounds of a black bear. The grunts scared me enough to make me slide faster. The backpack's detachable, clip-on side pocket, containing my copy of *Walden*, banged against the cliff as I plunged toward a black gully and soared toward the bushes.

After crashing, painfully, to the ground, I bundled myself in my nylon rain pants and windbreaker, put the hood on, and tore through an acre of invasive thorns. It was like rushing through a pile of wildcats. The bushes ripped my legs and shins, drawing blood. I pushed west and wound up on a dry and sandy hill. The sound of a rushing stream turned out to be traffic noise. I was tired and thirsty now, with blood running into my socks, but at least I'd gotten out. I emerged onto the highway just in time for the sunset. "We did it, Henry," I said aloud.

I took off my pack to assess the damages. I had fresh cuts all over me. My bottle of frontier whiskey was, remarkably, intact. I'd stowed it in the pack's interior. But when I reached for the side pocket where I'd stored the book, I found that the entire pocket, and my copy of *Walden*, was gone. The rosebushes had claimed it. A desolate feeling overtook me. A book is a book. Its loss shouldn't matter. But certain copies are talismans.

Big rigs came rolling. It was dark now. I decided to stick out my thumb and hitchhike back to Whitesburg, Kentucky, where they have lodging and good food, not to mention more bourbon. I hoped the truckers would disregard the bloodstains on my socks, the dirt on my face, the rips in my pack, and the red scrapes on my arms and legs. But first I looked back to the black ridge I'd slid down. I looked up at the mountain I'd escaped and traced my finger along the slope and down a stream. I thought of the rosebushes and, somewhere inside them, the greasy old book that had brought me out there in the first place.

Thoreau's stay in his rustic retreat yielded one of the great outdoor classics of American literature. But who can say what essays and books he might have written if he'd ventured into the woods of far upstate New York to a place that he'd only read and marveled about?

In the 1840s, Thoreau was amazed to find that outsiders got lost in those dark forests without help from paid wilderness guides. "New-York [*sic*] has a wilderness within her own borders," he marveled. "And though the sailors of Europe are familiar with the soundings of her Hudson . . . an Indian is still necessary to guide her scientific men" through its forests. His friend Ralph Waldo Emerson set out to visit those woods, but Thoreau never dared.

The name of that wild and mysterious place was the Adirondacks.

2

Exploring the Sewards with Zippy

[This] country, which signifies the Dismal Wilderness . . . is a triangular, high mountainous Tract, very little known to the Europeans. . . . It is said to be a broken unpracticable Tract: I own I could never learn any Thing about it.

—Thomas Pownall, 1784

The ludicrous incident, the careless joke, the thrilling story, the eager chase, are all in place in the forest . . .

—Joel Tyler Headley, 1849

I have generally gone into the woods weakened in body and depressed in mind.

—S. H. Hammond, 1857

Tom, my kind, tough-talking, exuberantly profane therapist, gave me a quizzical look as I sat on his spongy couch in Santa Cruz, California, and talked about my upcoming camping trip to the Adirondacks. We were halfway through the emergency session when he said, "Your normal state is hypervigilance. That's your baseline. What is not familiar to you is any kind of respite. If you catch yourself relaxing even for one moment, you always try to find some way to fuck it up."

"But what if I climb the wrong mountain?" I said. "What if I talk to the wrong people? Or float on the wrong lake?" I tried to explain that the

Adirondacks are the Fertile Crescent of American camping. This mountainous region in far upstate New York was an essential stop on my camping odyssey because it is one of the first wildernesses that large numbers of nineteenth-century Americans fled toward, not out of, because they were feeling overworked, miserable, and hoping to change their lives. Now I feared something would go wrong and my trip would be in vain. Just getting there from Santa Cruz would be a serious undertaking, involving two plane rides and an international border crossing. The closest major airport was in Montreal. After going to such trouble, I didn't want to settle for an ersatz experience.

"Okay," Tom said. "But you don't have to pin the success or failure of your trip on any one person or place. Who knows what's gonna happen? You have to give yourself over to chance."

"But chance is the one thing I'm trying to avoid."

"Look," he said. "Maybe you get out there and you won't find Old Smokey Joe, who lives in a fucking pine tree, and you've got to stand in the middle of the crick and call him down. 'Hey, Joe? You up there?' Or maybe you won't see Screamin' Sarah, who lives in a goddamn glacier on a mountaintop, and you've got to climb a rope to see her. You've got this core anxiety, Dan, and you're always adding layer after layer to the core because that's what you do! You'll find any reason to make yourself anxious. You have to let some of those things go. Maybe you get out there and you *don't* get to ride the ponies. Maybe you go out there and you don't get to see the white buffalo of the Adirondacks."

"But I don't want to ride the ponies," I said. "And I'm pretty sure they don't have buffaloes of any kind in the Adirondacks."

"Good," said Tom. "Those are two things you can cross right off your list."

Tom is a good therapist, but even he could not cure me of my monomania. Every camping journey needs a pilgrimage. To my mind, there was no better place for this than the distant, forbidding Adirondacks. This forest remained a terra incognita even while large cities were rising in the Northeast. Eighteenth-century maps represented it as a blank between Lake Ontario and Lake Champlain. It remained that way into the mid-1800s. Even the Algonquians and Mohawks spent only part of each year there. The winters were dreadful. Then spring came, and vicious biting bugs hatched to feast on human blood. Besides, the soil was poor and hardpan.

Conditions were murderous for livestock; catamounts and timber wolves lived in the woods. In 1794 a merchant named John Brown bought two hundred thousand acres close to the area now known as Old Forge but had a hard time convincing anyone to live there. His son-in-law did not help when he wrote that the "region was so barren a crow would shed tears of sorrow flying over it." That same son-in-law, by the way, tried to establish a settlement and mining operation there and ended up committing suicide. Early northeastern pioneers took one look at the place and kept rolling westward.

All that initial fear and revulsion led to a remarkable preservation. Although mining and timber interests started making inroads in the nineteenth century, the mountains and forests were mostly unspoiled and unexplored at the time Americans began to change their minds about the wild. In the American imagination, the great forests, which the Puritans considered the literal dwelling places of the archdevil Azazel, began to seem a touch less howling, terrifying, and psychosis-inducing, thanks in part to the influence of European Romantic philosophers and the American transcendentalists, whose leader, Ralph Waldo Emerson, went there to camp in 1858 on Follensby Pond.

I wanted to get the full effect of the real Adirondacks, which, from what I'd heard again and again, can make a man feel, paradoxically, strong yet childlike, a kindergartener trapped in the body of a lumberjack. Up in the

Ralph Waldo Emerson (1803–1882)

wild North Woods, Emerson had a chance to test out his idea that the woods are a place where a man "casts off his years, as the snake his slough, and at what period soever of life, is always a child."

To make my trip as historically authentic as possible, I wanted to follow a classic nineteenth-century template. For starters, I would bring my family with me, but I would make sure to stow them in a cabin in the woods of Keene, New York, beneath the High Peaks, while I exercised manly pursuits in the woods. I even hired a real wilderness guide, just like the Romantic-era Adirondack campers used to do. The best guides were skilled hunters, fishermen, lumbermen, animal trackers, boatmen, weather pattern readers, and way finders trained in the arts of woodcraft. Gentlemen campers of the Adirondacks—who were known in the nineteenth century as sports—were, for the most part, pampered intellectuals from large cities. They expected their camping guides to do almost all the donkeywork in camp, including some activities that most modern campers now associate with good fun, not drudgery. Guides had to gather firewood and chop trees to fuel the fire. They had to cook supper, put up instant and somewhat water-resistant shelters using foraged materials, warble out melodies on the harmonica, sing traditional songs, chat with clients, and tell tall tales by the hearth. The guides did all those things and more for two dollars a day. Even when adjusted for inflation, that works out to be a miserly forty dollars.

These days, paying somebody to camp with you and in some sense camp *for* you might sound louche, gratuitous, and silly, but it was once standard practice—and camping labors were only part of a guide's perceived value. Guides were also bodyguards, safety buffers between the delicate, powdered clients and the beautiful, savage forest. Those clients included a disproportionate number of lawyers and doctors who knew their way around forests about as well as a bog lemming understands probate law. These campers were not nearly as nature-fearing and -hating as the Puritans, but they weren't exactly careless and fearless nature boys like John Muir, either. Their attitude toward nature occupied a murky middle between absolute horror and domestic sublime, the sense that the woods were every bit as welcoming as your own living room. They wanted to get wild in the Adirondacks, but not too wild. A hired man with a guide boat allowed them to bring all the trappings of civilization they wanted, from fine wine to suits for dinner.

Besides, these guides added a sense of authenticity—or, to put it another way, city-slicker bragging rights—to any camping trip. The implication was that if you got a really lousy guide, you would see a lousy incarnation of the Adirondacks. Wealthy sports seeking the "real" Adirondacks vied for the services of sad-eyed Mitchell Sabattis (1823–1906), the masterful Abenaki tracker whose "eyes were clear and keen as those of a goshawk," according to one of his clients, and whose backcountry skills were unequaled.

One sport once saw Sabattis kissing his handmade guide boat as if wanting to make passionate love to it. The camper asked Sabattis what on earth he was doing. "Suckin' for holes," Sabattis replied. The famous guide was searching for leaks so he could caulk them with spruce gum and bits of rag. He could also follow the blood trails of deer through dimly lit forests and grease up his gun with animal fat. Men dominated the world of

Mitchell Sabattis (1823–1906)

wilderness guides, but there were a few women out there, too. Ann Telfer (1896–1975), a hunting guide based in Speculator, New York, could out-hike many of her male clients, was a crack shot with her 303 Savage, and "could carry a (dead) deer or a bear on her shoulders as well as a man," according to her daughters.

As I found out while doing my due diligence before the trip, hiring a backwoods helpmeet is not as much of a steal as it used to be. Securing the services of a New York State–licensed High Peaks guide would set me back almost a thousand dollars for a nonrefundable two-day campout for two people—me and my friend Michael, who also happens to be my editor and therefore, in some regards, my boss. Still, the price seemed worth it. With-out a guide, I could not have a real experience out there, or so I thought. I also wanted to know what it was like to pay somebody other than my ther-apist to act like my best pal.

Still, there was no denying that the guide, like Tom, my therapist, would be on the payroll, and I just had to wonder how that would change our quasi-friendship dynamics. In spite of all the confidence I place in him, Tom and I never get beers together, and I don't have his personal phone number, a fact that seems reasonable to me but also hurts my feelings. Would my relationship with the guide be compromised in a similar way? I also wondered if Michael's presence would add another degree of logistical and psychological complexity. I think of him as a friend and colleague, but I am, in a sense, on *his* payroll, too. I suspected we would have good fun together in the woods, but there was always some outside chance the campout would degenerate into a three-tiered power struggle in the remote wilderness with me in the middle. Was that going to be weird?

In the course of worrying about all these esoteric things, and obsessing about the trip's logistics, I neglected to undertake a certain basic all-important task—but, unfortunately, I did not realize this until one fateful late-August afternoon when I staggered, sleepy and unexpectedly alone, into the Montreal airport after forty-eight hours of flight delays and cancella-tions, an unscheduled layover, and dozens of other reversals, large and small, including my entire family's last-minute decision not to accompany me on my Adirondack trip; the mess with the airlines had upset them so much that they backed out at the last second. It must be said that my mounting obsession with the Adirondacks—my constant poring over old journals and books, my endless staring at pictures of moose eating willow shoots in the gloaming—had started to drive my wife insane.

After not showering or sleeping for two days, my skin pale, my shirt unbuttoned, my hair standing on end, I was a fright when I arrived at the Montreal airport. Jelly bags wobbled beneath my eyes. I was babbling to myself. In this addled state, I approached the counter at the airport's Hertz rent-a-car booth and showed the suit-wearing, spymaster novel–reading clerk my driver's license. He was the gatekeeper, my last obstacle to the mountains. I smiled at him and tried to be polite, but when I slid my license to him across the counter, he took one glance at it and slid it back to me.

"I will not rent a car to you," he sniffed.

"You what?" I said, entertaining the possibility that he was messing with me. When his sour expression remained, I tried to explain that the car was reserved in my wife's name. "Sorry for the confusion, but it's all just a matter of . . ."

"That is not the problem," he said. "Look here. Your license expired ten months ago! You have been driving your car illegally. Please step out of the line."

My eyelids fluttered. My tongue seemed to plump in my mouth, making speech difficult. "This can't be real," I said. "No, no, no, no, no. I can't get there without a car. I have a guided campout leaving at the crack of dawn tomorrow. My boss is going on the trip. This is an unbelievably important business trip for me. You have no idea how many people I will let down. I have appointments in every corner of the Adirondacks. All spread apart. It's, like, six-point-one million acres. Without a car, I'm completely screwed."

"If they pull you over, they will *impound* our vehicle, sir, and we will be held liable. Step out of the line."

I took a few steps away from the counter and sat on the filthy floor. I must have been a sight, because two French-speaking Québécois children stepped up and took cell phone pictures of me. It was sinking in that I would *never* see the Adirondacks now. This was my fault, all mine. I flirted with the idea of calling Michael and asking him to drive five hours out of his way across a foreign border to retrieve me, but I didn't know how to reach him. I know this is going to sound pagan, and superstitious, but I started praying, and not to God. Instead I prayed to the ghosts of all the Adirondack figures whose traces I'd come so far to find: William H. H. "Adirondack" Murray, Theodore Roosevelt, George Washington Sears, and many others. Without a Ouija board, I tried to access their spirits, to have them work some miracle to get me to the Adirondacks. I stepped outside the Hertz office and into the airport parking lot. "You are my only chance," I shouted into the emptiness.

At that moment, I noticed a sickly green glow emanating from the farthest corner of the lot. It beckoned me. In a moment, a car rental agency in a freestanding glass booth came into view. Two employees stood there in the rental booth as if they had been waiting for me all along: an attractive fortyish woman with lustrous curly black hair and a scruffy man with shy eyes and puffy gray hair. They offered me a folding chair. I tried to explain my absurd situation. The woman rested a hand on my shoulders.

"I see you are experiencing great stress," said the woman, whose name tag read MARJORIE. "But remember: your situation is not life threatening."

"It isn't?" I said.

"You must put this in perspective," said the rumpled man, whose name tag read GEORGE. "The customer who came here just before you? We believe she is dying."

"What!"

"She wanted to rent a car with no clock," Marjorie said. "She wants no reminders of time."

"She doesn't want to know how much time she's got left," George added.

"She feels helpless," Marjorie said. "And when we feel helpless, we must all rely on faith alone. My poor son, he got so sick one day, I had to put his healing in God's hands. He got better."

"Oh, my goodness," I said, still hyperventilating. "This is the most philosophical car rental booth I've ever seen. I feel so shallow. Here I am losing my mind about a camping trip and people are dying."

"Don't worry," Marjorie said. "Use our phone. Make as many calls as you wish. The clouds for you are about to part."

"But . . . I have to call California. What about the international charges?"

"We don't mind," Marjorie said.

I looked at her to see if she was joking. She was not. Marjorie handed me the phone. On some bizarre impulse, I decided to call the California Department of Motor Vehicles to see if someone might fax me a new license, even though it is understaffed and its employees often surly, and even though I'd been driving my car illicitly for almost a year. The DMV put me on hold for an hour and a half, and all the while, to my astonishment, Marjorie didn't complain once about my hogging their line. The

DMV picked up at last. Trying not to sound frantic, I told the woman on the line that I was trapped in a foreign-ish country. Just this one time, would they please let me renew my license over the phone?

"Okay," the woman said.

"Okay?" I said. "Seriously? What do I owe you?"

"Nothing," she said.

I gave her the rental agency's fax number and hung up, shaking my head, wondering why everybody in Montreal was being so nice. But a couple of hours passed and no fax showed up. Marjorie and George let me sleep in the silver late-model Hyundai Sonata I'd, in the meantime, reserved but could never drive. They even gave me the keys so I could open and close the power windows for ventilation. An hour later, Marjorie and George had gone home for the night, but a young man from the company rapped on the car window. "Take the car and just go," he said.

"Huh?"

"The boss says it's okay. We'll charge the card when you bring it back."

"But . . . did the fax ever show up?"

"No."

"But . . . what if I get pulled over by the cops?"

"You won't," he said, and waved me away, smiling.

As I rolled through Montreal, checking the rearview for cops, it occurred to me that all this must have happened for a very good reason. Perhaps the Hertz rental office, with its horrid, flickering yellow lights and bureaucratic efficiency, was meant to evoke the soul-crushing workplaces and impersonal city life that first drove recreational campers into the Adirondacks to begin with. And perhaps I was supposed to be a shambles upon arrival. The Adirondacks are a famous healing place, an American Lourdes, but a man cannot take the cure when he is well. Besides, getting there in the old days was a colossal pain. Stagecoach journeys on washboard roads provided "a remarkable sense of loosened joints, sore spots and general fracture," a nineteenth-century traveler observed. It comforted me greatly to remember that the difficulty of my voyage and my scrambled state of mind, followed by the sudden lifting of my woes and cares, placed me squarely inside a tradition that dated back almost two hundred years.

For the past few months I'd been reading memoirs of gentlemen who fell into soul paralysis in cities. Those men felt incomplete, and this was

literally true for the one-legged, British-born poet Charles Fenno Hoff-
man, who started a cultural trend when he limped into the Adirondacks in
the 1830s because he wanted to see "savage, stupendous" scenery. Failing to
climb Mount Marcy, he sat on the ground and sobbed bitter tears. In spite
of his disappointment, he came home raving about his wilderness guide,
"honest" John Cheney, "as stanch a hunter and as true and gentle a prac-
tiser of woodcraft as ever roamed the broad forest." Other addled campers soon followed. Before embarking on his first Adirondack campout in
the 1840s, the Reverend Joel T. Headley was such a shambolic mess that he
couldn't bring himself to say what was wrong with him in his own memoir, *The Adirondack, or Life in the Woods*, which was published in 1849,
and was an early example of the "immensely unhappy person finding
sudden redemption in the wilderness" literary subgenre that is still going
strong to this day. In the opening scene, Headley's doctor tells him he must
retreat to the deep woods or "_____" will happen. What does "_____"
even mean? Headley won't say. (Headley, by the way, inserts lots of strange
blank spaces throughout this memoir; in other sections of the book, he
identifies his companions as P_____, B_____n, Young Ar_____ld, and
Young S_____th.)

Headley does not go into much detail about the reasons for his abject
misery. He hints at a soul hunger, an "attack on the brain," and an "over-
wrought" mind that has weakened his spirit and disturbed his slumber.
Among his symptoms: a suffocating claustrophobia that "drove [him]
from the haunts of man"; a fear of the "printed page," although he doesn't
specify books or newspapers; and his worry that he was leading a one-sided
life, a condition he identified as "Einseitigkeit," which means bias, lopsid-
edness, or imbalance in German. The reverend had a mournful outlook.
"Such am I and such is every man," he writes. "Bewildered and stunned . . .
hurled against the rocks of discouragement. Life, life. How solemn and
mysterious thou art!" He believed the woods would do more than just cure
him. He hoped they would adjust his mental outlook and give him the
balance he lacked.

In the mid-nineteenth century, the concept of vacations, especially
wilderness vacations, had not yet entered the cultural mainstream. But
Reverend Headley, desperate for relief, packed up his India rubber leggings
and took a steamer and carriage to the Adirondacks, where he chopped
down a "brave old hemlock," apparently just for laughs. The experience

made him shiver with pleasure. "Hark!" he shouted at the tottering tree. "Crack! Crash! Crash!" The reverend slept in "shanties" and floated on lakes and rivers that passed between the mountains like living roads. There, his thoughts stopped their maddening swirl. His mind became "quiet and renovated." Soon he found the raptures he sought: "Green islands, beautiful as Elysian fields, rose out of the water as we advanced . . . and for a moment I seemed to have been transported into a new world." It amazed him that this Elysium could be found about 270 miles from Manhattan. "I was in the same State of which New York was the emporium, whose myriad spires pierced the heavens."

I wanted to be just like Joel Headley and see what he'd seen, and now at last I had my chance. He and other nineteenth-century Romantic campers and hikers found freedom and ecstasy in the woods. Though the Adirondacks seemed foreign to them, their explorations felt like an awakening and homecoming, a return of the spirit. Leaning into gorges, staring down precipices, climbing ancient peaks, they glimpsed the infinite.

Beyond the windshield, the famous mountains I'd been reading about for so many months came into view for the first time. I rolled down the window on that fine August day. "Beautiful, beautiful!" I shouted. The faraway peaks were slate-blue/gray with faint, scalloped edges. They clumped together to form an enormous dome. The closer mountains had thick green coats with notches, knobby bumps, and tubercles all over them. Many of the mountains had "slides," parallel rows of vertical scrapes that looked like the throat grooves on a humpback whale. I pulled over at a rest stop, stepped on the mucky greensward, and marveled at the scenery. This was the Empire State, but the bars on my cell phone had all gone away. I'd crossed the fabled "blue line," the boundary for the six-million-acre area known as Adirondack Park. A silver-blue dragonfly bumped my ear. A toad jumped onto my boot. *Welcome to the green world*, these wild things seemed to say. Light-headedness and an inexplicable energy came over me. It felt as though someone had slipped me an espresso with a horse tranquilizer fizzing at the bottom of the cup.

There is no entrance station, no ranger waving you through. You just drive on in. Adirondack Park is a hodgepodge of public and private interests. It has never been, and most likely never will be, a national park. The blue line surrounds boreal wetlands, trackless woods, sedge bogs, fourteen major rivers, and mountain ranges that are part of a state preserve and will remain "forever wild." In such places, campers sometimes go missing. Bobcats, beavers, star-nosed moles, and a few rarely seen moose have the run of the place. The blue line also encompasses one hundred thirty thousand year-round residents, small towns, ballparks, ski lifts, mobile homes, cities, prisons, a number of Stewart's Shops, a water safari theme park, and a mini-golf course with replicas of the Liberty Bell, a New York City subway car, and a giant lobster.

In spite of all that sprawl and development, the Adirondacks still feels like "away" if you know where to look. This was clear from the moment I returned to the highway and headed toward the small VRBO cabin my family had reserved in the woods near Keene Valley. Exits grew farther apart. The road steepened. Back roads led to enormous anthracite rocks pushing up above the green and rolling countryside. Keene Valley was some kind of afterlife. Swallows chased one another over plush meadows that led to the bases of hills so thick with growth they looked impenetrable. Side streets dead-ended at unframed Hudson River School landscapes: a waterfall feathering off a distant cliff; a boulder with a louse-size hiker on it; and glory beams falling from the spaces between the clouds, lighting up a church, a general store, and an outdoor gear shop. In the Noon Mark Diner, they had every kind of pie.

My absent family's cabin was just where it was supposed to be, at the end of a gravel road in the woods, a house key in the lockbox, fresh white cheddar and eggs in the refrigerator, a rainproof map of the western High Peaks on the coffee table, and a copy of Wes Anderson's *The Fantastic Mr. Fox* cued up in the DVD player. Outside, an Adirondack chair faced the mountains. A porch swing creaked. I closed my eyes, half expecting to wake up from sleep. No reality could match this dream.

It was hard to stay unconscious for long. Every hour, I woke up frantic with excitement about the guided trip that was leaving at dawn that morning. What would my guide look like? I hoped he resembled Alvah Dunning (1816–1902), whose skills as a huntsman and woodsman almost made up for the fact that he could not tell you who was president of the United States or, according to one account, whether the earth was round or flat. Or perhaps he'd have more in common with the legendary Orson Schofield "Old Mountain" Phelps (1817–1905), whose beard resembled rain clouds, whose clothes "seemed to have been put on him once and for all, like the bark of a tree, a long time ago," according to the writer Charles

Dudley Warner, and who once remarked that "soap is a thing I hain't no kinder use for."

Next morning, only my lack of a valid license prevented me from gunning that motor and driving at eighty miles an hour on the back roads to Lake Placid. I pulled over in front of the guide house near the High Peaks Cyclery store on Main Street and waited for my grand old archetype to show up, preferably someone with a beard, a backwoods brogue, and a tam-o'-shanter. In front of the guide house, I saw my friend Michael, whose neatly trimmed black beard and mustache made him look Victorian. Beside him stood a middle-aged fellow with a full head of spiky hair, a silver loop through his left earlobe, a thick green bandanna, and a leg tattoo showing a hybrid between a bat-winged dragon and a woman with stupendous breasts. She was devouring a yin-and-yang symbol. I remember thinking to myself, *Who is that unsavory character?* I sure wished the scruffy, tough-looking fellow would clear off and make way for my wilderness guide. Still, I didn't want to be rude, so I went out to greet Michael and say hello to this stranger. His name was Zippy.

After he introduced himself, Zippy said, "I'm your guide."

My shock was palpable. Nothing except for my extreme relief and gratitude just to be in the Adirondacks at all could muffle my initial reaction. Where was his pipe, his woolen coat, and his walking staff carved from the lateral branch of an old-growth hemlock?

Zippy, at age fifty, had a youthful and weathered face. His leg muscles were ropy from having climbed every one of the Adirondacks' famous forty-six "High Peaks"—that is, mountains that were originally thought to be higher than four thousand feet. He'd climbed them not just once, but almost twice; he was just three peaks short of becoming a "double-forty-sixer." It was reassuring to see he had an official badge on his pack that read NEW YORK STATE LICENSED GUIDE 6944, DEPARTMENT OF ENVIRONMENTAL CONSERVATION; he told me he'd earned it after taking multiple tests and receiving training as an emergency medical technician. It pained me a bit to hear that he was not Adirondacks born and raised—he came from a city in Connecticut—but I had to give him a pass on this when I remembered that several classic guides were also transplants, including "Old Mountain" Phelps, a native Vermonter. Though his given name was Andrew Seligmann, Zippy was his *nom de trail* because he zipped from place to place. "I am a High Peaks guide," Zippy told us with apparent pride. "I don't fish or hunt. I don't have that kind of license, but if you want to go off the beaten trail, and do some crazy stuff, and go to some crazy places you'd never go unless you were a maniac, which I happen to be, I'm your man. So what do you want to do? What do you want to see?"

Michael told him he wanted to go somewhere "as steep and away" as possible. I told Zippy I wanted a place that met all the accepted standards of Romantic-style "sublime and beautiful" scenery—in other words, that perfect admixture of Gothic peaks and glassy lakes corresponding to scenery aesthetics outlined by the influential Irish philosopher Edmund Burke. Zippy looked at me for a brief moment as if I were soft in the head, but then he took out a weatherproof map and pointed to the Seward Range. I'd heard of it because it is, apparently, a magnet for unprepared whistle-heads. A story had been circulating online about an Albany man who got stranded there in 2012 because his cell phone batteries lacked the juice to run his navigation app. He had just enough power to make one distress call. A team got him out and his name got in the papers, which must have made him wish they'd left him out there to rot. I figured the remoteness of that area would justify our trouble and expense. I longed to know what it meant to be authentically helpless, utterly dependent on a camping guide to get us through.

Zippy laid out the agenda. That morning, we'd drive to the Seward Range, hike for a couple of hours, and set up camp at the first-come, first-served Ward Brook Lean-to, a few miles from a dirt road parking area, unless somebody grabbed it beforehand. After setting up camp in our sturdy lean-to, we'd bag Seymour Mountain, one of the High Peaks. The second and final day was wide open. I vowed we would use that day to do something as crazy and as dangerous as possible. To evoke the true spirit of the Adirondack campout, I needed at least a small dose of pleasurable fear.

But first it was time to indulge. On most backpacking trips, you have to watch every ounce of pack weight, but not when you've got a Sherpa carrying a large amount of your equipment and food. On the way to the mountains, we ran wild in a supermarket. With Zippy pushing that cart, Michael and I scampered alongside him, grabbing everything we wanted, including luscious strawberry Pop Tarts, a bloody, shrink-wrapped New York steak, and a sack of purple potatoes. I was overcome with a child-like sensibility that reminded me of my first day in kindergarten, that unbeatable combination of expectation and infantilization. I wanted to yell to everyone in the store that we were going on an actual wilderness hike with a real live guide. Michael grabbed a huge jar of peanut butter, a great big pack of tortillas, and one of those bottles of Welch's grape jelly that stands on its own like a statuette. Forget your granola. We were going to eat like crossbred Cornish hogs out there.

Our excess was authentic. Early Adirondack campers didn't have to eat Slim Jims, dextrose tablets, gorp, and cryogenic Stroganoff with tubes of broiled gluten and mummified peas. They had at least one guide apiece to carry belongings and food from forest to forest in sturdy flat-bottomed guide boats. In 1858 one Adirondack campout dinner included "venison broiled, roasted and fried, pork and beans, a course of finer game consisting of frogs' hind legs, capped off with a dessert of pancake and rice pudding, coffee, cigars, whiskey, brandy, and a delicious glass of West India Shrub (a kind of alcoholic punch), the recollection of which still makes the teeth water."

Zippy brought a pack for each of us, sleeping bags, and tents in case we got shut out of that lean-to. There was no need to bring much water because Zippy had a filter; we could pump as we went. Zippy gave us just enough items to fill the backpacks we'd borrowed from the guide house in Lake Placid, but he would bear the heaviest load by far. He squished the food into two bear-proof containers and drove us to Corey's Road, between Saranac and Tupper Lakes, past luxuriant stands of red spruce. We arrived at the trailhead, packed up, and got out. The woods were rocky, steep and even lovelier than I expected. When I say "lovely," I'm talking about a combination of sense impressions that would be impossible to photograph: the raspberry herbal tea aroma of balsam, the comforting *shplotch* of my boots on hummocky ground, the mossy toupees on the boulders, the loping gait of our guide. My pack creaked as it swayed on its hinges. It sounded like crickets. A biting bug attacked while we were walking. For all I knew, that particular bug was a distant descendant of an insect that attacked Ralph Waldo Emerson. In deference to history, I let it feast on me and refrained from swatting it. Blackfly season was over by then. I considered that chomp a rare treat.

The forest got dense and dark. Zippy picked up the pace. He was some kind of Olympic champion talker.

"I am not a rich man, but I have a pickup truck, a motorbike, and I guide," he told me. As he knew full well, there were worse ways to make a living. He used to work at an Adirondack "character development" school, which was based in Saranac Lake and served troubled kids. The camp shut down in 2012 after a ten-year run. "The Adirondacks are a pretty rough place to bring kids," Zippy said. "It is steep, gnarly, slippery. You could get lost in a second. Mosquitoes? Blackflies? Deerflies? This is a terrible area to bring people for therapy."

The mountains, bad as they were for the troubled youths, helped Zippy center himself. He had another tattoo, close to his navel (viewings available upon request), showing Winnie-the-Pooh and Piglet walking together into a yin-and-yang symbol instead of the sun. "It represents innocence, without complicating thoughts," he explained. The woods helped him attain that state of mind. The tattoo, however, looked smeared. "I've got to get this redone," he said.

We walked for several miles into a dense thicket. House-size rocks leaned together, forming damp alcoves. White-tailed deer flashed through the forest. As we hiked along, Zippy entertained us with stories and lore and scenery explanations. Every once in a while he would point out some monstrous "glacial erratic," the gigantic boulders he characterized as "glacier poop" because the great ice sheets dropped them here many millennia ago. The original Adirondack guides liked to regale sports with exaggerated tales of deadly standoffs with cougars and wolves in these woods, although these animal encounters were quite rare. These days, the only wolf or cougar you will see in the Adirondacks are the stuffed dead ones at the Adirondack Museum out on Blue Mountain Lake. But Zippy had a few stories about some lesser creatures, including a raccoon that fell from a tree and hit its head, leaving it permanently foozled. "It was so badly brain-damaged, this couple adopted it as a pet, and they named it Nooccar—that's raccoon spelled backward," Zippy said. "They let Nooccar sleep in the bathroom, and it lived there. Nooccar's whole world was that bathroom! Have you ever seen a place trashed by a raccoon? God, it's disgusting."

When we arrived at the beautifully constructed lean-to, a three-sided hut open in the front to receive the warmth of the cook fire, a sense of well-being came over me. These structures had a long history. This one was a descendant of the original three-sided "shanties" of the Adirondacks. In the early days, camping sports did not have to bring a heavy canvas tent because a skilled guide could build a serviceable three-sided cabin on the spot. The process was simple; the sport picked a lovely stretch of woods. Then the guides whipped out axes and hatchets and started hacking the virgin forest.

Sports would laze around and marvel at the shacks rising up in the middle of the wilderness. It was all part of a grand performance, like watching mutton-chopped waiters in fancy restaurants assemble Waldorf salads tableside. Guides understood they were killing trees by peeling their bark and using the pieces as shingles. But it didn't matter, because the wilderness was considered an inexhaustible resource like coal, water, and passenger pigeons. Many of those instant shelters were often abandoned after just one campout, but the sturdiest served several parties of campers over a long period. Ours had little in common with those quickly assembled "shanties." It was a foursquare, handsome structure built by a state Department of Environmental Conservation work crew in the 1930s. I was grateful to see that a few things hadn't changed with time. For one, someone had left a battered communal journal in our shelter, a tradition that dates to the nineteenth century, when Adirondack wayfarers loved to pass the time filling the pages with inspiring words. What transcendental wisdom would I find between its well-worn covers? What authentic truths would it contain?

"If the spirit moves you, my friend, just pick an entry and read it out loud so we can hear it," said Zippy.

A feeling of joy overcame me. I took a deep breath, placed my finger in the middle of the page, and read the entry out loud in a nice booming voice. The author apparently was a woman who'd had anal sex in our lean-to while under the influence of hard drugs. "Today, we had a great day," she wrote. "It was blue skys [sic] and poop love tree Band-Aid pencil bag fermin dildo lean-to log butt sex stop bug shot up trail water. And then we had smores!"

I blushed a deep crimson as I put the book aside for some other camper to read. I will admit to being a bit of a prude about such literary styling. Still, it made me feel good that this anonymous Anaïs Nin of the Adirondacks— she had not signed her name—was at least having some fun out here, and in her own way experiencing Romantic rhapsodies.

After setting aside the trail porn, I headed out with Zippy and Michael for some Gothic scenery exploration, perhaps my best chance to access the Romantic frame of mind. With Zippy taking the middle, and Michael way out front, the three of us pulled ourselves by root, bough, and boulder on a steeply inclined and unmarked herd path to Seymour Mountain. On that rough way to the summit, you can see smooth hand- and finger-shaped markings worn in the rough bark of overhanging limbs; I called these the trees of trepidation, because thousands of Adirondack hikers had wrapped their hands around these branches to keep from tumbling off.

Zippy, to his credit, always waited for me, never patronized me or complained when I puffed, grunted, groaned, and wheezed up the mountain, pausing every so often to take a double-hit from my Xopenex inhaler. Balsam buds smelled like musk. I soaked my shirt with sweat. Zippy kept checking over his shoulder to make sure I hadn't had a coronary incident.

By the time we neared the summit, I was almost ready to lose myself in the Gothic experience. As I wrapped my fingers around another tree arm, my thoughts turned to the Romantic poet Alfred Billings Street, who journeyed to the Adirondacks in the 1850s and experienced the sublime, an odd combination of appreciation, enjoyment, swooning, and old-fashioned Puritan-style terror, the sort of thing we might experience during a horror movie or roller-coaster plunge. Sublimity is difficult to achieve because the pleasure and pain, sorrow and joy, are twined in a tight bundle. Street described his "sickening shock" when he climbed a forbidding overlook and peered down. "What a sight! Horrible and yet sublimely beautiful— no, not beautiful . . . all grandeur and terror."

While grunting my way to the summit, it was important for me to remember that those Romantics longed for unfiltered experience in the woods, which they considered a temple. Sometimes the sight of natural beauty led them to thoughts that seem, from our twenty-first-century vantage point, rather morbid. When Harriet Beecher Stowe visited Niagara Falls, roughly 270 miles west of the Adirondacks, in 1830, she longed to fling herself off the edge, not out of depression or sorrow, but out of pure joy. "I felt as if I could have gone over with the waters," she wrote. "It would be so beautiful a death; there could be no fear in it."

I was experiencing something close to that rapture and soul transport, if not the desire to fling myself off a precipice, by the time we reached the summit. Panting and perspiring, I stood with my companions and took a long plug of sweet, gravity-filtered stream water. To the west I saw Mounts Seward, Donaldson, and Emmons. The arrangement and shape of the peaks suggested an eastern timber wolf's snout in profile or perhaps an extinct catamount. Ampersand Lake was the eye. The windswept beauty of this place was almost more than I could bear. Even in my ecstasy, I could not resist pulling out my smartphone and turning it on, just so I could take a picture of all this loveliness and bring it home to my wife and child. In my camera viewfinder, I framed the view just perfectly, imagining the gilded edges of a picture in a museum.

You're here! I said to myself. *You aren't stuck in that airport anymore. You are doing this right now.* And just when my finger was about to press down and take the picture, a rectangular message icon popped up on the upper right-hand corner of the screen informing me that I owed $150 in library fines for an overdue book about a shy, list-making mouse named Wallace, which my little daughter didn't even like, and that my borrowing privileges were hereby suspended forever. I swore and stomped, and my anxiety returned full force.

Perhaps noticing how discombobulated I was, Zippy got me back to the spirit of the campout by offering me a tightly rolled peanut butter and jelly burrito and reenacting some hair-raising scenes from a rarely seen R-rated gross-out film called *Movie 43*. But this witty banter, diverting as it was, only increased my suspicion that the Romantic camping experience was irretrievable. No matter how I tried, those long-dead campers kept retreating into the mist. The cynicism of modern living contributed to my mental fog. Or perhaps this place was not quite the howling—or even barking, or softly purring—wilderness it used to be. After all, I'd seen plenty of people, including young children, and an unleashed Jack Russell terrier puppy, climbing the same slippery mountain that day without the benefit of a wilderness guide.

Yet I vowed to keep trying to find my Gothic release. So far, this campout had offered its share of perfect moments, but I wanted more. I wanted to embrace the Adirondack sublime—and I vowed to step up the search.

The wind began to blow.

We beat a quick retreat to the lean-to. Temperatures were falling rapidly.

"Everyone in camp must have a chore," Zippy announced when we arrived. Michael and I headed into the dense forest behind the lean-to to recover some deadwood. (It is illegal these days to use any other kind of wood in the 2.6 million acres of state land within the Adirondack Park; those protected areas are known as the Adirondack Forest Preserve.) Michael was in a state of transport and joy so profound that he started whistling "Habanera" from Bizet's *Carmen*. "I love that tune," Michael said. "It's so . . . saucy!"

As Michael kept on warbling out that melody—"ba-dump-bump-BUMP! Ba-doomp-boomp-BUMP!"—we hacked limbs with a rusty buck-saw we'd found in the lean-to, near that pornographic diary. Zippy lit the match, and the fire went whooshing, consuming dry timbers in an instant. Michael was merrymaking, nipping expensive scotch from a hip flask. Supper was sizzling in the pan. Purple potatoes frothed. Their starch made a rich foam. Zippy slopped a whole container of Land O'Lakes butter in the pan and flopped the steak on top of it. The light was fading, and for a while I was as *away* as any man could be. Now I chastised myself, gently. Perhaps I'd worried far too much about the power dynamic among the three of us, feeling like piggy-in-the-middle, with financial dependence skewing friendships, with money corrupting our camaraderie, and with everyone performing for one another like circus monkeys. Now we were getting some-where close to real rapport, and I just wanted everything to freeze then. I had the eerie sensation that no time had passed, that we were all in just the right position to form an iconic scene straight out of an old-time painting, our

Camping in the Woods: "A Good Time Coming" by Arthur Fitzwilliam Tait (1819–1905), 1862. This painting shows a nineteenth-century camping scene with two sports, one standing, one seated, taking their leisure while a guide stands between them, cooking a meal. A second guide lurks in the background, awaiting orders. The slapdash structure behind them is a classic lean-to, open to receive the warmth of the flames.

guide between us, me sitting on the planks of that lean-to, Michael standing to my right, holding his stainless steel container of spirits.

Michael and I became little kids again, playing at frontier living. Our lack of self-consciousness spoke to the power of the Adirondack guide: a good one brings the party, projects bonhomie on any campout, and turns grown men into happy and dependent tots. Even the great Ralph Waldo Emerson, for all his claims of self-reliance, regressed to a borderline kindergarten state when camping in 1858 out at Follensby Pond, less than ten miles from where we bivouacked with Zippy. If you saw the guest list at that monthlong wilderness adventure—now known as the Philosophers' Camp—among them, Oliver Wendell Holmes Sr.'s brother, John, renowned Harvard scientist Louis Agassiz, the poet James Russell Lowell and his two nephews Charles and James, who would both die in the Civil War, and Judge Ebenezer Hoar, who became attorney general for President Ulysses S. Grant, you'd think these men would have pooled their brainpower to cure dread diseases, discover new species, change the world forever with their shared brilliance, and create fantastic works of art in the forest. You would be wrong. Some of these men did some botanizing, and Agassiz was thrilled to discover an unfamiliar kind of freshwater sponge, but for the most part they took their leisure. While I doubt any of them hung out their unspeakable socks to dry in front of one another or romped half-naked as I did, they lost at least some of their self-consciousness. They removed their masks, shed their reserve, and embraced their hidden silliness, wonder, and sense of play.

In camp the men meditated, fished, lollygagged on the sandy beach, stared up to the tops of old-growth white pines two hundred feet high, and slept in bark and fir shanties with gigantic maples marking the center of camp. Emerson didn't mind the midges and blackflies too much; he thought of them as "protectors of this superb solitude from tourists . . . There is no settler within 12 miles of our camp." Here, Emerson suffused himself in the sentiments of his book-length essay *Nature*, published in 1836. William J. Stillman, the artist, explorer, and journalist who convened the camp, called the excursion an endless "play spell" in a "woods that played bo peep with us" in a "summer dream." All this was a grand illusion created by the guides, who slaved so that these gentlemen could take their leisure. Emerson marveled at the way the eminent campers and humble guides appeared to switch ranks in the woods. The hired hands were in charge, and the powerful "sports" were in their thrall.

Look to yourselves, ye polished gentlemen!
No city airs or arts pass current here.
Your rank is all reversed; let men of cloth
Bow to the stalwart churls in overalls:
They are the doctors of the wilderness,
And we the low-prized laymen.

Like a rusty shipwreck gathering mass at the bottom of the ocean, Emerson's 1858 campout gained weight over time. Eleven years before the Adirondacks became the center of America's first camping craze, and a decade before John Muir made his way into Yosemite Valley, these men helped get out the message that the woods were good for something other than timber and mineral extraction or potential farmland. "It was an early moment in the development of the idea that there was something sublime about nature," environmental writer Bill McKibben told the *New York Times* in 2008 after the Nature Conservancy bought a privately owned 14,600-acre parcel of Adirondacks land, including the three-mile-long Follensby Pond. "Nature was starting to play a less utilitarian function and a more aesthetic and intellectual one."

The fact that Emerson, the father of transcendentalism, had made the trip gave it credibility in the eyes of the other sports. But the campout was also frivolous by design, a pleasurable way to pass the time. That gleeful purposelessness made this high-minded wilderness conclave a bit more relatable to today's campers. Because of the guides' vigilance and care, the sports could spend their hours, in Emerson's words, "dissect[ing] the slain deer, weigh[ing] the trout's brain / Captur[ing] the lizard, salamander, shrew / Crab, mice, snail, dragon-fly, minnow, and moth," and enjoy the warmth of the "ductile fire." Emerson wrote about his immense respect for the guides, who allowed him to do all these things. Sometimes the campers showed no restraint about making their helpers do dangerous, fatuous tasks. One guide even risked death to scale a one-hundred-fifty-foot-high white pine just to grab an osprey egg so Agassiz could examine it. The guide found nothing but an empty nest, and drew the wrath of an osprey, which "wheeled and screamed" at him. Emerson never lectured at the guides; he conversed with them politely. But there was something patronizing about how he observed and analyzed them. Stillman, organizer of the campout, once wrote that Emerson regarded the guides as skilled "primitives."

In thinking them savages, Emerson could play at savagery himself, knowing the condition was temporary. It was fashionable at the time to think of regression and "primitive" living as a way to regain one's childhood and, in doing so, play out one's savage impulses, an exercise that allowed a man to become more civilized and manly than he was before. Some displays of boyhood and savagery could be downright hazardous. Emerson, as part of his regained childhood, developed an appreciation for firearms. Before the Adirondack campout, the poet Henry Wadsworth Longfellow was so horrified upon hearing that Emerson would have a shotgun with him that he refused to camp with the group at all. "Somebody will be shot!" he exclaimed.

But Emerson, thank goodness, did not plug any human beings on this trip. He didn't even bag a deer, a truly remarkable feat: guides made it almost impossible for anyone, no matter how hapless, not to shoot a deer. Back then, game laws were nonexistent or widely ignored, and jacklighting was a common, accepted practice, even among elitists. Jacklighting means shining a lantern or "jacklight" into the eyes of a deer to stun it into stillness and prevent the dazed creature from seeing the hunter behind the light source, taking aim. Unless the hunter got careless and scared the deer with a sudden noise, the animal would just stand there, waiting to be shot. Some camping guides also knew how to "hound" a deer into the water with a team of dogs, and then let a sport blast a few holes in it from the guide boat or, if his spirits were up, bash its poor head in with an oar. Certain expert guides could even sneak up on the deer when it was already trapped in the water, grab it by the tail, and hold on tight while the sport shot at it, missed, reloaded, and, if all else failed, gunned it down at close range. This technique was not much better than shooting heifers in a feedlot. This last, common practice was known as "tailing."

Though made illegal in 1897, these profligate hunting cheats apparently did not put much of a dent in the Adirondack deer population, in part because excessive logging had opened up more grazing areas for deer. Emerson's failure to bag a deer was extraordinary, but Stillman said the great man was probably glad, in retrospect, that he'd failed. Besides, he had more important matters on his mind, such as listening to the "croak" of the raven, the hoot of the owl, the "hammer" of the woodpecker, the "comic misery" inflicted by biting bugs, and the taste of "foaming ale" from a hunter's pan. He and his companions "fancied the light air / That circled freshly in their forest dress / Made them to boys again." Anyway, Emerson satisfied his juvenile impulses by shooting a "peetweet," a variety of sandpiper.

Such regression could happen only in unspoiled woods in the company of good friends who traveled to a place where no one could disturb them and sealed themselves away from the burdens and responsibilities of the modern world. That's why the campers picked a place that could be reached only by boat or a long and tortuous hike. In spite of their isolation, they did not always succeed in keeping the world at bay. Even in the mid-1800s, long before the invention of the satellite phone and many years before anyone started making Wi-Fi antennas out of empty Pringles containers, it was surprisingly hard to break free from technology and modernity. During the trip, the campers ran into another party, who regaled them with news of the laying out of the first transatlantic telegraph cable. Surprisingly, Emerson did not let this high-tech news hamper his enjoyment of the campout. In fact, he celebrated this "grand miracle," "this feat of wit, this triumph of mankind" with his fellow campers. He also used the news as an excuse to point out that his recreational campout was not exactly an escape from the urban world. If anything, it was a reassertion of that world to a forest setting.

"We flee away from cities, but we bring / The best of cities with us . . ."

Michael and I faced an unexpected intrusion of our own that night, and I reacted to it much less gracefully than Emerson.

Just when I was relishing my rare-cooked steak, and pretending it was a slab of tender Adirondack venison, a long-haired man rushed out of the woods from nowhere. After introducing himself hastily, he settled in front of the fire and interrogated us about our jobs and our alma maters. I was stunned. Who was this person? Why had he accosted us in this way? Why was he so curious about our pedigrees? At his insistence, I told him about my various work situations and where I'd gone to college. "Oh really?" he said. "I thought only successful people went there."

"Ouch!" I said.

"But Dan *is* successful," Michael said, perhaps a shade too defensively.

When he found out Michael's job, the man said, "Great! Have I got a book for you!" He was working on a dystopian fantasy novel—part Haruki

Murakami, part Mark Danielewski, part Stephen King, part Denis Johnson, part Kevin Brockmeier, but way better than all those people.

The stranger talked, seemingly without pausing for breath, and in one continuous sentence. I have a strong solidarity with the chatty authors of doomed projects; it humbles and pains me to think about the number of unpublished, frightful novels I've written, and may yet write. But this man, with his complicated sales pitch, yanked me out of my hard-earned Romantic camping trance. His elevator speech shattered my illusion that Michael was just my pal and we were out here by happenstance, just having fun. Suddenly I remembered that he was my editor. Oh, no! Was our friendship strictly transactional? Thank God for Zippy, who muscled the conversation right back to the topics of drinking and bushwhacking, returning to my dream of kinship untainted by financial quid pro quo, and sending the stranger back into the night from whence he came. Like Emerson's guides, Zippy had a great talent for erasing all self-consciousness.

Yet sometimes my role as a sport forced me into a "superior" position I did not want—and no matter how hard I tried to break free from the role, it ensnared me. I wanted to act like Zippy was one of the boys, but there were constant reminders that he wasn't. For instance, he refused to sample the meal he was preparing. Michael and I ate until our stomachs nearly popped. Even when the steak was practically peeping out of our throats, Zippy still kept saying, "No, no, no, I'll eat when you're all done." At one point he poured water on my hands after I'd used the outhouse. All this service was starting to make me feel strange. Who was I anyway? Commoner or Sun King? Zippy would accept no help at all as he washed the dirty dishes and created a special "sump pond" in a nearby stretch of dirt. Part of me resisted this behavior. I was paying him to act this way. Couldn't I force him to act like just another camping pal? "Can I help?" "No, no, no," he said.

Michael, I supposed, was more of a sporting personality—just going with the moment instead of overanalyzing it. But I couldn't stop myself. The fact that I was "on assignment" for Michael kept pushing me to ask questions that were more pointed and nosier than I would ever have asked if I had been out there for pure fun. Even though I knew this was happening, it was hard for me to stop. I finally just had to ask Zippy: "Isn't this whole thing just a little bit . . . awkward? The, um, situation we have here? Doesn't it drive you just a little bit batty sometimes? Like when you're working for

people what they wanted them to be. They never mention these
e a house somewhere and a wife and children and go to church
ordinary American lives." Terrie compared some of those play-
des to the principals in the *Duck Dynasty* reality show: "These
d guys with beards who live in swamps and have families but
as hell and shrewd and consciously manipulating that image, just
for all it is worth."

early accounts of Adirondack campouts conveniently over-
act that almost every guide was forced to do work on the side,
d. This was also true for Zippy, who worked for a high-end
esigner, doing installations, "Six-thousand-dollar curtains, eighty-
dollar rugs, the most beautiful stuff you've ever seen."

historical explanation intrigued and troubled me; I vowed not to
e sports he described, but the longer I lingered in the Adirondacks
y, the more I wondered if that sort of patronizing attitude arose
inevitably, from the business arrangement. Every time I found
ggering over some "folksy" thing Zippy said to make us laugh,
d if I was acting in a preordained, uncomfortably snobby way.

" Zippy said, after a long pause, "if you are in the service indus-
u live in the Adirondacks, it means you love the Adirondacks *a*
on't live here to make the big bucks. You live here because you
d it took years of struggling for me to get this far, years just to be
e here at all, after coming here as a stranger, and no one even
who I was. When you're a guide, you rest on your reputation, and
w up, people know about it. Let's say you bitched about me to
et's say you told him, 'Andy talks too much.'"

o wonder about this. How would his boss *not* know Zippy talked
, and why would that count against him? If we'd gotten a grumpy
rn guide instead of Zippy, that would have wrecked the whole
e for me. But Zippy wasn't through with his explanation.

as I'm concerned," he told me, "we all bleed the same blood, we
same sweat, feel the same feelings, you know what I mean? Let's
son is from a certain status? Okay? And let's say that person
be reprimanded. No, no, no. Not reprimanded. That's not the
d. Let's say enlightened. In that situation, I don't care who they
to them just like they were regular people.

ple want to abide by my safety guidelines and not come out here

someone who is really rich? I'd think th
there."

He didn't respond at first, so I asked wh
it over" him. Zippy—or so it seemed to me
trying to ruin the magic trick.

Suddenly I realized the deadfall trap I'd
It was his job to do what I wanted him to do
"make conversation," and there I was, ask
that seemed to make him uncomfortable.
rogations, even though, for all I knew, his
questions was compromised by the fact t
asking him whether he felt beholden to me
doing the very thing I was asking him abo
out of the question. Zippy gave me a skepti

"For someone who is very rich, I've nev
"It's never gotten out of hand. I've been doi
I used to be a service manager for a Toyota

"Well, yes, but a Toyota dealership mai
with the customer for forty-eight hours ai
all night long . . ."

I could kid myself about all this, but t
weight. There I was, seeking my "authentic
found it I didn't know what to do with it. Tl
been in a precarious position out here beca
pendent Adirondackers who could live off tl
winters and bad bugs, only to find themse
baggers who, in turn, relied on them utte
have been equally uncomfortable for the s
ists, unused to taking orders but out of th
In their writings about the campouts, the s
make their guides look like so many New
to make their backwoods journeys appear
to their readers.

"In a lot of ways, the Adirondack guide i
Adirondacks historian Philip Terrie told me
my trip. "There is practically nothing in th
think we can clearly say that the writers, tl

and act like an idiot, they are welcome, and I can accommodate anybody," Zippy continued. "It's your agenda I try to fulfill. What do you want to do and how can I help you achieve that goal? If people are pricks, if they're supercilious—well, that's just a social issue. You know, guiding—it used to be more like the *Titanic*: upper class, lower class, and steerage. These days everybody just comes out to have a good time. Nobody's special. In the old days, there was a social class thing, but if it got bad, the guides didn't care, because they were cocky back then. 'Okay, wanna be an idiot? I'll just leave you out here, and no one will ever find you!'"

Zippy's answer more than satisfied me, but as the night wore on, my neurosis changed course. Rather than obsess anymore about the compromised nature of our relationship, I began to obsess that our campout was not extreme enough to justify his presence in the first place. I turned to Zippy and saw the outline of his sleeping bag flash in the firelight. I asked if he could take us somewhere extreme, the kind of place that would have made the early Romantic campers tremble with a combination of excitement and fear. Zippy laughed because he had a place in mind.

"You're gonna have to be careful, though," he told us. "You're gonna get scraped. You're gonna have to cover up your extremities. This is going to be the real thing."

"Authentic?" I said, brightening up.

"You'd better believe it," he said.

The next morning, we arrived at a trackless wood up a steep hill containing overgrowth so dense I could barely look through it. Zippy gave the opposite of a pep talk. "This is going to be gnarly," he said. He'd brought along a GPS but questioned its usefulness; the contours were so tight they were difficult to read.

"It's pretty serious," he said. "We're gonna shoot for this brook right here. Looks like we will go up a mixed forest. We will follow the brook as far as it goes and see how close we can get to Ouluska Pass. I've never tried this one before. No trail. We'll just play the game as we go. But first let's eat some breakfast."

He let loose with a Snidely Whiplash laugh.

Moments later, we left the trail. Zippy went in first. He stepped off the path into a forest so dense I lost sight of the man in no time. You'd think the woods had swallowed him, spiky hairdo, Winnie-the-Pooh tattoo, maniacal expression, and all. We followed his voice into a wonderland of purple mushrooms, yellow-bellied salamanders, and old-growth eastern white cedars towering above us. Ahead of me, I could see the dense clutches of scratching branches, the uneven ground, and the matted fallen leaves concealing natural deadfall traps. "Cover your eyes in here; branches will try and gouge you," we heard Zippy say. "Watch out for your ankles; there are holes in the ground, and you can't see them. Watch for turtles; those are rocks that move and twist your ankle and roll you down. We're talking kung fu science, big time. If you're close enough to someone in front of you, be careful of flyback."

In a classic Adirondack bushwhack, the bushes do most of the whacking. Every time I took a step, a spruce or hemlock whipped me across the face with a tree branch or kneed me in the groin. No matter where I walked, I could not trust the forest floor. Sometimes I would plant my foot on a piece of solid land, only to watch my leg vanish into a "femur snapper," a mud hole buried under fallen branches and leaves. Again and again, my body would slam down to the ground like a sack of onions. Roots wrapped my legs. Natural trip wires extended from tree to tree.

I clawed my way out of a tight and slimy passage between two trees, only to wind up tangled in "cripple brush," a kind of mountain balsam that crowds around you. I freed myself, only to place my foot on a "turtle" rock that sent me flying face-first into a clutch of witch hobble, also known as moosewood or hunter's headache. Zippy had warned me all about it in camp: "If someone tripped over it, it means they either are, or are not, a witch; I can't remember which."

This bushwhack gave me a little perspective on what those early Adirondack adventurers must have faced. Michael and Zippy were nowhere to be seen. A creeping chill came over me. Which way was up? Which way was down? Where was the stream? Where were my companions? People still vanish in the Adirondacks.

At that moment, with the other two nowhere to be seen, I could just imagine myself lying in some undiscovered location with witch hobble growing through my clavicle.

"Michael," I yelled. "MICHAEL! Zippy. *Where are you, Zippy! Zippy, Zippy, Zippy!*"

"Right here," Zippy said. He was close by the whole time, but hidden from sight.

My relief was so immense I wanted to cry, but it seemed unsportsman-like, so I followed him and Michael out of the woods to a row of bumpy rock terraces and boulders. A brook dribbled over them, filling a series of shallow pools. Zippy looked in the water. "Dan," he said. "You need to see this."

Water striders skimmed the pool. Their legs were crooked spindles. As they chased one another, invisible fibers on their feet dimpled the water, dis-placing it, adding oblong shapes to their shadows on the bottom. As I mar-veled at this, a hemlock shed red-brown needles into the water. I watched them land on piles of spinning foam. I lay on a carpet of sphagnum at the edge of a rock, breathed out the last of the panic from my lungs, and covered myself with balsam boughs. Now I was starting to understand. Fresh from my memory of getting momentarily lost in the woods, I felt an oddly enjoy-able electric current course down my spine and into my fingers. It occurred to me that we campers hadn't really abandoned the old Puritan fear of the woods. That feeling of menace is always waiting in the background—which might explain the lingering popularity of bad-things-happening-in-the-woods movies, from *Friday the 13th* to *The Blair Witch Project*. Those Romantic campers did not abandon that panic. They merely modulated it, and somehow made it pleasurable, by knowing that the guide would not let anything really horrible happen to them.

"Anyone can come out here if you can read a map," Zippy said. "The difference is the wilderness is not the wilderness anymore. But if your equipment fails, if your GPS doesn't work, then you are in a true wilderness situation. The Adirondacks are still wild, as you can see right here. I can get lost easily. Just imagine. If you parked yourself up on the shoulder of a mountain, right about there." He pointed east of the stream, into a track-less area. "And let's say you wanted to be a hermit somewhere, and you had no obvious fires, and left no traces. And let's say you slipped and fell and hit your head. No one would find you. I guarantee you, no more than forty people have ever stood on the spot where you're lying down right now. You could disappear."

3

Camping the Crazy Away

Now, in the North Woods, owing to their marvelous water communication, you do all your sporting from your boat . . . This takes
from recreation every trace of toil. You have all the excitement of
sporting, without any attending physical weariness. Ah, what a
luxury it is . . .

—William "Adirondack" Murray, 1869

It seems unquestioned now that the white man has developed
the white plague since he became a house animal, and the natural cure of open-air life should be assiduously cultivated. No man
who sleeps out ever gets [a] nervous breakdown.

—Ernest Thompson Seton, 1915

After my sauntering in the Sewards with Zippy and Michael came to an
end, I retired to the Lake Placid Pub and Brewery and nursed an Ubu
English Strong Ale, my thigh muscles twitching, my arms and legs covered
with scratches and bug chomps. Happy, sweaty campers piled into the
lakeside bar, emptying pitchers of red, brown, black, and pale yellow brews
and regaling one another with lean-to tales. I was filled with satisfaction,
but it wasn't long before my brain began to squirm with unmet goals.

So far on my historic camping adventure I'd chased the specters of
Romantic campers through rows of hemlocks. Sometimes I almost caught
them. While in the woods, I'd watched ogre shadow shapes dance around

a campfire, observed a slab of meat jump around in a frying pan, woken up with my feet sticking out of a lean-to, felt the same night winds that blew through Romantic campsites, heard the same creek gurgles, and plowed through the same skin-shredding plants as on a classic bushwhack. But an enormous piece was missing: that tricky middle period when sleeping under the stars became less of a high-minded religious pursuit for a small and exclusive group of God-seeking wilderness tourists or a place for transcendentalists such as Ralph Waldo Emerson to evoke and re-create their boyhoods.

While I admired and envied those people, I wanted to get a better sense of how and when camping started to edge a little closer to its earthy, secular present-day self. When did camping begin to expand far beyond the domain of a small, self-selecting group of people and start to become a passion for ordinary middle-class schnooks like me?

Don't misunderstand me: I would welcome the chance to meet God on a windswept ridge, but I'm not necessarily counting on it; and I'd just as soon pull a bottle of chocolate stout from a campground cooler, eat a few s'mores, take in the ranger talk at the amphitheater, watch the sunset, zip myself up in my tent, and go straight to bed.

It seemed to me that only one man could give me a tactile sense of that time in the late nineteenth century, when camping got just a bit more homey and casual and enjoyed its first taste of mass appeal. But getting in contact with Joe Hackett, the most famous living old-style Adirondack fishing guide, was a bit like trying to schedule an appointment with one of his super-famous, wealthy, powerful clients.

Hackett has retreated into the backwoods with various U.S. presidents, an English prime minister, a chairman of the Federal Reserve, and a certain conservative Supreme Court justice who insists that Hackett call him Clarence. He charges premium rates. "I couldn't afford my own services," he told me over the phone. He also told me, sadly, that "someone would have to die" to free up a spot on his schedule so I could camp with him that summer.

He was kind enough, though, to offer up a few hours of idle "lily dipping" on a guide boat, free of charge. On the phone, I told him that I wanted to spend the morning with him in a part of Adirondack Park that time had forgotten, a place that looked *exactly* as it did in the years after the Civil War. He knew just the spot, and it was only a short drive in his pickup truck from the Noon Mark Diner. Soon we were out on a wobbly old guide boat, and Hackett was rowing me through the mists of Lower Ausable Lake, with Giant Mountain and the Gothics massing over us.

Hackett had a faint brown mustache, a bit of a paunch, and a slight, permanent stoop after so many years of lugging guide boats on dry "carries" between lakes and rivers. He has lived in the Adirondacks for fifty years. "I'm fifty-seven," he told me, "But my back is eighty-nine." He had a button-down pale yellow shirt, a brown beaver-felt hat that shed rain, and a hand-woven pack basket in the middle of the boat. A loon broke the silence. The call was a mixture of wolf howl, owl hoot, and kookaburra laughter, with loads of Elvis Presley "Heartbreak Hotel" reverb. Sudden and loud, it just about scared me out of my comfort-waist cargo pants.

The mountains formed an acoustic bowl, heightening the spooky echoes. Underwater grasses rasped against the boat, which a craftsman had made by hand in the 1880s by cutting L-shaped ribs from dug-up spruce roots. The ribs attached to a bottom board of pine planks secured with parallel rows of copper tacks. Hackett took me back to a time when these boats were the only way to get through this forbidding terrain. We drifted near the mouth of an ice cave, a natural tunnel where frost and icicles glazed the floor and ceiling. The cave blew cold gusts at us.

A black-headed silver-throated loon bobbed up in front of us. "To hunters, the call of the loon is the sound of spring coming," Hackett said, facing me as he rowed backward.

His ancient oarlocks made a sound like peeping birds. The "cranky" (meaning a little off balance or wobbly) craft dated to a time when camping became a more mixed experience: still somewhat religious but also avowedly secular and profane. Hackett himself struck me as a comforting blend of both impulses. He had a fervor for the forest combined with a surprising, earthy bluntness; as we rowed along, he told me that people love to camp because it is a chance to abandon restraint. "When you camp, you can burp, scratch your ass, let your hair down, and nobody gives you a hard time about it," he said.

His clients are trying to escape their stressful lives. They aren't seeking pantheistic transformation. They just want to go out there and get close to nature. Some get a little too close. "I had one guy who tried to pick up a skunk," said Hackett, who grew up in the area, just ten miles or so from where he was rowing me out. "We were going into the High Peaks, and he thought it was a cat and went over to pick it up, and he got it really bad.

You can't wash that off, you know. Vinegar is the only thing they say works. We had no vinegar. He was choked up, coughing, in pretty bad shape."

His clients may be seeking bliss in the forest, but it is not necessarily the spiritual kind. "I had one guy who came up with two Italian models and spent the whole weekend in the tent," Hackett told me. "I ended up fishing by myself. I didn't mind. You know, I was having a grand time, and quite obviously he was, too."

As we drifted through the water, it was easy to imagine the pull this lovely place had for repressed Victorian campers, who must have been eager to flee their stuffy parlors. I sensed this especially when we made landfall at a peninsula with a private camp that included the finest lean-to I've ever seen, with soft balsam needles for bedding. The well-used fire pit was cold, but it kicked up a warm scent when I stepped around it. I breathed in this mixture of odors and felt careless again. Hackett sat beside me in front of the fire pit, put his hands on his knees, and sighed. "That is the thing about those old camps, a mustiness to them, that smell of wood smoke and mud and bug dope and wet woolies all together."

While admiring the peaks rising almost vertically from the water's edge, I imagined we were back in a time when life was improving for Americans, at least for the comfortable classes. They had every reason to be happy. A middle class was forming. The War Between the States was over, and people had bicycles. Factories boomed. Railroads reached across the country for the first time. Toilet paper and typewriters were becoming available. What more could they possibly want?

Those developments, however, could not stop a devastating plague of neuroses from sweeping the nation, especially the Eastern Seaboard. If anything, all those new creature comforts seemed to increase the psychic devastation. The alleged mental disease, which entered American medical literature in 1869, was called neurasthenia.

Perhaps this perceived ailment was the end result of nature deprivation combined with jarring lifestyle changes. Like never before, Americans were bolting their breakfasts, yanking on their trousers, and racing to the morning commute. The dawn of the industrial age coincided with a time of risk avoidance and aversion to pain. Existence, for the first time in American history, was becoming predictable and numbing. Boring church services were squeezing out the fire-and-brimstone variety. Rational thought was staging a tedious comeback. Work was stultifying, life was pragmatic, and God was strictly optional. A deadening of the spirit was taking place. Prosperity had come, and it was boring as hell.

"For the late Victorian bourgeoisie, intense experience, whether physical or emotional, seemed a lost possibility," wrote historian T. J. Jackson Lears in his book *No Place of Grace*.

It all added up to a perceived cultural vampirism. Modern life was sucking all the vitality away. Newspapers ran frightening illustrations of neurasthenia sufferers who looked like walking corpses. Those ghastly pictures appeared alongside advertisements for suspect nostrums, including Paine's Celery Compound, an alleged cure for "exhaustion of nerve force."

Melancholy and stress had been drawing recreational campers ever since the early nineteenth century. But apparently the afflictions had become more toxic and complicated since the days when the Reverend Joel Headley fled to the Adirondacks in the 1840s.

While Headley's list of campout-inducing mental miseries was very modest, the symptoms of neurasthenia went on and on. Neurasthenics hated wide-open spaces. Then again, they despised enclosed spaces. Neurasthenics thought men were scary and women were terrifying. They feared everything, including fear. As the century progressed, doctors expanded

This vintage 1899 image of a sluggish and miserable neurasthenia victim
was part of a popular advertisement for Paine's Celery Compound,
a nostrum that was marketed as a blood cleanser.

the list of symptoms to include rotten teeth, which was not surprising, considering the sugary Coca-Cola with real cocaine prescribed to cure their "sick headaches, neuralgia, hysteria and melancholy." Neurotics suffered from "local spasms," overwhelming sexual excitement, underwhelming sexual boredom, ticklishness, and the cramps.

When the twentieth century dawned, pundits claimed neurasthenia was getting even worse. In 1906 in New York State alone, 6,046 people were thought to have died of "nervous collapse," amounting to nearly 10 percent of the state's overall deaths that year.

Neurasthenia was considered a bane of the well-to-do and of the middle class. Physicians blamed it for everything from murder-suicides to maritime accidents.

Dr. George Miller Beard, the great popularizer of neurasthenia and a self-diagnosed sufferer himself, believed the general cause was modern living. Another influential physician, Landon Carter Gray, blamed overwork—not the physical kind, but the enervating sort that took place in offices. While there is something smug about a perceived ailment that afflicts mostly "brain workers" and reasonably well off people, there is no denying that wrenching changes in American life were leaving scores of people from all social classes feeling more anxious.

Americans for the first time found themselves confronting the "time clock," the dreadful device that forced them to "punch in," and then "punch out" when the workday was done, introducing the era of being "on" and "off" the clock. The days of instant communication were already upon them. "We are in great haste to construct a magnetic telegraph from Maine to Texas," Henry David Thoreau warned in *Walden* back in 1854. "But Maine and Texas, it may be, have nothing important to communicate." Perhaps it was no coincidence that the completion of the First Transcontinental Railroad and the entry of the word *neurasthenia* into American popular culture both took place in 1869. The great railways offered speed and regimentation in the guise of convenience. "We do not ride on the railroad; it rides upon us," Thoreau observed.

Neurasthenics were willing to go through any torture or fad diet to make their mental miseries go away. They took freezing-cold ocean baths, tried shock therapy, and took up arts and crafts. They ate coal tar and guzzled all kinds of stinky nostrums, including extract of cow brains. Afflicted children downed milk and water by the gallon and were subjected to painful full-body rubbings. Some neurotics tried faith healing, spas, binge eating, and starvation. They joined work communes and quasimilitaristic organizations. Some suffered "cures" that were worse than the diagnosis. Dr. Beard, for instance, advised patients to endure a procedure in which beef juice, milk, or "defibrinated blood" was injected into their bottoms, a process called "rectal alimentation." Bad as it seems, it is not so different from today's "accelerated detox" programs at fancy spas, which often involve juice fasts and colonic cleansings.

Americans should at least be grateful that Dr. Beard also recommended vacations in the mountains, including the Adirondacks. Though he didn't use the word *camping*, it was strongly implicit. (It's unfortunate, however, that this cure-all landed so far down on his list of remedies, which also included ingesting arsenic, huffing nitrous oxide, and eating strychnine.) Around the same time, an idealistic and relentlessly self-promoting man came along who had a similar notion—and his words would have an enormous effect on recreational camping history. Without quite realizing what he was doing, this fellow would trigger America's first mad rush to the woods. For a short while, he was the reigning hero of the campsite, a Pied Piper of the backwoods, before his fans turned on him.

His name was William H. H. "Adirondack" Murray. Chances are you've never heard of this man unless you are a history-minded camping fanatic. There is no statue, no shrine in his memory.

Saying a regretful good-bye to Joe Hackett after our all-too-brief Lower Ausable Lake excursion, I drove to Raquette Lake, where I stood on the waterfront, hoping to borrow a rowboat while steering clear of some kids pelting one another with a beach ball and trying to ignore their tough-looking dad, who was shaving his shoulder hair with what appeared to be a butcher knife. The people at the dock gave me some sad news: the clock had just struck 5:00 p.m., which meant I was just in time to be too late to row a rented boat to Osprey Island, an unruly tuft of green land rising from the blue. Shaggy trees grew to a rim of smooth rocks around its shore. The isle's reflection was a perfect pyramid of green.

The rounded hump of land was close enough to shore so I could imagine the well-dressed and handsome Boston minister William H. H. Murray entertaining guests and setting up tents with his wife, Isadora, who

William H. H. Murray, 1840–1904

used to flounce around on the grass in a crimson jacket. According to a contemporary account by a man who visited them on the island, she looked quite "comely."

Murray himself was a shameless striver almost from the time he was born. He grew up on a farm in humble circumstances. "There has never been a rich rascal in our family!" he once bragged.

When he showed up at Yale to study, fifteen miles from his home in Guilford, Connecticut, he had less than five dollars in his pocket and only a pair of carpetbags to hold his clothes. Despite this humble arrival, he earned a reputation as a mesmerizing speaker and fierce debater who overcame a childhood speech impediment. Yet Murray could be fuddleheaded, and the pull of the woods sometimes threatened to derail his ambitions as a minister. Even as he rose up in the ranks in various New England churches, he wanted to haul off and shoot some deer. This habit did not always endear him to his flock. At least once, he shocked his parishioners in rural Washington, Connecticut, by rushing back out of breath and sweaty from a romp in the woods. He propped his rifle on a church wall, ascended the pulpit in his velveteen hunting breeches, and started up preaching as if nothing had happened. He didn't apologize or acknowledge the incident until the end of the service. In one of his writings, he had the gall to suggest that a wilderness vacation would do his parishioners at least as much good as church services. Yet Murray had ardent fans as well as people who thought he was a weirdo and a disgrace to the pulpit. By the time he was twenty-eight, he had become the minister for Boston's exclusive and formerly moribund Park Street Congregational Church, a house of worship so hidebound and joyless that people called it the Brimstone Corner.

Murray's huge popularity put an end to embarrassing rows of empty pews and made him a mini-celebrity. Park Street went from a local joke to a cultural touchstone.

"His church has been lifted to a level of near-universal observation," a popular magazine raved. "Murray's influence is beyond calculation."

Jealous Bostonians ridiculed Murray for the "nasal twang" of his speech; they branded him "the vocal horror from Connecticut." But that early mixture of praise and hatred was nothing compared to what happened in April 1869, when Murray published a best-selling book, *Adventures in the Wilderness, or Camp-Life in the Adirondacks*, only a year after taking the job at Park Street. This was a memoir, guidebook, and travelogue, with jaunty writing and vivid descriptions of trout, deer, and crashing waterfalls. "Ah me, the nights I have passed in the woods! How they haunt me with their sweet, suggestive memories of silence and repose!" (Adirondack Murray was fond of exclamation points.)

Murray's popular newspaper columns, in which he wrote about the sporting life, and his vigorous treatment of an immensely appealing subject, made the book a success. He knew his audience. He made his readers feel like he was opening the doors of their cramped little offices and talking directly in their ears. "A city life . . . is a grinding kind of life," said Murray, who knew what it was like to go from a simple existence on a farm to the rush of a big city. "It wrinkles the face and whitens the head . . . It destroys individuality and makes a man to be no more than an ant."

Murray offered his fans an escape, and he took pains to make camping seem as easy and simple as possible. He promised that a week in the Adirondack woods would cure every physical and mental ailment. He showed them where to find the best wilderness guides and listed their names. He told them where to bag the best deer, and even named the hotel where they could eat the fluffiest pancakes. The creeks were full of "eager fish." He even made the North Woods bugs seem like nothing more than a passing nuisance—an assessment that must have shocked anyone who had ever encountered the nibbling bloodsuckers of upstate New York. To this day, savvy visitors regard the region's blackflies with such dread that they plan their trips accordingly, and you will find most camping areas deserted in May and June. The blackfly will bite through clothes, break the skin, and squirt enzymes that work as anticoagulants, allowing the flies to pump and slurp from punctured capillaries. Yet Murray claimed that blackflies were "the most harmless and the least vexatious of the insect family." This borderline cutesy description is much different from an earlier account by Reverend Headley, who "was compelled to fling down my rod and run" during a blackfly attack, "for the blood was pouring in rivulets from my neck, face, and hands."

Murray disavowed such stories: the blackfly of legend was "a myth," he insisted, "a monster existing only in men's feverish imaginations." Trust me, he seemed to say. There was nothing to worry about in his North Woods, only "a thousand sources of invigoration" and a marvelous sleep that "woos you as the shadows deepen along the lake, and retains you in its gentle embrace until frightened away by the guide's merry call to breakfast."

Aside from his puzzling decision to defang a hated insect, Murray did himself a disservice by playing down the chaos hardwired into almost any camping experience. Most of us know just how wrong a camping trip can go. Murray was courting disbelief by making the backwoods seem as predictable as a stay in a country hotel.

Other aspects of his book are more admirable, including his exhortation for women to go camping alongside their men. This stance was unusual and defiant during a period when camping was often for men only, and Victorian doctors urged women to build up their constitutions by taking the "Weir Mitchell Rest Cure," which involved lying around in bed for at least a month, and avoiding all strenuous activities such as reading and writing, which might damage a lady's delicate constitution.

"Murray was the earliest outdoor advocate for women and children," wrote Harry V. Radford, a noted explorer, in a biographical appreciation published after Murray's death. Radford, who was fated to be speared to death by Eskimos in Canada in 1912, called Murray a camping revolutionary who dared to question its traditional demographic. While there is no way of knowing how many women answered his call, Murray's words made a huge impression on the respected journalist Kate Field, who took a three-week campout in the Adirondacks in the summer of 1869 with several women friends and loved every moment of it. "To come into the Wilderness and *not* camp out would be to me as unnatural as to bathe in a diver's water-proof suit," Field said.

Field and her daring friends took along a large stash of "sea biscuits," condensed milk, potted meats, maple sugar, and vegetables packed in cans. With a guide to help them, they spent three weeks camping and hunting, and refused to let the "blackflies, musketoes, and midges" harm their morale. "Days come, days go, and life grows richer, fuller, until the . . . old harness and bit become the bête noire of existence," Field wrote.

That experience marked Field's conversion into a camping fanatic. She went on to write popular columns aimed at women who were "willing to be tanned, freckled, and even made to resemble antique statuary" by facing the wild for a little while. She used her massive readership in such outlets as the *New-York Tribune*, the *Boston Post*, and *New York Herald* to praise "Adirondack" Murray, and to taunt and cajole women to abandon their sheltered lives for a spell. "Helter skelter, off with silks, kid gloves, and linen collars, on with bloomers, stout boots, and felt hat," she told them.

It's tempting to praise Murray as some kind of protofeminist for reaching people such as Field. But his come-on to female campers, while commendable and brave, was just part of his broader argument that the Adirondack campout, thanks to the presence of the hardworking guides, was such a passive experience that anyone—invalids, children, and even, God help us, women—could enjoy it. There was no need for strenuous exercise because a boatman would take you anywhere you wished, he said. The guide boat erased any need for the disgraceful activity that Americans now refer to as "backpacking." William H. H. Murray used a dismissive word to describe it: *tramping*. It would be another century before millions of Americans came to think that backpacking/camping were variations on the same activity. "How the thorns lacerate you!" Murray said, referring to the miseries of tramping. "How the brambles tear your clothes and pierce your flesh! I would not walk two miles through such a country for all the trout that swim!"

Murray's praise of the Adirondacks was sincere, but it created a reality distortion field for thousands of people. There are no reliable estimates of how many greenhorns folded up their three-piece suits; put on their hoop skirts; packed up their trunks; left Philadelphia, Boston, and New York City; and headed out in search of an easy vacation. But there is no denying that the number was much too high for the Adirondacks' feeble tourist infrastructure to accommodate them all.

Those campers sought bliss and an uncomplicated escape from their messy lives. They rushed out in search of an Adirondacks that existed mostly in Murray's head. What they found was the actual Adirondacks: steep, soggy, and unforgiving. Campers were badly frightened even when they strayed just a few feet from their lodgings. They shouted in panic at the sight of fresh deer tracks and even their own footprints. Some ladies tripped and fell in mud. Too scared to camp out on their own, some hung around the hotels; it was one of the earliest examples of Americans attempting to "get away from it all," only to find themselves facing a mob of people with the same notion. After a while, these would-be campers, derided as "Murray's Fools" in the newspapers, began to curse that stumblebum William H. H. Murray, who had lured them into the forest in the first place. Their curses soon gave way, however, to squeals of terror when the wicked bugs turned out to be "utterly beyond the comprehension of those who have not been there," as the writer Ralph Wing observed.

In his book, the hapless Murray assured his readers that the biting insects would be gone by July, but the summer of 1869 was cooler than usual, which lengthened the bug season; the chewing and gleeful chomping continued well into August.

Adirondack blackfly (actual size)

Blackflies circled, waiting to strike. They flew up men's noses and buzzed in ladies' bloomers. Panicking campers smeared pine tar all over their bodies, thinking it would stop the pricking and bleeding.

Crowds of would-be campers found out that all the great wilderness guides had been booked. Then the merely good ones were booked, and pretty soon people were hiring local drunks with no wilderness experience to guide them. Hotels were fully occupied. Even the barns were full. One desperate New Yorker—or so the oft-repeated story goes—was forced to spend the night on an old, scratched-up pool table in lieu of a hotel bed. After waking up the next morning angry and tired, with an aching back, he was handed a bill for the modern-day equivalent of eighty-five dollars.

So the backlash began. The August 1870 edition of *Harper's New Monthly* ran an editorial cartoon showing an Adirondack sportsman drowned in a swamp, his fishing rod lying next to his floating hat. A group of curious woodland animals gather around the deceased camper, while wondering at the book that lies on dry ground next to the mud puddle: a well-thumbed copy of William H. H. Murray's *Adventures in the Wilderness*. The headline of the cartoon was "The Dismal Wilderness." Murray was becoming the jackass of the year.

One prolific Murray hater, who wrote under the pen name Wachusett, sneered about Adirondack ladies "in a rain storm, faces and hands dripping with tar and oil (to keep the bugs away), mosquito bites smarting on wrists and temples, the boots soaked through and through, the reserve stockings in the carpet bag equally."

In a much angrier passage, Wachusett accused Murray of hard-selling a deadly dream for serious consumptives whose self-curing trips to the Adirondacks would only lead to the "the bitterest disappointment, bringing perhaps an accelerated death in its train." Wachusett was likely referring to a statement in Murray's book in which he describes a consumptive who arrived at the Adirondacks near death but came out healthy and "bronzed as an Indian." *New York Times* correspondent William Chapman White later wrote that Murray had created a "stampede" of "bitter people. They cried, 'Liar! Murray wrote a re-lieable book. In it he lies over and over!'"

Murray retained some bold defenders, Kate Field included. Confronting the critics who accused him of causing an ugly stampede, she argued that Murray "never dreamed of such results, or he would have walked through a fiery furnace before giving to the public his impressions of wood-life."

His few defenders were not enough, however, to save his reputation. Male aristocratic hunters wrote sarcastic columns accusing Murray of bringing a bunch of carpetbaggers to the Adirondacks and drawing unwanted females into their midst. Some manly sportsmen suggested that the women trashed their beloved woods with discarded parasols "and bits of lingerie," according to a story in *Forest and Stream* magazine.

Suddenly Murray was no longer considered a camping hero; people were picking apart every aspect of his book and using his own words to unmake him.

After trying in vain to reach Osprey Island, I gave up and made for a Murray landmark with darker connotations. Buttermilk Falls, just off North Point Road along the Raquette River, was wide and vigorous and kicked up such a mad froth that its bubbles clumped together, turning the water milky white and thick, until it resembled a runny yogurt-based smoothie.

Descending on foot, I followed the watery roar down a slick hillside until I saw it. Tourists gathered in clumps beside the cataract with boulders jagging out of it. I kept staring at the waterfall and thinking, *There is no way in hell that someone could run a guide boat over that nasty waterfall and not get shredded into a hundred pieces.* But Murray, in a florid and much-quoted part of *Adventures,* claimed that he and his noble guide ran the falls in a guide boat in the 1860s. (In the book, he renames the place "Phantom Falls.") "Down, down we went. O, how we shot along that tremulous plain of quivering water," Murray recalled. "Quivering like a frightened fish," his guide boat plummeted down "like a pointed stake hurled from the hand." The boat overturned at the bottom, but Murray and his guide swam to safety.

As I stood in the mist, I asked everyone around me the same question: would it be possible to float a big, clunky 1800s-style wooden guide boat over that waterfall without getting smashed to death? Nearly every one of the people there gave me variations of "hell, no." "Yeah, sure," said an older gentleman, who lived down the road, in Long Lake. "Float a guide boat over those rocks, then come back and try that backward. Then try the same thing with Noah's Ark while you're at it."

Murray would have been chagrined to hear these things. Widespread doubts about his waterfall plunge only did further damage to his reputation, in spite of the brief and cautious disclaimer that he appended to his story, asking readers to believe as little or as much of it as they wished. He must have realized his enemies were seeking any excuse to discredit him. The blowback maddened him. "The great, ignorant stay-at-home egotistic world laughed and jeered and tried to roar the book down," he later complained.

Murray blamed the privileged hunters and his enemies in the press for killing his best-selling book's momentum. "[T]he little book, which had been selling at a rate of 500 a week . . . suddenly dropped to five volumes a week and was dead, apparently beyond the hope of resurrection." He said that those who tried to "yell me down" knew full well that he stood to lose "all that made life worth living."

Murray decided to fight back against his "calumniators." In October 1869 he wrote an angry editorial in the *New-York Tribune*. His main complaint was that his critics were a bunch of elitists. He wanted to democratize camping, while they wanted to keep the woods as their private pleasure grounds. In the piece, he thundered back at the aristocratic hunters who thought the North Woods belonged to them. Those snooty huntsmen derided the middle-class campers as unprepared, unworthy, and vulgar: "I have no sympathy at all with those two or three hundred gentlemen who would selfishly monopolize the Adirondack Wilderness for their own exclusive amusement and benefit. Indeed I do not look at the Wilderness as belonging to sportsmen or any class; it belongs to the country at large." He criticized certain campers who showed up to the rugged wilderness "dressed as for a promenade along Broadway, or a day's picnic."

Murray tried to regain his stature. He went on the lecture circuit and delivered, more than five hundred times, to a total of about half a million people, speeches about camping in the Adirondacks and the glories of the wilderness. He continued to sell his dreamy visions of the North Woods to the public. Yet he never recovered from the embarrassment and outrage he faced in the summer of '69.

When reading about Murray's life, I often wanted to jump into the pages and urge him to move to his beloved Adirondacks and build a life there. Instead, he had a few ill-conceived ventures that had only the most tenuous connection with camping in the pines; for a while he had a racehorse named Adirondacks. His marriage to Isadora fell apart in 1886, back when divorce was a scandal. He spent some time at a ranch in Texas, and at one low point he shucked oysters in a dimly lit low-rent Montreal restaurant that sold no beer. The Adirondack historian Alfred Donaldson remarked that Murray "served the doughnut and the mince pie [as eagerly] as he ever served religious pabulum" during his days as a preacher. One journalist from the *San Francisco Chronicle* snidely reported that the once-handsome Murray had become sedentary, overweight, and prone to wearing goofy clothes. At least in Montreal, he had a little bit of late-career attention as part of Buffalo Bill's Wild West show, but it didn't seem to do much for him. You can see a photo of Murray posed next to Sitting Bull and Buffalo Bill, looking thoroughly burned out, exhausted, and annoyed. That is quite a fate for the person some consider the "Father of American camping" and whose book, according to the writer Wendell Phillips, "kindled a thousand campfires."

This is a real shame because Murray, in spite of his faults, was an original. Around the time his book came out, Americans were beginning to embrace the idea of camping as a leisure pursuit that was *not* idle, and just coming around to the idea that intense physical exertion in the outdoors might be good for the soul. Murray not only preached such views from the pulpit; he lived them. For me, the most striking and original aspect of Murray's camping philosophy is its secular quality. Among America's very earliest camping enthusiasts were Presbyterians and Methodists, who gathered at "camp meetings" in big tents for services. Before long there were also Chautauqua campout events, initially in upstate New York, starting out as practicums for religious school teachers, then evolving later in the century into edifying entertainment, sylvan precursors to today's TED talks. These early campers deserve credit for pioneering the "value added" campout, in which campers come away with something other than just a relaxing good time. Yet Murray was among the first to promote camping for camping's sake—not to shoot a deer, not to catch a fish, not to catch up with Jesus, but for the self-evident thrill of it all.

Late in life, Murray again returned to the lecture circuit and entertained crowds with sincere if sickly sweet stories about John Norton, a fanciful guide and trapper who embodied the spirit of the North Woods. Murray made enough money from those talks to buy back the family farm in Guilford, Connecticut, but his profile was greatly diminished. He died at age sixty-four in the room where he was born, on a farm with a giant buttonwood tree rising over the house.

Even in death, he got little respect; some obituary notices were catty. "An Erratic Career," one headline read. Another obit called him a hypocrite and morally suspect, perhaps a reference to his divorce. Over time, his writings were forgotten and he became irrelevant. Even at the turn of the century, people were disregarding him. "Neither lake nor mountain commemorates the name of him who opened the eyes of the world to this grand sanatorium and pleasure ground!" one of his admirers fulminated in 1906. By the end of the century, better maps, more roads, and self-guided wilderness adventure campers such as George Washington Sears, aka Nessmuk, were reducing the power and influence of wilderness guides in the Adirondacks and elsewhere; the kind of camping that Murray espoused was becoming passé. But in some respects Murray was ahead of his time.

He praised the healing vapors coming from Adirondack trees, one hundred fifty years before Japanese scientists prepared rigorous studies about the impacts of "forest bathing," which decreases stress, lowers depression, and bolsters the immune system. The studies also showed that emanations from certain trees could heal the body. Just as Murray rhapsodized about the life-giving properties of "air . . . laden with the mingled perfume of cedar, of balsam," science writer Jim Robbins has expounded on "medicinal mists" that contain "antiviral, antifungal, antibiotic," and anticarcinogenic properties. I can't help but wonder if it's time for a brand-new Murray to rise up again and cause another massive retreat into the woods.

In case you haven't noticed, Victorian afflictions are staging a grand revival. Measles has returned, thanks to close quarters and vaccination-averse parents. So have scurvy, mumps, scarlet fever, polio, public shaming, and gout. These days, "neurasthenia" is considered an outmoded diagnosis; it's just too sweeping and general for anyone to take seriously. Yet the conditions that triggered that alleged neurotic plague are still here, albeit in a somewhat different form. We twenty-first-century Americans have recapitulated the Victorian "shock of the new" that followed the Civil War. Doctors of the nineteenth century blamed the unprecedented speed of communications and the barrage of information from the first wide-circulation newspapers and magazines, not to mention "the monotony of routinized subdivided labor." I wonder what neurasthenia popularizer George Miller Beard would have said about our twenty-four-hour news cycle and our digital beepers and gadgets attached to our person all day long like prisoner bracelets. And forget the time clock; these days, some companies use biometric fingerprint scanners and cloud computer technology to make sure the person who punches the clock and breaks for lunch is really you.

It is enough to make me wonder if this nervous plague ever went away at all. I don't want to come across as technophobic. I get along with technology just fine. My father was part of America's first high-tech boom and helped transport one of the first powerful computers to Sweden at a time when those things were so humongous they took up an entire room. I use apps to identify birdcalls. I obsess over Internet stories about Adirondack historic figures. My problem comes from feeling that I'm always on call, that there's *no escape* from the message "ping" that has become the twenty-first-century equivalent of the foreman calling time.

T. M. Luhrmann, a professor of anthropology at Stanford University and a contributing opinion writer to the *New York Times*, wrote that one in five Americans had anxiety disorders in 2015. "We spend over $2 billion a year on anti-anxiety medications," she wrote. "There are many explanations for these nerves: a bad job market, less cohesive communities, the constant self-comparison that is social media." Luhrmann cited a World Mental Health Survey suggesting that out of fourteen countries surveyed, Americans had "more clinically significant levels of anxiety." The study found that we're more neurotic than the Nigerians, the Lebanese, and the Ukrainians. Just as George Miller Beard believed neurasthenia was an American disease, Luhrmann suggests there is something culturally specific about real and perceived twenty-first-century anxiety—she mentions the uniquely American quality of visualizing the mind "as an interior place that demands . . . constant attention," along with the fervent belief in somatized unhappiness: "Americans believe that excessive sadness makes us sick."

While some of us might laugh at the idea of neurasthenia today and all that fin de siècle soul anemia, in some sense we should all be grateful for Dr. George Miller Beard and his silly overreaching disease. After all, a diagnosed neurasthenic and asthmatic weakling by the name of Theodore Roosevelt first came to the newly trendy Adirondacks as a child in the early 1870s, not long before Murray put the area on the recreational map. Roosevelt would go on to change camping forever, with his calls for the strenuous life and his preservation of millions of acres where we camp today, from the Grand Canyon of Arizona to the Pinnacles of California.

In my final days in the North Woods, taking my cue from that first generation of survivalist campers who went out into the woods with no guides, I tried a bit of self-guided exploration. Searching for the peaks and forests

Roosevelt once haunted, I hiked into a summer storm with my rainproof map whipping against my face. In three days, I tramped ninety miles. I climbed creek beds and fell into countless mud holes, which I called "cha-wangachunks" for the matchless sound they made when they pulled my boots clean off. (The Adirondack Park specializes in mud: squirty mud, caked mud, mud that turns your socks the color of a blood orange.) I sipped rainwater from my upturned survival hat; slipped on sharp rocks and bloodied my knees. I followed stepping stones along soupy-green creeks through colonnades of hemlock and balsam. I loved all of this. The Adirondacks brought the pain. I sucked it right up.

On the last day, and in spite of warnings from a taciturn outdoor-store clerk who said I might not make it out before the sky went black, I made a try for the summit of Mount Marcy, the highest point in New York State. Unseen insects made loud and ugly crepitations, which sounded like emergency sprinkler systems in office complexes. In a couple of places, the trail was a rushing brown river. A damp butterfly alit on my hat. Spiderwebs hung in the branches of old hemlocks. Raindrops hung in the spinnerets. No matter how steep it got, or slippery, there was always some old codger marching beside me in the rain with his telescoping walking stick and toddler-age grandkids. It is impossible to hike such a mountain on a damp day and not feel the ghosts peering over your shoulder. I felt spooked at all turns, but never thought of quitting.

By California and Alaska standards, Marcy, elevation 5,344 feet, is a midget, but it plays a grandiose role in camping history.

On a different route, but on a comparably drizzly day, on September 13, 1901, Vice President Theodore Roosevelt climbed the same peak in what must have been a state of profound misgiving. A violent anarchist named Leon Czolgosz had shot a couple of bullets into the chest of Roosevelt's boss, President William McKinley, a classic Victorian gentlemen who had an urgent request for his advisers: "My wife—Be careful . . . how you tell her—oh, be careful!" before collapsing in a heap.

At the time of the attack, Roosevelt was attending a luncheon on Lake Champlain. He received an alarming phone call; Czolgosz had fooled the president with a nasty trick: extending a hankie-covered hand for the president to shake. McKinley assumed the hankie was just a bandage, but it concealed a .32-caliber Iver Johnson revolver. Roosevelt hurried to Buffalo to stay by the president's side, but after a while McKinley's advisers told

Theodore Roosevelt (1858–1919)

Roosevelt to get lost. Apparently they were scared that the sight of Roosevelt skulking by the president's bedside would rattle the public.

Roosevelt thought he was doing his duty as a good American when he fled Buffalo and joined his family in the Adirondacks while his boss lay moaning in bed, gangrene setting in day by day. In the mood for a "bully walk," and not knowing that the president was near death, he set out to climb Mount Marcy in spite of the mists and ominous darkening sky.

Roosevelt knew the Adirondacks well. His parents had vacationed there since the 1870s—likely because of Adirondack Murray's blockbuster book—bringing along their sickly, nerdy, and asthmatic child nicknamed "Teedie." Fancy getaway hotels were springing up, but little Teedie was never content just to laze around upscale Paul Smith's Hotel on Lower Saint Regis Lake. Instead, he wanted to get out into the forest, trudge through the hummocky swamps, ford the area's beguiling and "very crooked streams," climb mountains, and listen for the howl of an eastern timber wolf. During these family trips in his youth and childhood, and into his college years, he would take strenuous hikes and camp in the forest, always in the company of a watchful paid Canadian guide named Moses Sawyer, who was so good at his job and knew so much about the forest that other envious and admiring guides referred to him as a "seven-sided son-of-a-bitch."

Roosevelt's parents had good reason to fret about Teedie. Sometimes he could be smart-stupid—brilliant on the one hand, but absentminded. As one story goes, he was such a sickly child that his parents sometimes feared for his life. The future president had terrible colds as a boy, and once griped that he felt as if he had "a toothache in my stomach." His asthma was so awful he had to sleep sitting up to avoid suffocation. In his own words, even a "very slight" attack made it hard for him to speak "without blowing up like an abridged edition of a hippopotamus." Aside from this, Teedie, who would one day lead the Rough Riders charge up San Juan Hill in Santiago de Cuba, was so puny that a group of toughs once gave him a thumping and called him a sissy. At the time, he did little to endear himself to potential friends: he'd walk around with various critter specimens, including smelly dead bats, in the pockets of grease-smeared outfits, giving off the acrid stink of the arsenic he used to preserve these mammals.

Such a childhood was a most unlikely beginning for a man so tough and boundlessly energetic that he once played ninety-one games of tennis in the same day and was known to shake thousands of hands at political events without tiring. Even as an older man, after his presidency was over, he not only survived a bullet in the chest but continued his speech as scheduled in spite of the blood seeping through his jacket. How did he go from a limp noodle to a superman? Sawyer, his camping guide, deserves at least some of the credit. While Teedie's parents were frightened at the idea of their child climbing Adirondack peaks, they gave him more license if Sawyer was around to watch over him. Teedie was so appreciative of Sawyer's help that he gave the guide a prized gift: four of the dead birds Teedie had gunned down in the woods for the sake of science. (Many a North Woods bird met its doom at the wrong side of young Roosevelt's gun during those tramps through the forest.) If Sawyer found this present touching, his reaction must have been short-lived; Sawyer's cat, not realizing the birds had been treated with arsenic, attempted to eat them and dropped dead.

Fortunately, that little incident did not weaken their companionableness. Even in the future president's college years, he and Sawyer remained chums, and "By the time Roosevelt returned to Harvard in September 1877 for his sophomore year, he was ruddy-cheeked, bronzed, hardened, and strangely handsome, and his asthma was in remission," writes Douglas Brinkley in his Roosevelt biography, *The Wilderness Warrior*.

The Adirondack adventures did more than just strengthen Roosevelt's body. They also changed the way people perceived him. He learned a valuable lesson in the woods: if you defy expectations, face the night winds, stalk through the underbrush, and make a bed of balsam branches in wild country, you will win the respect of city people.

A decade later he learned that the rugged landscape of the West had even more cultural cachet than the North Woods and would help him as he made his way through the treacherous world of American politics. After traveling out to the Dakotas in the 1880s, he not only lessened the misery of his asthma, but also helped fight back against the political enemies who derided him as effeminate and called him "Jane Dandy," "Punkin-Lily," and "Young Squirt."

"He left New York a 'shrill eunuch,' as he was called by the press, and came back fit and masculinized," writes Tom Lutz in his history of the period, *American Nervousness*.

Roosevelt never forgot how much the outdoors did to shore up his happiness, his constitution, and his stature. From an early age, he vowed to use political power to set aside wild places where other people might camp and build up their spirits. Perhaps as a way of acknowledging how the North Woods shaped him, in 1899 Roosevelt, while serving as governor of New York, had the state buy up nearly seventy thousand acres of land to add to the forest reserves in the Adirondacks and the Catskills. He would go on to become America's greatest "camping president," establishing one hundred fifty national forests, eighteen national monuments, and five new national parks, while standing up to cattlemen, lumber interests, and mining bullies.

Yet he would never have had the power or the means to do so if not for the events that transpired that blustery day on the slopes of Mount Marcy. When he first gained the summit, all of New York State lay beneath him, but he could hardly see any of it.

I shared in his frustration. On top of the bare mountain, I saw nothing but clouds. I saw only raindrop-speckled Stonehenge rocks beneath my feet with dark seams running through them, everything the same gray pallor except for the grainy blue mist that enshrouded the summit.

I was all alone up there except for a sheepish-looking young couple sitting on a boulder just below me, their arms wrapped up in each other's mummy bags. They looked like a Romantic and ecstatic pair, the sort who might wish to make love in a hurricane. "How long do you plan on staying?" the man grunted at me. "Not long," I told them. No matter. The wind was blowing in my face and I was losing sensation in my toes. Time to descend. Too bad I didn't stay long enough for the clouds to break apart as they did for Roosevelt, revealing a view that was almost more than he could bear. "Beautiful country, beautiful country!" he shouted again and again.

Roosevelt took his time. He had no idea that a messenger, at that moment, was racing up the slopes of Marcy with dire news. While he rested a few hundred feet below the summit, on the shore of Lake Tear of the Clouds, and enjoyed a light snack of tinned ox tongue, the messenger arrived. The man had sprinted a dozen miles over harsh terrain and wore such a pained expression that Roosevelt didn't need to read the telegram to know what it said. He read it anyway:

```
THE PRESIDENT IS CRITICALLY ILL
HIS CONDITION IS GRAVE
OXYGEN IS BEING GIVEN
ABSOLUTELY NO HOPE
```

While the puzzled and breathless messenger stood there waiting for a response, Roosevelt finished reading the telegram and then went right back to his lunch, looking calm, with no visible change to his expression or demeanor.

Then he made up for his hesitation by rushing down the slopes. (I hope he didn't bonk into as many trees as I did on the way down.) When he reached the Tahawus Club, an even direr message awaited him:

```
THE PRESIDENT APPEARS TO BE DYING AND MEMBERS
OF THE CABINET IN BUFFALO THINK YOU SHOULD LOSE
NO TIME COMING
```

Roosevelt fled the Adirondack region in a buckboard wagon that night. Though he had no way of knowing it, he became the next president of the United States at 2:15 that morning, September 14, 1901.

I didn't have as much of a reason to hurry; I was only scared about being caught in the dark and getting chilled by the endless rain. Somehow I mud-surfed and jog-walked myself back to the parking lot in Keene Valley at twilight. Exhausted but happy, I jumped in my car and drove back toward Montreal through the evening mist.

In the city of Plattsburgh, New York, twenty miles south of the Canadian border, I searched for a motel and reasonable food. I found one motel, but it looked run-down, so I backed up and out of the parking lot and onto a major road. Apparently I enjoyed the sensation of backing up so much that I just kept on doing that, unthinkingly, for a hundred yards or so, wondering why the city was passing by my windshield in the entirely wrong direction.

A police siren came whooping up behind me. I was horrified. As you will remember, I had borrowed this rental car somewhat illegally, with no up-to-date driver's license, in Montreal. I prayed to the ghosts of the Adirondacks: "Don't let this police officer impound my car!"

I pulled to the side of the road. The policeman lingered in his car for a long while, as if he were doing a Sudoku puzzle in there. At long last he walked over, ever so slowly, and shined his heavy flashlight in my face. I unrolled the window. He gave me a pained and puzzled look and asked if I had been drinking. I shook my head forcefully. "Sir," he said. "You were going backwards. On a major road. You could have been hit by a truck."

He looked more baffled than angry. I kept waiting for him to ask for my driver's license but, to my great surprise, he did not say a word about it. Perhaps the spirits of the Adirondacks had clouded his brain and stayed his tongue.

Instead, he let me off with a stern warning about sloppy driving, recommended a good motel, turned off his flashlight, and drove off into the drizzly night.

Hero of Camping: George Washington Sears

Camping in the Shade of Nessmuk

George Washington Sears, aka Nessmuk (December 2, 1821–May 1, 1890), was not a fine figure of a man. In the most famous photo of him, Sears has sunken eyes. His ill-fitting overcoat bunches around his body. He grasps the stock of a rifle so long that the muzzle extends beyond the camera's view. Sears has a pointy mustache, a crusty beard shaped like a cowcatcher, and a bemused expression. "Hurry up, take your stupid picture. Let me off of this damn stepstool right now," he seems to be saying. At various times, Sears, a cobbler by trade, suffered from ailments ranging from pleurisy to tuberculosis to maybe even syphilis, according to one biographer. "He was a little man, about five feet nothing . . . but one of those thin, wiry fellows without an ounce of fat who looks as old at forty as they do a score of years later," his contemporary Fred Mather recalled. "Divested of clothing, he was nearly as big as a pound of soap after a hard day's washing."

But Sears went on to be one of the greatest camping innovators and popularizers of the 1880s. He may have been weakly, living and dying in poverty, but he had camping talent in spades, with a cockiness to match. "To myself I sometimes appear as a wild Indian or an old Berserker, masquerading under the guise of a nineteenth-century American," he said, sounding at turns like Whitman and Melville. "When the strait jacket of civilization becomes too oppressive, I throw it off, betake myself to savagery, and there loaf and

George Washington Sears, circa 1880, was one of America's greatest campers, and a popular outdoors writer, but he never cashed in on his fame and died in poverty.

refresh my soul." He stripped his life to the elements like a burlier version of Thoreau. "I love a horse, a gun, a dog, a trout and a pretty girl," he said. "I hate a pothunter, a trout-liar and a whiskey-guzzling sportsman. I smoke and take an occasional glass of wine and never lie about my hunting and fishing exploits more than the occasion seems to demand."

A century before Ray Jardine and the ultra-ultra-light packers conquered the Pacific Crest Trail with their homemade backpacks, Sears went "featherweight" into the forest with little more than a tent, a shirt, a blanket bag, a rifle, a rod, a kettle, a dish, and a bit of coffee—all weighing a total of fifteen pounds. Sears went on three great camping and boating journeys in the Adirondacks, but it was his third and most audacious trip, in 1883, that made him a legend at age sixty-one.

The boat that transported him, the *Sairy Gamp*, is perfectly preserved and currently resides in the Adirondack Museum in Blue Mountain Lake, New York, where it is on permanent loan from the Smithsonian. Visit the boat, and you won't believe how shrimpy it is. The nine-foot-long canoe, the handiwork of innovative boat maker J. Henry Rushton of Canton, New York, weighs ten and a half pounds. It is so puny its wizened pilot could lift it with one hand.

Staring at its ribs and the symmetrical rows of copper fastener heads, try to imagine this boat's captain rowing with the spindly two-bladed oar he called his "pudding stick." Sears, in a sublimely nerdy literary inside joke, named the craft after Sarah "Sairey" Gamp, the alcoholic nurse in the Charles Dickens novel *Martin Chuzzlewit*, although he slightly changed the spelling of her first name. Frightened the boat would sink and drown him, he named it after a character that "took no water." Few people thought he would finish, or even survive, his planned 266-mile perilous boat journey through the Adirondacks. Some of his friends took out a five-thousand-dollar life insurance policy on him, assuming he'd die. Sears found their lack of faith disturbing. "It wouldn't take a strong rope to hang me, but a bear trap on one leg and a grindstone on the other wouldn't drown me in ten fathoms," he replied. Out in the woods and waters, he got caught in drenching rainstorms. On a thirteen-mile muddy "carry," he wore the *Sairy Gamp* on his head like a cap. On the way, he slathered himself with a mixture of "three oz. pure tar, two oz. castor oil, one oz. oil pennyroyal" simmered together, to fend off insects. Somehow he survived. "I once said in *Forest and Stream* that I was trying to find out how light a canoe it took to drown a man," he remarked after the journey. "I never shall know. The *Sairy Gamp* has only ducked me once in a six weeks' cruise, and that by my own carelessness."

Sears was revolutionary in the sense that he took survivalist notions and repackaged them for a mass audience of pleasure campers. "We do not go to the green waters to rough it," he once remarked. "We go to smooth it. We get it rough enough at home, in towns and cities . . ."

Yet this tough little man had a certain mournful aspect. Though he prided himself on his populism and independence, he never lost his envy for the rich "outers" and sports who could go out and camp in a high style he could never afford. He lazed in the forest, feasted on "crisp trout," and fancied himself the happiest man alive—until he came across rich men's camps so lovely and well appointed that it made his heart hurt; "I never feel the lack of wealth so sadly . . ." he remembered.

Sears had a half-wretched, half-blissful childhood. Born in South Oxford, Massachusetts, in 1821, one year after the elderly Daniel Boone died in his sleep, Sears was one of ten children. His family sent him off to work long hours at a lakeside mill when he was only eight years old. The only thing that stopped him from going insane was the forest outside the factory. When the mill got shuttered, Sears slipped into the backwoods and hung out with a Narragansett who taught him how to survive. That encounter doomed him to a life of adventure, and it gave him his pen name, Nessmuk, which he borrowed from his Native American friend.

That childhood pal helped him amass the skill set that Sears shared with the world in his 1884 classic *Woodcraft and Camping*, a trove of technical information conveyed in prose so personable it sounds as if Sears were whispering it in your ear while sitting beside one of his "rough bark lean-tos" warming himself by a fire. He advised his readers to "go light; the lighter the better, so that you have the simplest material for health, comfort and enjoyment."

4

Acts of Transmission

Seriously, is it good for men and women and children to swarm together in cities and stay there, keep staying there, till their instincts are so far perverted that they lose all taste for their natural element, the wide world out-of-doors?

—Horace Kephart, 1906

I was out in Butano State Park on a forested ridge above the coastal town of Pescadero, California, muttering curse words, making faces, and failing to light a basic cook fire. My four-year-old daughter, Julianna, was shivering. The only decent fires I've lit in my life have been accidental, including the blaze I made in my backyard when I was nine years old and meting out vengeance on red ants with a tripod-mounted magnifying glass. All these years later, in the darkening forest, I could not understand why my family had appointed me fire maker. It must have had something to do with gendered campground task expectations.

Quail nattered in the bushes. A dripping fog settled on the dogwoods and second-growth redwoods. I lit another match. Smoke rose, along with an acrid odor, but there was no warmth there, no light, no fire. The wind picked up. My wife, Amy, looked nervous as she sipped from a twenty-four-ounce can of Modelo Especial. "Too cold here," she said. "We should leave. Do we really want to subject our daughter to danger and inconvenience on her first camping trip?" She took a swig. "Then again, we don't really want her to think we're quitters. Then again, I don't want her to hate camping because she stayed here and was miserable."

There was no denying it: I was the reason this campout was so cold. I started panicking. Now I puffed my cheeks like a bellows and rearranged the sticks and logs in all sorts of fancy formations, but the flames would not catch. A raw chicken habanero mango sausage stared me down. My daughter began to whimper from hunger. "Is there going to be a fire, Daddy?" she said, tugging my hand.

"Soon," I said, lying.

My shame stuck in my throat like a piece of Slim Jim. I was not much older than Julianna when my father first took our family camping in the eastern Sierra Nevada. I remember him breaking branches over his legs, cutting wood with a pocket saw, and arranging the logs in an A-frame. He flicked a lighter, the whole thing went up in an instant, and I thought to myself, *There stands a man!*

My parents were getting old, and I knew they would not be around forever. I wanted to pass down the love of camping they'd taught me all those years ago. At this point, that was never going to happen. I was losing all credibility with my daughter. A week before our Butano campout, Amy, Julianna, and I spent a chilly night in a yurt in another forest. It was supposed to be a baby step. That evening, our neighbors one yurt over from us raised a roaring bonfire and roasted seven chickens on a spit at the same time. I had to sit there, embarrassed, listening to the grease from the chicken skin drip and crackle while my daughter's teeth chattered and my campfire coughed black ash.

At the time of our campout in Butano, my daughter was going through a shy phase. Social interactions exhausted her sometimes. Sounding like a modern-day William "Adirondack" Murray, I'd told her that camping would relax her. "If you are feeling sad, if you're all knotted up, all you've got to do is find a pretty forest and set up your tent," I said. "That's the cure. That's how you get your tension out."

"Or I could just kick somebody," Julianna replied.

Before this campout, I swore to her I'd make a "fantastic fire" at Butano. Now she was hopping up and down to keep warm. I poked and prodded the dead fire. "Come on, come on, do something!" I said to the kindling. Unless something or someone intervened, Julianna would never camp again. She'd grow up to work for Big Coal.

Staring into that pile of sticks, I rued the fact that it was possible for me, with my modern gear and pocket stoves, to have hiked the Pacific Crest Trail and not know how to light a fire. I love modern gear; I collect it. Yet it has built a bubble around me in the forest. The wilderness is my kingdom of heaven, but sometimes I wonder if I've entered it under false pretenses. All my high-tech gadgetry serves the same role that wilderness guides such as Orson "Mountain" Phelps served in the Adirondacks: it has built a buffer between me and the wild. Still, there are times when the barrier falls down and exposes me in all my ignorance.

Amy tried to fix the fire, but it was too far gone. "I need a break," I told Julianna. "Give me a second. I'll return at some point."

Abandoning the fire pit, I walked to our dinged-up Toyota Corolla, which was parked beneath a crooked tree overlooking a vernal pool full of newts, twigs, and drowned redwoods. I popped the trunk in search of more fire starter, but the only camping-related item I could find was an old, olive-drab book called *Camping and Woodcraft*, written by a fellow named Horace Sowers Kephart. This library copy dated to 1921. Though it seemed ancient, with its translucent pages, delicate as onionskin, this was a revised and expanded version of the original text published in 1906 as *The Book of Camping and Woodcraft*. I'd brought along the book for distraction and entertainment after reading about it in *American Frontiersman* magazine one afternoon at Rite Aid. I thought I should have it handy on my first, real family campout, but only so I could snigger at its masculine posturing and anachronistic advice.

I'd spent a few lazy evenings at home chuckling over Kephart's hyperspecific ideas about barbecuing "tender squirrels" on spits cut from stout pieces of wood and about the tastiest methods for cooking raccoon. "Remove the 'kernels' [scent glands] under each front leg and on either side of spine in small of back," Kephart advised. "Stuff with dressing like a turkey ... Roast to a delicate brown." I'd smiled at Kephart's exhaustive inventory of forgotten camping implements with names such as gibcroke, wambec, wangan stick, and kekauviscou saster (a sort of pothook).

Now, in the Butano State Park campground, with my stomach gurgling and my wife looking at me with that "you married up" expression on her face, I wondered if this goofy Kephart might have some wild ideas about building a cook fire. I thumbed through the book's index and, sure enough, found a reference to fire building. When I turned to the campfire section of the book, Horace Kephart switched places with me. Now he was the one laughing. *Get that smile off your face and let's take a look at your pathetic excuse for a campfire*, he seemed to be saying.

"If we rake together a pile of leaves, cover it higgledy-piggledy with dead twigs and branches picked up at random, and set a match to it, the odds are that it will result in nothing but a quick blaze that soon dies down to a smudge," he wrote. "One glance at a camper's fire tells you what kind of woodsman he is."

Well, thanks a lot, Horace Kephart. He struck me as peevish and mean. I wanted to throw the book across the forest, or drop it in the vernal pool and let it float among the newts. But I kept on reading. Kephart said my fire was an abomination. Then he told me how to save it. A simple fix would not do. This fire required a radical revision. *Start over*, he seemed to say. *Take everything out of that fire pit, including the fire starter. That's cheating. Get it out of there.*

Doing as Kephart advised, I began again. His surefire recipe did not exactly make for scintillating reading, but something told me to follow it to the letter or it wouldn't work.

> First get in plenty of wood and kindling . . . If you can find two large flat rocks, or several small ones of even height, use them as andirons. [I had no idea what an andiron was, but followed the procedure as closely as possible.] Otherwise lay down two short cuts off a five- or six-inch log, facing you and about three feet apart. On these rocks or billets, [what the hell are billets?] lay two four-foot logs parallel, and several inches apart, as rests for your utensils. Arrange the kindling between and under them, with small sticks laid across the top of the logs, a couple of long ones lengthwise, then more short ones across, another pair lengthwise, and thicker short ones across. Then light it.

I did as I was told. Amy and Julianna stood by my side and watched. I dropped a lit match into the kindling and waited. And waited some more. And nothing happened. Of course it didn't. What a joke. Thanks for embarrassing me in front of my family, Horace Kephart. I looked over to my wife and child and put my hands in the air. "Maybe Pescadero has a pizzeria," Amy said in a lemony tone.

Then a stroke of crimson appeared in the fire ring.

I heard a rushing sound, followed by a loud *ka-BOOM*! The logs and kindling burst into flames. When I shouted in surprise, the fire flattened itself like a scolded dog. But the fire wasn't flinching. It was only resting for a couple of seconds, gathering strength.

Then it pulled in a series of deep breaths; it doubled, tripled, quadrupled, until the flames threatened to jump from the circle. I could smell the essential oils in the pinewood, the trapped gases leaking out. In an instant, I went from worrying about no dinner at all to praying I wouldn't burn down the redwoods.

I placed the sausages on the metal grille and lowered it onto the heat. The metal turned the color of a maraschino cherry. The sausages popped. Fat silked out of their casings and dripped on the coals, making the flames go *snicker-snack*. Amy looked thunderstruck. Two moonfaced children from a neighboring campsite walked out of the shadows to stare. Thanks to Mr. Kephart, I was everybody's hero. We filled our bellies with hot food, and then we ate the most glorious s'mores I've ever had, the middles so soft my daughter thought we were serving her warmed-up gobs of sugared cream cheese.

After our meal, the fire seemed to go out, but hours later, after we'd all gone to sleep, a coastal breeze stirred the embers and brought the flames to life again.

The brightness made me cover my eyes as I lay on the Therm-A-Rest thinking the sun had risen. It took me a while to realize that the light was coming from the fire, making a sound like shirts on a clothesline in a strong wind. I had no witnesses, but I felt as if Kephart himself were sitting beside me by the hearth, warming his hobnail boots, sipping frontier whiskey from his favorite tin cup—though he would have had to come a long way to share my fire. He died in a car wreck on a mountain road outside Bryson City, North Carolina, on April 2, 1931.

The classic portrait shot of Horace Kephart shows him taking his leisure beneath a shady tree in the Smoky Mountains. A felt hat covers his thinning hair. He's knotted a handkerchief around his long and tendinous neck.

Kephart looks weary and self-satisfied. Perhaps he's mugging for the good friend who took the picture, the Japanese American photographer

Horace Kephart (1862–1931), dean of American camping

George Masa. In the picture, Kephart is in his element, camping out, enjoying the pastime that gave him a reprieve from the "Blue Devils" that assailed him all his life.

As I would learn later on, the simplistic picture I had in my head of Kephart—stout backwoodsman, big-bearded, barrel-chested—was inaccurate. Friends and family members well understood that Kephart was a sensitive and charming wreck, alternately full of rapture and misery and often drunk.

Brought up in rural Iowa, Kephart loved books and the wild, and never understood why he had to choose between them. He wanted to bridge two

different roles: the urbanite and the barbarian, the geek and the survivalist, the fussbudget and the berserker. City life hated him, and he hated it
back. Its phoniness disgusted him. Still, he wished he could pick out the
things he loved about civilization, including the fine arts, and haul them
into the forest with him. "Imagine Boston or Florence set in the midst of
the Yellowstone Park," he said in his twenties. "When a fellow wanted to, he
could go the Public Library or the Opera . . . he could walk right out into
the primeval truth of things and cuss the universe of shams—be Samuel
Johnson and Daniel Boone by turns!"

Kephart was cautious and soft-spoken, sometimes awkward and retiring, nothing at all like the flamboyant woodcrafters on television now. "I
know no games, tell no stories . . . can't joke, guess riddles, dance, flirt, or
even sit gracefully," the young Kephart said. "I can't talk nonsense with
strangers, and I won't . . . it is the hardest thing in the world for me to
entertain a stranger when feeling that I'm on my good behavior."

For years he tried to moderate his wild impulses, balancing the need to
be a "gentleman and a scholar," against the transporting fun of nailing "an
eight-inch bull's eye at 200 yards, off-hand." When he couldn't get out to
the forest, the bottle was his favorite escape. Alcohol comforted him and
turned him into a raconteur, but it also contributed to his unhappiness
and, eventually, his joblessness.

Before his big spinout, Kephart had a fine career in libraries, which gave
him his first enjoyable outlet for the tinkering skills, exacting classification
systems, and cataloging talents he would later impose on the camping
world. Though he loved his bookish pursuits, he wondered what good they
would serve in a crisis. The world of words lacked the solidity, the thrills,
and the immediacy of a forest. The woods kept calling to him, even as he
rose to the highest rank in his field, becoming an assistant librarian at Yale,
then taking the top job at the prestigious St. Louis Mercantile Library
in 1890.

Peers respected him, and he published influential articles and essays
with such titles as "Paste for Labels, with a Word About Writing Inks."
But his family and responsibilities tugged him one way, and the woods
tugged him the other. By the late 1890s, children and camping gear threatened to crowd him out of his own house. At some point he encountered
Woodcraft, by George Washington Sears, better known as Nessmuk. Apparently that slender volume, first published in 1884, had the same effect on

Kephart that *Walden* had on me: it unhinged him. Its combination of survival skills and entertainment increased his love for the forest. Soon Kephart's shelves groaned with all his pelts and axes, every one of them arranged just so. Rifles hogged his wall space.

Two uniquely American impulses kept jostling at Kephart, making it impossible for him to live a tidy and respectable life anymore. The first was neurasthenia, which made him duck out on his wife and six children at turns and go on benders. The second was woodcraft, which Kephart defined as "The art of getting along well in the wilderness by utilizing nature's storehouse."

Unlike today's backpackers, who are "just passing through" and often lack the gear, the skills, or the wherewithal to occupy a forest indefinitely, woodcraft masters tried to make the woods into their smoking parlors, their kitchens, their bedrooms. Unlike William "Adirondack" Murray and all his talk of wilderness guides, this new breed of adventurers wouldn't dream of paying someone else to do all the hard work for them. Why outsource their good times?

They wanted no filter between them and the wild. Instead, they wanted to gain the technique they needed to stay out there for as long as they wished. Books could help them, but there was no substitute for great mentors and experience. Urban living had destroyed the old artisan traditions, but they could rediscover them by learning woodcraft at the hand of an old master. Though they bore the strong influence of the dirt-poor Nessmuk, many of these "campaigners" were well off, and had the leisure time they needed to learn difficult skills. Woodcraft campers obsessed about the best ways to build a snare. They perfected the "keen-eyed silent stalking" after a deer and "the thrill of the chase." They read the contours of the foothills like scholars poring over lines of text. The best of these campers augured weather with a glance at the sky, tanned a buck's hide to a silky smoothness using the enzymes of its liquefied brains, and made slap-up meals in the deepest woods with nothing but a hatchet, a flint stone, a loop of steel, and a cast-iron skillet. These skills turned the forest into a giant play scape. On the surface the woodcrafters were trying to be more manly, but part of the thrill was a chance to live out never-ending boyhoods.

The backwoods life was the only one that Kephart could tolerate, but it took him a long while to figure out how to make a living from it. Until then, he was trapped in the city and continued to deteriorate. The woods distracted him so much, and led to such chronic absenteeism, that the Mercantile Library forced his resignation in the fall of 1903.

Soon afterward, Kephart entered his tailspin at age forty-one. The worst of it happened in the middle of March 1904. On a trip with a few friends in the wilds of Missouri, about fifty miles from downtown St. Louis, Kephart lost his mind.

He and his pals had done some "good shooting" and were about to head home. But bad weather came in and rocked their steamboat. The waters of Establishment Creek bulged against their banks. Kephart was already on edge, and the wind and rain made him frantic. At 1:30 a.m., he jumped out of bed, screaming about dynamite-laden Sicilian terrorists on the roof wanting to blow them all out of the water.

His friends thought he was joking, right up to the moment Kephart pulled out a shotgun and started blasting away at the top of the steamboat, thinking he was picking off phantom southern Italians. His friends got him back to St. Louis, but his delusions continued. Showing a disregard for privacy that rivals our twenty-first-century paparazzi, St. Louis newspapers ran detailed descriptions of Kephart's spinout. "Kephart Lost Mind on Hunting Trip," one headline read.

Kephart was not press savvy. He let a reporter interview him in his sickbed, and he accused his camping and fishing friends of becoming "fiends" who'd used him as a puppet, controlling his emotions and body with a magic battery that made raindrops talk and turned trees and birds against him. One newspaper transcribed and printed the contents of a suicide note Kephart handed a bartender, addressed to the Mercantile Library that had fired him.

His breakdown drove him to make an extreme decision. Kephart, the same man who intervened to save my awful cook fire and, in the process, gave me one of the most memorable family campouts, turned his back on his own family.

After a layover with his parents in Dayton, Ohio, he headed to the Smokies, home to his ancestors, seeking the "Back of Beyond." For a while he camped on Dicks Creek, about forty miles west of Asheville, North Carolina, then occupied an empty cabin on Hazel Creek, the largest creek on the North Carolina side of what is now the Great Smoky Mountains National Park. This cabin became a primary staging ground for the book I'd brought to Butano State Park. Kephart never claimed the woods were an easy fix. He admitted that "when supper would be over and black night closed in on my hermitage, and the owls began calling all the blue devils of the woods, one needed some indoor occupation to keep . . . in good cheer."

Fortunately, he had plenty of "occupation" to distract him. Taking a cue from his idol, Nessmuk, Kephart researched and wrote *Camping and Woodcraft*. The book, now in its seventieth printing, drew from the woodcraft and folklore of the Southern Appalachian highlands, combined it with tidbits passed down from frontiersmen, early-nineteenth-century mountain men, and of course the Native American scouts who influenced them, and placed it in the hands of the pleasure camper.

A spirit of newfound freedom comes across in every page, along with a cranky libertarianism. Kephart, who dedicated the book to "the shade of Nessmuk in the happy hunting ground," made it clear that his book was *not* for the sort of pasty, risk-averse wimps who hired camping guides. "Personally, I would rather get lost now and then than be forever hanging on a guide's coat tail," Kephart writes.

The book addresses a hunger for direct experience, with a strong emphasis on going at your own pace and doing it all yourself. Many "sports" of the nineteenth century handed most of the hard work and camp chores over to their guides. Kephart, though, understood the difference between soulful work and meaningless labor. Tasks that were stultifying in the cities seemed clean and new in the woods. Even dishwashing could be joyful. Rather than scouring a greasy frying pan, Kephart advised campers to "pour it nearly full of water, place it level over the coals, and let it boil over. Then pick it up, give a quick flirt to empty it, and hang it up." Has any other outdoor writer in history used the word *flirt* in a dishwashing description?

In Kephart's hands, even a crisis in the woods might turn into a good laugh. Unlike "Adirondack" Murray, who concealed the most unpleasant elements of the camp, Kephart celebrated even the scary moments. "For there is a seamy side to camp life, as to everything else," he writes. "Even in the best of camps, things do happen sometimes that are enough to make a saint swear silently through his teeth. But no one is fit for such life who cannot turn ordinary ill-luck into a joke, and bear downright calamity like a gentleman."

More than just a crack shot, Kephart could write like crazy, so his book and his "outing" columns in prestigious magazines found a wide audience. He became the undisputed "Dean of Camping," the most accomplished, articulate woodsman during a period that history-minded camping fanatics now regard as the Golden Age of Camping, which began in the 1880s and continued into the 1930s. This was a time before synthetics and dehydrated food pellets, when camping smelled good and tasted great. No deteriorating nylon, no neoprene soles, just leather, wool, wood, and cotton.

These campers prided themselves on their survival skills, but that was not the point. Many campcraft books from that era had a requisite "How to Stay Alive in Adverse Situations" section that always seemed like a half-hearted attempt to impose gravitas on a book that was supposed to be a lark. Come on! How many times did your average late-nineteenth-century or early-twentieth-century recreational camper have to build a deadfall trap to avoid starvation? The same principle holds true even now, with survival or "tactical" camping books wrestling with doomsday scenarios. I don't mean to suggest that these skills are not important. We should all be so lucky to survive a plane crash in the Yukon with a skilled wildcrafter by our side. But the relentless emphasis on survival belies the fact that the skills in these books are, for the most part, meant to facilitate good times and a sense of freedom in the forest, peak oil and dirty bombs be damned.

What we now regard as "classic camping" came of age at a time when daily life was becoming impersonal, when a farmer's yield was becoming "an abstract commodity" instead of a point of pride. Kephart's contemporary Ernest Thompson Seton, the woodcraft genius and Boy Scouts of America inspiration, called civilization a "gratuitous failure." This was a time of "rationalized, technological organization," which led to "a disorienting sense of caprice and lost rootedness," wrote historian Philip Joseph Deloria in his book *Playing Indian*. "The soldier who once could see his enemy aiming at him now died blissfully ignorant, blown apart by a gun fired from miles away. In the mine and the mill, machines maimed and claimed lives randomly." Against this backdrop, old-time campers celebrated their own intimate version of "the authentic."

In such impersonal times, Kephart, though strict and unstinting in so many ways, left plenty of room for quirky individuality in his campout writings. Though he knew how to go "feather-weight" if he must, and ridiculed "tyros" for bringing along silly and unnecessary gear, he also understood that some people brought useless items to the camp as a kind of fetish or security blanket. Campers comforted themselves by taking along "a chunk of rosin," a shaving mug, or "a derringer that no one could hit anything with."

Kephart himself refused to camp without his own comfort object: a porcelain teacup with a broken-off handle. "Many's the time it has almost slipped from my fingers and dropped upon a rock; many's the gibe I have suffered for its dear sake. But I do love it. Hot indeed must be the sun, tangled the trail and weary the miles before I forsake thee, O my frail, cool-lipped, but ardent tea cup!"

In making such allowances, Kephart put a premium on human comfort, psychological and physical. His camps were supposed to feel inviting. Imagine the scene: ditty bags, handkerchiefs, scarves, chairs, camp boxes and wooden trunks, carbide gas lamps, jackknives, billy cans, piles of rifles, a deer carcass strung up in a tree branch, the scent of bannock bread wafting from a Dutch oven sitting on a bed of coals with more coals piled on top of it, steam rising from a stockpot full of "skillagalee," a fish, fowl, vegetable, and rice stew that any passing "hungry varlet" could enjoy.

The skinny and rangy Kephart loved to cook his meals over an open fire: pork fritters in bubbling fat, fried bacon sliced thin, basted canvasback duck with butter and bacon, cream gravies, cranberry sauces, canned salmon on toast, buckwheat cakes, strong coffee, and apple dumplings and doughnuts cooked hot to order.

Kephart was judicious about what he killed. He never bagged more than he needed, and much of his writing has a protoconservationist bent. He was a scold about sloppy fires that might run loose and turn into wildcat blazes. Like Nessmuk before him, he took aim at game hogs. Yet even the most skilled and sensitive woodcrafters abided by rules that were far less stringent than today's "Leave No Trace" (LNT) standards, while the worst of them were LGBT (Leave a Great Big Trace). Read Kephart's book and you'll hear trees crash to the ground. You'll watch a few deer get turned inside out, and see a turtle get bopped on the head and ushered into the stew pot. Treading lightly in the forest was considered judicious and gentlemanly, but it was never the point. In the days before the environmental movement, even the most forward-thinking of those adventure campers thought of forests as places for a man (and they were mostly men) to spread out. Even the tents sprawled in all directions, using a complicated arrangement of stakes, hitches, and guylines. Some were made out of cotton "duck" or the highly coveted material called "balloon silk," with such a tight weave that it kept out most of the rain, perhaps with additional help from paraffin wax or a solution of arsenic that dyed the fabric light green. Open-faced "Baker tents" received the campfire heat. This was an unrushed form of camping. It took forever to set up camp—and forever to dismantle it, but so what? Campers filled the time telling stories. "There are no friendships like those that are made under canvas," Kephart observed.

To this robust classic camping scene, Kephart added authoritativeness, a meticulousness, and a gleefully dweeby preoccupation with (if not all-out fetishization of) specialized camping gear. He and his fans were not exactly primitivists; nor were they anticonsumerist fanatics. If anything, they embraced the technology of the era: the telescoping cots, the fancy camp stoves, the nesting mess kits, and, later, the automobile.

Even now, Kephart's work and many of his ideas are remarkably free of Victorian dust, with the exception of two brief but unfortunate passages. In one instance, in relation to a ginger tea recipe, he mentions a "plantation darky," and he makes some crass observations about "Chinamen," whom he describes as a robotic race of people. In moments like this, I just want to bop him upside the head with his own book. "In regard to race, Horace Kephart was, unfortunately, like many if not most of us, a creature of his times," the Kephart historian George Ellison told me.

Too bad I can't mentally excise these unfortunate words from a book that remains indispensable in the campground, and not just for me. There's a strong Kephart cult out there right now, and it's especially strong in the Southlands. Two celebrated Golden Age–style campers and respected primitive skills experts, David Wescott and Steve Watts, draw attention to Kephart's work and use it as a mainstay in their painstakingly re-created Golden Age campsites. "I came up in the fifties, using a bunch of old gear," Watts told me when we talked on the phone. "Of course I went through the whole backpacking revolution in the seventies, and that was fun. Colin Fletcher was God, as far as I was concerned. But I remember being up on the Appalachian Trail one night in a little tent, warm as I could be, with a great down sleeping bag in wintertime, looking at twelve hours of darkness. And there I am, stuck in this little Starlite tent, and it just wasn't fun."

In comparison, when Watts spends the night in a Golden Age–style "Whelen" tent—a classic canvas shelter designed by Colonel Townsend Whelen in the 1920s—"I can stand up and put my pants on like a human being instead of just waddling around. It's a really pleasant way to camp. Isn't that what it's supposed to be?"

Those who associate camping in the old style with used army tents that "leak like a sieve" are missing out, Wescott told me. "When we set up a traditional canvas tent it is warm and cozy and rainproof." He also mentioned the durability of the old-time gear. "The average tent built today is supposed to last for twenty-one nights of camping, and after that they fall apart," he grumbled.

Watts and Wescott have a special affection for Kephart. They make appearances at a Kephart Days celebration that takes place in various locations in North Carolina. Re-creators can bring back the old-time camping in exquisite detail because camping writers, including Kephart, left behind such exhaustive instructions.

Camping and Woodcraft was enough for one lifetime, but Kephart, while on permanent hiatus in North Carolina, also amassed enough material to write another classic, *Our Southern Highlanders* (1913), a loving, stylized account of modern-time pioneers in the Smokies. He also pushed for the formation of the Great Smoky Mountains National Park and was an early inspiration for the Appalachian Trail, which runs from Georgia to Maine.

Kephart remained active in woodcraft all his life; surely he would have made even more of an impact on the camping world if he had not decided to go out on a hooch run with one of his writing pals, Fiswoode Tarleton, on the night of April 2, 1931. On the return trip, the cab they were riding in flipped over. The driver escaped serious injury, but Kephart was crushed to death. He was sixty-eight years old. Tarleton also died at the scene.

Kephart, unlike "Adirondack" Murray, did not wind up in the InSink-Erator of camping memory. The American Scouting movement came along and championed his work for years, introducing new generations to the ideas of the "Dean of Camping" and his hero Nessmuk.

5

Clash of the Neckerchiefs

Walk seven miles in two hours. Single-paddle a canoe one mile in twenty minutes. Know how to splice a rope and lash a rope end. Make a rubbing-stick fire with tools by himself. Set up a tepee . . . Know twenty-five native wild birds. Know ten native wild quadrupeds. Know thirty forest trees or shrubs. Know and show use of five medicinal herbs. Be sunburnt from head to feet.

—Ernest Thompson Seton, rules for "Tried Warriors,"
in his *Manual of the Woodcraft Indians*, 1915

I distrust people who tell me they have no regrets. I have a thousand. One is my decision to quit the Boy Scouts of America (BSA) after two hours and fifteen minutes in the organization. I wish someone had put a steadying hand on my shoulder and told me to push through my initial discomfort with the troop meeting. When you're twelve years old, so many adults already seem like cryptofascists, even when they're not wearing neckerchiefs, twill breeches, epaulets, badges, and web belts.

I only realized my mistake in quitting the BSA thirteen years after the fact, while hiking in the San Gabriel Mountains of California. The Pacific Crest Trail climbs most of Mount Baden-Powell, named after the Boy Scouts founder and British general Robert Stephenson Smyth Baden-Powell. I fell in line with a Scouting party heading for the summit. Their packs were spotless and packed just so. I was stooping over, splotchy, buzzing with flies, and singing Motörhead songs. They were clean, smiling, and laughing wildly, and if I'm remembering this correctly a few of them were even yodeling. "I love to go a-wandering / Along the mountain track! . . . Val-deri! Val-dera! / With a knapsack on my back."

Those kids were on a pilgrimage to the mountaintop, where they would find an obelisk bearing an inscription in Baden-Powell's honor. Perhaps they, like me, simply assumed he was the organization's sole father figure and grand master.

I was wrong to have such a simpleminded notion of the group's origins. As I've now come to realize from delving more deeply into my camping project, American camping history is contradictory, complicated, and full of intrigue, like any good campfire tale. So our Scouting story must not begin with a British general. It must start with a long, lanky man with a big, furry Friedrich Nietzsche mustache. His name was Ernest Thompson Seton—misunderstood, gleeful, and tortured at turns, with great big ideas and bigger hair, a bottomless love for the forest, and a lifelong disdain for personal grooming. He was, in other words, your typical male Victorian camper, only more so. "Seton's corporeal presence was preceded through his life by his smell," one of his biographers, John H. Wadland, reports. "He seldom shaved or bathed. His wild and shaggy locks, like untended sails, luffed madly in the breeze."

Seton was born in England, like his Scouting cohort and future genteel antagonist General Robert Baden-Powell, but the sudden failure of his

Ernest Thompson Seton, aka Black Wolf (1860–1946)

father's shipping business, precipitated in part by a pirate raid, forced his family's abrupt move to Canada in 1866. Nature reached out to Seton, but city living, and the unwanted attention of schoolyard ruffians, roiled him. As a child, he fought furiously on the playground, and when someone or something made him angry, his eyes crossed. That hot temper became a liability when he entered adulthood. But he was also one of the camping world's most affectionate and persuasive teachers, and a great student of wildlife and woodcraft. Birds entranced Seton so much that he once counted every feather on a grackle's wing. Though he was full of uncontrollable passions, something about the wild made him slow down a little and take his time. That patience, and his powers of observation, ultimately helped him find his way as a wildlife illustrator and a successful writer of children's books, portraying animals in tragic and empathetic ways. The sight of an animal in distress made his heart hurt; as a youth he looked from the window of a train and saw a pack of domesticated dogs tear into a Canadian wolf. In the eyes of that defiant creature, he saw himself: alone, a victim, at odds with so-called civilized forces. Later in life, while in New Mexico, he stalked and snared a gigantic wolf called Lobo, an experience so heartrending it turned him into a conservationist. Seton dubbed himself "Black Wolf." After killing Lobo, he began to draw a realistic paw print beside his name every time he inscribed a book or signed his correspondence.

Bullies of all kinds made him sick, but of all the brutes in the world, he hated three the most. The first was George Armstrong Custer, for his crimes against Native Americans. The second was St. Paul the Apostle, who urged women to submit to their husbands without complaint, creating a reliable template of misery for Seton's hagridden and mousy mother, who bore eleven children. But the man Seton hated most was his father, Joseph Logan Thompson, whom he considered "a worthless loafer, a petty swindler, a wife-beater, and a child-murderer" on his best days. He also declared his dad "the most selfish person I ever heard of in history or in fiction."

As someone who buys camping gear compulsively on Father's Day, and whose own father triggered his deep love of camping and his desire to transmit this value to his daughter, I can't help but notice that quite a few Victorian-age impresarios of camping had agonizing fatherhood issues. Some had tormented relationships with their dads, or had a strained relationship with fatherhood itself, or else they lost their fathers early on. John

Muir's dad beat him and almost worked him to death on the family farm in Wisconsin. The elder Muir's joyless Christianity gave Muir Jr. something to camp against during his rapture-filled explorations of Yosemite. George Washington Sears and Horace Kephart both ditched their families.

There are, of course, important exceptions. For instance, Henry David Thoreau got along fine with his father, John Thoreau, a noted pencil maker; and Theodore Roosevelt always said his father was the finest man he'd ever met. If anything, his father's advice when TR was a puny youngster contributed to his love of the outdoors. "Theodore," his father told him in 1870, "you have the mind but you have not the body, and without the help of the body[,] the mind cannot go as far as it should. I am giving you the tools, but it is up to you to make your body. It is hard drudgery to make one's body[,] but I know you will do it." To this, Theodore replied, "I'll make my body!"—a decision that led to many of his life-changing and constitution-building campouts.

Still, I've seen enough examples, including some more recent instances, to wonder if there is a relationship between the desire to camp out and tortured fatherhood. The much-married, philandering Edward Abbey skipped out on his kids, although he settled down and became a family man later in life. Cheryl Strayed, author of the most popular camping-centric memoir of the twenty-first century, wrote about her abusive and neglectful father. It is worth mentioning that my own first great hero of camping, my father, lost his own dad when he was three months old. Truly, there is a fatherhood deprivation epidemic in the camping world.

Seton's fatherhood-related issues were so extreme that he stands apart, and not just because he claimed his dad liked to whip his kids with a slipper and a riding crop for measly infractions. On Seton's twenty-first birthday, his father presented him with an itemized bill for services rendered. By Seton's account, his skinflint papa had been keeping track of every cent he'd spent on Seton's behalf, every grudging grocery and school supply bill, even the cost of Seton's delivery at the maternity ward. Now he wanted to be paid back the grand sum of $537.50. (There is something especially spiteful and cruel about those fifty cents.) Unless Seton paid the cash right away, his dad would charge him 6 percent interest per annum. Seton was anguished, "utterly staggered," he said. "Oh, the blackness of that moment!"

Whether or not the story is true, there is no doubt that Seton believed his dad to be monstrous, and that this helped form his personality, and influenced his involvement with youth camping. It also drove him toward financial independence. Seton wrote and illustrated a series of children's books full of animal stories that made him rich, in particular a volume called *Wild Animals I Have Known*, published in 1898. This "real-life" nature collection sent his young readers into raptures, but annoyed the esteemed naturalist John Burroughs, who grouped Seton along with other popular "nature fakers," whose anthropomorphized nature stories strained credulity. Seton wanted his readers to see animals as sentient beings deserving of their compassion, but sometimes he went too far. In one passage, his ingenious foxes trick dogs into running in front of trains and getting squashed. In his devastating piece in the March 1903 issue of the *Atlantic Monthly*, Burroughs joked that Seton should have named his book *Wild Animals I Alone Have Known*. Seton was far from the worst offender. Another writer, Charles G. D. Roberts, told some much juicier whoppers, including his story about an eagle that dies in midair, then floats, like a glider, back to earth. So Seton got caught up in the controversy. Even President Theodore Roosevelt ridiculed the "yellow journalists of the woods." Seton claimed he was vindicated during a dinner with Burroughs, when he confronted the naturalist, who (in Seton's telling) broke down in tears with guilt over what he'd written.

Though he faced a certain amount of public humiliation for *Wild Animals I Have Known*, the book changed his lifestyle. By 1901 he had enough money to branch out from his freelance writing career. He'd bought a two-hundred-acre property in Cos Cob, Connecticut, near tony Greenwich, and settled with his wife, Grace Gallatin Seton-Thompson. There he built a mansion called Wyndygoul, which means "Windy Gulch" in Scottish. Using artificial means, he made the property appear more "wild" than it had any reason to be, importing deer and squirrels and even damming a stream to turn a swamp into an instant lake. The native species weren't always nice to these introduced creatures. Huge snapping turtles rose from the depths to devour Seton's waterfowl. But the worst invasion came from neighboring humans. When Seton had workmen build a fence around the property, he hoped to keep roaming dogs at bay. In the process, he antagonized a group of pitiless and foulmouthed teen hooligans, who considered Seton's property their turf.

One day, Seton was making his rounds when he saw that the teens had left offensive pictures and inscriptions on his fence. The images were so appalling that "not even a Sunday paper" would have printed them, Seton cheekily remarked. Another time, he caught them vandalizing his property. A different man might have cursed out those boys, or even fired a warning shot over their heads, but Seton's hot temper did not extend to the youth of America. He decided to take a polite and careful approach.

"Now, boys," he called out. "I don't know who had painted this gate, and I do not wish to know. But if *you* know, I wish you would ask him to stop." The kids burst into laughter, screamed, hollered, then came back to write even worse messages on the fence.

Instead of thrashing those kids, Seton had another solution in mind. Like many other adults at the time, he worried that "the American boy [was] rapidly becoming flat chested, and his chief amusement [was] smoking cigarettes and shooting craps." How far he had fallen from the time of the frontier boy a century before, living on small farms, knowing nature, and being "respectful and obedient to his elders." Seton, responding to the same impulses that had inspired Horace Kephart's retreat to the woods, believed nature had curative powers. He didn't think modern youth was inherently rotten; modernity rotted them out. "[Boys] have badness thrusted upon them," he observed, adding that "not one boy in a thousand" is born bad.

Seton decided to visit the nearest school, assuming the young rapscallions were enrolled there. Instead of demanding that their teachers punish the children, he made them into his experimental camping hamsters. He would use tents, the forest around Wyndygoul, "war dances," call-and-response chants, and a blazing fire in a hearts-and-minds campaign.

In April 1902, with the school's permission, he invited local schoolboys over twelve years old to swim in his snapping turtle–infested lake, gobble his food, and camp "Indian-style" with him on the same land they'd once trashed. He extended the invitation to twenty kids, but more than twice that number showed up. For the next two days, they danced around the fire, chanted, banged drums, and skinny-dipped. Then they went off to sleep in tepee-style tents. Seton named himself the "medicine man" of a group he called the Woodcraft Indians, though all his young "braves" were white and middle class.

The transformation, he said, was immediate. "Instead of forty-two little reprobates, doing all the mischief they could to me and mine, I had

forty-two staunch friends who all turned out to be 'high class citizens,'"
Seton said. On the face of it, that strategy makes no sense. How can the
neighborhood's rich eccentric turn a bunch of hooligans into respectable
moderns almost overnight by encouraging them to run wild?

Seton had some corroboration for his views. Over the next few years,
when his Woodcraft Indians were gaining momentum in America, teachers and parents, and Seton himself, became devotees of a psychologist and
professor named G. Stanley Hall. If you are a parent of an active teen,
surely there have been moments when the words "Brute! Savage! Not quite
fully human!" flashed through your brain. Hall led American parents to
believe that their teenaged sons were either savages or a remarkable simu-
lation of them. Hall thought that men "recapitulated" the stages of human
social evolution from savagery to hunter-gatherer period to present-day
civilization as they aged from infancy to adulthood. Their savagery by itself
was not the problem. Modern life had "kidnapped" their youth, yanking
them out of the natural order, disrupting and arresting their evolutionary cycle. No wonder boys acted like the grunting denizens of the Stone
Age; that's what they were. The only way to free boys from savagery's
prison was to let them sound their barbaric "yawp" in a supervised environment. Only then could they return to society, make lots of money, be
patriotic, and raise wholesome families. That is where recreational camping fit into the picture.

Hall's is the Victorian take on the same child-development issues we
fret about even now. The author Richard Louv gained a national audience
with his 2005 book, *Last Child in the Woods: Saving Our Children from
Nature-Deficit Disorder*, about the estrangement of youth from the outdoors in the technological age. "The society is telling kids unconsciously
that nature's in the past," Louv told National Public Radio in May 2005. "It
really doesn't count anymore, that the future is in electronics, and besides,
the bogeyman is in the woods." In another interview, a year later, Louv
described hiking into some mountains near San Diego with hardened gang
members. He watched as the gangsters' blank expressions and city-induced
cynicism gave way to playfulness and wonder. In a similar fashion, Hall
wanted parents to expose their sons to "primitive" pursuits in the forest.
Seton encouraged his young charges to run wild, but he had no desire to
turn them into peewee anarchists. "Don't rebel," Seton told the boys. "Don't
kindle a wild fire; protect the song-birds; don't make a dirty camp; don't

bring firearms of any kind into the camps of those under fourteen; keep the game laws; no smoking (for those under eighteen); no firewater in camp; play fair; word of honor is sacred."

As a man-child himself, Seton was skilled at developing activities he knew his young male charges would love. In his book *The Birch-Bark Roll of the Woodcraft Indians*, he created a comprehensive set of rankings, rules, codes, and games designed to enchant them. The Woodcraft Indian "tribes" ruled themselves, much like the kids in *Lord of the Flies*, but without the bloodletting. They could earn "scalps" made of horsehair, and appoint their own "wampum chief." Seton knew that the trappings and ceremonies of ancient cultures would add necessary weight to the boys' feelings of transport and joy. Part of that "serious" appeal came from his relentless cherry-picking and simplification of native customs.

Seton's sympathy for America's original inhabitants was genuine— among his friends was a Native American doctor who treated the Indian victims of the Wounded Knee Massacre. Seton spent years studying Native American hand signs, yet he saw nothing wrong with building a youth encampment that was a hodgepodge of Blackfoot, Algonquin, Cheyenne, and Sioux influences. Just in case you were wondering about all those fake Native American–sounding names that sometimes grace the signs of private summer camps on American lakes even now, with phonetic spellings containing goofy puns, look back to those Victorian, quasi-Indian white camping impresarios for the source of all that kitsch.

The Woodcraft Indians was not a moneymaking venture for Seton. He had all the comfort and wealth he needed from his writings and illustrations. Did his terrible standoff with his own dad influence his desire to be a surrogate father for the kids of strangers? Maybe. All we know for sure is that Seton wanted to give boys the best of his childhood. He wanted to distill all his escapes into the woods, his fort making and snare building, into a program that lasted for years. Hoping to give that experience to as many boys as possible, he longed for a larger presence in America's Scouting scene, and daydreamed about extending his reach overseas. Perhaps these desires explain why Seton then made a boneheaded move he would regret for the rest of his life. Looking for some like-minded champion who might sympathize with his ideas, join forces with him, and help him spread his Woodcraft Indians model to other parts of the world, Seton sent a copy of *The Birch-Bark Roll of the Woodcraft Indians* to an Englishman named

Robert Baden-Powell (1857–1941)

Robert Baden-Powell. The book was a compendium of Seton's best ideas about Scouting, outlining the "constitution, laws, games and deeds" of his vigorous young "braves."

If Seton was a Black Wolf, Baden-Powell was more like a charming and playful fox: crafty and cunning, a careful trickster, and a bit of a shape-shifter, even in terms of his gender.

Baden-Powell, like Seton, was a native Englishman, but that's about all they had in common. Born in London in 1857, Baden-Powell lost his father, the controversial professor and clergyman Baden Powell, when he was only three years old. The young Baden-Powell never forgot the stories he heard about his dad, who sympathized with Darwin's views and spoke out against absolutist ideas about the world's creation. For this he was isolated, embarrassed, and branded a heretic. All his life, Robert Baden-Powell maintained a strong distaste for the clergy. The absence of his father also pushed him closer to his domineering mother. One of his biographers, Tim Jeal, speculates about the impact the death of his father had on Baden-Powell's future Scouting. "A lifetime's obsessive concern with manhood [and] manliness" was one result, along with constant concerns about the lessons and wisdom his father would have transmitted to him if he'd lived a longer life.

In spite of this early loss, Baden-Powell had an indomitable spirit of fun and good cheer, a strong sense of self, and an element of mischief; his preoccupation with masculinity did not stop him from messing with gender roles in graceful and flamboyant ways. Ever since his school days, the future champion of knot tying, fire making, and other alpha male activities was known for dressing up in ladies' clothing and dancing onstage to wild applause. In his army days, he had no qualms about taking on the role of "landlady" or "the waterman's wife." Well-known for his falsetto, he could even sing like a woman if he so desired. Skirt dancing was one of his specialties. It should be noted, however, that there were no women in the British military at the time, so someone had to play those roles.

As an adult, the man who would embody an organization that fostered so much male bonding had an all-consuming bond of his own: with a grown man named Kenneth McLaren, whom he called "the Boy." Tim Jeal reports that the two lavished gifts on each other, and were despondent when apart. There is no way of knowing if Baden-Powell and "the Boy" were gay. "It is . . . dangerous to impose one era's values and standards of conduct on another," writes Peter Applebome in his history-minded Scouting memoir, *Scout's Honor*. In those times, men could have passionate friendships with other men without reproach. Biographer Jeal also writes that Baden-Powell often spoke of the naked female form as if it were the most revolting thing imaginable, and the naked male form as gorgeous and sacred. He once said that two men "could be just as happy living together as any man and woman." At one point in his book, Jeal makes a strong pronouncement: "The available evidence points inexorably to the conclusion that Baden-Powell was a repressed homosexual."

There has been widespread speculation but no definitive proof. It's also true that Baden-Powell charmed and courted a number of ladies. He may have broken the heart of Girl Scouts of America (GSUSA) founder Juliette Gordon Low when he married a much younger woman, Olave St. Clair Soames. But Jeal's bold statements about Baden-Powell's sexuality are striking, especially considering the future furor over gays in the Boy Scouts, the group Baden-Powell helped create. Until 2013, gay youth were banned from the BSA, and only in 2015 was the ban on openly gay adult leaders finally lifted. In her 2012 *New York Times* opinion piece, "The Rainbow Merit Badge," contributor Brooke Allen said Baden-Powell's life is "a poignant story that should be known. This man who gave so much to so many suffered from the forces of repression and taboo. It is unfortunate that the American branch of the movement he founded should perpetuate them."

Baden-Powell got married in 1912, at age fifty-five. "[A]fter dispensing with the messy unpleasantness of sex," Baden-Powell was able to achieve "a warm, comradely union with the woman who became his partner in Scouting," Applebome wrote. He also referenced Baden-Powell's less-than-romantic mention of marriage in his autobiography. Referring to the process of choosing a Scouting guide for a dangerous mission, Baden-Powell once said, "The selection is one that cannot be lightly made. It is as bad as choosing a horse—or a wife. There is a lot depending on it."

Whether or not there is any merit to the claims that he lived a secret life in a British society that would have thrown him into jail if he'd relaxed his vigilance, Baden-Powell was undoubtedly brave, crafty, cunning, and resourceful, with a storied military career. He made his reputation while stationed in South Africa at the dawn of the twentieth century. The Boers, hardy farmers of Dutch extraction, known for their skills at horseback riding and their deadly competence with firearms, resented the British troops in the Transvaal. In October 1899, Baden-Powell came under siege in Mafeking, a collection of modest tin huts on the blazing-hot veldt. He used feints and trickery to make his Boer marauders think the defenders had much more weaponry and larger numbers than they really had. In doing so, Baden-Powell and the other fighters, though badly outmanned and outgunned, held off the attackers for an astonishing 219 days. The Boers finally launched a head-on assault, but the defenders defeated them. Then the British cavalry rode in and drove the Boers away. Baden-Powell's countrymen were so thrilled at his achievements that *maffick* earned an entry in *Webster's Dictionary*. The word, even now, means "to celebrate with boisterous rejoicing and hilarious behavior."

By the time he returned to England, Baden-Powell was a general and a national hero with a huge platform and built-in audience for his ideas about Scouting for boys. The notion came, in part, because of his profound anxieties about new generations of "loafers and wasters." He wanted to give them spirit, military discipline, and camaraderie, but in an enjoyable way. At the time, the dreary Boys' Brigades ruled the Scouting scene. In 1907, Baden-Powell tested out his ideas by inviting twenty-two boys to camp on Brownsea Island. He made sure they came from different social classes, and kept the atmosphere light. He had them chant things like "Invooboo! Yah bo! Invooboo," in loud call-and-response demonstrations. They stalked animals in patrols named the Curlews, Ravens, Wolves, and Bulls, and camped in repurposed army tents. Baden-Powell called them to order, sounding out blasts on a koodoo horn from Africa.

By all accounts, it was great fun. Yet for all his popularity, Baden-Powell was about to make a lifelong enemy of Ernest Thompson Seton.

The troubles started when Seton mailed him a copy of his *Birch-Bark Roll*, outlining his ideas for the Woodcraft Indians and adding loving and exacting descriptions of games. It's easy to imagine Baden-Powell ripping open that package as if it were a box of sweetmeats. He devoured the book, and for a short while, Seton and General Baden-Powell seemed like comrades. It looked as if they might even do some wonderful things together for young people all across the world. But that joyful, mutually respectful working relationship was not to be.

The rupture came in 1908, when Baden-Powell followed up his success at Brownsea with a best-selling book, *Scouting for Boys*, his first truly coherent and detailed expression of his Boy Scout ideas.

Though Baden-Powell was a military man, *Scouting for Boys* is about much more than discipline. It is goofy, enjoyable, specific, *and* demanding, a bit like Horace Kephart for adolescents, with an added dose of morality, patriotism, and upright behavioral suggestions. It's all here: how you tie a knot, how you use your axe, how you should act (always in a polite and genteel manner), and how to sneak up on a deer. The message is consistent: Purify your mind. Respect old people. Don't touch yourself in an unclean manner. What else would any self-respecting English boy really need to know about life?

Scouting even had its own cosmology, including a quasi–Ten Commandments: "A Scout's honor is to be trusted. A Scout is loyal to the Queen, his country, his parents, his employers and those under him," and so on. Baden-Powell made sure not to overdo the dour materials. He always leavened the serious bits with hilarity. "Laugh as much as you can," he advised. "It does you good."

The boys loved it. Ernest Thompson Seton, not so much.

After reading the book, Seton was, apparently, apoplectic. He later said that he was "astounded to find all my ideas taken, all my games appropriated, disguised with new names, the essentials of my plan utilized, and not a word of acknowledgment." He sent a concerned but polite letter to Baden-Powell, who apologized—sort of. Perhaps Seton expected an abject letter, begging his forgiveness. But Baden-Powell's apology was a bowl of lukewarm and watery oatmeal. "I much regret that I should have omitted mentioning the source of several of the games."

This apology mollified Seton a little bit. But he was a temperamental and wounded man who could not leave off. The little cut in the relationship of these two camping giants began to fester. Was Seton right to be so mad? Was Baden-Powell being sincere, not disingenuous and slimy, when he kept putting those little hedges in his apologies? The answer depends in part on whether you're a Seton or Baden-Powell fan boy. Regardless of one's affiliation, there are a few striking if not uncanny similarities between *The Birch-Bark Roll* and Baden-Powell's book, including the way the boys rise up through the ranks through tests, and can gain a high honor that might be taken away and attained once more: a bundle of horsehair, or "scalp," for Seton's Indians and the First Class Badge of Scouting for Baden-Powell.

Seton was not wrong to feel he had been misused; there are some serious overlaps between some of the games, too. In fairness, Baden-Powell, apparently, cribbed from everybody, and drew copiously from his own background in military reconnaissance. *Scouting for Boys* wasn't even his first book on the subject. And it must be said that Seton simply lacked Baden-Powell's formidable salesmanship and schmoozing skills. Baden-Powell's genius at repackaging his own and other people's ideas for maximum impact, enjoyment, and appeal cannot be denied. The Woodcraft Indians just weren't catching on like Baden-Powell's Boy Scout concept. It was only a matter of time before the Scouts spread to America. At first Baden-Powell was, at least publicly, reluctant to see the Boy Scouts launch in the United States. He didn't want to create the impression that he was stomping into the domain of Seton's Woodcraft Indians. But Baden-Powell's Scouting book was so popular that the matter was taken out of his hands. By the time the Boy Scouts of America launched in 1910, Baden-Powell's project was on the verge of becoming a global phenomenon. Looking to avoid any more static, the Boy Scouts of America was careful to name Seton "chief scout" and brought in yet another strong-willed man who also considered himself the true "Father of Scouting."

Daniel Carter Beard (1850–1941)

His name was Daniel "Uncle Dan" Carter Beard, an Ohio-born, Kentucky-raised illustrator and freelance writer besotted with America's pioneer past. His *American Boy's Handy Book* (1882) was an instant outdoor classic that showed boys how to make everything from homemade bows, arrows, and minnow buckets to kites designed to fight in gleefully nasty aerial battles. Beard loathed big business and plutocrats, and he was resolutely anti-wimp. "We want *no* Molly Coddles," he said. His motto for his young charges was a Crockettesque quote: "Be always sure you are right, then go ahead." Like the Black Wolf, Uncle Dan had some peculiarities. For instance, he was always flinging tomahawks for fun, even when he reached his dotage, and welcomed every day with a freezing-cold bath, which roused him into song: "It's a mighty pretty morning, good Lord, good Lord. The devil's mad, and I am glad. He missed a soul he thought he had, good Lord, good Lord!" He once proclaimed that all mosquitoes were "Bolsheviks" and was fond of blunt sayings, such as: "This was a good country in the past. It is a good country today. It will be a good country tomorrow *unless we fail it.*" Like Seton, Uncle Dan was also a well-known artist; most famously, he contributed his artwork to the first edition of *A Connecticut Yankee in King Arthur's Court,* by Mark Twain. It helped that the two of them had a similar oil-of-vitriol sense of humor. "Yes, it was a fortunate hour that I went netting for lighting bugs and caught a meteor," Twain said of Beard's work, adding that he hoped his illustrator "lived forever."

In 1905, five years before the launch of the BSA, Uncle Dan rolled out a group of his own, the Sons of Daniel Boone, a rowdy little precursor to the Boy Scouts. Instead of playing at "savages" like the Woodcraft Indians, they acted like frontiersmen. Instead of tribes, he had "stockades." Instead of dressing up his boys in Indian finery, they wore brown overalls, hunting shirts, and buckskin chaps. They even pretended to fight off and kill boys pretending to be Indians, setting up an instant silly rivalry between Beard and Seton. For all his enthusiasm, however, Uncle Dan never turned the group into a major cultural force. Baden-Powell's growing organization outclassed him and threatened to make him a marginal figure in the outdoors unless he faced reality and joined forces with the BSA.

Baden-Powell was very careful to express his gratitude toward Seton and Beard in public, although the two of them often felt outmaneuvered and undervalued. At a gala ceremony at the Waldorf-Astoria hotel in Manhattan in September of 1910, Seton, perhaps under duress, and maybe through clenched teeth, was on hand to introduce Baden-Powell as the "Father of Scouting." Then, in a statement that is either gracious and kind or mushy, icky, and disingenuous, Baden-Powell said, "You have made a little mistake, Mr. Seton, in your remarks to the effect that I am the Father of this idea of Scouting for Boys. I may say that you are the Father of it, or that Dan Beard is the Father. There are many Fathers. I am only one of the Uncles, I might say." The audience loved this show of unity. The Boy Scouts were an immediate wild success in America. "There are already 150,000 lads enrolled in the Boy Scouts of America, though the organization is only a few months old," the *New York Times* reported in October 1910.

But the organization continued to push aside Seton's ideas. He couldn't stand the way the Boy Scouts picked and chose certain aspects of his Woodcraft Indians, discarding the rest. In his view, the group was losing its tasty wood smoke flavor and its love of the forest while drifting toward jackbooted militarism. He had good reason for complaining, but Seton was so abrasive and whiny in his jeremiads that potential allies turned on him. In spite of Uncle Dan's lingering annoyance at Baden-Powell, he joined in the dog-piling against Seton, denouncing him as a mealymouthed pacifist, and made fun of him for refusing to renounce his British citizenship and become a naturalized U.S. citizen while serving as BSA chief scout. He also went after Seton for speaking angrily about American foreign policy. In 1915, five years after the BSA's inception in the United States, Beard wrote a snippy personal memo that included a blow-by-blow comparison between himself and Seton.

Mr. Dan Beard	Mr. Ernest Thompson Seton
Christian	Pagan
Whiteman	Indian
Democratic Government	Monarchy
"That the American flag is beautiful."	"That it is the ugliest among nations."
"That the pioneers were clean and moral men."	"That the American pioneers were scalawags and low types."

Seton's stubborn convictions led to an image problem for the BSA during the buildup to America's involvement in World War I. With jingoism in the air, Seton's pacifist views offended some powerful people who influenced the Scouts, including Theodore Roosevelt, who did not name Seton but had him in mind in an angry letter sent to the BSA: "It is my understanding that as part of the wicked and degrading pacifist agitation of the last few years, certain leaders [in the BSA] . . . have used the Boy Scout organization as a medium for . . . pacifist literature," interfering with military training. The former president growled that any Boy Scout "who is not trained actively and affirmatively that it is his duty to bear arms for the country in time of need is at least negatively trained to be a sissy."

Roosevelt was an irresistible force. His speeches and writings about the need to "stave off effeminacy" had set the tone for boys' groups even before the launch of the BSA. By then, Seton had yet another cause for his rancor: James E. West, the chubby, cleft-chinned executive head of the Boy Scouts, whom Seton denounced as a joyless, wonky prig (in so many words). As Seton summed up the evolution of the Scouts, "Seton started it; Baden-Powell boomed it; West killed it." Seton also called West "a lawyer . . . with great executive ability but without knowledge of the activities of boys . . . and who, I might say, has never seen the blue sky in his life."

West responded in kind, all but branding Seton a traitor, a man "in harmony with the views of anarchists."

After holding a press conference to announce his resignation in late 1915—he had sent a letter of resignation months earlier, but for some unknown reason it didn't take—Seton stayed active with his Woodcraft Indians. His stature nevertheless faded over time. While he still has a strong following with camping revivalists, it is Baden-Powell who lives on in the American imagination as the "founder of the Boy Scouts." But the movement would not have the same outdoorsy feel, its focus on old-time fun in the forest, without the contributions of Seton and Beard. Seton's influence was far-ranging, even if the name is no longer familiar.

In comparison to the twisty-turny saga of the Boy Scouts, the story of the early Girl Scouts of America is much more straightforward, with one undisputed mother of the movement. Yet the GSUSA's founding visionary, Juliette Gordon Low, nicknamed Daisy as a child, had much in common with Ernest Thompson Seton. Both drew from painful memories when they built their play scapes in the woods for American youth. In an era when men wanted their wives to be feminine and dependent, Low urged girls to own their destinies.

Growing up in Savannah, Georgia, Daisy exhibited the same willfulness, eccentricity, and idealism that would sustain her later in life, along with a brave inclination toward inclusiveness that might have something to do with her divided household: her father fought for the Confederacy in the Civil War, while her mother, born in Chicago, was antislavery. Her mother was so chummy with the Union side that General Sherman himself stopped over for social calls several times in Savannah, following his three-hundred-mile march of destruction through the South. The young Daisy was fearless even then, and loved interrogating Union troops. When one of them was hanging out in her house, Daisy speculated out loud about his missing arm. The soldier told her, "Got it shot off by a Rebel." "I s'pose my father did it," Daisy said. "He shot lots of Yankees."

Bold and brazen from an early age, Daisy was also an impetuous do-gooder. Sometimes her early efforts to be helpful led to pitiful situations, such as the time she tried to remove a friend's freckles surgically. On another occasion she hoped to revive a dead dog by dragging its body onto her mother's bed and working it over with a "medicinal electric wand." In her girlhood, she formed a crude precursor to the Girl Scouts, an organization called the Helpful Hands Club, which sought to help needy children by making clothing for them. Unfortunately the girls were incompetent seamstresses. The outfits fell apart when the kids put them on. This extreme shoddiness earned Low's organization an unwanted nickname: the Helpless Hands Club. Her biographer Stacy Cordery wrote that there is "some evidence that Daisy rescued a three-year-old from drowning when she herself was only eight . . . surely the wisdom of being prepared for an emergency was not lost on her."

But that early wisdom was not enough to keep her from making a decision that derailed her. She went to the finest private schools, enjoyed the advantages of being a member of a well-off family, and became a debutante, but her youthful impulsiveness led her into an exhausting and miserable marriage to a ne'er-do-well who took advantage of her trust. Such is the power of physical attraction. On the day of her lavish wedding to the rakishly handsome William Mackay Low in 1886, she was injured in a bizarre incident that served as an omen of things to come. Daisy and William, a gambler, horseman, playboy, and heir to a large fortune, had boarded their carriage, and were about to be whisked off to their honeymoon, when revelers started pelting them with rice. That custom is supposed to bring good luck and prosperity to the happy couple. Not so this time. One of those rice grains lodged itself deep inside Juliette Low's inner ear, causing her excruciating pain. That grain of rice would permanently damage her hearing and contribute to her near deafness later in life.

If Daisy thought of that rice as a harbinger of a future unhappy life with William, she did not act on the hunch. She stayed married for nineteen childless and mostly unhappy years. When William began cheating on her without bothering to cover it up, Daisy was furious and devastated, and wrote about the "dregs of the bitterness of life." By 1900, most everyone in Daisy's circle knew about the philandering. She decided to pursue divorce proceedings, even though it was sure to cause a scandal. Her husband dropped dead in 1905 before the divorce was finalized, though. Before his demise, he took the time to make funeral arrangements that seemed designed to make Daisy feel even worse. For one thing, he arranged to have his mistress's love letters piled on top of his corpse before it was lowered into the grave. For another, he made arrangements to leave almost all his money to his lover, while giving his widow only a modest monthly "allowance." Stunned and more humiliated than before, Daisy contested the will and got most of the money owed her as widow, but she lacked a plan. She'd wasted her youth as someone's unhappy helpmeet. What was she supposed to do now that she was single and had all this money but no purpose? At a time when homemaking and child rearing were the most respectable jobs for women and alternatives were rare, there wasn't much of a future for a middle-aged widow with bad hearing and no kids.

Yet Daisy soon found her purpose, which appeared in the form of none other than Robert Baden-Powell. When they met in May 1911, sitting across the table from each other at a luncheon, the Boy Scouts was having great success in America and England but would not accommodate the six thousand girls who attempted to join. Instead, Baden-Powell arranged for his sister, Agnes Baden-Powell, to form an English spin-off group called the Girl Guides. Daisy wanted to form her own group in the United States but had only a murky idea about how to run it. As a start, she organized a Girl Guides troop in Scotland. Brimming with energy and resolve, Daisy returned to Savannah in 1912 and telephoned her cousin Nina Pape, insisting that she "come right over! I've got something for the girls of Savannah, and all America, and all the world, and we're going to start it tonight."

Daisy and this fledgling group of eighteen members wanted to set themselves apart from the Girl Guides in Great Britain and jettisoned

Juliette Gordon Low (1860–1927)

"Guides" for "Scouts." That year, the most influential girls' group in U.S. history was born. Low was a great networker and persuader, and when people resisted her entreaties, she cocked her "deaf ear" toward them and kept pounding away at their resolve. In addition to her actual partial deafness, Daisy cultivated the selective deafness that served her well when angry male opposition rose up to shout her down. The intimidating and bureaucratic Boy Scouts executive director James E. West, the same man who caused such heartache for Ernest Thompson Seton, thundered against the Girl Scouts. In those days, when people were much too prim to throw around words like *lesbianism*, West accused Daisy of converting girls into tomboys while allowing her scouts to "ape" the BSA's khaki uniforms. He also said that Daisy "trivialized" and "sissified" the Boy Scouts by using the word *scout* in her group's name.

At the same time, Daisy faced aggressive competition from the Camp Fire Girls, a group that was founded in 1910, with help from West himself, and that described itself as "Hard as Nails and Dipped in Sunshine." In terms of its activities, the group was quite similar to the Girl Scouts, with its focus on hard work, camp craft, patriotism, and "the joy of primitive living" combined with kitchen skills. Camp Fire Girls had to learn a variety of vintage camping hacks, from making a bed on the ground to tying a "squaw hitch" and various "trick knots," building a tree house, and erecting an "Indian tepee." They had to know how to "prepare a gruel, a cereal, an eggnog, and milk toast and arrange an invalid's tray attractively" and "Roast, broil, fricassee, [and] boil" meats. But the Camp Fire Girls, in its original incarnation, used ecology and Native American garb mostly as a way to expound upon the glories of housewifery. Daisy well understood that most of her young charges would go on to be housewives. Yet she was determined to give them a little something extra that would help them fend for themselves in case those marriages collapsed—a few essential survival skills combined with the power of sisterhood. She had girls climbing trees, lighting fires, and doing strenuous exercises in the woods at a time when these behaviors were considered unseemly for females; in those days, women's basketball was considered so shocking that Daisy was forced to hang up privacy curtains when her Girl Scouts played.

Even the name of Daisy's group reflected her bolder sensibility. At a time when the word *scouting* had an exclusively male and warlike connotation, she dared to call her girls Scouts. She must have known there would be a backlash. Camp Fire Girls cofounder Luther Gulick declared that it was "utterly and fundamentally evil" for the Girl Scouts to copy the Boy Scouts. Daisy refused to listen. When forced to do so, she leaned on her pal Baden-Powell for moral and political support, putting the "Hero of Mafeking" in an awkward position. He wasn't too crazy about the name "Girl Scouts," either.

Daisy was no radical, no activist or revolutionary. If anything, she was a cautious agent of change. She knew how to "play the game" and cater to gender expectations. The inaugural Girl Scouts handbook, *How Girls Can Help Their Country*, published in 1913, has some inevitable disclaimers and cautious hedges: "No one wants women to be soldiers." There are sections on tidiness, needlework, child care, and of course housework. But much of the book is indistinguishable from any boyish woodcraft camping book published around the same time. It tells its young readers to pursue careers as stockbrokers, architects, or aviators if they dare. The book uses camping, and outdoor activities in general, as a means to give the girls the courage to take on life's problems and pursue their ambitions, and foster a sense of self-assurance that would spill over into their home lives and possible careers. She also prepared the girls for a future in conservation, telling them that it was "more in their power than men to prevent waste."

The manual also tells girls not to fear snakes, how to use semaphores, cut kindling, repel mosquitoes with citronella, stalk through a forest undetected, stay calm when lost, and shoot a gun "for means of defense should an emergency arise." The handbook includes paramilitary maneuvers in the woods and explicit instructions for subduing and restraining a burglar. All they needed was eight inches of strong cord.

"Make a slip-knot at each end of your cord . . . Place him face downwards, and bend his knees," the book advises. "Pass both feet under the string, and he will be unable to get away."

Girls loved these passages, and they could not resist Daisy's charisma. "She was *electrical*, or something like that . . . people fell for her," one early Girl Scout reported.

The Girl Scouts took pains to hide their subversive bent. They were hyperpatriotic. During World War I they hawked war bonds, made trench candles, and mastered some tricky drill formations. But they were not afraid to tweak stereotypes. In a 1917 editorial, the Girl Scout magazine *The Rally* dared to confront chauvinist male educators who sought to keep girls "too under cover, too much confined to books, too little free to engage in sports that might spoil their clothes. All healthy girls have resented this violently, and endured the title 'tomboy,' if only they could have the chance of the tomboy's free movements and fresh air."

The Girl Scouts were also inclusive for the times, embracing girls from all social backgrounds. The strategy worked. By 1920, more than 50,000 girls had signed on to the GSUSA. Within another ten years, the group was 275,000 girls strong. The group was never all white. The first African American troop began in 1912 and the first Native American troop in 1921. It took the GSUSA a few more decades before it embraced integration although, to its credit, the Girl Scouts made meaningful steps in that direction in the 1950s, before the modern civil rights movement became widespread. And the group, at least in its recent history, has sidestepped the gay exclusion controversy that dogged the Boy Scouts. The GSUSA did not take an official position on lesbians in its scouting troops until the 1980s; at that point the organization stated that "while the Girl Scouts does not recruit lesbians, it does not discriminate or intrude into personal matters."

Its open embrace was an expansion strategy. By the time Daisy was buried in her full Girl Scout uniform in 1927, her group had grown from a small troop of curious girls to a national force with hundreds of thousands of young members. Since then, the group has become synonymous with fearless womanhood, with a roster of former GSUSA scouts that includes Taylor Swift, Gloria Steinem, Madeleine Albright, Hillary Rodham Clinton, Dakota Fanning, Sandra Day O'Connor, Nancy Reagan, Martha Stewart, Venus Williams, Condoleezza Rice, and Laura Bush. GSUSA also had a strong presence in my household, which only increased my regret about not joining the Boy Scouts; I remember being in awe of my sister as she packed up her enormous Girl Scouts duffel bag and headed off to adventures on mountain ridges and desert plateaus. She remembered resting, sunburned, on a bank of the Colorado River at night, "watching the constellations spin and spin and spin." Her moments of rapture as a Girl Scout later led me to kidnap her duffel bag and hold on to it to this very day.

Daisy was not alone in leading girls and women on a march into the woods. On their own, in groups, in cars, on horses, or on their own power, women were finding their way into the male-dominated camping world.

Hero of Camping: The S'more

*The Curious History of a
Hegemonic Campground Treat*

One of my proudest camping moments involved an elderly French lady who wandered into my Sierra Nevada car camp one night in high heels, with clanking jewelry and a fruity perfume with notes of menthol. She wanted to know why I was squishing flame-roasted marshmallows against a cracker with Hershey's chocolate. The woman had a disapproving look, and I could not understand one word she was saying, but she communicated her thoughts with frantic hand gestures. If memory serves, this woman was wearing Chanel and foundation makeup on national forest land. She was well put together, but when I gave her her first taste of s'mores she fell apart. "Fondant!" she shouted as she jumped around my campfire. "Fondant, fondant, fondant, fondant!"

A cultural transmission took place that night. The woman just about cleared me out of my Jet-Puffed marshmallows. I owe that rapturous moment to the Girl Scouts, who gave the world the first and most popular recipe for "some mores" in a 1927 Girl Scouts manual, *Tramping and Trailing with the Girl Scouts*. The candy sandwich was a standout in a cooking section that included a baleful concoction called the Spotted Dog, consisting of mushy brown rice, water, salt, and "seeded raisins." The original Girl Scouts s'more recipe calls for sixteen graham crackers, eight bars plain chocolate ("any of the good plain brands broken in two"), and sixteen marshmallows. "Toast two marshmallows over the coals to a crisp gooey state and then put them inside a graham cracker and chocolate bar sandwich," the Scouts advised.

No one seems to know if the Girl Scouts devised the recipe themselves. At the time the guidebook came out, this combination of ingredients was well known to the American public in the Mallomar cookie, which came out in 1913, and in Moon Pies, which debuted in 1917. I like to think that the clever and joyous Girl Scouts pioneered the idea of applying heat. After all, this organization was well versed in the art of improvisation and repurposing. These are the same girls who hoarded peach pits to be used in American soldiers' gas masks in World War I. The burnt pits were turned into a special charcoal that was placed in the masks and mixed with antigas chemicals, according to Francis Andrew March and Richard Joseph Beamish in their *History of the World War: An Authentic Narrative of the World's Greatest War Including the Treaty of Peace and the League of Nations Covenant*. In other words, the girls understood that great results can come from homely ingredients, even the normally repulsive graham cracker.

Let's face it. If there were no such thing as s'mores, the graham cracker would have no right to exist. (No, graham cracker piecrust does not count. It falls apart and tastes like sawdust, while compromising the cracker's one redeeming virtue: its ability to serve as an architectural support for melting marshmallows.) Not only that, but the graham cracker has a creepy provenance. Truly, the s'more has rescued it from oblivion.

These days, if you were to go online and type "s'mores" and "orgasm" into a search engine, you would get 174,000 results, with findings such as "s'mores cookie equals orgasm in Pyrex," and "Ben and Jerry's S'mores equals edible orgasm." You will even find an Urban Dictionary entry called *s'morgasm*. In light of this, it is striking that the graham cracker was originally intended as an early-nineteenth-century cure for bawdy urges and a deterrent to masturbation.

American Presbyterian minister and joyless food activist Sylvester Graham (1794–1851) was either the inventor of or the inspiration behind the graham cracker. Whether or not he baked the wafer that bears his name is open to question, but "it was originally produced with his health principles in mind," wrote Kyla Wazana Tompkins in her alarming essay "Sylvester Graham's Imperial Dietetics." At the very least, Graham, the most influential health food diet proponent of the early nineteenth century, came up with a recommended list of ingredients for the cracker, originally made of "coarsely-ground, unbolted wheat" and "a little molasses or sugar." The texture was gritty and rough, but it wasn't supposed to be pleasant. Graham thought that eating a gruel or cracker made from his "farinaceous" flour would stop young males from a bad habit that would drain their "spinal marrow," give them apoplexy, cause their teeth to drop from their gums, and make their lithe young bodies "dwarfish and crooked."

Graham himself was the product of unbearable urges; he had sixteen brothers and sisters. This did not stop him from preaching his message to anyone who would listen. Strange as his beliefs may seem now, he was not considered a freak; nor were his views spontaneous or even original. It appears that Graham was an admirer of the book *Onania: Or the Heinous Sin of Self-Pollution, and All Its Frightful Consequences*, and his views appealed to health enthusiasts worried about the moral fiber and laziness of nineteenth-century boys. These, by the way, are the same concerns that led to the beginning of youth camping later in the century. As the historian T. J. Jackson Lears points out, a lot of these fears of self-abuse had to do with cultural anxieties about discipline and self-control, and not just sex.

One of the first places to serve the graham cracker was Oberlin College, starting in the early 1830s. School staff offered the flavorless wafers along with fruit, gruel, rice, and vegetables, all washed down with cold water. (Coincidentally, in another bit of graham cracker/American camping history, John Muir subsisted on graham crackers when he was an impoverished college student in Wisconsin during the early 1860s.) These graham cracker dinners at Oberlin were revolting, and so were the students: they staged an insurrection, charged out of the cafeteria, and to spite the administration gorged themselves on red meat in private boardinghouses. These rebellious scholars prevailed: the college discontinued the Sylvester Graham–inspired regimen after finding it "inadequate to the demands of the human system as at present developed."

While Graham had followers, he was also controversial, and some of the backlash against him was borderline violent; he was so passionate about home-ground whole wheat, and spoke so stridently against the evils of pure white flour, that at one of his speeches, in Boston in 1837, a group of bakers rioted and dumped loads of whole wheat flour on the people lined up to hear Graham's lecture. His negative image carried on through the decades. When American food manufacturers began mass-producing the crackers at the beginning of the twentieth century, several cookie makers printed the word *graham* in lowercase on their packaging, perhaps to distance themselves from Graham.

Coincidentally, while Americans were figuring out ways to make the graham cracker more palatable, they were also puzzling over the fate of the marshmallow. In the beginning, only mom-and-pop confectioners made them from scratch at home. Candy makers sold them in tins. Then, in the early twentieth century, they started appearing in scores of recipes. In a 1916 issue of *La Estrella*, a newspaper in Las Cruces, New Mexico, the food writer Nellie Maxwell introduced an early s'mores-like snack made of marshmallows and dipped in peppermint fondant, baked to perfection and placed on salted wafers. Some of the recipes seem desperate, as if the chefs had inherited several wagonloads of marshmallows and were trying to dispose of them. One writer instructed readers to serve marshmallows as an appetizer, with "boiled salad dressing" poured on them. A newspaper in Brownsville, Texas, printed a recipe for cabbage salad with crushed pineapple, chopped marshmallows, four tablespoons of mayonnaise, and a dollop of chili sauce.

Then along came the Imperial Candy Company, which launched the "Campfire Marshmallow" in 1917, taking advantage of the brand-new cultural trend of holding marshmallow roasts on the beach. It was inevitable that someone was going to come along and try to goose the deliciousness of these marshmallows by adding other flavors and textures.

So this leaves one final question unanswered: Why do s'mores almost always contain Hershey milk chocolate? The answer, it seems, has to do with Hershey's muscular presence at the time s'mores were invented. Milton Hershey pioneered "the mass-produced chocolate bar" in 1900. "There were other chocolate manufacturers, but Hershey was there first and was the biggest and best known," candy historian Samira Kawash told me. Though early s'more recipes don't specify Hershey's, they didn't have to; Hershey's was pretty much all there was.

"As for our own day, have you seen any other brands of single-wrapped chocolate bars lately?" Kawash said. She pointed out that the candy industry underwent a dramatic consolidation beginning in the 1960s, and basically left only two standing. "Hershey, with its chocolate bars, and Mars, with its other kinds of bars," Kawash said. "So even if you wanted to use another bar, you'd be pretty hard-pressed to find one. Also, there is probably a story about the scoring of the Hershey bar." Kawash was referring to the Hershey bar's famous and recently trademarked grid design, which allows campers to snap it into twelve suspiciously s'more-sized parallelograms, which are called "pips."

These days, the s'more is hegemonic in camping. Out in the Paws Up glamping resort in Montana, where renting a tent can cost thousands of dollars a night, you can opt for a "s'mores butler" to roast them for you. Glamping Girl, a website that promotes upscale camping, includes a recipe for "S'moretini Shooters," consisting of marshmallow, whipped cream, or cake-flavored vodka, Godiva chocolate liqueur, Bailey's Irish Cream liqueur, chocolate syrup, half-and-half, graham cracker crumbs, and "vanilla frosting for glass rimming."

But what about the awkward portmanteau word *s'more*? The Girl Scouts seemed to know they were marketing something irresistible to the masses. These days, even the lowly unheated marshmallow has become part of a cultural catchphrase for temptation: "the

Marshmallow Test." Around 1970, Stanford researcher Walter Mischel started using the marshmallow, or some other treat, as part of a longitudinal study that linked delayed gratification with long-term success.

No wonder a combination of marshmallow and silky milk chocolate, on a platform of cracker that provides stability, architecture, and a shattering crunch, can send children and adults into a fugue state. Perhaps aware of future generations eating these treats until they fell face forward into the campfire in a diabetic coma, the Girl Scouts included a plea for moderation at the end of their recipe: "Though it tastes like 'some more,' one is really enough."

6

Wild Victorian Ladies

They talk about a woman's sphere, as though it had a limit. There's not a place in earth or heaven. There's not a task to mankind given . . . without a woman in it.

—Kate Field, journalist, nineteenth-century camper

In 2008, I was in Portland, Oregon, on a book tour to support my Pacific Crest Trail memoir, *The Cactus Eaters*. My talk was set to begin at 7:00 p.m., and I was getting twitchy, because it was 6:45, there were forty seats, and all but ten were empty. I hid in the children's section and watched the bookstore staff round people up and practically shove them into the folding chairs. Five minutes before 7:00, fifteen more people sat down. Two drew my special attention: a stringy-haired teen who sat in the center of the third row, only to bury his face in a manga book, and an athletic blonde who appeared to be in her early thirties. She was wearing, if memory serves, a Polartec-type dark fleece zip-up jacket. I enjoy guessing the occupations of audience members to amuse myself and ease my nerves. During my reading, I picked up on this woman's stillness and watchfulness, and her talent for deep listening. She was most definitely a child behavioral psychologist, a career guidance counselor, or an animal trainer. After the talk, she waited in line to have me sign her copy of my book.

"You live and work around here?" I asked her, eager to test out my hunch about her job.

"Yes," she said. "In Portland." She mentioned her husband and two young children.

"What's your work out here?"

"I'm a writer."

"Cool. Part time?"

"Full time," she said, with just a little bit of an authoritative edge to her voice.

"Really? *So cool*. What's your husband's job?"

She told me he made documentaries.

"Oh, my goodness," I said. "And you can survive with those jobs?"

"So far," she said.

"Nice. What's your name?"

"Cheryl Strayed," she said.

"Really?" I said. I'd read a bunch of her work. I'd even studied her essays in graduate school. But this healthy, seemingly centered woman looked nothing like the pale and haggard vision I'd conjured from her essays, which mentioned hard living and drugs. "You're not what I expected," I blurted out. She laughed, and told me she had similar reactions from time to time. Certain readers seem to expect whips and chains, she told me. "I'm a soccer mom!"

I stopped talking to her for a moment, walked up to the live microphone, and addressed the stragglers in the crowd. "Hey, everyone, guess what? Cheryl Strayed is in the house. Cheryl Strayed, the writer? She's got skills!"

She smiled indulgently. A couple of people gave me blank stares, then went right back to browsing the aisles. No one had any idea who she was.

We wound up talking for a couple of hours at a Chili's restaurant in the charmless mall that contained the bookstore. Cheryl Strayed ordered no food or beer. She accepted one limp french fry after I urged her to try it. She wanted to tell me about a book she was drafting. It involved a long walk on the Pacific Crest Trail. From the sound of it, a lot of the book had to do with her mom and her past. She hadn't decided how much weight to give the trail, or how the pieces of the narrative were going to talk to one another and fit together. Just before my sloppy meal was over, she looked at the remains of my terrible burger. "Don't you know that Portland is one of the great food cities of America?" she said.

"Now you tell me," I said, feeling the onset of a stomachache.

We continued our Chili's conversation over the next few months, through a series of long e-mails. She gave me more information about her work-in-progress and confessed a touch of nervousness. How were people going to respond to her work? I came to believe that certain testy members of the Pacific Crest Trail community and perhaps the rest of America would gang up on her. Even now, in the twenty-first century, the story of a woman camping and hiking alone feels like a provocative gesture to certain people, a jab at the status quo. "*Wild* is certainly about hiking the PCT," she told me during one long online missive,

> but it's also really very much a memoir about my life *before* the hike. There are long, long "flashback" passages, and what goes on inside of me is in some ways more front and central than the trail (though of course the trail is huge in the book, too—when you read it, you'll see what I mean). Plus—oh, and *this* is going to drive those PCT purists nuts!—I did not thru-hike the trail. I hiked about twelve hundred miles of it. That's a *long way*. How this idea formed that if you didn't hike the whole thing you somehow didn't really hike the trail is utterly absurd. I never intended to hike the whole thing. I set out to spend about a hundred days on the trail, and that's what I did. It was hard, amazing, and life changing. I wasn't prepared for the hike (this too will incite the hiker purists!), but I learned a lot. And that, of course, is the story. Or at least part of it.

I sent her a long and sympathetic e-mail, and she sent me one in return when I vented about my experiences with online haters and trolls. Years passed. We fell out of regular e-mail and Facebook communication. When her book was released, it did not turn out to be the disaster I worried it might be. It did not get buried beneath a pile of hatred and male opprobrium. It became one of the best-selling memoirs of all time, and certainly the best-selling book that devotes so many pages to an American woman's solo camping adventure. As the book climbed to the top of the list and was made into a feature film, it occurred to me that *Wild* was lucky to have been published in the twenty-first century. Of course, the huge success of this book was much more than a question of its timeliness. Strayed wrote a beautiful, candid, and unsparing work, an unsentimental and gripping story of redemption in the wilderness. But it also occurred to me that if she had been born in, say, 1819, the work, regardless of its quality, would have enjoyed a small private printing at best. At the time her book came out, I had been reading my way through a teetering pile of redemptive wilderness memoirs dating to the 1830s. It occurred to me that the basic shape and setup of *Wild*—a troubled Romantic travels into the wilderness seeking not an escape from the world but a different way to engage with it—is part of a long-standing literary tradition. It's just that this redemptive journey was, until recently, an exclusively male and elitist endeavor. It occurred to me that my prediction about the anti-*Wild* backlash was out of step with twenty-first-century reality: America loves an underdog, and I doubt *Wild* would resonate with readers in quite the same way if it were about a male trust-funder slack-packing the trail with an entourage of mules and support vehicles. *Wild* is provocative in part because it rewrites and dramatically recasts a familiar template.

Back in the 1840s, the Reverend Joel Headley helped create a popular model for the find-yourself-while-camping-in-the-woods genre when he became well known for writing about an "attack on the brain" that drove him into the Adirondacks. Looking at the notoriety Headley's book received, I had to wonder: What about the women and *their* attacks of the brain? What did they do? At a time when *feminine* and *weak* were synonyms, and men considered themselves masters of the camp, how did these women cope with the double standard without going crazy? What, if any, tentative steps did they make to nudge America just a little bit closer toward *Wild*, toward the notion that women could be considered adventurers outdoors in their own right, strong and independent and not just the helpmates of male campers?

The more I snooped into that period, the more it became clear that women were not just sitting back in their parlors or sprawled (genteelly, of course) on their fainting couches and meekly accepting the idea that forests belonged to male explorers. I was surprised to find that many American women refused to stay home while the men went off and set up their "fixed camps" in the forest, cooked stews, erected wall tents, and jacklit deer. Women dragged themselves through canyons and explored slippery caverns with sputtering lanterns in their hands and flat-bottomed shoes on their feet.

There are photos of women staring down from the tops of remote mountains in the Cascades with footwear that would be hazardous anywhere, even on a city sidewalk. They have clunky walking sticks and rifles in their arms and smiles on their faces. One iconic photo from 1909 shows a group of adventurous women in full-length Victorian dresses and ridiculous cone-shaped hats standing on Pikes Peak and holding aloft a great big billowing sign reading VOTES FOR WOMEN. This photo op was staged years

This scary peak in western Washington would frighten away most campers,
but it could not stop this mid-nineteenth-century woman from scaling its
hazardous heights, while decked out in a smothering dress and insensible
shoes and risking accidental suicide by firearm.

before a woman's right to vote became the law of the land in the United
States. Camping and climbing women regarded the woods and the mountains as more than just recreational space. They were also places where
women could make a political statement, raising a feminist banner on top of
a giant phallic symbol. "The history of American women is about the fight for
freedom, but it's less a war against oppressive men than a struggle to straighten
out the perpetually mixed message about women's roles that was accepted by
almost everybody of both genders," wrote Gail Collins in her *America's
Women: 400 Years of Dolls, Drudges, Helpmates, and Heroines.* Such was the
case in the woods, where women learned to write their own rule book.

It took a long while for those women to make headway in the forest.
When recreational camping started in this country, it was like one big frat
house. Men flocked to the forest so they could spend time in the company
of other men. Proper ladies were told to stay at home. In the years after the
Civil War, affluent women had a certain amount of power and social status in luxurious resorts and upscale hotels, often to the resentment of their
husbands, but their status in the woods was lowly.

America's population was less than 40 million in 1870. By 1920 the number had climbed to 105 million, and most people were living in cities. As the feminist historian Nancy C. Unger points out in her book *Beyond Nature's Housekeepers: American Women in Environmental History*, only fourteen cities in 1870 had populations of 100,000 or more. In 1920 nearly seventy cities were that big or larger. In 1890 the superintendent of the U.S. Census declared the American frontier closed. Three years later, the historian Frederick Jackson Turner panicked men when he spoke about the loss of the frontier lifestyle, which Turner insisted gave Americans (read: white male Americans) their unique and rugged character, a certain coarseness and strength "combined with acuteness and acquisitiveness; that practical inventive turn of mind, quick to find expedients; that masterful grasp of material things . . . that restless, nervous energy; that dominant individualism."

Men, pining for that idealized version of pioneer times, full of male camaraderie and minus the untidy parts such as typhoid, disembowelments by grizzly bears, and cholera, felt diminished and rootless. Mentorships and apprenticeships were dying. Fewer men devoted their lives to craft traditions. It was possible to live out one's whole life without milking a cow or making something by hand or setting foot in the woods. Not as many livelihoods were considered earthy and manly anymore. This was a time when American men feared any potential challenge to their influence and control.

Where could they go where they could swear and smoke and behave as they believed real men should behave, far from the efforts of women to control and "civilize" them? These men set out to make the entire outdoors into their private cigar lounge. Even the names of landscape features reflected that masculine desire. Mountains in the Victorian era were considered manly and robust, while lakes were female and nurturing. Water bodies were passive, reflective, and empathetic. Landmark names, therefore, fell in line with this idea. Often, the few exceptions to the rule were sexualized in rude ways—for instance, Twin Teats, Nellie's Nipple, the Grand Tetons, and Squaw Nipple Peak. When someone dared name a peak in Inyo County Mount Alice, the name was quickly changed to something deemed much more appropriate for the times: Temple Crag.

Any sort of long walk was considered out of the question for respectable ladies. In those times, doctors commonly thought that exercise would sicken any female—a woman's doing the equivalent of the Pacific Crest Trail would have qualified as madness or a form of suicide—even while books and articles claimed that outdoor activities could cure middle- and upper-class men of neurasthenia. Certain medical experts thought that such strenuous, sweat-inducing activities actually worsened hysteria in women, making them "delicate and high-strung, subject to fits of anxiety or even hysteria that could erupt at any time," wrote Sheila M. Rothman in her book *Women's Proper Place: A History of Changing Ideals and Practices, 1870 to the Present.* "By virtue of their anatomy, all women were susceptible and therefore had to avoid anxiety-producing and enervating situations."

The prevailing women's fashions, which emphasized bulky and concealing garments, added yet another layer of physical confinement. Women were more likely to be harmed just by standing around wearing the standard-issue clothing of the day—crushingly tight whalebone corsets and thick, misery-inducing skirts—than by climbing a mountain in more sensible attire. Their clothes were so restrictive that the pioneering female doctors of the time started to notice the side effects of Victorian fashion, among them, corset-induced "displaced or prolapsed uterus, atrophy of abdominal muscles, damage to the liver, displacement of the stomach and intestines, and constriction of the chest and ribs."

Another strong disincentive to camping out was the fact that there was no such thing as a sanitary pad, Nancy C. Unger, a professor at Santa Clara University, told me when I called her up to discuss her book. "Most of the women out in the woods at that time were in their reproductive years," Unger told me. "No wonder so many of them did not want to go camping. I get so impatient with the idea that women were too fastidious to go out there. They had to deal not only with their periods, but with this uber emphasis on women's modesty, a pressure on them that men didn't have to face. The first disposable pad didn't come along until the 1920s. Instead, the women were forced to use rags, which were not designed for the contours of the female body. They move around. That's why lots of women often took to bed for a couple of days when they were having their periods. The rags were inconvenient, and they were not disposable. If women camped, they had to consider laundering their rags and wonder: Will there be water in the campsite? Will it be raining? Where will we dry them?"

Fortunately, the second half of the century brought new opportunities for women in the woods. A few strong-willed men stood up for their right to be in the forest at all, including, as we have seen, the first great camping popularizer, William "Adirondack" Murray. Even women's clothes became a touch less constraining. Out in the forest, starting in the late 1850s, a few daring women left their terrible corsets at home and donned ankle- or knee-length trousers called "bloomers," that mid-nineteenth-century innovation that is stifling to contemporary eyes but was much more comfortable and freeing than standard-issue dresses. Women were also more likely to stop by a sporting goods store and pick up an "outing skirt" that they could unbutton down the front if they got too hot. Naturally, some men were shocked and disgusted to see such things, but for some women that was the whole point. "We learned . . . to wear our short skirts and high hob-nailed boots . . . as though we had been born to the joy of them," wrote editor Harriet Monroe about a trip to California's Kern River in 1908. The scandal felt wonderful to her. People acted as if she were "a barbarian and a communist," she later boasted. Without those tight clothes pressing on their guts, women could even enjoy hearty flame-roasted food in the forest and stuff themselves for the first time.

Still, the clothing brought only a measure of freedom. If a woman camped in a party of men, she was supposed to fall uncomplainingly into the role of housewife, becoming camp cook as soon as the sun started sinking. Even if the women managed to have some burly adventures, they were expected to keep quiet about them. It was considered unseemly for ladies to talk about their feats of tramping and climbing. While Cheryl Strayed worried, many years later, that hiking "purists" (a predominantly male group) would feel she hadn't hiked "enough" of the enormous PCT, Victorian camping women were, if anything, discouraged from writing about their acts of bravado at all. The more miles they walked, the more mountains they bagged, the more they were told to understate their accomplishments.

Some were forced to sublimate their desires by living vicariously through men. We've all heard of John Muir, but it's a lesser-known fact that a strong-willed and super-smart woman named Jeanne Carr greatly influenced him. The wife of Ezra Carr, one of Muir's professors at the University of Wisconsin, not only curated Muir's reading list but also encouraged and helped shape his writing voice. She gave a sterling recommendation of Muir to Ralph Waldo Emerson, who ended up hanging out with Muir for a short while in Yosemite in 1871. Muir was her pet project, and she was Muir's perfect audience long before he had a mass readership. He was always trying out ideas on her, and reporting back from campouts and explorations. Without Carr's guiding hand, perhaps Muir would have lived all his days as an eccentric hermit in Yosemite instead of moving out of the valley later in the 1870s and changing the world. "As a feminist, [Carr] disliked many of the duties exacted from a housewife in High Victorian America," wrote Stephen Fox in his book *The American Conservation Movement: John Muir and His Legacy.* "She hated fashion and housework . . . she felt her life ebbing out in little dribs and drabs . . . She envied [Muir's] freedom . . . 'Write as often as you can,'" she told him. "'Your letters keep up my faith that I shall lead just such a life myself sometime.'"

But there was a surprising upside to being a wild lady of the nineteenth and early twentieth centuries. Some women used male stereotypes of their behavior and interests to their advantage. "Botanizing" was considered an admirable pastime for women, so it gave women license to go sauntering into the woods and mountains. Bringing along a plant press was a kind of passport for them to go wherever in the wilderness they pleased. If a man came along and asked what on earth they were doing so far afield, these respectable ladies could whip out some of their dried rhododendrons and tell the man, in all seriousness, that they were advancing the causes of science and ecology. Since women were considered more virtuous and in tune with "Mother Nature" than men, they were among America's first credible preservationists.

This association between women and preservation had its inevitable downside. Men who opposed wilderness could always twist around the image of female weakness and use it against any enemy who stood up to them. During the buildup to John Muir's humiliating defeat at Hetch Hetchy Valley (the pristine area of Yosemite National Park that he attempted to save from a campaign to impound the Tuolumne River and create a new reservoir to serve San Francisco), development interests slandered him as "impotent and feminine." In a political cartoon that appeared in the December 13, 1909, issue of the San Francisco *Call*, the great preservationist is shown in dowdy drag, desperately trying to sweep away the floodwaters of Hetch Hetchy with a dust broom.

There was only one way for adventurous women to deal with this strong link between womanhood and weakness. They had to ignore it. In the late nineteenth century, it became more common for all-female camping parties to head into the woods for fun. Starting in the 1880s, a boisterous group of "artistic, Avant garde" well-off female campers called the Merry Tramps of Oakland headed for the coasts and forests together in Calistoga,

Sweeping Back the Flood

The San Francisco *Call* used this image to embarrass
John Muir for his campaign to save Hetch Hetchy.

Sonoma County, and the San Gabriel Mountains of California. They were
not exactly steely-eyed survivalists dragging themselves up Mount Hood.
If anything, they qualified as America's original-issue glamour campers,
heading toward the forests in beautifully appointed Pullman cars with
enormous suitcases, fine liquors, and comfortable bedding. This gleeful
group posed for photos while holding hands, making a daisy chain around
a giant Pacific Coast redwood. They slept on fine feather beds hauled into
huge wall tents, with stacks of rifles piled in front of their vestibules. They
hired small armies of Chinese cooks to prepare their breakfasts, lunches,
and dinners. Yet even this escape to the woods could not let them flee all
domestic responsibilities; there are photos of Merry Tramps wearing all
their finery while stooped over a sinkful of dishes, soap bubbles floating as
the women scrub and clean.

The Merry Tramps had safety in numbers—in certain photos, there
are so many of them that not all of the campers can squish into the

camera's view—but other women preferred to travel in pairs or face the woods alone.

More than a century before Cheryl Strayed wrote about her encounters with strangers along the Pacific Crest Trail, including a run-in with a sexually menacing and boorish hunter, newspapers all across America wrote about the incredible camping and long-distance hiking exploits of thirty-six-year-old Norwegian immigrant Helga Estby, who lit out on May 5, 1896, from Spokane, Washington, on a walking journey across America, leaving her husband, Ole, and eight of her children behind on the farm. She and her eighteen-year-old daughter, Clara, both wearing heavy skirts, planned to walk thirty-five hundred miles to New York City on the promise of a cash reward; anonymous sponsors had put up ten thousand dollars and said the money was theirs to claim if they made it to Manhattan within seven months of their departure. Apparently their shadowy benefactors had something to do with the fashion industry, and were hoping Estby and her daughter would "prove the physical endurance of women, at a time when many still considered it fashionable to be dependent and weak," wrote Estby's biographer, Linda Lawrence Hunt. In an early instance of product placement, the sponsor also forced Helga Estby to wear a certain "bicycle skirt" for part of the walk.

Estby knew the risks on the road and in the forests. She was packing a Smith and Wesson revolver, some pepper spray, a lantern, a compass, and a map. Young Clara brought along her curling iron. The circumstances of Clara's birth are still mysterious; Helga Estby became pregnant when she was only fifteen, which has led to speculation that she was raped while working as a housemaid. Helga and Clara Estby took lodging when they could, but they did a lot of camping on their transcontinental journey. This was not a vacation for them. The Estbys were lagging on their mortgage payments, and Helga Estby was trying to save the family farm, which had been threatened with foreclosure. When a newspaper reporter cornered Estby and asked why she kept walking on, "Well, to make money" was her pragmatic response.

Trying to avoid getting lost, they followed the railroad tracks on their journey to the east. They faced danger at every turn, but these were no women to mess with. A menacing vagrant shadowed them through the mountains near La Grande, Oregon, until Helga Estby finally pulled out her Smith and Wesson and blasted a hole through his leg.

The journey was an adrenaline rush for the mother-daughter team, especially when the two ended up staggering through the jagged lava beds and scrubland of southern Idaho. They slept out in the Red Desert of Wyoming, which was swarming with antelope and grizzlies.

They thrilled to the sounds of the night wind and narrowly escaped a gray mountain lion "as big as a man" that followed them for twelve miles. "Being acquainted with the animal's traits, we knew they never attacked from behind and never except by running and springing upon a victim," explained Helga Estby to a reporter. But the biggest danger was a robber near Denver, Colorado, who tried to attack the women, only to get a face full of pepper spray so painful that he fell to the ground and tumbled down a slope. "I knocked him down," Helga Estby bragged later on. A gang of would-be assailants from Chicago had to beg for clemency when the women attacked them with bug powder. The mother-and-daughter team pressed on with their walk, and refused to give up, but a rude surprise awaited them at the finish line.

At the end of *Wild*, Cheryl Strayed meets the love of her life. Trail's end

Helga Estby and her teenage daughter Clara packing heat,
holding a dagger, and getting wild in 1896.

was different for Estby. The sponsor cheated her and Clara out of the promised cash award on the flimsy grounds that they missed their arrival deadline in New York City by eighteen days, in part because Clara had fallen and hurt herself in Colorado. The two apparently had to beg for funds from a sympathetic railroad magnate just to get back home, and by the time they did two of Estby's children had died of diphtheria.

Estby won no points for heroism, only public shaming and sour faces. She received no meaningful posthumous recognition until history buffs rediscovered her in the early 2000s. Linda Lawrence Hunt blames Estby's long-standing obscurity on neglect, willful or otherwise. "She broke the central code of her culture, in this case that 'mothers belong in the home,'" Hunt writes, speculating about the reason that Estby's story remained untold, even within her own family, for seventy years. Or Perhaps Estby was compelled to silence herself because her trip was controversial and she did not wish to create more family strife.

Whatever the circumstances, Estby, unlike Strayed, did not have a chance to tell her story in detail—her letters and unpublished manuscript are now lost. Fortunately, some other camping women have left vivid recollections of their journeys into the unknown. One of the best is Kathryn Hulme's wonderfully written 1928 outdoor memoir, *How's the Road?*, which reflects on the newfound freedom women found in the outdoors because of the invention and mass popularity of the automobile. Suddenly women did not necessarily have to tag along on a macho campout in the high peaks of the White Mountains or the Adirondacks to get their taste of the wild (and scrub someone else's dishes). Now their wheezing metal contraptions could get them to the edge of the wilderness unaccompanied or with other women.

In the summer of 1923, Hulme and her friend Tuny set out on a 5,444-mile cross-country auto-camping journey from New York City to San Francisco. Along the way, the America they saw seemed foreign and wild; the Wisconsin dells were a lingering frontier. "[P]oising on top of a hill, the head-lights focused on the brow of the next hill, [and] leaving the dell through which we were to plunge, a mystery of black nothingness," Hulme writes. Deep in the Badlands of South Dakota, she and Tuny piloted a roadster named Reggie into a river but seriously misjudged the water's depth and power. Rolling through strong currents in the deepening waters, the tires lost contact with the river bottom. Reggie began to float. "Liquid mud flew as high as the windshield," Hulme wrote. "Reggie was swimming. Reggie was chocolate-covered from top to bottom. I had received a mouthful of gumbo [mud] when I shouted in midstream. Our license plates were obliterated."

The territory of men was just as hazardous as any mud wallow or river bottom. Hulme and Tuny slept on prairies, in Canadian forests, and on mountain meadows in Yellowstone and Glacier National Parks, resilient in the face of bad weather, busybodies, and unbelievers. People in towns found it odd that two women would dare to auto-camp without men. Hulme mentioned the "kind, motherly" henlike women who accosted them in small towns and directed them, endlessly, to the nearest YWCA. When Hulme and Tuny got a flat in a small and isolated town, they had just barely started to fix it when four boys showed up out of nowhere and elbowed them aside without asking permission. "Tuny and I stood around looking helpless and grateful," Hulme recalled. "It always pained us . . . Tuny and I were both good mechanics, capable of making any repair on the car."

Granted, Hulme wasn't backcountry hiking like Strayed, but one could argue that her auto-camping journey was a small step in the direction of a twenty-first-century woman's solo hike. The author reveled in the freedom of the outdoors. Like Thelma and Louise in the successful 1991 eponymous film, Hulme and Tuny were bold, independent, on the lam from boredom, and fated to run into many of the same problems that bedeviled the characters played by Susan Sarandon and Geena Davis: the endless come-ons of confidence men (most of them not as good-looking as Brad Pitt), sexual menace, and constant unwanted offers of help. "We had many experiences with the 'assisting' man camper who thinks that when a woman gets anything more complicated than an egg-beater in her hand, she is to be watched carefully," Hulme said more than ninety years before Rebecca Solnit published her nonfiction book *Men Explain Things to Me*.

One night, Hulme and Tuny camped out on an open prairie where two cowboys drove up and teased them about the tiny pistol they'd brought to protect themselves against varmints and assailants. One of the cowboys pulled out a revolver "fully fourteen inches long" just to mock them. The men finally left. "We climbed into our sleeping bags early and lay listening to all the twilight noises of the prairie," Hulme remembered. "The stars were suspended. I had never realized there were so many. They seemed frighteningly close overhead." Coyotes howled. "Would they ever come near us?" Tuny asked from her sleeping bag. "Never . . . they are cowards!' the author reassured her. She was talking about varmints. She might as well have been talking about cowboys. Hulme undercut that first scary encounter by mentioning that the cowboys drove up, while they were sleeping, and left them "a jar of cream and six eggs," but the message is clear: in spite of that final gift of food, those cowboys went out of their way to let the women know they were encroaching on the territory of men.

Hulme's book contains moments of fear, sexual peril (and titillation), and camaraderie that reminded me time and again of *Wild*. What puzzles me is the fact that Hulme, who went on to become a best-selling author in 1956 with her novel *The Nun's Story*, either could not succeed in having the camping memoir published or didn't even try. It was privately printed. Looking back from a twenty-first-century perspective, and with our libraries crammed with excellent outdoor memoirs written by women (Sara Wheeler, Terry Tempest Williams, Kira Salak, among many others), I find her reticence (or bad luck) unfortunate. Her book has a mischievous, revelatory quality that Hulme might have suppressed had she known the book would be available to the public. Or perhaps that provocative aspect stopped it from being published in the first place.

Aside from invading the territory of men, a few brave women authors even tried to muscle in on the male-dominated woodcraft tradition. When Kathrene G. Pinkerton published *Woodcraft for Women* in 1924, she was hoping to teach women the art of thriving in the forest. While some of the book has a compromised quality, with advice about bolstering male spirits with a bracing pot of tea, the book challenged women to experience the same joy and release that their husbands took for granted in camp.

"When a passion for hunting and uninhabited regions led Daniel Boone from his Yadkin farm to his adventurous life as hunter and trapper, he did not take his wife with him," she noted. "Somehow, out of neglect, arose the impression that woods joys were for men alone. Gradually a few women discovered that the lazy drifting down a pine and rock-bound stream calms feminine as well as masculine nerves." Pinkerton aimed to correct the problem of "isolated" female camping enthusiasts being forced to camp out as "passive observers" while the men had all the fun, and to stop men from squashing the spirit of joyful exploration in women. In a crafty and careful way, Pinkerton dared the women of America to follow their adventurous impulses by learning "the joy of maps," overcoming the terror of being lost, and using the woods as an "enchanted playground."

Another grand instigator was Grace Gallatin Seton-Thompson

(1872–1959), wife of woodcraft genius Ernest Thompson Seton. She was every bit as wilderness-loving as her husband. Even more important, she drew links between women in the wilderness and their self-worth. Her self-effacingly titled *A Woman Tenderfoot in the Rockies*, published in 1900, was disguised as a memoir, but it is nothing less than a call for female independence in the wild. Seton-Thompson wanted women to know "the charm of the glorious freedom, the quick rushing blood, the bounding motion, the joy of the living and of the doing."

She chastised any woman who would miss out on a deluxe camping holiday on horseback because of vanity: "Is it really so that most women say no to camp life because they are afraid of being uncomfortable and looking unbeautiful? There is no reason why a woman should make a freak of herself even if she is going to rough it; as a matter of fact I do not rough it, I go for enjoyment and leave out all possible discomforts."

Seton-Thompson promised nothing less than a grand transformation of any woman who ventured into the forest. "Now this is the end," she writes, marveling at her own change from a coddled socialite to a survivalist. "It is three years since I first became a woman-who-goes-hunting-with-her-husband. I have lived on jerked deer and alkali water . . . nesting among vast pines where none but the four-footed had been before. I have been sung asleep a hundred times by the coyote's evening lullaby. I have driven a four-in-hand over corduroy roads and ridden horseback over the pathless vast wilds of the continent's backbone." Aside from preaching camping, she told women exactly what to bring, from eiderdown sleeping bags to enamel casserole dishes, and how to "keep your nerve" if they get lost.

Seton-Thompson's marriage to her famous husband ended badly, with cross-accusations of cheating, and Ernest Seton taking up with his much-younger secretary. The two split up for good in 1935.

But Seton-Thompson stayed active in the women's rights movement all her life, and she was unstinting in her support for women's suffrage. "Wealth allowed her to choose her own way," wrote the author Dorcas Miller in a remembrance of Seton-Thompson. "She was not financially dependent on her husband; to the contrary, in the early years of their marriage, he was dependent on her."

Women have gone from a barely noticeable presence in camping to comprising nearly half the campers out in the forests today, according to the latest statistics from the Outdoor Foundation, the nonprofit group that represents the outdoor gear industry. Savvy outdoor gear companies are marketing brands exclusively to women. All-women campouts, from Yosemite to Alaska, have become a burgeoning presence. Meanwhile, Camp-Out, a members-only private camp reserved exclusively for women, has gained a following in Henrico, Virginia. The all-women proviso is so strictly enforced that the website contains an advisory warning that "There may be men on the land to clean the porta-potties. This usually is in the mornings."

Perhaps these are signs that Victorian mores and standards have been upended. It's also possible that these trips are a form of rebellion against gender-based modes of interpreting wilderness. Women may be reacting to a state of affairs described by experiential educator Karen Warren, who claims, "Social conditioning inundates a woman with the insistent message that the woods is no place for her."

Those messages are hard to resist even now. Nancy C. Unger, the feminist scholar whose research inspired this chapter, admitted to me that she sometimes falls back, almost unthinkingly, on traditional roles when camping out, and recalls vividly how much her mom hated camping with her family because she ended up doing all the same chores she did at home, but in a wilderness setting, while the rest of the family tramped off to the waterfall.

If those attitudes are still with us today, then so is the spirit of these long-gone wild Victorian ladies. In spite of all the discouragement and double standards, and without the promise of an audience or the assurance that their words would make their way in the world, these women still took it upon themselves to climb mountains, hike on their own, and camp with other women.

In doing so, they claimed a piece of the wild for themselves.

All these years later, women have a large presence in America's forests. Yet, in other ways, the American wild—and, in particular, our national parks—still put up invisible barriers for certain user groups who don't always feel welcome there, or who have come to believe that these places are not safe or inviting for them.

One winter, I set out to talk to a group of adventurous youth, and some hardworking outdoor activists who are doing their utmost to change the woefully lopsided demographics of recreational camping.

7

Gator Girls

We descend from people who had that connection—that visceral, emotional, physical, spiritual connection to the earth.
—Shelton Johnson, author, hiker,
African American ranger at Yosemite National Park

I was getting ready to board a minivan bound for the Everglades when I saw a teenage girl with long black hair standing under a light pole with a lizard on her head. She had no idea the lizard was there. The girl had an ingratiating awkwardness. She was holding a fuzzy yellow backpack shaped like the Pikachu rodent from the Pokémon franchise. She blinked through black-rimmed spectacles and talked with friends at a rate of roughly 347 words a minute, in well-developed paragraphs no less. *Voilà*, I thought. *A confidante!*

I was in Miami because I wanted to camp in a national park with one of the least represented groups in American camping today: African American and Hispanic youth from the urban core. The girls, aged thirteen to nineteen years old, looked pent up and jittery on that muggy winter night. The temperature was eighty-two degrees. Their open-toed shoes sparkled. One wore a hoodie. Another wore a T-shirt with twinkling stars and smiling birds. This was new for me. Most people I see in camp look like the folks you would meet at a Shriners' convention or a Phish concert.

I had no specific agenda for this campout; nor did I plan to draw sweeping conclusions from my experience, or suggest that these campers represented their respective ethnic groups. I just wanted to let the journey unfold, see what happened, and (with the advance consent of the campers, whom I'd met several days before at an orientation meeting in their Miami high school) get their feelings about this trip as it took place. What did it mean for them to be in a wild place? Did it feel like an escape? Was it fun? Enlightening? Mind-expanding? A form of torture?

Demographic boredom had brought me there. I had hiked the Pacific Crest Trail in 1993 and 1994 and seen no people of color on the footpath. The participation gap complicates my ideals about what recreational camping is supposed to be, why it exists, and whom it's for. In 1869, William "Adirondack" Murray tried to democratize sleeping under the stars for pleasure and wanted to broaden its appeal. He stood up to the small group of elitist hunters who dominated the North Woods, and he was ridiculed and marginalized for his efforts. The homogeneity of too many twenty-first-century campgrounds made me wonder how much progress we've made since the day of Murray's Fools.

Also, as a person who loves camping, I can't help but view the ethnicity gap as a threat to the outdoors. In a 2012 study in the *Annals of the Association of American Geographers* (AAG), Joe Weber and Selima Sultana warn that the demographics of national park visitation, not just in terms of camping but even the act of driving up to the park, snapping a few photos, and going home, could become an existential issue for government-protected wild places. National parks had nearly 293 million visitors in 2014, an all-time record high. Yet if we were to measure these annual figures on a per capita basis, looking at park visits as a share of the rapidly growing U.S. population, national park visitation is roughly 20 percent lower than it was in 1987, according to a Property and Environment Research Center report. Those numbers could (and should) be a lot higher.

"If [non-Caucasian] visits to the national park system continue to be low, then future visitors, funding, and overall support for the parks could . . . decrease and hence the survival of 'America's best idea' becomes critical," the AAG report reads. Here, I'm using the term *non-Caucasian* instead of *minority* because, perhaps as soon as 2044, the white population in the United States will become the minority, according to the U.S. Census Bureau.

The numbers speak for themselves. As of this writing, more than 80 percent of U.S. campers are white, 8 percent are Hispanic, 6 percent are Asian/Pacific Islander, and 4 percent are black, according to the Outdoor

Foundation, America's leading outdoor recreation lobby. In America's national parks, four out of five visitors are white. Meanwhile, the website Stuff White People Like lists camping as the 128th whitest activity in America, right behind riding Vespas and reading Maurice Sendak's *Where the Wild Things Are* to our children.

While trying to suss out *why* certain individuals within certain ethnic groups avoid camping, I must, of course, allow for tremendous differences of opinion within any given ethnic group. There is also room for my own hypocrisy. I can think, for example, of many white people I've met who despise the very idea of camping, in particular my mother-in-law, and of the storytelling and typecasting that can go on within any ethnic group. For example, a writing teacher of mine who, like me, happens to be Jewish used to tease me about my love for the outdoors. She told me that camping and long-distance hiking were "Christian pleasures." I've met several Jewish people who have told me that Jews "don't camp." Perhaps they are responding to the stereotype that Jews are urbanites and that wilderness is foreign to us—a notion that has nothing to do with my day-to-day reality and fails to take into consideration the religious summer camps that play a strong role in Jewish cultural identity.

Having said this, I, nevertheless, wish to call attention to certain concerns that pop up again and again in blogs and articles by African Americans, Hispanics, and members of other groups, exploring the reasons for the outdoor diversity gap. Some writers have grappled with a fearful cultural memory of the outdoors that contributes to the perception that camping is unsafe. In an online column, "Camping While Black," journalist Deb Pleasants, who is African American, wrote about her father cautioning her that "blacks don't camp." She thought his fears were unwarranted and a bit silly, until she camped with her family in Minnesota and saw a neighboring camper display a large Confederate flag. Other writers have voiced their concerns about traveling to the campground: just getting to a scenic spot might require a drive through isolated rural towns where white xenophobes and rednecks may dwell. Writers have also mentioned the persistent worry that campgrounds will not accommodate their needs, and the idea that camping is regressive, a step backward toward the rural lives of poverty left behind long ago.

I've also heard complaints about media-perpetuated myths that black people and Latinos, for example, do not engage with the outdoors at all—myths that somehow discount as natural activities picnics, fishing trips, day hikes, trips to urban "green spaces" including city parks, and other outdoor experiences closer to home. Others grumble about the portrayal of blacks and Hispanics in the outdoors on TV and in movies. "The only time you see African Americans in the woods in the movies, sorry to say, is, number one, we're being killed first [in a horror movie] or it's slavery time," the African American writer and outdoor recreation enthusiast Eliss Cucchiara told me during a phone conversation. "This feeds the notion of 'this is why black people should not go into the woods, because they will be killed or eaten.'" It's easy to corroborate Cucchiara's views. Consider the 1997 action movie *The Edge*, in which Alec Baldwin, Anthony Hopkins, and the Africa American actor Harold Perrineau play characters who match wits with a man-eating grizzly in the Alaskan wild. Guess which one gets ripped apart and devoured?

Activists and recreational enthusiasts have made inroads since I pitched my first tent long ago. You will now find Asian American camping Meetup groups, and African American and Hispanic outreach groups, not to mention environmental organizations that sponsor city children from various backgrounds and ethnicities who wish to go on camping expeditions. The National Park Service, which is 80 percent white, has responded to concerns about the participation gap with cultural literacy and sensitivity programs, and has promoted park sites dedicated to African American history and culture. Outdoor Afro, a nationwide network of African American outdoors enthusiasts and advocates, has teamed with NPS staff to institute an "African Americans in the National Parks Day." Still, there is much work yet to be done. In 1924 the NPS's founding director, Stephen Mather, envisioned the great outdoors as a melting pot. It's more like a fondue pot full of white cheese.

I was eager to explore this situation in some modest way, but now that I had flown all the way out there from San Jose, California, and embedded myself with this group of young campers, a morbid self-consciousness overcame me. I didn't know what to say to these kids. The barrier, I now suspect, had more to do with age difference than ethnic background or even socioeconomics. They were teenagers, and I've always been old. All the elements that make up the life of your average teen, from rebellion to slang to trendy music, baffled me when I was a teen myself. The alienation has increased with time. Aside from all this, I was surprised and dismayed to learn, upon my arrival, that the campers would all be girls.

I'd assumed, without asking anybody, that the camping trip would be coed. As it turns out, the Miami chapter of Inspiring Connections Outdoors (ICO), the group that organized the Everglades excursion, conducts campouts restricted to one gender because the volunteers believe that girls and boys behave differently in mixed groups and can have a more enjoyable and less self-conscious and more trouble-free experience in all-girl, all-boy camping situations. It comforted me to know that I would, at least, never be on my own with the girls—which would look mighty sketchy, I feared—because there would be two adult female volunteers from ICO and an adult female staff worker from Urgent, Inc., the nonprofit organization that works with the girls in Miami.

The three of them would be on hand at all times, organizing excursions and supervising every activity. Still, it felt a little odd to be the much-older white guy hanging out with his reporter's notebook and pen and recorder while trying, somehow, to "blend in." Out in that Miami parking lot, I fought an urge to flee.

Then I saw the lizard on the girl's head, and I thought, *Hooray. Potential icebreaker.*

The lizard peeked from the curtains of her hair, pulled back inside, and showed up moments later on a different part of her skull. I thought, *This is going to be very bad. This girl is from a paved environment, which means that she is, most likely, alienated from the natural world. She'll run her fingers through her hair, discover the lizard, and scream. Maybe it will bite her for good measure.* I had no choice but to walk over there and save her.

I'd met this seventeen-year-old girl, whose name was Meena,* only briefly at the camping orientation meeting held at a local high school a few days before the trip. Now I walked on over. "Don't be scared," I told her. "But there's a big fat lizard in your hair."

"Could you get him out?" Meena said. "Yes, please get him out. I would like to see him."

I reached into her hair.

"Hold still," I said.

"There's a lizard on my head," she said. "And I'm so glad to hear it. I'm actually really calm right now because I used to catch lizards when I was little. My family used to live in Ocala, which is a very rural community, before we moved to Miami. I used to have geckos big and small climbing

---

* The names and identifying characteristics of minors appearing in this chapter have been changed.

all over me. I attract them, I guess, especially the baby ones, and there used to be these little animals that ate baby geckos. My friends and I used to chase away all the birds so the lizard eggs could hatch in peace . . ."

"Just hold still, please."

". . . and that's why I don't get squeamish. I'm used to it by now, swimming with fishes, catching creatures. A snake, for example, is nothing I'm scared of. We owned an acre. All you saw was trees. You would have to walk out to the road just to see civilization. I have seen deer, possums, bats. A big spider hung outside my window for the longest time. It never left, and it had blue and black dots on its back and eight long legs that were black and yellow, and it had very big fangs. First time I saw him, I opened my window and freaked out because he was inside, so I ran away, but after a while you get the courage. I walked up to the spider. I said, 'Hello there. You again. Keep doing what you're doing. Good job.'"

Meena's mother is a tax preparer from the Dominican Republic. Her father is a computer repairman from Puerto Rico. I found it striking that a girl so full of speech could have parents with such quiet occupations. I untangled the lizard from Meena's hair and showed it to her. "Aw," she said. The lizard crawled on her hand. "That is just such a nice-looking lizard," she said. "A really cute one. We should release him in the high grass somewhere where he'll have a higher chance of survival."

She crouched in the grass and put the lizard down. "I am so glad you noticed it," she said. "Or else we would have had a little friend with us in the minivan."

"Yeah," I told her. "And maybe it would have gotten squashed in there."

"Oh no," Meena said, wincing. "No. Not squashed! I don't even want to think about that."

It was my first faux pas, and the trip hadn't started yet. I took an involuntary gulp of air, as if trying to suck the offending statement into my mouth. Meena turned around and began talking with someone else. *Oh great*, I thought. I'd found and lost my one camping trip comrade. As a former teenager, I remember the adolescent tendency to cut conversations off without warning or explanation, but I also remember the painful sensitivity, the miscues and overreactions. There was always some chance I'd antagonized her with my heedless comment about the crushed lizard.

Two minivans were going to the Everglades, and Meena, to my disappointment, was about to board the one I wouldn't be traveling in. I had done this to myself. How do you gain and lose an acquaintanceship in four and a half minutes? This was like middle school all over again. Then something occurred to me: if I felt out of place among the teenagers, I could only imagine how some of these kids would feel when we hit the Everglades. The park encroaches on Miami-Dade County, which has 2.6 million people, roughly one out of five of them African Americans, and three out of five of them Latinos. In spite of those numbers, 98 percent of Everglades visitors in the winter and spring tourist seasons (when the temperatures and bugs are not ferocious) are white, according to the 2008 edition of the Everglades National Park Visitor Study. I'd taken a straw poll at the campout orientation meeting several days before and found that most of the girls had never camped in a national park or even set foot inside one, two had never camped anywhere, and several of the returning campers had camped only at Virginia Key Beach, an African American heritage site five miles from Miami.

Out of the darkness walked Chelsea, one of the girls who'd never camped anywhere. She'd never tasted s'mores.

Tall and long-armed, Chelsea had high cheekbones and wore her hair in intricate plaits. Her mom and dad did not want her on that trip. Chelsea had a sweet and guileless expression, and though she was feeling nervous, she found her parents' disapproval amusing. "My father is an orderly at a hospital," she'd told me. "He *is* orderly, you know what I mean?" She burst out laughing, her hair flying every which way. "He just doesn't get that I would want to do this. He told me, 'Black people don't camp.' But camping is like sports. You see some white basketball players, don't you? It's not all black. You'll see some Chinese basketball players. No one in my family has ever gone camping. When my dad found out, he was like, 'No, no, no, no, no, no, no, no, why are you going? You can go in the backyard or watch the Nature Channel.' I guess he thinks it's dangerous because it *is* the Everglades, and the Everglades has crocodiles and poisonous snakes and spiders."

She was right about that. I'd glanced at our Everglades itinerary and was surprised to see that it included a three-hour wilderness canoe trip on Nine Mile Pond, which has a robust alligator population, especially in winter. "Look for floating logs with eyes," an online travel brochure advised. The brochure failed to mention that the pond was also home to a monster crocodile named Croczilla, who'd been spotted several times that year, stretched out on the shore of the pond. One eyewitness claimed that the creature was twenty feet long.

Chelsea told me she was scared to see the Everglades, but only a little bit. Mostly she couldn't wait to get there. The swamps would be a welcome distraction, she told me. "There is peace on my street in Miami. Quiet. Calm. No trouble. Go farther from my street, and it just gets crazy. The ghetto is close to my neighborhood. The people there could do way better for themselves. They settle for what they have. It's like they don't want to improve their circumstances."

Now Chelsea wanted to see some stars and have a chance to reflect on her life so far. "In the city, you don't get to think. You just do."

Chelsea was not assigned to my minivan. Instead, I had to ride with three girls I didn't know, including Jaliyah, who stood near the vans and fiddled with her orange hoop earrings. She had a sleeveless green shirt, pink sandals, an imperious expression on her face, and spray-treated red-and-orange-tinted hair that defied gravity. Some of the other campers had a year or two on her, but Jaliyah's stronger build and broad shoulders made her look older. She was always whispering things to friends, and they would double up laughing. A girl named Crystal rarely left her side. She was like some kind of teenage aide-de-camp to Jaliyah. They'd chitchat for a while, fall into companionable silences, and communicate with looks and gestures.

I'd talked with Jaliyah momentarily at orientation. She'd told me that her mother was a nurse and her father was a caregiver in a residential facility. Neither one of them wanted her to go to the Everglades. "Oh, they don't like it at all. They think a bear's gonna come after me." She rolled her eyes. "I told them they're not gonna *try* to put us in any danger." Jaliyah had never camped before, but unlike Chelsea she showed no sign of nervousness and no trace of visible excitement. She had a real edge to her. I'd have to impress her as soon as I could, because she was the key to my fitting in with the other kids. They deferred to her. Perhaps if I won over Jaliyah, the others would fall in line and accept me, too, and I'd find some comfortable place within the clique. It was a question of choosing the right moment to make a positive impression.

By 8:00 p.m. we were out on the highway in a silver Toyota Sienna LE with WOMEN FOR OBAMA and DOGS AGAINST ROMNEY stickers on the rear bumper. We were stopping and starting in traffic and pulling a U-Haul full of rotisserie chicken; fried chicken; turkey pastrami; taco fixings, including ground turkey for the filling; sausage links; sugar cookies; red and green grapes; pickles; a tub of hummus; a two-pound chocolate crème cake; several banana bunches; and a large container of Chips Ahoy! Candy Blasts cookies—among many other foodstuffs. In other words, this was not going to be a survival hike with backpacks, sucrose tablets, and Nature Valley granola bars. Hip-hop thumped at medium volume. The driver, Karen Kerr, the trip leader, who is white, wanted the kids to feel comfortable, so she'd let them choose the station. The unanimous choice was WEDR-FM, 99 JAMZ. An ambient rap song—I found out, after the fact, that it was "Stoner," by Young Thug—thrummed in the sound system. Jaliyah seemed to have memorized not just the words to every song but the phrasing, the sound effects, the beats, everything. She and Crystal sat in back with Ariane, who was easygoing and, from what I'd observed, everyone's favorite. She spoke with a French accent. Ariane had immigrated to the United States from Brittany seven years before. Her dad is American Indian, her mom is of African ancestry, and her parents met in France, which makes Ariane an Afro-Franco Native American. Much of the girls' mumbling was incomprehensible—they were talking teenager—but sometimes I could make out a phrase or two: "Oh yes, I do know that boy. He is a dog. I don't even like him that much, but he will definitely look at your booty."

It just felt voyeuristic and wrong to be sitting there in the front seat taking in all this gossip and chitchat and contributing nothing. My initial plan to travel as a detached observer while watching these kids make their way in the wild was starting to feel off-kilter to me now, and a little hinky. It felt as if I were trying to squash each girl onto a glass slide and put her under a microscope. I didn't want that anymore. Now I wanted to fit in, interact, inspire, and become just another one of the girls.

But I didn't know how to start. At least I had an easy rapport with Karen, who was ruddy and athletic, with blondish-gray hair and a gentle voice; she looked quite a bit younger than sixty-seven. Karen had let me stay in her air-conditioned trailer near her house in South Miami for several days while she was getting ready for the trip. She lives with her thirty-year-old son, one of her five children—three of them "bios," as she calls them, and two adopted black children: a daughter, who lives in Ireland now, and a son, who died of complications related to AIDS in 2011. He was difficult, and his life was a struggle even in infancy; Karen told me he had methadone and heroin in his bloodstream at the time he was born, and also became addicted to chemicals the doctors pumped into him to wean him off those drugs. He was a talented dancer, but a severe learning disability made it hard for him to read.

Back in Miami, Karen had told me of that son's itinerant lifestyle, his promiscuity, her constant struggles to get through to him, and her caring for him at home before he passed away. "You know, I always thought if we could do just one more thing, we could have saved him." The loss stays with her all the time. "The way I see it, [my adopted children] were with me for a limited time," she said. "And I did all I could for them." She feels the same way when she's working with other people's children. "I know there is a difference between my kids and other people's kids, but when I work with a kid or I'm teaching a kid or I'm taking care of a kid, he's my child."

Karen chairs the Miami chapter of ICO, a Sierra Club affiliate that takes more than fourteen thousand youth from fifty-three cities across the United States on nature outings ranging from trail restoration projects to whitewater rafting trips. The participating youth are mostly low income. (ICO used to stand for Inner City Outings, but a number of chairpeople, including Karen, felt the term *inner city* was pejorative, stigmatizing the campers.)

Each ICO chapter raises money to cover excursion costs for the youth. This particular trip would cost the Miami chapter six hundred dollars. ICO targets youth who would not, for economic or other reasons, go on outdoor excursions. Karen retired in 2009 after selling off her day care center in Kendall, Florida. Now she can devote her full attention to running these camping trips, writing grant applications, and seeking donations from foundations and from businesses that sell sports equipment. The Sierra Club must approve all donor stores and companies. "We wouldn't go to Shell Oil for funds," Karen told me. She always teams with a non-profit partner organization that works with youths. The girls on this particular trip are all part of an urban youth empowerment program called Rites of Passage, which uses camping (along with arts, culture, and media) to build character and smooth the girls' path to adulthood. Their mentor in that program is an African American woman.

Karen's young charges are often confused when she tells them she isn't paid to supervise these camping trips. Some of them think she must be kooky to accept such an arrangement. But she loves these trips, and believes she is sharing something irresistible with people who cannot afford camping trips in the wild. "Have you ever gone to a restaurant and had something that tasted just exquisite?" she'd told me. "And you say to yourself, 'If only other people would try it, they would love it, too?'"

Now, as we drove past strip malls, bodegas, Creole bakeries, grocery stores, and welfare check–cashing operations, I wondered if Karen's role as an authority figure complicated her ability to relate to the campers. Just as I was ruminating about this, Jaliyah, in the backseat, put Karen to the test. Within the first half hour of our journey to the Everglades, she had flouted, forgotten, or misunderstood the electronics ban. The kids were not supposed to use their cell phones. If there were emergencies, Karen could call parents on her own cell phone, and all the parents had Karen's personal number. In spite of this edict, Jaliyah was murmuring into her phone. I recognized her voice immediately.

"Okay, who is talking on her cell phone?" Karen asked. Jaliyah kept right on whispering in an animated way. "Dan," Karen said. "Do me a favor. Look back there and see who's talking on a cell phone."

I was torn. I wanted to help Karen, but I didn't want to alienate the teenage leader of the pack so early on in the trip; nor did I want to come across as a big fat snitch. After I looked back and saw Jaliyah yakking away, I turned to Karen and baldly lied.

"Sorry," I said. "I can't see who's talking."

Karen glanced at me and pulled off the highway onto the left-side shoulder. I thought I was going to get busted for fibbing, but it turned out we were lost; the lady in the GPS was giving wrong directions, and Karen had to pull out a map. While we were idling on the highway's wide shoulder, she reached back into the darkness. "Give me the cell phone," she said, extending her right hand toward Jaliyah.

"Wait, was I not supposed to bring it?" said Jaliyah, deadpan. There was a standoff, all eyes on them, but Karen and Jaliyah reached a truce. Karen did not take the phone, and Jaliyah put it in her pocket.

Soon we were driving again. Now that I had avoided ratting out Jaliyah, I decided to step on up and insert myself into her conversation with her friends as smoothly as possible. A confident male voice rapped from the radio. In the lyrics of the hip-hop song, the vocalist talked about asylum being purchased and "running up" on somebody named Yeezy.

I turned to face the girls. "Jaliyah?" I said, more loudly than I'd intended. "Um . . . who's singing on the radio?"

There was silence for a few seconds. Jaliyah leaned forward and looked at me. "Are you talking to me?"

"Yes," I said. "The song they're playing. Right now, on the radio? Is this a local group? You know, a local band from Miami?"

There was total silence for a few seconds, and somebody snickered, and Jaliyah said, "What did you say?"

"This radio station," I said. "Ninety-nine JAMZ. Do they play local regional groups? Is this a local band we're listening to right now? I've never heard this before."

"That's Jay Z," Jaliyah said very slowly. "And Kanye West."

"Oh," I said, feeling the redness burning in my cheeks. "I've definitely heard of those bands before. Those hip-hop artists, I mean. I have no further questions."

There were a few sneezes of unsuccessfully suppressed laughter in the backseat. I couldn't believe how badly I'd screwed up that interaction. *That's it*, I vowed to myself. *No more dumb-ass mistakes!*

The conversation in the back of the minivan was lively and boisterous right up to the moment when Karen turned off the highway onto a dark, narrow road through farmland. We drove past corn, tomato, and strawberry fields and a bean-packing factory. The van's headlights lit a stack of pallets, throwing slasher-movie shadows on the blacktop. No one so much as cleared her throat.

"Is everybody okay back there?" I said.

No one responded. Clearly the girls were scared out of their minds. A few miles later we saw the Everglades National Park entrance sign etched in a chunk of coral. The minivan made its slow, bumpy way down the asphalt strip into Long Pine Key Campground, which was hemmed in by slash pines. Crickets rasped. Bullfrogs burped. Palmettos clapped their fronds in the trade winds. The girls' eyes went wide. Karen looked around to make sure there weren't squatters in our spot, a large flat clearing with picnic tables and a jungle forming a wall around it. My eyes were on the girls' faces. I wanted to ease their panic and smooth their transition from urban to wild life any way I could. I got out of the van and watched the campers get used to their surroundings. With the exception of the smiling, contented Meena (the bespectacled chatty girl with the lizard on her head), everyone looked jumpy. "Where am I going to sleep?" said Chelsea, walking into the blackness.

Jaliyah stepped from the minivan and tightened up her mouth as if she'd just tasted something overly citrusy. The temperature had dropped to seventy degrees. She had a sweater but did not put it on. Instead she rubbed her shoulders for warmth. She took out a bottle of Woodsman repellent and dosed herself with so much bug spray that a noxious chemical cloud rose around her and settled. She moved the spray bottle back and forth across her arms, legs, and shoulders twice. Her eyes watered and blinked.

"Don't breathe in, Jaliyah!" Meena said. Jaliyah just glowered.

I didn't like how this was going. I began to experience a vicarious uneasiness. It must have been something parental, this urge to make everything okay. In that moment, I was grateful to Meena, who directed our attention to the night sky. In the absence of city lights, and before the ICO volunteers lit the powerful Coleman lanterns, the stars were alarmingly close and enormous. The sky seemed to press down on the girls. Even Jaliyah stopped squashing bugs while pouting and looked heavenward. Chelsea stood knock-kneed, shivering, her head tilted as far back as it could go.

"What's your sign?" Meena said.

"Taurus," Chelsea said.

"Well, you're in luck because there's a bull over there," Meena said, pointing to the shining cluster that suggested the face, horns, shoulders, hooves, and midsection of a bull. "That's your constellation overhead. Too bad the clouds are blowing in. Now I can only see the torso."

"What's a torso?" shouted Jordan, a skinny and tomboyish thirteen-year-old camper whose mother was from Belize. For a while, the girls stood in the cooling air, crimping their necks and connecting glow dots. Ariane, the Afro-Franco Native American girl, broke the silence. She was standing near Jennifer, a Puerto Rican girl I hadn't met.

"I hear you can buy a star now," Ariane said, looking up. "Isn't that crazy?"

"That *is* crazy," Jennifer said. "They'll probably turn around and resell that same damn star to hundreds of people."

Time to set up our tents. One more chance to make myself useful and blend in with the kids. Maybe I'd said dumb things and maybe I needed to watch myself a bit more, but at least I could fall back on my years of experience as a camper. Surely there was something I could do to make their time here more enjoyable. When the girls broke into two groups and put up two big, white five-person tents, I tried to stake them down in the ground, but the soil was so full of rocks and roots that it was no use. As I kept on hammering, the girls vanished into the tents. I heard one say, "I'm really scared about leaving my things. I don't want them to get stolen. Things like that happen when you camp. People take stuff." "Look. I'm standing *right here*, and I can tell you that *no one* is going to take your stuff," said a voice that was, unmistakably, Jaliyah's. "Believe me. I *do not want your shit!*"

It sounded pretty tense in there, so when the topic turned, momentarily, to literature and reading, I was very happy to keep the conversation going in that direction. How cool that the kids liked fiction. I liked novels, too! The girls in the tent were talking about William Golding's *Lord of the Flies*, a required book for their high school lit classes, while I stood outside still trying to figure out how to knock the tent pegs into the ground. "*Lord of the Flies*! That was my favorite book in high school!" I shouted out. "I thought it was so amazing how the kids all reverted and turned primitive at the end. I remember getting scared when they killed Simon. And the part when they dropped the rock on Piggy? That freaked me out so badly when I was in high school."

Someone gasped inside the tent. "That's what happens?" said the voice. "Oh, my God! I knew it! I knew they were going to turn primitive and kill each other!"

No, no, no, I thought to myself. Good Lord. Not again! Having realized I'd just ruined the ending of an assigned book the girls hadn't even finished yet, I retreated through the campground to let the whole thing blow over for a little while. As I roamed through the camp, just trying to steer clear of everybody, I almost collided with Crystal, the girl who was usually hanging around with Jaliyah. Now she was all on her own and standing in front of a large gas stove. "Mr. Dan," she said as I passed by. "Do you want to light the stove?"

"*Yes!*" I said, seizing the chance. Crystal handed me a lighter. I flicked it and tried to light the stove, but nothing happened. I told Crystal there might be something wrong with the stove, or her lighter was messed up. Crystal gave me a confused look, reached over, and flicked the lighter herself. The stove was hot and roaring in no time.

As I retreated to the outside edge of the camp, maybe one hundred feet from where the girls were sleeping, it occurred to me that Crystal didn't want or need my help. She'd only been trying to give me a purpose and make me feel included.

I set up my tent far away from the girls. I wanted to give them their space. Soon it was dinnertime, and when we'd all finished our enormous, belly-busting suppers of rotisserie chicken and chocolate cake, I suggested that we hunt for alligators. Karen liked the idea. So did Miss Candice, a counselor from Urgent, Inc., the nonprofit group that worked with the girls in Miami, and who was so wild-haired, youthful, and ebullient that I mistook her initially for one of the girls. With Karen's approval, I'd brought red cellophane to wrap across the beams of the girls' flashlights. I'd heard from a good friend out in New York City that the red tint prevented creatures from noticing you while you watched them. I was glad to see that Meena was thrilled about this plan and had no trouble rallying the others.

"We're going on a nature walk!" she said, and the girls followed without comment down the brief muddy path from the campground to the lake. Some were wearing closed-toed shoes. A few, to my dismay, were wearing bejeweled flip-flops. Most looked skeptical, hugged themselves, and stuck closely together. Only Meena strayed far from the pack. Soon she was out in front and had vanished into the black.

"Meena, where are you?" I said, but there was no answer as we approached a silver-glazed lake with slash pines growing around it. In a moment I could see Meena's silhouette near the water's edge, looking down. "The water's so nice and calm," she said. "I hear them, though. I sense their presence."

"Whose presence?" I asked.

"Alligators," she said. "I feel one looking at me right now. You know that feeling you get, that . . . extrasensory perception sort of feeling, that shiver down your neck when you know something's staring at you?"

All the girls got quiet.

"Something in that water sees me," Meena said. "Not taking its eyes off me. I can't see him, but I know he's there."

The girls shone their cellophane-wrapped lights in each other's frightened faces, and Meena kept leaning over that water, just begging to be eaten. I could feel a ripple of fear go from girl to girl to girl.

At that moment, a loud something in that dark forest *krick-kracked* and *snicker-snacked* through the underbrush.

"What the hell was that?" someone whispered, and we all looked around, desperately, for the source of the awful sound. We were trying to recover from the first noise when another unseen creature opened its big wet mouth and said, *Bwaaaaaaaaaaaaaaaaark!* All of us just about wet our pants right then. The girls all screamed, except Meena. They fell all over each other laughing, shrieking, and slipping and sliding in inadequate footwear. "Mr. Dan," Chelsea said, tapping me hard on the shoulder. "We want to go back to the campground *right now*. Can we please go?"

I thought, *Well, goddamn, these girls are so well behaved they're request-ing my permission not to be eaten alive?*

"Yes!" I said. "Of course. We'll all go," and off we went, trying not to slip in the lakeside mud and fighting our way up that steep path with our red-tinted beams shining on the tree trunks. I was just as scared as the kids, and pretending not to be. All of us were trying to put as much dis-tance between ourselves and the lake as possible except Meena, who lingered for a while, trailing her beam on the black water.

8

Nine Mile Pond

That's what I love about crocodiles. They are the most powerful apex predators!

—Steve Irwin, *The Crocodile Hunter*, October 1991

When we rose the next morning and rubbed the sleep out of our eyes, I looked in the clearing and saw for the first time in my life a campsite full of black and Hispanic kids. While I would like to report how startling and inspiring this was, my actual reaction was a bit more prosaic. It just seemed like a bunch of young people in the woods having fun. I saw a girl whose parents had come from Belize, and another whose parents had moved from Puerto Rico, and another who hailed from El Salvador and told me that cities always got her down and hemmed her in "because I get these incredible urges to climb the tallest trees, and nobody can stop me." They were eating French toast and playing cards. Miss Candice, the counselor from the nonprofit agency, who is part Brazilian, was painting temporary henna tattoos on the Puerto Rican girl's hands and wrists.

Jaliyah had such a sour expression on her face that I could not resist walking over there and asking how she liked the campout so far.

She gave me the teenage eye roll. "Oh, it's *nice*," she said. "It's been *fun*."

She went on a bit of a rant when I asked about how she'd slept in camp. "Oh, it's just ugly, the thought of being there in that *thing*."

"What thing?"

"That tent," she said. "There's dirt in there! That's where I lay my head. That just makes no sense to me. And there are no showers. And the bathrooms, they're like two hundred feet away. I guess this is a survival trip. I'll just have to survive, I guess. I hope I do survive. I am a survivor."

Chelsea walked over and told me she'd gotten scared in the middle of the night. "Where am I? Why can't I see anything? Why is it so dark?" The fear subsided, at least a little bit, when she saw the nylon-wrapped clumps of snoring sleepmates and realized she wasn't on her own in a forbidding forest. Only Meena looked completely refreshed. I was starting to wonder if the slash pines and the swamp were her milieu.

The abundant food was a corrective against the expected first night of restless slumber. Karen understood the unspoken rule of camping: you might put the kids on the finest bedrolls, show them the highest mountain, show them a bottomless lake, but the food had better be great, because that's what they will remember and talk about. Feed them slop, and they won't forgive you. But now that they'd survived a night in a tent and had a good breakfast, the kids had yet another reason to be jittery.

The canoe trip on the gator-infested pond was coming up that morning. I'd decided not to remind the kids about all the armored reptiles in the water. Instead, I asked them, "How many of you can swim?" Only three girls raised their hands. Among the nonswimmers were Chelsea and Jaliyah. I couldn't believe it. It wasn't the fact that they couldn't swim that bothered me. What rattled me was the fact they couldn't swim and yet they had agreed to ride around in flimsy metal boats on a pond with living dinosaurs. Suppose the boat tipped over and they fell in?

Karen and I drove out to the pond with Jaliyah, Crystal, and Ariane, who looked out the window at groups of retirement-age snowbirds standing next to their RVs. License plates read COLORADO, ONTARIO, and MICHIGAN. In 2015, a year after I went on the campout, the New York Times reported that the "vast majority" of national park visitors were "white and aging." In the Long Pine Key Campground, the average age seemed to be sixty-five, and every camper, outside of my little group, was Caucasian. None of the girls muttered a word about any of this except Ariane, who saw a pink man with an impressive potbelly rising and falling beneath his white undershirt, which only reached down to his chest. "Oh. My. God," she said as she looked at him. The man waved to the girls and smiled. The girls returned the wave but not the smile. I couldn't help but wonder just what it would be like to camp in a park and see crowds of people who did not look like me. However, I made a point of not asking the kids the question, "Is it weird to be here with all these white folks?" If I had asked them this, I would have fallen into a trap of my own creation, making the kids feel self-conscious and freakish for visiting the outdoors, the problem that had brought me out here in the first place.

Though I didn't interrogate the girls about feeling out of place, I'd been doing some digging about this issue. Around the time of the campout, I'd been corresponding with Audrey Peterman, a prominent Jamaican-born outdoors enthusiast and advocate who lives in Fort Lauderdale. She uses speeches, conferences, and television appearances to get the word out about the great outdoors while calling attention to the need for better national park outreach campaigns targeting nonwhites. She and her husband, Frank Peterman, went on a national parks camping odyssey in the mid-1990s and were dismayed to see so few people of color out there. "I felt really affronted because I knew the reason," Peterman told me during a phone conversation. "When we told our friends and family that we were going to go out and hike and camp in the woods alone, they were really alarmed. Terrified, in fact. Some of my friends' friends brought out their collection of guns. They said, 'You're going to arm yourself if you're doing this crazy thing. White people are not going to expect to see you out there and you're not going to be welcome.' A lot of that fear and antipathy has been passed down generationally. Grandparents tell grandchildren of what used to happen. Many who had not experienced the aggression personally still had a cultural memory. [But] I felt affronted because this is *our* country and we all pay taxes. National parks belong to the American people."

African Americans and Hispanics are not the only ethnic groups affected by the "participation gap." Native Americans, the United States' original campers, and Asian Americans make up only a small percentage of today's campers. But African Americans are unique in the sense that a large body of writing and scholarship, much of it written by black people, has been building up around the issue, especially over the past two decades. One of the most outspoken voices is the African American environmental historian Dianne Glave, whose 2010 book *Rooted in the Earth* addresses the fraught as well as the uplifting aspects of black environmental history in this country.

The book is unflinching when it talks about the atrocities that brought about "a shapeless, lingering fear" that continues to haunt many urban African Americans. Wilderness, she explains, has troublesome connotations for the descendants of African American lynching victims in southern forests and of exploited workers in the mostly black labor force that toiled in the turpentine camps of the South for low pay and in unsafe conditions. During the first Great Migration, starting in about 1910, millions of black Americans fled the rural South for industrial careers in the Midwest, leaving behind a life close to the land that meant hardship and toil.

Other writers have pinpointed ways that certain ethnic groups, especially African Americans, have faced years of exclusion in the American outdoors, and some of the worst examples have taken place there in Florida, where segregated "separate but equal" state parks facilities were common in the 1950s and into the early 1960s. A few of the girls on the Everglades trip had camped on Virginia Key Beach, which used to be a "colored only" recreation area, starting in the 1940s. African Americans had to rally for the right to swim and sunbathe there. Even the national parks were not immune to Jim Crow. "Within the large Western national parks, established in the early twentieth century, African-Americans weren't particularly welcome," *Slate* magazine reported in 2013. In an interview, Terence Young, a geography professor and American camping historian, mentioned that early-twentieth-century park administrators had a "conscious, but unpublicized policy of discouraging visits by African Americans, [who were], in the opinion of administration, 'conspicuous . . . objected to by other visitors . . . [and] impossible to serve.'"

Black camping families driving their cars to Virginia's Shenandoah National Park in 1940 were confronted with an unsubtle hand-carved sign, mounted on wooden posts directing them to the LEWIS MOUNTAIN NEGRO AREA, with "separate but equal" camping, coffee shop, and cottages. This was the result of a jurisdictional quirk; the state of Virginia originally owned the land and, upon donating it to the National Park Service, it insisted that the NPS impose Jim Crow laws. The park was desegregated in 1942.

Yet there is another side to the story of African Americans and the land, as Glave points out. African Americans have a rich parallel environmental history that is every bit as valid and powerful as the negative connotations. During slavery, "African Americans actively sought healing, kinship, resources, escape, refuge and salvation in the land," she wrote.

Brandon Harris, an African American independent filmmaker, film critic, and contributor to the *New Yorker*, referred to the survival issue in his essay for Talking Points Memo, published in December 2014, called "Why Is Camping a White Thing? A Few *Wild* Theories." In his piece, and in a raucous and freewheeling phone conversation with me a few months after his story came out, Harris recounted several startling but little-known stories about black people camping in extreme situations.

"For many blacks in the antebellum south, camping skills were essential," Harris wrote. "The faintest hope of freedom depended on surviving in the forests of the deep, still-wild south upon escaping from bondage, as some hundred thousand African-not-yet-Americans did between 1810 and 1850. Mentions of rock shelters and bluff tops, which were used as hideouts and improvised camp sites, course through many of the most significant fugitive slave narratives, from Frederick Douglass to Sojourner Truth and onward. The ability to manipulate fire and navigate was often the difference between life and death. The railways one imagines when first hearing the term 'underground railroad' were in fact swamps and streams, caves and rivers."

Over the phone, Harris went into greater detail, talking about the escaped slaves who fled to the Great Dismal Swamp when it was a million-acre expanse of forbidding marshland overlapping southeastern Virginia and northeastern North Carolina. Somehow they dwelled there for years, using the scariest aspects of the land to their great advantage. "Slave trackers would try to retrieve their property, and this was a bridge too far," Harris told me. "They were not willing to go there. 'If you want to go live in the swamp, we will leave you the fuck alone!' I think it is really remarkable. It's like the stuff of a Dave Chappelle skit. But it's real."

While talking to Harris, it seemed to me that this counternarrative would be irresistible if more people knew about it. Gaze into the pages of camping history and you will find an African American mountain man named James Beckwourth, a former slave. Shelton Johnson, an African American Yosemite National Park ranger who grew up in Detroit, has pointed out that members of two African American U.S. Army regiments, known as the Buffalo Soldiers, were some of the first park rangers between

1899 and 1904. "This puts African Americans at the very beginning of national park history," Johnson said in an interview with NBC News. "If you don't know you have cultural roots in the parks, then you're not going to feel a sense of ownership in them." Black-owned and -patronized private campgrounds and lakeside resorts became popular in the Midwest after the Great Migration.

So why is it, I asked Harris, that there continues to be a participation gap? He mentioned black friends of his who love camping, and a few others "who really don't give a shit about it." When I mentioned to him the African American activists who are working hard to connect more black people to outdoor experiences, and who, like Peterman, remind us that national parks belong to us all, Harris said, "I can't speak to those people's feelings. I think that you are right to suggest we should all have access to these public grounds, for the commons. We have this wonderful bounty that we have all collectively stolen from the Native Americans, so we want to make that available to everybody, you know?"

Harris, who let loose with a mordant laugh, was right to mention this painful issue. The establishment of national parks such as Yellowstone and Yosemite coincided with those parks' native populations being kicked out of their own territory. The history of American camping started off with a cruel irony; America's first occupants were dispossessed of the land that belonged to them, only to be informed that they could visit it, and dwell on it briefly, but never make their home there again. "But in all seriousness," Harris continued, "I do think the commons are important. People who live near Yellowstone National Park are going to have more access to it. I am happy as a taxpayer and as an American to pay for that wonderful space, which is our shared heritage. But, likewise, I am hoping that the same individuals [who support national parks with taxes] would also support high-speed rail and intercity transportation that allows us to limit congestion and pollute the planet less."

Activists and scholars have given us a strong sense of the problem's scope. So what is being done about it? Certain well-meaning Caucasian pals of mine have asked me whether I'm imposing the "white value" of camping on nonwhites. When I hear such criticisms, all I can do is point to the growing number of activist groups who are putting forth the strong message that the outdoors is for everyone. But my discussions with leaders such as Audrey Peterman, and with Jose González, coordinator of the outreach group Latino Outdoors, also make me wonder if I'm skewing the diversity issue a bit by focusing so much on the camping angle. González told me that when he's engaging Latino youth in the outdoors, he avoids setting up a strict "continuum" in which one form of engagement with nature is considered better or purer than others. He sees value in bringing children out to suburban parks, just as he sees value in taking them out to the wilderness. "If they want to go to wilderness, we can build that for them," he said. "But I'm not pushing them to say their real goal is to do a five-day backpacking trip."

As we crossed the saw grass marshes, prairies, sloughs, and ridges and made our way to Nine Mile Pond, the girls hummed along with Rick Ross, Drake, Beyoncé, and 2 Chainz. The Everglades were nothing at all like the pictures I had in my head. I'd imagined impenetrable jungle, no visibility anywhere, but the Everglades, if anything, had far too *much* visibility. Its toasted-brown and olive-drab prairies were so flat they gave me a vertiginous feeling, as if I might fall off the earth. The open spaces looked featureless at first glance. Marjory Stoneman Douglas wrote of a "vast glittering openness, wider than the enormous visible round of the horizon." Every time I looked out the window, a new discordant feature revealed itself. Unruly tufts of trees and land rose from the saw grass in brown and green clumps. Wood storks hunched. Their skin was slack and baggy. Their pickled faces reminded me of apple dolls cured with salt and lemon and left in the sun too long. Sometimes the land broke into canals and pools. Alligators drifted. Snouts and eyes skimmed the water. Black tails swung below the surface.

In no time we'd arrived at Nine Mile Pond, where Winston Walters, an African American volunteer for ICO, was waiting for us near the water. That morning, he'd hauled out the canoes from Karen's house in South Miami. I'd been corresponding with Winston by phone and e-mail for a few weeks. Winston had grown up on a Jamaican farm where he spent his days raising chickens, rabbits, and herbs, roaming green hills of mahogany and cedar, and searching for stray goats hiding in little caves. Nature felt like his living room.

Winston had a faint wisp of a mustache and carried one of the biggest survival knives I'd seen in some time. He was muscular and slim, which subtracted a few years; I took him for thirty-four, but he's fifty. Winston was in love with camping and the outdoors and liked introducing kids to the wild, especially when they lived in concrete environments and didn't have much money to get out there. He'd signed on with Miami ICO because the volunteers are mostly white and he wanted young campers to have more adult mentors who looked like them. He told me it had been a consistent struggle to recruit other black camping trip leaders, a fact that he attributed to "black people in America being tied historically to the land in ways they don't necessarily want to be tied to." In stating this, Winston was reiterating a point I'd heard other outdoor activists share with me. But Winston had a unique take on this subject. He told me that this cultural trepidation, while strong among many of the parents, didn't necessarily have much of an effect on the kids on his camping trips, perhaps because their elders' attitudes did not have the chance to set and harden, or perhaps because the oral histories that caused so much ambivalence and pain hadn't been passed down to them yet.

Winston mentioned that all the girls on this particular trip had the food and the use of gear for free, but for most people, camping can be expensive, and economics can be a serious barrier. But he doesn't think income is always the major deterrent to black Americans who dislike or fear camping. "Certainly, [cost] is a factor, but really, I see the same resistance whether they are low income or middle class. A big part of it is just exposure. Folks just have this sense that if you are outdoors, it's going to be hard, tough, dirty, buggy. That's all they've been exposed to through the media."

The kids that camp with ICO are from different circumstances and neighborhoods. There is a mix of middle-class, lower-middle-class, and poor kids. Winston lives in Overtown, a traditionally black neighborhood that is home to many of the youth he's camped with through ICO. When I typed "Overtown" in Google, I found some positive stories about revitalization efforts and neighborhood pride, but first I had to scroll through a list of Miami tourist warnings and exploitative "ghetto tour" YouTube videos first. Overtown has a striking mixture of vitality and blight, cultural treasures and menace. It's home to the newly renovated Lyric Theatre and the work of the legendary collage artist and painter Purvis Young. It also has its share of random shootings and drive-bys and often makes the papers for all the wrong reasons.

Winston oversees a research lab that specializes in spinal cord injuries at the University of Miami. He lives within biking distance from his job. His handsome Key West–style condo is reasonably priced by Miami standards, but he felt conflicted when the home owners association got approval for funding to build a fence around the eighty-unit development, walling it off from its surroundings. "This development was initially conceived to elevate the neighborhood around it, not separate from it."

On the other hand, he does not feel entirely safe anymore. "It's complicated," he told me. "As my seven-year-old daughter gets older, I have had to wonder whether I want to rent my place and live somewhere else until she can handle herself, because I worry that something is going to happen to her when she chooses to walk out the door and down the street. I am not suggesting that this happens all the time, but I fear it because I think something *can* happen. We hear gunshots quite often while we are here at home. And every once in a while, something happens in this little enclave."

In the summer of 2014, one of his neighbors was on his porch, talking on a cell phone and not paying attention, when a couple of youths walked up to him, robbed him, and sauntered into the housing project next door across the street. That year, Winston and a few other home owners were meeting with a contractor, talking about where they might put up the entrance gate, when two cars sped past and the passengers shot at their rivals with automatic weapons.

"People have had bullets lodged in their walls," Winston told me. "A lot of it is random, and a lot of it is just because of where we are. Who knows? Maybe a stray bullet meant for somebody else may find you."

And though he sometimes calls the police because of incidents in his high-crime area, Winston said his relationship with them is complicated and a bit "schizophrenic." He is alarmed by recent shootings of black residents by police in Miami. In 2013, the U.S. Justice Department, after reviewing thirty-three police shootings between 2008 and 2011, concluded that a number of those killings were unjustified. Among the dead were seven black men shot by police within an eight-month period.

Winston spoke of problems close to home. "There was a spate of police shootings in [Overtown] in the space of two years, and there was a huge uproar in the community," Winston said, speaking of events that unfolded in 2013 and 2014. But he said the incidents were not well publicized because they took place before August of 2014, when a white police offer shot and killed Michael Brown, an unarmed black teenager, in Ferguson, Missouri, setting off nationwide protests.

In light of these tragedies, "I try to be very aware of where I am" when police are present, Winston said. "I walk with purpose, as they say, and make sure I look like I am going somewhere as opposed to nonchalant loitering or whatever." Several campers on ICO-sponsored trips, and in particular the boys, have shared their fears of the police with him. "We talk to the kids about this and make sure they understand the things they need to do or not do, whether it is provoke or in any way precipitate an incident. We are all painfully aware that things can go south, things can escalate, things can get really, *really* bad in an instant," he said.

The ICO camping trips are not just an escape for the kids, in other words. They're an escape for Winston, too. Sometimes the campers don't realize they're safer here than they are in town, he told me. "It's sometimes amazing to me: these kids are totally fine walking around after dark where they live, and when we're camping in the dark in the Everglades, they're scared. For me, it's the reverse."

Above all else, he just wants the kids to feel comfortable out there. But Jaliyah, as she made her slow way from the car toward the boats in Nine Mile Pond, looked anything but relaxed, and not for reasons that Winston could do anything about.

She walked to the canoes lined up near the water and paused to cringe at her reflection in a car window. "My hair looks ratchet," I heard her say.

"Jaliyah," I told her, hoping my reassurances would make up for my Jay Z/Kanye West shellacking. "Your hair does not look wretched at all."

She gave me a look that could cut glass. "I didn't say my hair looks wretched," she said. "I said my hair looks *ratchet*."

Jaliyah told me the fear of *ratchet-ness* kept many of her friends and her two sisters out of the woods. "My sisters would never do something like this because they all use flat irons to straighten their hair, and hair spray, you know. The air out here is just no good for hairspray, that's all. I decided to go anyways because my friends are going. But then I come all the way out here and there's no electrical outlet and no showers, and my hair. My hair!"

For the first time, Jaliyah, this bulwark of snark, seemed vulnerable. Then I remembered she couldn't swim, and I thought, *Well, damn, if she's this upset about her hair, no way in hell is she ever going to get into that canoe.* Even I wasn't thrilled about going out on the lake, knowing Croc-zilla was lurking.

But I underestimated her.

Winston was her canoe partner, and his confidence was infectious. She got right into that wobbly boat without protest.

The excursion leaders took every safety precaution. All the girls and adults put on life jackets. Karen wrestled one of the canoes into the lake. She made sure every girl had at least one adult with her in any given canoe. Meena got in the middle of my canoe. On the one hand, I was delighted that Meena had, apparently, forgotten my thoughtless remark about the squashed dead lizard. On the other hand, I had to know one thing for sure: "Meena, can you swim?" I'd taken that straw poll so hastily, and the kids had raised their hands in the air so briefly, that I didn't have a clear sense of who answered yes and no. Meena frowned at me. "Of course I can swim," she said.

My fears assuaged, at least for the next few seconds, I took the front, Karen took the back, and the three of us pushed out into open water.

The four canoes creaked toward mangrove islands in the distance. If the girls were afraid, they did not show it, not even when the canoe flotilla wobbled single file into a dark mangrove tunnel with turns so tight and forest cover so dense I couldn't see what was happening to the boats ahead of us. For all I knew, Croczilla was in front of us somewhere, overturning canoes, gulping volunteers and girls. My boat made a hollow thunk as it banged an underwater rock. It was way too quiet for a fleet of noisy girls. All I heard was the slow and steady slip-slop of warm pond water against the sides of our canoe.

I sighed with relief when the mangrove channels widened and I saw, at long last, Winston and Jaliyah making their way through the maze. Jali-yah looked ferocious and in her element. She was smashing water with her paddle. Every time she stroked it, the canoe surged forward, almost as if it had an outboard motor. It wasn't clear if she was enjoying herself or if she was attacking that pond, trying to beat its face in.

There were hoots of encouragement and peals of laughter when one of the canoes, piloted by Miss Candice, the counselor from the non-profit group in Miami that worked with the girls, ran aground on a muddy mangrove island. As comfortable as she was with the kids, she was not much of a canoeist and was getting her fair share of loud teasing, which she suffered with good cheer. Her crew members, including Ariane, tried desperately to extricate themselves from that mucky hillock, only to run aground again, provoking screams of laughter from other boaters. "Row, row, row yer boat!" shouted Meena to Ariane. "I'm trying to encourage you."

"You aren't helping," Ariane shouted back.

The warm water was thick with periphyton, pulpy clumps of algae, microbes, and fungus in loose-knit mats of white, brown, and light green. Leggy spiders walked on the floating blobs. Meena reached in the pond, pinched some of the organic goop between her fingers, and showed it to me. It smelled like algae and looked like cat vomit. She scooped up a nice big handful. Water oozed out of it when she squeezed.

Meena alternated between entertaining, instructing, and frightening me out of my wits. Once, she pointed toward a clump of rock and vegetation. "Oh, my God. I see an alligator at eye level over there, a fat one, so close to us, coming toward us."

I looked and saw nothing. Karen told me not to worry. "If you think an alligator is coming toward you, it is probably coming toward something else and you're just in the way." A low belching came from the lake. I felt a little zing down my spine, but Meena laughed and said it was only a bullfrog. "You've got to learn to hear the difference," she told me. "That was only a croak. Real gators groan, you know. A groan is more like a *brrrrr*. It comes from the throat. Alligators aren't everywhere. They only hang out in certain places."

Meena wasn't quite done unnerving me just yet. We left the mangrove islands behind and had just reentered a big stretch of open water, heading back toward shore, when she took her right hand off the paddle's handle and let her pale fingers drift just below the surface of the water. I was horrified.

She wiggled her juicy digits. Our canoe drifted over a splotchy black shape maybe fifteen feet below us, probably just a shadow from our boat, a slimy rock, or perhaps a clump of underwater bladderwort.

But the shape was huge, and there was always some possibility, no matter how small, that it was Croczilla coming for his afternoon hors d'oeuvres.

Winston had told me emphatically that there had never been an incident involving crocs or gators on these ICO Miami outings, although "a couple of times folks have seen alligators and gotten freaked out and for-got the basic rule that they are not going to bother you unless you actually jump on top of the alligator or get between a mother and its babies. Other-wise, they don't want anything to do with you." Yet Winston, for all I knew, did not know about the monster croc. I just kept thinking, *Meena, get your hand out of that water right now before something bites you.* Air bubbles drifted from the pond's dark bottom and popped one by one. I asked Meena, "Aren't you afraid of alligators? Are you afraid of anything at all?"

She withdrew her fingers from the pond. "Actually," she said, "I fear alligators more than anything. But I guess I'm the kind of person who embraces fears to get past them. You know who I admire? Steve Irwin. The crocodile hunter, may he rest in peace. He faced fears every day. Imagine. Hunting crocodiles, and then he got killed by some stingray! What I wouldn't give to follow in his footsteps. What I wouldn't give to have an Australian accent. What I wouldn't give to have an underwater infrared camera to spy on the alligators right now."

I looked down, uneasily, at the churning water, but now that she'd pulled her fingers from that lake, her peaceful concentration, and her skill as a boater, eased my mind. It was surprising and disconcerting to realize that Meena's calm and reassuring presence in the boat was the only thing that kept me from surrendering to fear.

Meena seemed to pick up on this. "My point is," she said, "you can acknowledge fear, you can name your fear, but you can't let fear overcome you or rule you. I've always had personal fears of heights and the dark, but the fear of the wilderness is something different. You are basically travel-ing into the unknown. Everything is unpredictable. You could come across a predator. There is a chance of getting poison ivy, or stung by an unknown insect that can be poisonous. And for all we know, our canoe could cap-size."

"So why do you have faith that all those bad things won't happen?" I said.

"I don't know," she said. "I guess I have faith in the unknown."

As we drifted toward shore, Meena spoke about her ambitions for the future. She enjoyed biology—though she said she was not so hot on math—and longed to be a croc tracker and conservationist, but such jobs were hard to come by, so she was thinking about becoming a forensic pathologist, warming up cold cases for the FBI. Still, it was hard for me to imagine Meena ever pulling away from her beloved reptiles. You could even say they consumed her. Sure enough, as we made our way slowly toward dry land, we saw a medium-size tubby alligator lollygagging on the shore, torso visible, eyes shut tight, and its tail below the muddy surface. Meena got out of the boat and rushed right over to it, as though she were greeting an old pal from middle school. She stopped when she was about fifteen feet away from the beast.

"I wonder how big that alligator is," said Meena. "It looks like a six-footer. Maybe bigger. Or a little smaller. I'd love to go over there and measure it."

"Please don't measure it!" I said.

That afternoon a rainstorm swept the Everglades. All the kids took cover. I'd hoped the counselors knew what they were doing and that the tents they'd brought were seam-sealed and rain-proofed like mine. After all, I'd traveled thousands of miles with this tent, and it was built to withstand any condition. Then my tent flipped over and flooded with me inside it. I shouted and moaned as the water poured through my "sealed" seams as if through the holes in a colander. When the storm broke, the kids were treated to the spectacle of me standing in the mud, turning my tent upside down as I thrashed all the dirt and muck out of it. A steady mist was falling, and the campground was quiet. No one was out and about, except of course Meena, who tromped past my tent, looking straight ahead. *Oh, no*, I thought. *What is she up to now?* I called out to her. "Where are you going?"

"Rain brings gators!" she called back to me.

Lake-bound, Meena followed the path toward the shoreline. I worried the rainstorm would return and soak me, but I didn't want her to do something rash and get gobbled, so I followed her. Meena's prints led me to a muddy bank, where I found her among the slash pines, staring into the water. A juvenile gator, maybe five feet long, floated near the rim of the lake, its eyes on Meena, its green-black brow above the surface. For a while we stood there and watched bubbles form around the humps on its head and the scutes of its armor as it drifted closer.

"You are looking at an American alligator," Meena said. "You want to know who gets hurt by alligators? Entertainers—alligator wrestlers. They stick their heads in the jaws and take their heads out just before it closes.

The reason they always get injuries is because the sweat falls down and lands on one of the sensors in the gators' mouths, which are very sensitive, so that signals the gators to clamp their mouth shut."

"No way," I said.

"An alligator's bite has God knows how much pressure! It was tested. It had the highest, I forget; it had one of highest percentages of pressure of any other creature's bite—the amount of speed, force, and power—and of course they have their deadly death roll. When they hold on to you and they start rolling, the only way to get out of that roll is to turn and roll *with* the alligator. The only way to not lose your arm or limb or anything is to roll with the gator. It takes at least four handgun bullets to penetrate an alligator's skull because it's said to be as hard as steel. At close range. It's that tough."

"Uh-huh," I said, thinking to myself, *This kid's got some imagination. How do you roll with a gator?*

"Seriously. The only way to kill an alligator is attack its underbelly."

After a while, it stopped drizzling and the mist broke. The sun began to set. I nudged the conversation in another direction, asking what a normal day was like in the city, and how she liked living there.

"How would you even define 'normal'?" she said. "I'm a teenager. When you're my age, there is no such thing as normal."

When she was through with staring at the gator, we made our slow way together across the squishy trail toward camp.

Then we looked back for a moment to see if the gator was still there. It was looking at Meena. The sunset left long and bloody ribbons on the water.

It was the last night of the trip, so I decided to stop trying to impress anyone, get their secrets, blend in, or have any more "bright ideas" to "help out." Instead, I'd concentrate my full attention on building, and feeding, the best fire I could, and letting the flames do the rest. For once I achieved my goal, with help from Horace Kephart's campfire recipe, printed on a piece of paper, and an assist from a female ICO volunteer with a strong German accent. Karen sat at the picnic table, where she squished flame-melted marshmallows between graham crackers and graded each kid's s'more from A through F, with higher grades for maximum gooeyness, a system that delighted the girls, who turned it into a cutthroat competition. Chelsea got ready to heat up her marshmallow but she didn't know how to do it.

"Roast it like a chicken," Meena advised her.

After lancing her marshmallow on a pointy metal stick, Chelsea waggled it too close to the red coals. It caught fire immediately. She tried to put it out by blowing on it, but her dainty puffs only made the conflagration worse; in no time at all, the marshmallow was a full-on fireball. "I don't want my plaits to catch fire," I heard her say. She was laughing, but I detected panic.

She puffed on it once more. The marshmallow kept on blazing.

"Oh, come on," Jaliyah said. "What the hell do you think you're doing? Don't blow it out cute. Blow it out for real!"

By the time Chelsea got that marshmallow to stop burning, it was a sorry sight indeed. Imagine cinders with gooey gunk in the core. Karen still gave her a low A. Chelsea took her first bite and closed her eyes, and as she chewed she gestured wildly with her free hand. I asked how she liked it, and she just laughed and moaned.

Sugar and darkness made the evening wild. There was lots of gossip and small talk and random silliness and henna painting on people's ankles, arms, and hands. When the kids at last got quiet, Miss Candice, the counselor from the Miami nonprofit agency, with square-framed eyeglasses and flowing garments and chakra stones in her pockets, commenced a fireside ritual. We were all supposed to take a fear or an obstacle we each had, write it on a slip of paper, and toss it on the fire. I didn't want to take part; it seemed like a hippie-style rip-off of Rosh Hashanah minus the gravitas. Besides, I had no desire to embarrass myself anymore. Still, I joined in for the typical teenage reason: everybody else was doing it.

Crystal went first, and though she scribbled her words with an intense expression on her face, she wouldn't share what she burned.

Then they got to Meena, and she said, "I need to stop living in a fantasy world." Looking somber, she leaned over and dropped the paper into the flames.

No one said a word, but Meena in that instant went from the most revelatory of all the girl campers to the biggest cipher on the trip. Not that it was any of my business, but since she had gone public with her confession, I couldn't help but wonder which part was the fantasy: the alligator she'd claimed to see in the middle of the pond but that I couldn't, the dream of being a croc hunter, the fallback plan to be a forensic pathologist, or the list of alligator "facts" she'd told me by the pond? Not that it even mattered. I wished I could have told her that seventeen is no age to *stop* living in a dream world. Dwelling in my own personal Neverland was the only thing that prevented me from losing my mind when I was in high school.

Besides, I knew her love of nature was no fantasy. Winston had noticed it, too. Once, when he was helping to supervise a previous campout on Virginia Key Beach, he'd been sleeping in a hammock next to the water, heard a noise, woke up, and saw Meena looking out at the spreading sunrise. By her side were her sleepy friends. She hadn't let them miss out on that beauty. I remembered all those crazy factoids that Meena told me about gators after the trip was long over and did some scientific sleuthing. Every one of her bizarre-sounding alligator "facts" turned out to be true.

As I waited in front of that fire, I didn't have much time to puzzle over Meena and what she'd said, because it was my turn. I thought about how scared I was on the canoe ride and about the girls' bravery. "I wish not to be fearful," I said. I wrote "FEAR" on my paper, crumpled it up, and tossed it in the flames.

Then it was Jaliyah's turn. She wrote something on her paper slip, frowning, and when she'd finished, she picked up the slip and held it close to her face. "Are you listening to me?" she said to the words on the paper. "You aren't shit! You are *never* gonna be shit." I did not look at the paper, but I strongly suspected it contained the name of a boyfriend, or other rogue male, who had treated her poorly. She dropped the paper on the fire, which flashed white and red. She shook her head and muttered, "I *hate* boys."

Karen, the trip leader, went last. She faced the girls. "Now, I know I'm a lot older than you," she said. "And some of you might think of me as an old lady, but I still fall in love, I still date, and I still get my heart broken sometimes. And there's this man. He's been in and out of my life for a while now. It's been going on too long. So I think it's time to reach over and put his name in the fire."

She reached over and dropped the paper; it caught the flames, and the kids went wild. Karen received the loudest cheers of the night.

The girls on the campout had no Wi-Fi access, no Instagram, no Whats-App, no Snapchat, no Tumblr, no Yik Yak. All they had was a couple of lanterns and a fading fire, so they sat and talked and played card games (including Go Fish and Cheat, which Jaliyah renamed Bullshit) until the moon rose. As the evening wore on, they gathered around the hot coals and told ghost stories.

Miss Candice told a long, confusing, creepy one and acted out scenes from the movie version of *The Shining*. Jordan, the skinny and androgynous thirteen-year-old with tight-clipped hair, told some spooky stories that stopped as soon as they began. "There was this guy," Jordan said. "He walks through the forest, and he saw this bad thing that blocked him so he couldn't go around it, so he says, 'I need to go somewhere. Could you step out of the way?' The thing slits his neck, and my mom told me that story so I'd never go outside. In Belize, where my family is from, they used to tell the children, 'You have to come in before dark because this guy on a horse, he's a ghost, and he used to steal little children.' His feet are backward, though. He's short and he's from Mexico, and he has a sombrero and he always has his machete."

"How funny," Meena said. "Does he walk backward?"

"No, he walks forward, but his feet are on backward. When he was little, they chopped off his feet. Or something like that."

At that moment, I had a memory jolt. A couple of days before, I'd chatted with Jordan's mother, Samantha, in the Miami parking lot where the kids were getting ready to board minivans for the Everglades. Samantha, who'd moved to the United States twenty-five years ago at age thirteen, admitted she was glad to get some peace in the house for a weekend but was mystified that Jordan would want to camp.

"Camping just seems like going backward," Samantha had told me. "That's how we lived in Belize. We were housed, I didn't live in a camp, but the river was down the hill, and there were no paved streets. When I came to America for the first time, I thought it looked like a big Christmas tree. I kept saying, 'The lights!' Imagine if you had to light a fire, not for fun, but that's what you had to do or you'd go hungry, and before you finished you'd smell from smoke, the cooking smells were on you, your hair was singed. And having to walk to school no matter how far and having animals bother you. You carry the water. Carry the bucket. My daughter never had to do that for her family. It was a way of life for me every day. If she had had to live like that . . ." Her voice trailed off.

Yet here was Jordan, camping in spite of the history and scary stories, and not just camping, but camping like crazy. Jordan sang louder than anybody else when she led the girls in a rousing rendition of "The Campfire Song Song" from the *SpongeBob SquarePants* TV show, the one where you sing as quickly as possible and see who tongue-trips first. As Jordan clapped out the rhythm, I couldn't help but think of the backward-footed monster covering his ears and beating a retreat to the swamps.

Next morning, in the final hours of the trip, Karen Kerr sat at a picnic table and talked about the environmental destruction of the Everglades and what the girls could do about it. She mentioned the draining of the swamps. She talked about the invasive pythons that were gobbling native fauna, including raccoons. Jaliyah frowned and glanced at the treetops for snakes. Her look of defiance made me snort with laughter.

During a break in the discussion, I turned to Jaliyah. "I want to thank you," I said. "For making me laugh during this trip. I think you're some kind of stand-up comedienne."

"You make me very happy when you say that," she said.

I asked her what she thought about the trip.

"Oh, I loved it," she said, before clarifying that she was only referring to select moments of the experience. "I have never seen so many stars." She especially liked the canoe trip on the lake. "I murdered it," she said. "I did well." She told me the campout was a nice escape from her usual life in Liberty City, her neighborhood in Miami. She likes going to high school in Little Haiti well enough. "I mean, it's nothing bad for me; it's just a regular place." She likes her classes, especially math and science. Jaliyah wants to be a chemical engineer. "Chemistry's such a stable subject," she said. "Theories do change over time, but everything is there for you at any moment. In chemistry you will find predictable patterns. Chemistry is a central science."

Then she returns to her neighborhood after school and it's not so stable. The same month as the campout, the *Miami Herald* ran a story about three girls, ten, fifteen, and eighteen years old, who were caught in a drive-by shooting a few blocks from Jaliyah's home; bullets grazed the teens, and one bullet hit the ten-year-old in the arm. "When I'm home, I don't come outside; I stay in my home. I'm scared of the people, the thugs, the wannabe thugs, the guns, the gunshots, and whatnot," Jaliyah said. "Nobody see your face, you can't get killed. I just want to stay out of trouble. I don't want to risk getting into *any* kind of problems. I don't want to be in Liberty

City anymore. Especially with my little brother. I want him to leave there, too, 'cause he can't be with those boys. I'm not going to leave Miami, but if I can, I'll move out to the suburbs. My little brother, my mom kept him in the house all his life. That's good. I'm glad she did. And she put him in a private school in Little Haiti. That's what he should be doing. During the day, I go out, but I don't go out for fun, just to go to the park, walk around or whatever? No way. I'm not doing that with you." Then she got quiet and looked away, which I took as a strong signal not to prod her any further about what she'd told me. So I decided to stay in safe territory and ask her something else: Given her difficult experiences in the city, wouldn't she jump at the chance to go camping again and get away from all that?

"*No!*" was her sharp reply.

"Really?" I said. "Why not? You were just telling me about life in your neighborhood. It seems like it's so much safer out here compared to . . ."

"Because I couldn't use my cell phone. Because I couldn't call my mom. No electrical outlet? That was just hell. That just made me want to fight. Not having use of a cell phone for that long? I mean, that was, by far, the worst experience of my life."

The girls experienced the full potential of American camping on that one trip: enjoyment and frustration, fear and adventure, discomfort and s'mores. Their experience was all about engagement as well as preservation and ecology. Karen wanted the campers to experience the awe of nature so they might stand up and fight for it later on. That's why, during the final portion of the trip, she put a special emphasis on the forces that threaten the Everglades. In doing so, Karen and the campers were following a long-standing American tradition: bearing witness to environmental degradation while sleeping under the stars. At the turn of the century, America's quintessential camper, John Muir, had a similar strategy in mind when he traveled through Yosemite with an illustrious and influential camping partner.

9

The Odd Couple

I never before had so interesting, hearty, and manly a companion.
I fairly fell in love with him.

—John Muir in 1903, writing about Theodore Roosevelt

On the second night of his Yosemite camping trip in May 1903, John Muir decided to burn down a five-hundred-year-old tree just for fun. He must have guessed that this act of recreational arson would delight his camping companion, who was in his midforties but sometimes acted like a kindergartner.

Muir dipped a tree branch into the bonfire close to their bedding, in a quiet spot sheltered from the winds off Glacier Point. He tramped through the snow, lit the isolated pine, and watched it turn it into a pillar of flame. Overcome, he danced a Scottish jig around the tree. This is surprising behavior for a man who adored trees so much that he once made an English tourist "fairly jump . . . with fright" when she asked Muir if giant California sequoias would make good lumber for furniture. Muir gave her a ferocious look and replied, "Would you murder your own children?" In his defense, the lit-up pine was already dead, and besides, he had good reason to impress his camping partner, President Theodore Roosevelt, who loved conflagrations almost as much as he loved shooting things.

Muir would do most anything, even torch a tree, to lure this powerful man closer to the preservationist cause. What was one dead snag compared to the living forests of America?

The two campers had been riding hard through a snowstorm all day long to reach their camping spot, but they had plenty of energy left over. When he saw Muir reeling around the flames, Roosevelt started jumping around, too. "Hurrah, hurrah," Roosevelt shouted. "That's a candle it took five hundred years to make. Hurrah for Yosemite, Mr. Muir!" At another point, Roosevelt reportedly shouted out, "This is bully!" It's easy to imagine Roosevelt leaping in the snow, casting long shadows, his pince-nez spectacles barely clinging to the side planes of his nose. Roosevelt woke the next morning in a state of bliss, with half a foot of snow on his blankets. "I passed one of the pleasantest nights of my life," he remembered.

Hoping to do some "forest good" for California, Muir had agreed to delay a long-planned overseas botanizing trip for a chance to camp with the president. He thought of it as a lobbying session. Roosevelt had his own motives. Though his enthusiasm for the mountains was overwhelming, and his admiration of Muir was genuine, perhaps he was being a touch disingenuous when he told Muir he'd wanted to "drop politics absolutely for four days and just be out in the open with you." At the time, Muir was the wilderness It boy of the northeastern establishment, the literary wild man of the moment. He imparted a sense of wilderness cool to everyone who brushed against him; Roosevelt burnished his reputation by playing up his nature boy image, which he'd built up, painstakingly, along with his physical strength, through a series of camping and ranching adventures.

Both men must have known the strategic importance of this campout. Yet one of the great joys and sorrows of camping is its unpredictable nature. Campouts create their own mysterious agenda. Throughout the weekend, the two of them would show their humanity in surprising ways, with gaffes, insults, enthusiasms, and complaints. The campout was more than just a historic meeting of minds. It was also a chance for them to peel back the layers of their own mythologies for a short while.

What a fine thing it would be to turn myself into a field mouse and observe their campout from the right-side pocket of Muir's trousers. Since it would take magic to achieve such a thing in the first place, I would also give my mouse self opposable thumbs, minuscule notebooks, and wee little fountain pens so I could jot down their every utterance. Alas, no authoritative source about the campout exists; we must rely on small potsherds of information from the campers and their various hangers-on. Yet those scraps give us tantalizing glimpses of real people.

At the time of the campout, Muir, at age sixty-five, was one of America's most articulate and popular defenders of untrammeled places, a passionate camper and woodsman who used little or no gear to conquer western peaks that others considered unclimbable. Like "Adirondack" Murray before him, charming thousands of people into the North Woods in the early 1870s, Muir, starting in the late 1880s, helped popularize camping and climbing in the western wild with his sublime essays and newspaper columns. "Climb the mountains and get their good tidings," he wrote in 1901. "Nature's peace will flow into you as sunshine flows into trees. The winds will blow their own freshness into you, and the storms their energy, while cares will drop away from you like the leaves of Autumn." He spoke to the tired brainworkers, and they listened. With their bedrolls, tents, and walking sticks, they fled their offices in Los Angeles, San Francisco, and Sacramento and headed for the Sierra Nevada.

Unlike many of his nature writing and camping contemporaries, Muir didn't fill his notebooks with stories about gunning things down. Instead, he brought creatures and trees to exuberant life. Muir reveled in the owl, "prince of lunatics," and the "tap-a-rap" sound of the woodpecker; the "soft-breathing" of the night wind; and the "fine musical sparrow half-chatter, half chirp" of the squirrels and the "thumping sounds" of their fallen cones. He watched the sparks from his campfires "stream off like comets or in round star-like worlds from a sun." Each spark "echoed clear and sharp, producing a remarkable effect, like the popping of muskets let off irregularly by practicing recruits." The smallest details in camp could not escape his gaze, not even "the glad, hilarious energy" of the Yosemite grasshopper, or "the curves he described in the air." Convinced that every aspect of life was "hitched to everything else," he glimpsed the divine in every spider and centipede. In the woods of California, Muir listened to imagined orchestras, "a flutter of leaves like the clapping of small hands." Along with the sounds, he breathed in "the rosiny pine and spicy fir," the "fragrant violets" and the sweaty funk of "plushy bogs in which a thousand herbs are soaked." Those who read Muir camped through him. They could watch the landscape being formed, step by step, and see ancient processes doing their slow and patient work.

Muir had reason to believe that Roosevelt was a fellow traveler. Both believed humanity could not survive without wildness. Both despised "malefactors of great wealth" (dishonest land speculators, rapacious lumbermen, real estate fraudsters, and corrupt business interests) for despoiling the West. Roosevelt equated forests with nationalism. Let the snide Europeans have their opera houses and museums; their man-made wonders could never compete with Bridalveil Fall or El Capitan.

Yet Muir needed Roosevelt's help. At the time of their campout, Yosemite Valley was not part of Yosemite National Park. It was a land grant administered with casual indifference by the state of California. In 1889, Muir had gone on a pivotal camping trip with his good friend the influential magazine editor Robert Underwood Johnson and found the site overrun, a disgusting mess. A mere 650 people per year visited Yosemite from the mid-1850s through the 1860s. By 1890, when Congress designated it a national park, it was a major tourist destination, in no small part because of Muir himself. Many of those wilderness adventurers must have read Muir's passionate stories in national magazines, celebrating the area's glory, urging for protections against lumber and mineral interests. Now it needed protection from people who were wrecking the valley by catering to the visitors' worst impulses and trying to enrich themselves in the process. Ugly surprises awaited Johnson and Muir at every turn: a rank saloon, cattle fences everywhere, too many tree stumps, the land plowed over. They came across a pigsty so aromatic that Muir wondered if it would leave a permanent stink on the rocks. Outside the park's boundaries, sheep nibbled wild grasses and flowers down to stubs. Muir, a Sierra foothills shepherd in his younger days, called them "hoofed locusts." People were crawling all over Yosemite. Archival photos show dapper dandies and women with feathered caps, ribboned walking staffs, and long dresses making their way up steep rocks leading to the high peaks.

Honoring such a glorious place and protecting it were two different things, as Muir well understood. The intimate camping trip with Roosevelt was Muir's chance to change the rules about wild places, or at least to nudge them in the right direction.

Both campers, to their great credit, took pains not to make this a press junket. As soon as they arrived in a grove of ancient sequoias on their first day in Yosemite, Roosevelt immediately dismissed his large entourage. He sent Secret Service agents, press corps members, and cavalrymen to the Wawona Hotel, where the waitstaff was preparing a lavish dinner in Roosevelt's honor, having no idea he was going to brush them off and sleep outdoors with Muir.

Freed of their escorts, Roosevelt and Muir rode their horses deep into the woods. The two of them had much to talk about, from the future of the forests to the natural forces that had formed Yosemite Valley and the lands around it. The first night, they roughed it easy at the ancient Mariposa Grove, which, like the valley, was not part of Yosemite National Park at the time. Muir used evergreen boughs to soften the president's bedding before he lay down beneath the Grizzly Giant sequoia tree, which stands more than two hundred feet tall, with a girth of ninety-five feet at the base. It was, apparently, named after the native bears that once roamed California, though the tree's lumpy and gnarled appearance also earned it the nickname "Grizzled Giant" over the years.

Roosevelt brought no tent with him, just a tarp, but he held off the cold with a pile of forty woolen blankets. "It was clear weather, and we lay in the open, the enormous cinnamon-colored trunks rising about us like the columns of a vaster and more beautiful cathedral than was ever conceived by any human architect," Roosevelt remembered.

Yet these two men did not camp entirely on their own, and for that, we campers should all be grateful. Perhaps they wouldn't have survived the trip if they had been allowed to head out there unattended. Roosevelt and Muir, although they were two of the most soulful and influential campers in history, were not so hot at camping from a strictly technical standpoint. In terms of their skills in forests, including their ability to stay safe and comfy in wilderness areas, Horace Kephart and Nessmuk would have trounced them. C. Hart Merriam, a friend of Muir's, once said that Muir "knew less about camping than almost any man I have ever camped with."

Muir often seemed "foolishly indifferent" to dangers and discomforts on the trail, the distinguished Muir biographer Donald Worster wrote. "Often he set off into the backcountry without sufficient gear or left too late in the day for common sense. He had to endure long periods with little food. All his life he gave little thought to hypothermia or a new bout of malaria or a crippling fall a long way from help. While many assumed that he was a master of survival techniques, someone always to be depended on, Merriam found him to be a negligent hiker who too often let his passion overcome his judgment."

Perhaps Merriam's assessment is a bit unfair. Somehow Muir survived

in woodland tramps and on so many daring climbs in spite of his impulsiveness. "Perhaps he knew more [about camping] than he was given credit
for," Worster told me. But sometimes he could be insensitive to the wants
and needs of companions in the forest. A couple of decades before his campout with Roosevelt, Muir traveled to Yosemite with his wife, Louie Strent-
zel Muir. At one point, she was struggling up a mountain. Hoping to speed
her ascent, Muir gave her a push with a stick. Needless to say, she never
traveled to the wilderness with her husband again.

Roosevelt also had his shortcomings as a camper. In an 1890 visit to
Yellowstone with his family, he camped at 7,500 feet above sea level on a
chilly September day, with his wife Edith and his sister Corinne. They
brought ridiculously thin blankets that did nothing to hold back the cold.
Their drinking water froze in a pail. It was safe to say the man had not done
his due diligence. Later, Edith got thrown off a horse; apparently no one
called for medical help. "[F]or all his scientific knowledge, Theodore was a
reckless escort in the wilderness," writes Douglas Brinkley in his book *The
Wilderness Warrior*.

Thank goodness Muir and Roosevelt had professional help in camp,
including a seasoned mountaineer, wilderness guide, and ranger named
Archie Leonard and an outstanding cook named Charles Leidig. Muir was
infamous for his camping meals, which sometimes included a hard heel
of stale bread with tea. His carbohydrate-rich and paltry food was part of
his system of extreme self-deprivation, which helped facilitate his woozy
ecstasies on mountaintops. Yet, with Leidig in charge, Roosevelt gorged
himself on beefsteak and chicken, and washed it down with black coffee.

Posing for an iconic photo at the halfway point of the camping trip,
Muir and Roosevelt stood with their backs to a thirty-two-hundred-foot
drop at Glacier Point. If the two men had toppled over, it would have
taken a good fourteen seconds for them to hit bottom. Muir looks like a
dapper scarecrow in the picture, with a wildflower sprig in his buttonhole.
Roosevelt appears hale and determined, his legs anchored to the rock, his
square-jawed face shaded by a Stetson hat. There is an element of pure
ham to that photo. Both campers seem to revel in their legend and power.

But if you've ever camped for more than one day with anyone, you
know there will be tensions and cringe-inducing moments. At one point
in the trip, the president grumped at Muir for slipping a flower into Roosevelt's lapel without his permission, and he bellowed at his helpers to

Theodore Roosevelt and John Muir took a few moments from their campout
to pose for photographs at Glacier Point. The two men camped nearby in an area
that was sheltered from the wind and woke up with snow on their blankets.

retrieve his misplaced suitcase. At another embarrassing juncture, the
hapless Muir, anticipating today's accidental "reply-all" e-mail humilia-
tions by more than a century, inadvertently showed Roosevelt a passage in
a letter ridiculing the president and his "sloppy, unintelligent interest in
forests." The letter also declared that Roosevelt was "altogether too much
under the influence of that creature [Gifford] Pinchot," the chief of the

U.S. Bureau of Forestry (later known as the Forest Service), whom Muir disliked. Muir showed Roosevelt the letter for another reason: its author had hoped Roosevelt would pass along personal messages to the emperor of China and the czar of Russia when he met with them that year. The president roared with laughter at the inadvertent insult. "John," he said. "Do you remember exactly the words in which this letter was couched?"

Muir looked flummoxed. "Good gracious!" he replied. "There was something unpleasant about you in it, wasn't there? I had forgotten. Give me the letter back."

Aside from that gaffe, they had another serious communication problem: both were jabber-jaws, accustomed to talking endlessly. Muir could talk a wolverine out of its muddy burrow. As for Roosevelt, a news reporter once likened him to Yellowstone's Old Faithful geyser, "his only rival in intermittent but continuous spouting." Nevertheless, the persistent Muir managed to "stuff" the president with stories about the trashed valley and the need to expand and increase protections for Yosemite National Park.

There was also a bit of back-and-forth jibing in camp. Roosevelt was stunned that Muir, Mr. Nature Boy, didn't know very much about birdcalls. At another unguarded moment in camp, Muir took a jab at his new pal. "Mr. Roosevelt," he said. "When are you going to get beyond the boyishness of killing things? Are you not getting far enough along to leave that off?"

To this, Roosevelt had the uncharacteristically lame reply: "Muir, I guess you are right." Of course, as we know, he continued to hunt, killing hundreds of big game animals in Africa on another camping trip of sorts, with his son Kermit.

As any camper knows, it's hard to cover up such personal differences for very long. The campout has a way of finding these little fissures, just as surely as a hard rainstorm will find the place where you forgot to seam-seal your Gore-Tex bivy sack. In some respects, these campmates were opposites. Roosevelt was fastidious about his appearance, while Muir, according to one account, had never shaved in his life. The president reveled in war making, while Muir had skedaddled up to Canada to avoid fighting in the Civil War. Roosevelt was highborn, while Muir was a lowlands Scotsman of modest means. Roosevelt saw no contradiction between his love of all things wild and his love of blowing them away with his rifle. In his boyhood in Dunbar, Scotland, Muir sometimes hurled pebbles at cats and took potshots at keening seagulls. He also disrupted birds' nests and swiped their eggs with glee—a memory that troubled him later on. After the family settled on Hickory Hill Farm in Wisconsin in 1857, young Johnnie, like most frontier boys, would shoot at just about anything unlucky enough to squeak, scuttle, or flap in front of him. Years later, Muir, in an unusual display of brutality, once strangled a cat accidentally while trying to wrest a songbird from its throat.

Yet Muir put his killing ways behind him as an adult. To him, campouts were about the camping itself—the feeling of getting lost in raptures in the forest. They were not means, or excuses, to stalk and hunt. To Roosevelt, camping out was about the prey and the chase, and while he put his gun down while visiting national parks, he wasn't happy about it. Muir thought hunting was regressive, while Roosevelt never lost his conviction that hunting animals made boys into men. Killing was fine with him—so long as it was thoughtful and well regulated. An admirer of Charles Darwin, he considered people just another creature—and why shouldn't the mammal with the shotgun and the frying pan prevail? When he plugged a creature and stuffed it, he also thought he was doing the species a good turn by committing its body to science or a museum diorama, increasing awareness of the creature and its habitat; in other words, by killing something, you might save it. Roosevelt, not without cause, linked hunting with preservation; he was a founding member of the Boone and Crockett Club, a group of well-heeled amateurs whose love of the hunt and desire to preserve wild habitats were equally passionate. Muir, for his part, once mourned over a dead bear and wanted people to cherish all kinds of wildlife.

Needless to say, Muir had no luck changing Roosevelt's ideas about shooting. Perhaps they had awkward silences as they sat there in camp, staring at each other, the unresolved issue hanging in the air before them.

Yet, for the most part, they seemed to have had a grand time in Yosemite.

Muir was once a professional hiking and botanizing guide in Yosemite, and he knew the area better than anyone else. Their itinerary included, among other places, a luxuriant meadow near Bridalveil Fall, where the campers discovered just how hard it was to get away from it all, even in 1903: more than a thousand well-wishers assailed them, chasing the campers on foot and in buggies. "These people annoy me," Roosevelt grumbled to Charles Leidig. "Can you get rid of them?"

In spite of that intrusion, Muir did a fine job of introducing Roosevelt to the area's wonders. Perhaps he was making up for a heartbreaking lost opportunity in 1871, when Ralph Waldo Emerson visited Yosemite and was enthusiastic about camping with Muir but backed out, apparently because his handlers were opposed to the great sixty-eight-year-old transcendentalist's sleeping rough outside. Muir begged Emerson to reconsider—"the mountains are calling; run away!" Muir said—but Emerson would never reexperience the camping raptures he enjoyed in the Adirondacks in 1858.

Muir said later on that he "fairly fell in love" with the president. They were united in their belief that the woods could cure the neurasthenic soul. The two of them were tireless alliance builders. The camping trip reaped great dividends for the preservationist cause. After the trip, Roosevelt gave an incendiary speech about despoiled California sequoia groves. Muir also convinced Roosevelt that Yosemite Valley and the Mariposa Grove, both part of the California State Grant, should fall under federal protection and become part of Yosemite National Park. "There can be nothing in the world more beautiful than the Yosemite, the groves of the giant sequoias," Roosevelt said. "[O]ur people should see to it that they are preserved for their children and their children's children forever, with their majestic beauty all unmarred." Aside from adding mightily to Yosemite, Roosevelt created five national parks, fifty-one federal bird reservations, and eighteen national monuments during his presidency. Perhaps his admiration for the views of John Muir influenced the president's decision to make the Petrified Forest a national monument in 1906 and to grant the Grand Canyon the same status in 1908.

The saving of Yosemite Valley was one of Muir's career highlights. In a sense, his whole life had built up to that point. He may have looked like a tramp in his younger days, with his ragged clothes, but he was as single-minded and ambitious as could be.

Muir, unlike the coddled "Teedie," survived a brutal childhood that prepared him for his extreme camping adventures and his grappling with politicians in adulthood. Those unhappy memories informed the rest of his days. The hardest work at the Muir family farm in Wisconsin went straight to young Johnnie, who blamed his "stunted" growth and "runt" status on exhausting manual labor. Once, he almost died from inhaling noxious gases while digging a deep well.

Yet Muir had a Puritan ethic and a boundless imagination. As a youth, he binged on books and invented various crazy gizmos late into the night, from a device that lopped the heads off gophers to a clockwork contraption that lifted up a bed and dumped its baffled occupant onto the floor. Think of it as an alarm clock in which the medium is shock and pain instead of loud noise. In an interview, Worster said that Muir had the "cultural genes" to be a great man of industry; he allowed the world of technology to postpone his entrance into the outdoor world, no matter how it called to him. Then a brutal setback forced him to change course.

In 1867, Muir was working after hours in an Indianapolis factory that made parts for carriages when the pointed end of a file jumped up and pierced his right eye. The stunned Muir remained at his worktable, cupping his eye as the vitreous humor drained into his hand. His vision in that eye went black, and for a while, in sympathetic reaction, his left eye went dark as well. The absolute emptiness was so terrifying it overrode any pain he might have felt. Even as he lay in his sick bed, the accident struck him as metaphorical. In tireless pursuit of prestige and money, he'd closed his eyes to life's grander possibilities.

So, like a cancer patient checking off a do-before-I-die list, Muir decided to be bold and embrace heedlessness. Taking a plant press, a book of poems by Robert Burns, a copy of Milton's *Paradise Lost*, and a pocket-size edition of the New Testament, he set out, on September 1, 1867, on a thousand-mile walk to Florida. He was twenty-nine. In his sojourns he dwelled among the stout Kentucky oaks and marched past armies of giant sunflowers. He crossed the Cumberland Mountains and traversed Georgia's river country. It was not just the great peaks and lakes that held him. He also loved mosses, ferns, and sprigs of life between the cracks in old stone walls. When he could not get a room in a private home or a dollar-a-day hotel, he made his bed in the open, under towering pines.

Muir, who had wild reddish ginger-brown hair and kindly blue eyes, ingratiated himself with everybody he met. He'd camp with anyone regardless of skin color or class, and he'd bed down anywhere. Even the Bonaventure graveyard outside Savannah, Georgia, struck him as so lovely, "almost any sensible person would choose to dwell here with the dead rather than with the lazy disorderly living."

Among tombstones, Muir rested for a while beneath "the great black arms" of live oak, close to a "coffee-colored stream," under the moonlight, with hard and spiny beetles crawling over his hands, his plant press on its side, no tent, no sleeping bag, no regrets, few possessions, and a burial mound for a pillow. Eagles called to him in the morning as he stuffed breakfast crackers in his mouth.

Anticipating by more than a century our country's preoccupation with "through-hiking" on long-distance paths, Muir followed his own psychic trailways. Onward he rambled through Florida swamps on a floral pilgrimage through "mangroves and mosses," sensing the alligators in the dark, hearing the "springy snap" of their jaws. "Honorable representatives of the great saurians of an older creation," he called out to them, "may you long enjoy your lilies and rushes, and be blessed now and then with a mouthful of terror-stricken man by way of dainty!"

On his way, he hobnobbed with former slaves, broke bread with swamp dwellers, and tried to explain his purpose to perplexed passersby. Someone asked if he could call himself a proper Christian, camping and tramping in this manner. Muir responded that a proper Christian reveled in *all* of God's creation—no skipovers, ever. Sometimes bands of brigands crossed his path but did not rob him; Muir had nothing worth taking.

At the Gulf Coast of Florida, he came down with a near-fatal case of malaria that weakened him during his brief trip to Cuba. Too weary to venture into the Cuban highlands, he began his "crooked" journey by boat to California. He showed up in San Francisco almost penniless on March 27, 1868. A single day in that bustling and dirty town was enough, and when he happened upon a man on the street and asked how he might escape the clamorous city, the fellow was confused: Where would you like to go anyhow? "To any place that is wild!" John Muir shot back.

On the ferry to Oakland, Muir met a Cockney named Chilwell, who agreed to accompany him on foot to Yosemite Valley. Heading from the East Bay, Muir could hardly comprehend his newfound "capacity for happiness." He gazed at the foothills of the "Monte Diablo range" to his left and the Santa Cruz Mountains to his distant right, "smooth and flowing, . . . covered with flowers growing close together in cloud-shaped companies, acres and hillsides in size, white, purple, and yellow." There was no going back to Wisconsin: "I am lost—absorbed—captivated with the divine and unfathomable loveliness and grandeur of nature."

His greatest adventures lay ahead of him. In Yosemite he embraced the meadows and mountains in a borderline sexual way. Has any other nature writer used the word *throbbing* quite so much (e.g., the "full, gushing,

JOHN MUIR
Lover of all living things. With the
exception of sheep.

John Muir (1838–1914)

throbbing glory" of the upper Yosemite and its "Shafts" of song, as well as
the "outside sprays" and the "whole massive column" and the "stupendous
unit of mountain power")? Muir was living proof that the rhapsodic camping ways of the early-nineteenth-century Romantics still had a place in the
backcountry. The age of rationalism and industry could not snuff out their
spirits. In his campouts and his stomps up mountains, he placed such terrific demands on his body and brain that these parts of him seemed to
cleave apart. Yet Muir felt a supreme unity when camping out. "No sane
man in the hands of Nature can doubt the doubleness of his life," he said.
On rough trails and on long bushwhacks, he practically starved himself
sometimes, but the result was "No pain here, no dull empty hours, no fear
of the past, no fear of the future." He got to the point where he'd close his
eyes and "dream . . . of glaciers."

The result was absolute freedom. Muir, unlike the woodcrafters of his
day, was no gear fetishist. "He never wore a coat" during his backcountry
scrambles, "because it impeded his arms, flapped in the wind, and was
liable to catch on bushes or rock outcroppings," one biographer, Stephen
Fox, tells us. "On the hardest climbs he stripped down to his drawers to
free his limbs completely."

He went ultralight, wearing thick-soled hobnail shoes instead of boots, which might shrink up on him. Sometimes he went all alone or mustered up a group of companions. Other times, he loaded up a few belongings on a mustang pony: a pot of tea, a couple of loaves of crusty bread, some blankets, and notebooks.

For most of his Yosemite years, he published nothing at all. Yosemite Valley was Muir's Walden Pond, his subject and proving ground, and while Thoreau wrote the template for this kind of wilderness adventure, Muir truly lived it. Even the cabin he used while working for James Mason Hutchings's lumber mill had a Walden-like quality; Muir, an ardent fan of Thoreau's, rerouted a stream so it flowed along an interior wall, providing habitat for frogs that clung to ferns working their way through the cracks; sometimes they serenaded him all night long.

Like Thoreau, who claimed he left the woods at Walden Pond for as good a reason as he entered them, Muir stopped living full-time in Yosemite Valley from the mid-1870s onward. Instead, he turned his attention from camping to writing. His pen gave him his first taste of power and influence. Through hard work, the man whom some Yosemite visitors once regarded as the silly, harmless hermit of the valley became a national force. In keeping with the times, Muir did not tell the full story of Yosemite in his essays and articles. He captured the imaginations of wilderness lovers by portraying Yosemite as God's own creation and, somewhat disingenuously, an unpeopled paradise, while skirting the inconvenient and tragic fact that this unpeopling happened by force; in 1851, soldiers in the Mariposa Battalion rode into Yosemite to drive out the Ahwaneechee, the Native American tribe that had lived in the area for centuries before the federal government anointed it as a national park. In that respect, Muir, unfortunately, was not at all unusual. Across the nation, new generations of nature lovers, including campers, had become caught up in the untouched virgin wilderness myth, an intoxicating legend that erased a long legacy of human beings occupying and altering the landscape.

To this day, Muir comes in for strong criticism for the role he played in "selling" the western woods and mountains as an Eden while marginalizing the original occupants. But even the staunchest critics of Muir might at least give him some credit for helping to stop those places from getting plowed over, and for the alliances he built to stop this from happening. Over time, the young, uncompromising Muir gave way to a consummate schmoozer and coalition builder. His feats of preservation would have been impossible without his cozy relationships with powerful men, including railroad magnate Edward Henry Harriman, or his abiding belief that the future of wilderness depended on state and federal government intervention.

The legends surrounding Muir warp the national memory of him. He was not some impoverished pilgrim sleeping in a one-room run-down shack or in the mouth of some slimy cave, elbowing aside the bears and the panthers so he could reach his bed of straw. Muir had knock-around clothes and was often poor in his youth, but when he married into wealth in 1880, and started running a highly profitable farm in Martinez, California, he never had to worry about money again. He lived for most of his post-Yosemite years in a beautiful and well-appointed 10,010-square-foot manor house. Instead of the raggedy clothes of his youth, he started to wear smart suits and fine shoes on fancy occasions. When people visited him, he offered cigars and wine. And while it is hard to picture Muir enjoying conveniences of any kind, his great big house had—God forbid—electricity. Also, back when California had fewer than thirty thousand phone subscribers statewide, Muir had a telephone. He even had a listed number: Red-63.

It is this version of Muir, not the endearing hermit of Yosemite Valley, who helped save America's forests, and who showed up to the Yosemite woods with Roosevelt in 1903. The two of them camped out hard for those three days, and vowed to keep in touch.

Roosevelt's love for wilderness, and his belief that it was the last hope for "overcivilized man," was genuine, as was his friendship with Muir. In 1906, just after the death of Louie, John Muir's wife of twenty-four years, Roosevelt sent his old camping friend a lovely and heartfelt letter. "I do not wish to intrude upon your grief," the president offered. "There is nothing that I can say that will be of any comfort. Get out among the mountains and the trees, friend, as soon as you can."

Roosevelt was writing from experience; when he was twenty-six, his wife and mother both passed away on the same day, leaving him so devastated that he wrote, "The light has gone out of my life." The future president drew a great big X through the page of his diary. The heartbreak pushed him out to the Badlands, where he camped and ranched his pain away.

Still, when it came to saving the wild places he loved best, Muir's sway over Roosevelt, and the influence of that magical campout in Yosemite, went only so far. Muir found this out while trying to fight the last preservation battle of his life. Once little more than a steep-hilled pueblo, San Francisco became a big, booming city during the gold rush, when its population ballooned. Occupying a peninsula bounded by saltwater on three sides, and dependent on springs and surface water, San Franciscans began their aggressive search for other, more reliable supplies in the late 1890s. Even before the Great Earthquake of 1906, city leaders had been eying the Tuolumne River, flowing through Yosemite, as a potential place to build a reservoir. Yet the quake and the ensuing fire drew wider political support for the idea of building a dam that would flood Hetch Hetchy Valley, well within the boundaries of Yosemite, as a potential spot for a reservoir. Muir was furious; while the leaders looked to Hetch Hetchy as a resource for their city, Muir saw the dam plan as a form of sacrilege; he considered Hetch Hetchy the wilder and equally beautiful sister of Yosemite Valley, a place where he loved to stand "waist deep in grass and flowers while the great pines sway dreamily." He called it an Eden of Mariposa tulips, orchids, iris, Sabine pine, incense cedar, wild cherry, trout pools, jagged gorges, and waterfalls that Muir likened to silvery scarves.

Muir appealed to Roosevelt for help, and in return he received a friendly and unhelpful letter in which the president stated his need to respect the public's will, whatever that turned out to be. As much as he loved wilderness and respected Muir, Roosevelt, at heart, was a utilitarian, more a conservationist who thought of forest as a "resource" than a preservationist who believed that all creatures and forests were sacred.

Seeming to talk out of both sides of his mustache, Roosevelt vowed that he would do "everything in my power to protect not only the Yosemite, which we have already protected, but other similar great natural beauties." Then came a very significant *but*: "*But* you must remember that it is out of the question permanently to protect them unless we have a certain degree of friendliness toward them on the part of the people of the State in which they are situated." If the feds should interfere in such cases, "the result will be bad." Then—painfully, at least for me—he refers back to the camping trip: "I wish I could see you in person; and how I do wish I were again with you camping under those great sequoias, in the snow under the silver firs." In the end, even other Californians could not prevail against the interests in San Francisco.

Theodore Roosevelt, the same crusading conservationist who wisely set aside great swathes of birding grounds in Florida and Puerto Rico to save them from feather barons and ladies' hat makers was also a proficient dam builder. At one point, before reconsidering his views, he thought it was a good idea to play God and gun down cougars and wolves to give ungulates a fighting chance at survival. By the time he and Muir went camping, Theodore Roosevelt was the world's best-known champion of wildlife and protecting wilderness, but his ardor never matched Muir's. Roosevelt became sick to his stomach when people cheapened old-growth redwoods in Santa Cruz by hanging signs on them, yet he did nothing to stop Hetch Hetchy from becoming a giant Sparkletts water container.

Muir, as usual, was able to round up influential supporters, including a number of powerful newspapers as well as preservation groups—and he did an especially fine job of rallying the support of women campers and wilderness protectors. His determined opponents were every bit as forceful and indignant as the people on his side. His old nemesis Forest Service chief Gifford Pinchot declared that the idea of wilderness for its own sake was simply wasteful. "Trees are a crop, just like corn."

The nasty debate must have taken Muir straight back to his youth on the farm in Wisconsin: is nature "useful" outside its productivity and what we can get out of it? James Phelan, a former San Francisco mayor, put Muir in his sights when he said, "To provide of the little children, men and women of the 800,000 population who swarm the shores of San Francisco Bay is a matter of much greater importance than encouraging a few who, in solitary loneliness, will sit on the peak of the Sierras loafing around the throne of the God of nature and singing his praise."

Hetch Hetchy is one major reason we remember the radical side of John Muir so well today; the controversy over it reawakened that quality in him. Hetch Hetchy was more than just a failed attempt to preserve part of Muir's wilderness temple. It was a grim reminder that national park status, without protections, was close to meaningless. If a city could take part of a national park, what use was the park designation? Hetch Hetchy was a momentous event for every camper in America because it was the first time that Americans really had to sit down and argue, passionately, about the use and meaning of wilderness.

Muir's defeat by the dam-building forces led to the organizing and vigilance that, in turn, led to the formation of the National Park Service in 1916, two years after Muir's death and three years after his defeat in the valley. As Ken Chowder points out in his book *Modern Maturity*, "In 1913, the time of the Hetch Hetchy decision, only a handful of conservation organizations existed; 40 years later the number was over 300."

Roosevelt himself did not authorize a bill giving the go-ahead for the dam construction; that task was left to President Woodrow Wilson, in 1913. Still, Roosevelt could have stopped the project with an executive order if he had so desired; his decision to stay out of the conflict and, in his words, avoid "the disagreeable position of seeming to interfere with the development of the state," must have awakened Muir and his many advisers to the limits of compromise.

It has been said that his defeat at Hetch Hetchy killed the heartbroken John Muir, who died in 1914 of pneumonia in Los Angeles. That is a bit simplistic, considering Muir undertook a strenuous trip to Alaska after the defeat—not the sort of thing that one would do while teetering at the edge of the grave. For another, Muir, in spite of his bitterness at this tremendous setback, seemed to understand how the decision would reverberate in history. Muir, in a vinegary way, tried to look to the upside of things: "[I]n spite of Satan & Co. some sort of compensation must surely come out of even this dark damn-dam-damnation."

He was right about that "compensation." The loss of Hetch Hetchy helped galvanize the movement behind the 1964 National Wilderness Preservation System, which preserved more than a hundred million acres of land. The battle also shored up his legend. Even earlier, it was a lesson for those fighting a dam in Echo Park, now Dinosaur National Monument, during the 1950s.

Muir, apparently, was not bitter toward Roosevelt after the battle, and Roosevelt continued to have warm feelings for him in return. In his elegy, Roosevelt paid tribute to his friend and occasional combatant, while mentioning the good their campout helped bring about: "[Muir] was . . . what few nature lovers are—a man able to influence contemporary thought and action on the subjects to which he had devoted his life. He was a great factor in influencing the thought of California and . . . the entire country . . . to secure the preservation of those great natural phenomena—wonderful canyons, giant trees, slopes of flower-spangled hillsides—which make California a veritable Garden of the Lord."

Muir and Roosevelt's campout, influential as it was, revealed a schism that divided even the people who loved wilderness the most. Roosevelt roused the spirit of preservation, yet presided over an America that had never been as built-up and industrial, lavish and wasteful. Modern times, like never before, were elbowing their way into the woods. It's not surprising that certain Americans were trying to capitalize on the desires of people who thought all that progress was happening too quickly. In 1913, the same year Muir lost his Hetch Hetchy battle, a very different sort of fight was taking place in the woods, involving a middle-aged, potbellied Yankee who retreated into the forests of Maine wearing nothing but a jockstrap. He gained thousands of fans by vowing to live like a caveman. He made a promise to his admirers: when he emerged from the forest two months later, he would be so well clothed in animal skins that he could walk a city street without causing offense.

His name was Joseph Knowles, and his camping trip would shock America.

Hero of Camping: Estwick Evans

The Craziest Thru Hiker of the
Early Nineteenth Century

Estwick Evans, an eccentric, bored, apparently burned-out New Hampshire lawyer, made headlines and caused consternation when he embarked on a borderline-suicidal four-thousand-mile "pedestrious" tour of America, starting with a seven hundred forty-four mile walk from New Hampshire into the western territories. Evans was trying to simplify his life and discover the essence of himself, thirty-five years before *Walden* came out. He embarked on America's ultimate thru hike adventure, a century and a half before Congress passed the National Trails System act of 1968, giving "national scenic trail" status to the Appalachian and Pacific Crest Trails.

The wind threw snowdrifts in Estwick Evans's face as he trudged away from his home in mid-February 1818 while dressed in thick robes of buffalo skin with bearskin trim and homemade moccasins on his feet. He loved the wilderness, but this was a time when most people found the forests terrifying. Evans took no chances. His camping gear included "a brace of pistols"; a long, thrusting dagger called a "dirk"; a small but lethal hatchet; and a six-foot rifle. If he happened upon some meager lodging, he would sleep on the bare floor with his hunting dogs Pomp and Tyger cuddled against him. On most nights, though, he took his rest in a tent, which he set up even in storms. Some people in town thought his camping tour was incomprehensible. "Some imagined me to be on a secret expedition for the government," he noted. Like Thoreau after him, Evans, who was antislavery, saw a link between camping and self-emancipation. As he walked across the country, the treatment of slaves struck him as a blight on the American soul. "Oh, cruel nation!" he wrote in his memoir. "Loh, detestable system! The oppressor is hateful to the eye of Heaven."

Evans was no lunatic. He was just a well-read, privileged gentleman who could afford to entertain romantic ideas about camping out. Like modern-day campers who revel in going out there and getting their noses cold for a while and then rushing back to their houses, Evans set out to experience "the pleasure of suffering and the novelty of danger." Giant

Estwick Evans, 1787–1866

flocks of geese rocketed over his head. Ancient forests rose above him. He waded through saline springs, squeezed through "gloomy" caverns, and stared for hours at "torpid" bats. He was woefully out of shape, his feet swelled up, and at one point he nearly froze to death. Near the dreaded Great Black Swamp of Ohio, a hungry wolf pack surrounded poor Pomp and Tyger, ripped them to pieces, and devoured them while Evans lay moaning in his tent, driven half mad by an "excruciating tooth ache," which temporarily deprived him, puzzlingly, of most of his sense of hearing. He had every reason to finish his campout in a bitter or mopey frame of mind. Instead, he returned full of rapture.

In all, he lugged forty pounds of pack weight "through deep snows and bogs and over many a tedious mountain." When asked why he would have done such a silly, treacherous thing, Evans said, "I wished to acquire the simplicity, native feelings and virtues of savage life . . . and to become a citizen of the world. . . . How great are the advantages of solitude!"

10

Night at Badger Spring

I am not interested in money, and my purpose is entirely scientific. I shall enter [a forest] naked and take with me absolutely nothing. I shall see absolutely no one. I shall keep a birch-bark record with charcoal of my progress and place it each week under a stump where a trapper will get it and send it to the *Sunday Post*.
—Joseph Knowles, 1913

[T]he simple life ain't so simple.
—Van Halen, "Runnin' with the Devil," 1978

My naked survival campout was going very well until I sat on a yellow jacket nest. It happened around half past noon, judging from the position of the sun.

At the time of the incident, I had been hanging around for about a half hour in a remote corner of the Santa Cruz Mountains on California's Central Coast. I was on a green and bushy hill, a steep forty-five-minute bushwhack from the nearest trail. My car was five miles away, on the side of a country road. In this untrammeled section of the Soquel Demonstration State Forest, I saw no fence posts or signs, no barbed wire, or any other indication that a human had been there in a long while.

I had no tent on me, no survival knife, flashlight, sleeping bag, underpants, water bottle, toilet paper, bug spray, or first-aid kit, and no way of calling out for help. I had brought my baby-blue Xopenex inhaler because

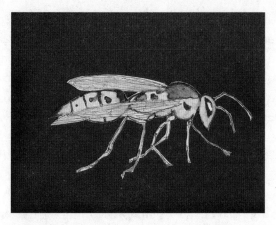

The yellow jacket can sting its victim multiple times.

I can't breathe without it. I'd also brought my prescription glasses and half a whole wheat peanut butter and honey sandwich, which slipped out of my hand and landed in a pile of deer scat the moment I arrived on the hill. Never mind. At dinnertime, I would forage for a tangy green plant called redwood sorrel, and see if I could find any sticky monkey flowers for dessert.

Still, the sandwich incident reminded me to be more careful. Even small mistakes would have consequences in a 2,681-acre state-administered forest reserve that would be deserted when the sun went down. Camping wasn't even allowed up there. I had had to get a special-use permit and sign a document promising that my family "under no circumstances" would sue California if something awful happened.

In those fleeting moments before the wasps arrived, I loosened up a bit, while maintaining my hypersensitivity to the woods around me. It felt so freeing to be naked in a place like this. I couldn't remember the last time I was that present inside my body. I spent a good long while just staring at my left arm, admiring it. I lifted it up and down, counting the freckles and the little blond hairs and examining the crease where the arm met my shoulder. I wriggled my toes in the mud, which was rich and crumbly and smelled like mold. Then I spent a while examining my gastrocnemius muscles. Tan oaks and second-growth redwoods shaded me from the sun as I walked barefoot through a luxuriant canopy of wild ginger and five-fingered ferns. I put my hands on my hips and breathed in. A glory beam lit up a clearing in the middle of the grove, the tree roots all knotted together, forming a circle. The wind whispered against my buttocks.

The only thing that bothered me just a little bit, and prevented me from relaxing too much, was the slight chance of encountering a cougar.

They lived there. I don't mean to suggest that they lived, exclusively, inside the Soquel Demonstration State Forest. Cougars roam around; they have places to go. Sometimes they even show up lost and confused in downtown Santa Cruz. But the forest is part of their habitat. I once attended a lecture by a mountain lion expert named Chris Wilmers, who said the chance of getting eaten by a mountain lion was less than the chance of impaling yourself accidentally with a toothbrush, the sort of thing that happens only in the *Final Destination* horror movie franchise. Still, you can't be too careful, so I made a point of scanning the treetops every once in a while for sunbathing apex predators with eyes the size of golf balls and yellowy slits for pupils. It did not occur to me that a much more immediate danger was hiding in the earth beneath my feet.

Feeling thirsty, I crept up the ridge to the source of Badger Spring, a few hundred feet away from the place where I would be sleeping for the night. There, I crouched, cupped my hands, and filled my belly with the most delicious spring water. I rubbed a little bit of that water in my hair and on my chin and dabbed some on the sides of my neck like eau de cologne. For all I knew, I was the first person to camp here ever. This was the first time a piece of forest ever really belonged to me. I let the forest soothe me. There was no separation between me and nature.

That's when I first heard the buzzing sound, like an electric current moving through a power line. The noises seemed to be coming up from below the ground. "Oh, no," I said out loud, because only one creature on earth made that particular *Bzzzzzzit*.

I stood up and brushed the dust and dirt off me. Too late. A dozen yellow jackets circled me, bobbing up and down in the air.

I knew from experience that yellow jackets are monstrous in a way that transcends mere cruelty. They are incapable even of indifference. It's very possible that they have no thoughts, just a bunch of white static. You cannot reason with bugs. I'd been stung before, badly, in Point Reyes, California. I went into mild shock, and my arms turned the color of Vienna sausages, the kind that come in jars. My wife had to sit by my side for hours and put a cold compress on my head because I was burning up.

No, I could not get stung again, even once, not while I was naked. And what if the yellow jackets stung me *down there*? What then?

I wanted to run, but that was not an option, because the ground was steep and uneven, full of little snags, rocks, roots, and gullies, and I had no shoes on.

The sound was loud now. Wasps everywhere. Keep calm. Don't panic. Just get to your tent and seal yourself in.

But there was no tent, no nothing in my camping spot, just a pile of leaves and a rotting log.

My chances of escape were slim, but I had to try. What choice did I have? I couldn't run, exactly, without scraping and bashing my feet and toes. The only option was to take a series of small but powerful uphill leaps as the yellow jackets closed in on me. With my hands cupped in front of the most vulnerable and sensitive region of my body, and my backside exposed to the fates, I bunny-hopped through the forest, screaming.

In those moments before the inevitable happened, my mind filled with nothing but fear. As I fled from the wasps, my decision to be out there in the first place suddenly seemed impulsive and absurd, the worst idea I'd ever had.

The fact is, I had never prepared so hard for any camping trip in my life. I'd hashed out every aspect for weeks in advance. I even chose the departure date, August 3, 2013, for its historic value. In the summer of 1913, one hundred years before I started my own nude survival experiment, the good people of Boston, Massachusetts, opened up their newspaper and saw a story that must have made them choke on their cream toast with prairie chicken.

Joe Knowles, a middle-aged Boston-based painter, wildlife illustrator, onetime hunting guide, and former navy man, declared that he would enter the Dead River wilderness of Maine, 250 miles north of the city, without a stitch of clothing on his doughy, five-foot-nine-inch corpus. Never mind that he was a chain-smoker and heavy drinker whose appearance did not inspire confidence. He had a nose like a crookneck squash and weighed 204 pounds, but he didn't seem to care. He would prove to America that he was a winner.

Even in the era of woodcraft and survivalism, his plan was audacious. For two months in the woods, he would dwell among the coon cats, meadow voles, and woodchucks, enjoying no contact with humans. Knowles would have no premade tools, books, implements, or weapons. To mark the days, the Nature Man, as he came to be known, would cut notches in a tree with a stone axe made of foraged materials. The woods would be his Walmart. If he got hungry, he'd kill an ungulate. In a year of assembly lines, slums, child labor, tenements, Stravinsky's *Rite of Spring*, difficult modernist fiction, the institution of the Federal Reserve Act, and America's first income tax, Joseph Knowles was going to live like it was fifty thousand years BC. By the time of his campout, many other Americans, most notably Theodore Roosevelt, had preached the importance of the "strenuous life" and living up to the grit and the resourcefulness of the pioneers. Knowles was trying to be the ultimate exemplar of that raw and adventurous lifestyle. And for a while, at least, people as far away as Chicago knew his name. His breathtaking naked camping stories got more attention than the 1913 World Series.

By being out there in the woods, I wanted to pay tribute to this man, and get a better sense of the excitement and misgivings he experienced firsthand. Most of all, I wanted to feel the "full freedom of life" that he describes so vividly in his writings about the camp. What would it be like, even for twenty-four hours, to do as Knowles did, taking up Thoreau's challenge of "Simplicity! Simplicity!" and pushing it to the logical extreme? I thought this campout would disprove all the ideas I'd accumulated about myself: that I'd lost my boldness, that I wasn't half the man I was when I walked the Pacific Crest Trail. It would also be a way to slough off all the useless pieces of camping equipment I'd accumulated over the years. His message resonated with me: an ordinary-looking middle-aged man could reinvent himself in the woods.

Knowles's underdog credentials were secure. He grew up poor and, in the grand tradition of many famous American campers, had the requisite lousy relationship with his dad, who bullied him. As a child, his peers taunted young Joe for snacking on sowbelly and using a lard pail as his lunch box. Now he had a chance to prove those schoolyard bullies wrong.

At 10:40 a.m. on August 4, 1913, Knowles took off his brown suit and stripped to a white cotton jockstrap, which he wore for propriety's sake. Now he looked pudgy and pale as he stood before the group of reporters and wilderness guides. He struck a few poses and flexed his muscles in the drizzle. "My body was already glistening with the rain, but it didn't bother me any," he remembered later on.

A doctor examined him. One well-wisher asked if he would like one last cigarette. Knowles accepted it, took a few puffs, and tossed it on the

Joseph Knowles strips down to his jockstrap in front of a group of well-wishers and curiosity seekers. Image from *Alone in the Wilderness*.

ground. This, in itself, was quite a cocky gesture; it must have been hard to give up a serious smoking habit just before a stressful and possibly life-threatening journey. Perhaps this final puff was a message to the crowd: *I am capable of anything. Willpower is only the beginning of what I can do.*

People in the crowd, especially the survivalist types, must have wondered why Knowles was so sure of himself. In the days before his departure, friends "literally begged me to abandon the idea," he said. What was Knowles's secret? Why was he so self-assured? People vanished in the Maine woods from time to time. Besides, without "bug dope," a sticky pre-DEET insect repellent consisting of pennyroyal boiled with pine tar and castor oil, Knowles would be defenseless against blackflies, which bit so hard they left welts and blood puddles. No problem; before the campout, Knowles, a native of rural Maine, planned to reach high elevations where mosquitos could not be found. He had been experimenting with natural repellents, including foraged mint leaves smeared all over his body.

In the final moments before his adventure, Knowles smiled at the onlookers. "See you later, boys!" he said, and walked away in his flimsy codpiece.

A local camp operator and a hunting guide tracked Knowles for a while, but they turned back after a few miles. Knowles, seeing that he'd lost his unwanted escorts, discarded the jock strap and headed off into the unknown.

Two months before my own naked campout, I took the first necessary step toward learning how to survive like Joseph Knowles: I went out and hired a wilderness consultant.

If I lived in any other city in America, finding someone to advise me on the art of nude camping might have been a challenge. But my home is in Santa Cruz, California, where you can find someone to teach you just about anything. If you're interested in soul retrieval and acupuncture for cats, we've got the expert for you. We once had a self-proclaimed "Breatharian" who claimed he could show people how to eat and gain sustenance from food odors (while leaving the food intact). He was gaining some traction until a story started circulating about him devouring a pot pie from 7-Eleven, followed by Twinkies and a Big Gulp.

One wonders how such wildly impractical people could get by even in the short term in a town where the median home price is $755,100. Here's my theory: Santa Cruz forces iconoclasts and creative-minded people to become extreme survivalists in one way or another. The few who can stay here in the long term without selling out or going broke must have a wiliness, resourcefulness, and endurance that would rival those of any naked camper on reality TV.

It did not take long for my search to lead me to Robin Bliss-Wagner, perhaps the wildest man in Santa Cruz. I met him during one of the all-day intensive wilderness skills classes that he teaches at the University of California, Santa Cruz campus. Robin is a dashing young man with long hair tied up in a loose ponytail. His aquiline nose reminded me of a goshawk's beak. Something about his eyes brought to mind an owl or a kestrel. It must have been his steady watchfulness, and the sense that he was casing out his surroundings at all times without comment, looking for any movements, disruptions, changes. I had the sense that Robin was taking note of everything and everyone, adding it to a mental Filofax that never ran out of pages.

Unlike the blustering Joe Knowles, Robin is soft-spoken, gentle, and humble, but he's a keen-eyed stalker of prey animals. He told me about the times he'd taken squirrels with a homemade bow and arrow. "They're just as good as chicken," he insisted.

Most of his interactions with animals are peaceful. He loves to observe them. Robin talked about holding himself so still in the Sierra Nevada foothills, willing himself to vanish, that black bears sauntered past him without giving him so much as a sniff. I asked if he'd camped out naked in the forest. "Several times," he told me. He once slept in the buff beneath a bunch of acacia pods, and though the air above him was frosty, he was steaming hot beneath his blanket of vegetation. He hones his skills through constant learning, and always seeks out people who know more than he does. Alongside his tracking mentor, Jon Young, a protégé of the survivalist, best-selling author, and animal tracker Tom Brown Jr., Robin traveled to Africa to learn wilderness skills from Kalahari Bushmen, who astounded him with their birdcall analysis. He remembered one instance in which a Bushman, hearing a bird's distress trills, said that he knew which animal was menacing the bird (a mongoose) and the direction of the predator's approach (from the southeast).

When I told him about my plans to do a survival campout in honor of a once-famous naked woodsman named Joe Knowles, Robin laughed. I detected no malice in his laughter, only enthusiasm and amused interest. He cautioned that his seven-hour session could teach me only so much about camping naked.

He and his students picked some green and spiny leaves of yarrow, a powerful coagulant; crush it in your mouth and secure it to your wound with a loop of buckskin and the bleeding will subside, Robin told me. He showed me a plant called mugwort, a delicate and fuzzy weed that makes excellent tinder and serves as a "coal enhancer" for friction fires. As we slipped in and out of forests overlooking the eco-brutalist buildings of UC Santa Cruz, he taught me how to take a carved wooden spindle, secure it to a piece of cord, tie the cord to both ends of a curving stick as long as his arm, and then work the stick back and forth in a blur of motion, making the spindle turn so fast it burned a hole in a piece of soft wood, creating a smoldering, peanut-size coal that Robin enrobed in mugwort and duff.

He blew his bundle gently, and *foof!*—there was fire. Speechless and amazed, I decided right then to hire him as my naked campout trainer. Robin became my frequent companion in the forests of Santa Cruz in the weeks leading up to the big event I called Knowles Day, the one hundredth anniversary of Knowles's campout. Robin taught me more than survival. Together we studied a tight piece of rabbit-fur-tufted bobcat shit. We chewed Douglas fir needles, chock-full of vitamin C. He showed me how to quiet my mind in troubled times by using a process called Owl Eyes. All you do is focus on the middle distance and still your brain so you notice the slightest swaying of a tree bough, a tremble in the underbrush, and the flicker of a bird's wing. In teaching me this skill, Robin enhanced my ability to *look*; while taking a hike on my own in between my training sessions, I saw, for the first time, an endangered Ohlone tiger beetle, its iridescent green shell rattling through the high grass at Moore Creek Preserve, in Santa Cruz. On one of our long walks in the woods together, I told Robin how much I despised certain animals and plants, and he asked which insect I hated most of all.

"Yellow jackets!" I said.

He gently admonished me for loathing wasps. Most of the time when they attack you, they are just protecting their young and following pure instinct, he said. Besides, they are janitors of the wild. He asked if I'd ever seen yellow jackets swarm around a carcass. If I looked closely enough, I'd see that each yellow jacket was carrying a small piece of meat ripped from the dead body. Somehow the thought of this brought little comfort.

"But how do I stop yellow jackets from stinging me?" I asked him.

He said that if I held my ear close to the ground, I could hear them buzzing. It was always good to scan the earth this way before digging around looking for vegetation to build a shelter.

"But what if they come after me?"

Robin smiled at my question. "Run!" he said. "Run like hell."

When Robin teaches intensive nature skills courses to adults and youth, he is responding to a "collective hunger" he shares with Americans who feel they have been separated from the land for far too long. While he was telling me about this primal need to be in natural areas, it occurred to me that it was this same longing that had led to Joe Knowles's massive fame a century before. That was a time when progress-addled people took solace in stories that highlighted the primitive in fantastical ways, including the Tarzan tales of Edgar Rice Burroughs. The nation was learning that technology and comfort had their limitations. A year before Knowles did his naked campout, the state-of-the-art and luxurious *Titanic* sank to the bottom of the ocean off the coast of Newfoundland, killing 1,517 people.

Knowles may have been fleeing the excesses of the twentieth century, but he made sure in advance that thousands of people would follow his every move in the woods. Before the campout, Knowles signed a deal with the *Boston Post*, a workingman's newspaper and the archrival of William Randolph Hearst's flashier *Sunday American*. For added authenticity, Knowles would write each report from the forest on a birch bark roll and include drawings of animals. Using burned bits of charcoal, he would scratch out and illustrate dispatches from the deep woods.

He was the whole picture, skilled but human and relatable, and because of his extreme subject matter, he had a built-in massive audience. In that sense, Knowles was America's first outdoor survival "reality star," predating by nearly a century the contemporary survivalist programming on television, including *Naked and Afraid*, a series featuring the exploits of naked campers trapped in jungles. Another recent example is a 2014 series called *Fat Guys in the Woods*, in which a group of marshmallowy and clueless men are led by soft-spoken, earnest-eyed survivalist Creek Stewart into a forest, where he teaches them to make friction fires, forage for wild grapes, and catch prey.

Those campouts are glorified publicity stunts, and so was Knowles's. But *Walden*, in some sense, was also a publicity stunt, an extreme gesture designed to inspire, confound, and provoke American readers. Knowles's admirers thought of him as a genuine woodsman, unlike those egghead transcendentalists who knew next to nothing about hard-core survival. Ralph Waldo Emerson and his buddies had to take along a wilderness guide for each member of their camping party in the Adirondacks. Knowles marketed himself as the real deal, a master of camping in its rawest form. One minister, interviewed by the *Post*, predicted that Knowles would "share the fame of [Henry] David Thoreau."

I longed for my own chance at naked camping glory, but was starting to wonder if it was ever going to happen. Robin was showing me how to do my experiment successfully. The trouble was, I couldn't figure out where the adventure should take place.

Originally I planned to do the trip in Maine, to honor Knowles, but decided it made more sense to camp nude near my hometown. Knowles, for all his bravery, made sure to camp in a forest he knew well. Why should I place myself in a completely unfamiliar landscape? As far as I could figure out, though, the only way I could do this locally would involve trespassing, which I did not want to do. I could just imagine the headlines in the *Santa Cruz Sentinel*: "Asthmatic Nudist Flashes Felton Grandmother; Deputies Summoned." The best approach would be camping on private property, where no one would hassle me, and I would break no state laws, as far as I knew. But it was hard to find a parcel that met my extensive needs, and none of my landed-gentry acquaintances would return my phone calls.

I decided to try my luck with the good people over at California State Parks, but they had serious reservations about letting me camp on public lands. One stumbling block was my planned display of nakedness, a misdemeanor in California, which had rules against anyone "willfully" and "lewdly . . . expos[ing] his person, or the private parts thereof." To make the trip more palatable, I agreed to put on a skimpy loincloth to avoid shocking anyone I might meet in the woods. I also discarded my original halfhearted plan to hunt squirrels with a primitive spear called an atlatl. Instead, I planned to take along a super-realistic squirrel toy I'd ordered on Amazon so I could practice "hunting" it instead. There are no state laws against killing something that never lived.

Yet the rangers would not be mollified, even when I decided not to build friction fires, which I was bad at doing anyway. One of them, who worked at the Wilder Ranch State Park in Santa Cruz, told me my plan to harvest plants and build a "foliate debris shelter" would violate state park laws by damaging wood, "and then when you write about it, you will encourage someone to do the same." I tried to assure him that I would attempt to follow "Leave No Trace" practices as closely as possible. I would merely displace some fallen deadwood and then put it back where it was. "I will only eat small handfuls of delicious wildflowers," I told him. "And I will attempt to harvest them in a sustainable manner."

The ranger would not change his mind.

I was just about to hang up the phone and forget this crazy campout altogether when the ranger said, "I just thought of something. Have you tried the Soquel Demonstration State Forest?"

The ranger's suggestion surprised me. I'd visited the place for a few hours with my wife; we took a hike there. It was dry, dusty, and hot, ringing with chain saws and smelling like sawdust. The place was also full of mountain bikers. Then I remembered that Knowles's experiment took place in a nonpristine forest chockablock with hunters' camps. The ranger told me that the rules regarding overnight campouts might be a little different at the "Demo Forest," because loggers "sustainably harvest" lumber there; in other words, the place doesn't pretend to be a howling wilderness.

Still, I was jumpy when I called the forest management office. What if they rejected me, too? They put me on hold forever, and while I was wait-ing, the voice mail system played a spooky old song called "A Forest," by the Cure, about a man who gets lost in the woods running after a girl who turns out to be an apparition: "The girl was never there." The spirit, it seems, is luring him to his doom. By the time the forest manager Angela Bernheisel got on the line, I was so unnerved by the song that I almost lost my chain of thought. Bernheisel listened to my elevator pitch without com-ment. Then she took me off guard with her sudden and enthusiastic yes. I felt elated on the one hand, and also had a sobering realization: "Good God, I'm actually going to have to do this thing."

She said she would make a special exemption to their no-camping rule because my campout sounded "educational." She cautioned me *not* to camp in a riparian corridor, where mountain lions love to hunt and where the temperature can drop to forty degrees Fahrenheit, even in summer— precisely the kind of place I needed to camp if I wanted access to clean water.

When Knowles Day arrived, in early August, I was feeling proud, sure of myself, and well prepared. *Cougars, schmougars*, I thought. Nothing was going to hurt me out there.

By then, I'd had one last intensive practice session with Robin. Just to make sure I was ready, the two of us had visited the Soquel Demonstration State Forest a week before the day I'd scheduled for my naked campout. He'd bushwhacked up the hill with me, led me to a reasonable spot for camping, and even helped me build part of the shelter I would occupy that night, though he left it up to me to complete the job. While I nibbled on a chicken burrito, Robin led me to good water just up the hill. He'd homed in on the source of the creek to minimize my chances of drinking runoff water infected with animal wastes.

I was as well prepared as I could ever be.

But my wife, Amy, did not like my idea one smidgen.

We'd been together for thirteen years by then. She knows I can be impulsive and self-sabotaging. Sometimes she thinks of herself as my unpaid life manager and, other times, as a topiary artist. I am her unruly tree; she is always making artful snips. In other words, Amy tries to motivate me when I'm apathetic, but she also tries to prune me back, especially when I'm obsessing about something she thinks will cause me harm. On the morning of my departure, she tried once more to talk me out of going, even while I was hauling out my loincloth and stuffing a few provisions into a cotton sheet I'd bought at a yard sale and cut in half.

Amy sighed. "I've been telling my friends about what you're doing, and they think it's weird, and not in a good way," she said as I was getting ready to leave. She pressed a peanut butter and honey sandwich in my hand and made me promise I'd eat it. "You were *never* supposed to push it this far," she said. "You told me you were going to go out and camp naked for one or two hours at the maximum. You weren't going to spend a whole day and night in a forest with no clothes on. I think your parents need to know about this right now."

"Please don't tell my parents," I said. "They're Jewish. They won't understand."

Only my daughter, four years old at the time, did not seem the least bit worried. She handed me a diagram she'd made of my shelter. In her mind, it had plenty of blankets, even a functioning toilet. If anything, she seemed thrilled for me. "Stay warm in your shelter, Daddy. Bring pillows. Don't get splinters."

I understood my wife's fear, but I had no choice. How was one hour going to give me even the dimmest sense of what Knowles experienced?

I arrived at the Soquel Demonstration State Forest at 10:00 a.m. in my scratched-up Toyota Corolla. The rural road and dark woods behind it seemed so remote to me then, though this place was only forty minutes from our dingy rental house in Santa Cruz and ten miles from Highway 17, which passes through the green mountains and links Santa Cruz with Silicon Valley. Up to thirty thousand commuters drive on it every day. Many of them toil in the tech industry. How strange to take such a highway to my own personal Stone Age.

Joe Knowles believed he was leading America back to Neolithic times. He would prove by example that man could achieve "vigor and energy and pleasure for the life led by the original cave men," wrote the *Chicago Tribune* in a 1913 news story that was a barely disguised fan letter to Knowles.

Now I wanted to follow Knowles into the forest. I parked my car near the entrance to the Soquel Demonstration State Forest. When I got out of the Corolla, I was wearing only tennis shoes and a loincloth, which I'd made from a flap of scratchy deer hide, a long and tapering strand of deer gut, and a sustainably harvested deer horn for a clasp. I'd bought these items for a total of $13.67 at a Santa Cruz leather store that caters to survivalists and bondage enthusiasts.

After stepping from the car, I noticed four squadrons of mountain bikers preparing for their morning ride; the Demo Forest is popular among fat-tire fanatics. Some of the cyclists were looking at me. On the dusty hood of my car, I unrolled half a cotton sheet, dropped a few survival items in the center of it, rolled it up tight, and draped it across my shoulders. I was just making sure the car doors were locked when a cyclist rode up to me with a look of grave concern.

"What do you think you're doing?" he said, looking me up and down.

Caught off guard, I tried to explain the historic nature of my naked camping project, its origins and specific precedents, harkening to survivalists in the early years of the twentieth century, when Americans revolted against modernity by embracing primitivism.

"That's fine," he said, "but you're crazy to leave your car on this road. We've got crackheads. They'll bust your windows. They'll cut your tires."

"You've got crackheads *and* cougars up here?"

"At least put your things in the trunk, where the crackheads won't see it. They'll steal everything. They'll sell it for drugs."

"All I've got is junk."

"Even junk!"

I did as the man told me to do, placing my daughter's eyeless, legless dolls, stick figure drawings, empty bottles of Tugaboos baby wash, and half-melted crayons in the trunk, alongside my balled-up socks and coffee-splattered back issues of *Poets and Writers*. Still, I felt discombobulated as I made my way toward my camping area. I couldn't stop thinking about the crackheads who haunted this area, although I just had to wonder if the cyclist meant "crankheads," which is a more sylvan demographic than crackheads. It took a little while, but I was able to center myself by taking deep breaths until I pushed those druggy car burglars out of my mind. Nothing I could do about it anyway. This was the chance of a lifetime. I couldn't blow it by worrying too much about a few meth zombies.

Car windows could be replaced, but this moment might never come again.

I jogged down the unpaved Hihn's Mill Road, a glorified dirt track, the sun breaking through redwoods at intervals. A bike-squashed snake lay in the dust like a rubber toy. Dozens of helmeted cyclists passed me by. I can't blame them for staring so contemptuously at a bald guy running down the road in a getup that looked exactly like the one Raquel Welch wore in *One Million Years B.C.*, minus the bikini top and sexual frisson. The loincloth was just my way of staying true to the primitive spirit of my survival camp-out without flouting California's public nudity laws.

After a while of jogging, I reached the bottom of the slope and saw the Badger Spring waterfall, about five miles downhill from the place where I'd parked the car. With every step, I imagined Robin was with me, giving advice. On the way, I remembered what he told me during our visit to this forest. When I arrived at my designated point of departure, I would rest for a moment, then leave the possessions I'd rolled inside the cotton sheet, including my flashlight, fleece jacket, bottled water, knife, and the lifelike stuffed squirrel toy, in the hollow of a redwood tree. Robin simply called this designated hiding place "X marks the spot," but I chose to call it the Tree of Cowardice, or the Chickenshit Tree; it would be waiting for me if I decided to "chicken out" of my naked camping adventure.

Yet this clever plan had a catch. If I decided the naked campout was too much for me, as long as there was light, I could make my way down from the steep and trackless woods, retrieve the flashlight and other gear, and hike right out. Once the sun went down, however, I would have no way of descending that heavily forested and treacherous hillside in pitch-black darkness and retrieving my gear. At that point, I would be stuck on the hilltop for the night.

At the bottom of the hill, I left the dirt road and found a suitable redwood to store my provisions. There I left my survival gear, including all my warm clothes. I also left the plushy squirrel toy I'd bought online from Amazon. Then I started hiking barefoot up the hill, but the ground was so sharp and poky that I decided to go back to the Chickenshit Tree and retrieve my sneakers. I was just reaching into it when a plague of unwanted rational thoughts began to assail me.

What are you doing? I said to myself. *You're going to freeze your ass off in your shelter! Don't just take your sneakers. Take all the rest of the gear with you! This is insane.*

Struggling with indecisiveness, I reached into the tree, scooped up all my clothes and equipment, and began hiking up into the forest, cradling my belongings in my arms. That's when another scolding voice began to shout in my head. *Coward. Fraudster. You are violating the rules you set for your own campout. Put it all back!* Reluctantly I hiked back to the Chicken-shit Tree. Though I could not bear to take off the sneakers, I left the wind-breaker, the knife, the map, the compass, the flashlight, the leggings, and even my fuzzy insulating jacket.

I took the squirrel.

For the next forty-five minutes, wearing only shoes and a loincloth, and still clutching the cotton sheet in my arms, I hiked my way up a slippery slope covered with tan oaks, a misleadingly named evergreen hardwood that is actually part of the beech family. Their trunks were gray and bumpy, like elephant skin. Their leaves were blue and waxy, with prickly edges. An exotic water mold, *Phytophthora ramorum*, had made them dry and spongy and ready to topple over. Sometimes I would reach out for one of their branches and try to pull myself up; the rotten wood broke off in my hand.

I tightened the clasp and readjusted the loincloth, which was slipping down my hips. Holding my head close to the ground, I used the spring's faint traces and the orientation of the slope to make my way toward the place Robin had selected as my camp. At times I felt lost; the forest seemed to swirl around me, giving me vertigo. A dark-eyed junco offered some much-needed encouragement from the bushes. "Neat, neat, neat!" he cried. "Thank you!" I cried back.

Rather than allowing myself to dwell on my misgivings, I focused on the insurgent cheekiness of my campout. I'd gone to extremes to keep my experiment pure. I'd brought no water filter, no water purification tablets of any kind. Of course, giardia was a real concern; I'd gotten a bad bout of it on the Pacific Crest Trail twenty years before, lost twenty-five pounds, and looked in some of my trail photos like the nut-brown, shriveled-up Mummies of Guanajuato. That's why I now scrambled as close to the source of Badger Spring as possible: the last thing I wanted was raw drinking water contaminated with creature turds.

Halfway up the hill, I entered a thick redwood grove. The time had arrived for me to ditch the loincloth and shoes. No more delays. No more excuses.

In a sunlit clearing between a fairy circle of slender redwoods, I reached down and undid the deer-horn clasp. With a Gypsy Rose Lee shimmy shake and a teasing twirl, I let the flimsy garment slide down my midsection, slip down my thighs, and puddle around my ankles. Then I removed my tennis shoes and buried them under a pile of rocks along with the loincloth—and then I was completely, gloriously naked.

The sun shimmered in the momentarily hushed forest. The leaves shivered in the Douglas firs and madrones. I walked onward, ever so slowly slipping through shrubs, mosses, sorrels, and crumbled wood the color of devil's food cake mix.

For the first time I really *smelled* a forest: the sweet and glorious rot of it, the chlorophyll and disintegration, the soapy scent of a ceanothus plant, the invigorating tang of fallen redwood needles. Tree limbs creaked like timbers at sea. I could feel the circular motion of air molecules scrubbing up and down my body like invisible loofahs.

The trees gave off a mentholated scent, which felt sharp, almost painful, in my nose. Planes flew out of San Jose airport and passed a few thousand feet above me. Hearing the rush of their engines and watching their vapor trails only added to the thrill of my isolation.

I took care with every step. Piles of leaves might conceal hollows where I could fall and wrench my ankle. I was relieved to come across my half-built debris shelter, which rested against a long and rotten redwood log. It was about seventy degrees outside. Every time a breeze passed through the woods and ruffled the remaining hairs on my head, my alertness sharpened.

A blue fly descended on me and nibbled the dead skin at the end of my index finger. It meant no harm. I did not kill it. Glory beams fell from the sky and lit the flat space at the bottom of a steep hill. I took a good long look at this lovely unloved place. This was the first time a campground really felt like *mine*. But this was no time to get sentimental. When that ball of fire sank below the horizon, I would have to be sealed inside my little shelter without a flashlight. Robin had told me that the moon tonight would be "sliver to none."

I distracted myself for a few blissful moments, making a spear thrower out of rocks, twigs, and grass and hurling projectiles at the lifeless toy squirrel. *Bam!* I scored a direct hit. After building up a thirst with my atlatl tossing, I put the squirrel back on the rotten log and went up to Badger Spring. A beetle scuttled past me, a suit of black armor protecting its squishy parts. Everything I stepped on or brushed against was so much spikier and sturdier than I was.

Soon I found the long, dark slit that contained the spring. I arrived at the spot where water burbled up from beneath a rock overhang. There, in the shade, I sat down apelike in mud. The water was sugary sweet and had a zinging mineral aftertaste. I dribbled water across my scalp. "Oooh la la!" I cried. I got down on my haunches and settled on the soft, dusty ground, trickled water down my chin—and that's when I heard the buzzing. Thinking at first that it was my fearful imagination or early-onset tinnitus, I ignored the sound until the humming got louder and more insistent.

In an instant the wasps were everywhere. In my defense, this was not one of those classic breast-shaped wasp nests, those bulbous, papery ones that dangle from tree branches. Burrowing California yellow jackets congregate in hollows and tunnels. They have enormous colonies and protect them aggressively. I managed to pluck one wasp off my shoulder and smash it on a rock. I had no way of knowing that my defensive violence would only worsen the situation. Lynn Kimsey, a professor of entomology at the University of California at Davis, told me after the fact that squishing a yellow jacket "releases all kinds of body odors" from the dead creature. If you've already disturbed the nest at that point, as I had done, the agitated insects will recognize the odor of their dead or damaged comrade. The smell of its broken body will "recruit" other wasps against you.

"Running is the *only* solution, because you will get stung a buttload of times if you don't," Kinsey informed me.

Angry yellow jackets, if so inclined, will chase you two hundred feet. I tried to escape, but did not go fast enough. The stings came all at once—*thwock, thwock, thwack!*

It felt like someone was splashing boiling broth on me. The corrosive liquid pain spread across my neck and shoulders, upper stomach area, hips and abdomen, but not—thank God—anywhere below my waist. By the time I reached the campsite, the little demons had stung me seven times. I was getting woozy; the forest was starting to wobble. I lay down in the cool soft dirt and rolled around for a good long while in pain, pressing clumps of earth against the swelling lumps on my neck and abdomen. At least the wasps had tired of tormenting me and returned to their hideaway. I moaned a lot, which did no good at all. My breath came up short, ragged, and labored. I could feel a great pressure bearing down on my chest. My legs seemed to be made of gelatin.

I wanted to get the hell out of there, but I could barely move; even in the daytime, with that much poison in my system, there was no way I could safely negotiate the half mile of steep, slanting, potentially neck-breaking stretches between here and Hihn's Mill Road. All I could do was lie there in a panic, hyperventilating, taking hits from my Xopenex inhaler, trying to open my airways, and every so often glancing at my useless cell phone, which I'd brought just to photograph my campout for anyone who needed proof. I watched the SEARCHING FOR RECEPTION message flashing on the upper right side of the screen.

I was much too hyped-up and dizzy to think of anything but my own escape from this situation, and what I would do if more wasps decided to sting me. After a while, I took some cold comfort in the knowledge that Joseph Knowles's first day in the woods was also painful, lonely, and dangerous.

In the first few hours of his campout, cold rain washed over his naked body, and there was no escaping from it. He crossed Bear Mountain, bare and shivering, arrived at Lost Pond, and soon had his first taste of real suffering. Brambles and bull thistle tore his skin. He limped through the underbrush, bleeding. None of the hype or his adoring fans could help him now. "My legs looked like they had been in a fight with a wildcat, to say nothing of how they felt," he wrote in a birch bark missive to his waiting public.

That night, he tried and failed to make a friction fire; the wood was too moist. He had no food, and no shelter to keep him out of the dampness. Knowles jogged through the woods all night long to keep his blood moving and to stay warm. "I must have run miles that night," he wrote.

He was so pumped up with adrenaline that he didn't feel sleepy. Just to pass the time, he found a tree limb and did some chin-ups.

"Daylight came very slowly," he reported.

As Knowles found out, time is relative when you're naked in the dirt. "What time is it now?" I wondered as I lay against the log, the stings still throbbing on my neck and on my sides, my head resting on a pile of leaves. My thoughts turned to something Robin had told me during our intensive training sessions: Calm yourself. Go to Owl Eyes. Focus on the middle distance. Pay attention to any disturbance or change or motion you see. Pay attention to the softest sound you can hear. Having no other choice, I tried Robin's method. After a while, my thoughts settled down, and my airways seemed to open up again. It was working. But just as I was entering a kind of limbo, made possible by a combination of self-hypnosis and a soporific dose of wasp poison, I noticed a flash of yellow.

A yellow jacket landed on the rotten log right next to my head.

She was perhaps three feet away from me.

"Go away," I whispered. "Please get out of here."

But she would not move.

I forced myself to stay motionless, and the wasp remained there on the log, an inch or two away from my useless squirrel toy. I considered taking hold of a nearby piece of wood and squashing the wasp, but it was much too risky.

Five minutes passed. The wasp still wasn't moving. Maybe she was building up her energy to attack me better.

Without knowing why, and because there was nothing else to do, I forced myself to take a good hard look at her. (The aggressive attackers in any yellow jacket colony are females.) Her girlfriends had all gone home by then. It was just the two of us. The wasp began to walk up the log. She looked wobbly. Perhaps I'd hurt her on my flight back to camp.

The yellow jacket twitched her antennae and settled down again. I'd never seen one close up like this. I was surprised at how damned pretty she was: yellow patches, racing stripes, black circles down her body, the delicate piping between her thorax and abdomen, and wings I could see right through. Her eyes were black and glossy. I remained that way in my cradle of tan oak leaves for a while, just staring at her. No detail was out of place. I marveled at her perfect stinger, the downy tufts on her head, and the branching lines on her wings.

I don't know how long I ogled her in this fashion. Do wasps sleep? This one seemed unconscious. Now was my chance to pick up a rock and end her life, but I didn't see the point. I grew sleepy and briefly napped. When I woke up, the yellow jacket was gone. Such was my loneliness that I wished she'd come back. She had gone in such a hurry.

It was getting dark. My hunger rumbled through me, but I had nothing to eat but redwood sorrel, which I stuffed into my palm, rolled up, and covered with even more redwood sorrel, pretending the glob of green mush

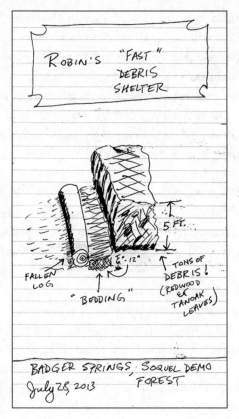

Robin Bliss-Wagner gave me a precise and elegant blueprint for building a debris shelter.

was a chicken burrito. Time to complete the shelter. I was barely cognizant enough to follow Robin's basic instructions.

When I call this thing a "shelter," I am being too kind. Really, it was just a heap of forest vegetation piled beneath and on top of me. It was fortunate that Robin and I had started this project with a few dozen armfuls of leaves during our "shakedown hike" the week before. To complete this glorified haystack, I spread my cotton half-sheet on the hill above camp, filled it with leaves, lugged it back, and repeated the process until I had a five-foot-high, seven-foot-long pile of duff and leaves that would serve as a mattress. This bedding would elevate me off the ground, saving my body heat and serving as a natural Therm-A-Rest.

In the two-foot-wide space between the pile and the rotting log, I fashioned a separate seven-foot-long, warm, thick "side pile" of leaves that I would pull over myself to use as a comforter, smothering me. In other words, I would be part of a sandwich: two piles of duff were the bread slices and I was the lunch meat. In theory, my trapped ambient heat would stop me from getting chilled. I had to force myself to lie down naked on the "mattress" pile; it was quite scratchy and itchy. Loose twigs twisted into my side.

Now came the tricky part: getting into "bed." First I covered up my face and head with the cotton sheet. Then I reached into the "comforter" pile and pulled the whole thing on top of me.

I was buried alive. I pushed up from the top of the comforter pile, pulled away the cotton sheet, and made a sort of blowhole, with my eyes, nose, and lips sticking out of it. Immediately I felt claustrophobic. I was going to have to sit there like a mummy in a sarcophagus all night long. The wasp stings still burned and itched, but I tried not to rub or scratch them; if I so much as twitched or tossed in my sleep, the pile was going to fall off, leaving me exposed. Still, the shelter had its advantages. Considering there was nothing to hold it together, no blanket securing it, no overstructure or framework of any kind to stop it from slipping apart, it did a fine job of keeping the elements away from me.

If my numb nose was any indication, it was getting nippy out there. There was something lovely and intimate about this sleeping arrangement. I was part of the forest floor and was not sealed away from it. It was surprisingly warm. But the wasp poison kept moving through my veins; my neck still ached with it. Perhaps it had even leached into my brain.

As night fell, I looked up into the forest canopy, high in the redwood fairy circle, and saw an inexplicable presence in the boughs: a glowing silvery substance that looked like a bunch of mysterious grapes, each dangling on a phosphorescent tentacle of fog.

The ghostly grapes shone from the inside. What the hell was that, I wondered. Was it alive? Was I having a rhapsodic vision?

The more I stared, the more the vision intensified. This was not an effect of the light; the sun was gone. Yet the gleam grew and flashed. Perhaps it was a group of spirits stuck in the branches—lost souls up there. I wished I understood what that quavering thing was. I've spoken to some naturalists since my campout, and they've given me all sorts of theories. Perhaps it was a colony of glow-in-the-dark mushrooms. Or maybe it was a bunch of banana slugs mating. But why would fungus quaver in the branches like gelatin and appear to float in midair? And why would orgiastic gastropods flash and glow in the night? I can't even explain it away as a hallucination,

This photo was taken in a forested area of Santa Cruz during one of my
one-on-one wilderness skills workshops with Robin Bliss-Wagner.
This is a preliminary version of the debris shelter that I would later build in
the Soquel Demonstration State Forest. Those are my feet sticking out of it.

simply because I sat there looking at it for so long, thinking about it, considering it, judging it, and yet it held its shape for half an hour.

Then the night began to eat away at those glorious glow grapes in the
trees. "No, no, don't go away," I called out to the mass of ectoplasmic goop.
"Stay right where you are. Please don't fade away! I have no other light."

It was no use.

One by one, the orbs extinguished themselves.

Soon the darkness was absolute.

Robin was right. The moon was just a fingernail.

The night grew blacker and I buried myself ever deeper in my debris shelter. As I settled in, I tried to find comfort in its musty, minty smell and its shape, which had responded to my form like a Posturepedic pillow, the material yielding to the contours of my body and creating a warm pocket of air around me.

I liked to think Old Joe Knowles would have been impressed with what I was doing. He, too, was able to recover from his initial struggles in the forest. The morning after his bad first night, Knowles "envied the hide" of a nearby doe. "I could not help thinking what a fine pair of chaps her hide would make and how good a strip of smoked venison would taste a little later. There before me was food and protection, food that millionaires would envy and clothing that would outwear the most costly suit the tailor could supply." Knowles spared her life, though, but only because the Fish and Game Commission, to his great annoyance, had refused him a hunting permit. Like me, having to struggle just to find a legal place to do my campout, Knowles chafed at bureaucratic hassles. How could mankind get primitive with modern rules standing in the way? "The first men of the forest were not handicapped by laws from an outside civilized world!" he snorted.

That second day, he managed to build a little dam and trap a few lethargic trout, which he caught but had no chance to eat; after he decided to store them in a stream until he figured out how to make a fire, a hungry mink came along and gobbled them. Knowles's legs and feet were in agony, but he calmed his thoughts and found some witchgrass, a fibrous weed with fuzzy stems. After picking as much of the plant as he could, he wove a dense mat, which he then fashioned into leggings, and used "the lining bark" of trees to make a pair of soft moccasins and a surprisingly comfortable shirt.

After a while, Knowles was able to make a fire to drive away the clouds of mosquitoes. Later on, he would admit to feelings of total desolation. "I did not experience any physical suffering to speak of, though I did suffer greatly in another way," he wrote in his memoir. "My suffering was purely mental and a hundredfold worse than any physical suffering

I experienced . . . It never occurred to me that I might be lonely . . . Time and again, those mental spells were almost too much for me. At those times I would vow that I would leave the forest the very next day."

Sometimes the temptation to stop the campout maddened him, especially on the day he ran into a backcountry guide who recognized him. "Hello, Joe," the man said. Using every bit of his resolve, Knowles walked the other way. Every time he was just about to give up, a thought would come to him: "Here is a chance to show that you are a man."

As the days progressed, he became glad he hadn't quit; he soon had some bragging points for his readers, including the yearling bear he caught in a deadfall trap. "I finally landed a blow on the bear's head that put an end to him," Knowles wrote on one of his birch bark scribbles. After preparing the hide, he now had a nifty robe. Never again would he be the Naked Man of the Woods.

The readers of the *Boston Post* adored this story so much that Knowles tried to outdo himself with every dispatch. He described an epic battle between two moose, and wrote about the day he stumbled across a still-warm deer, killed by a wildcat, supplying him with an unexpected windfall of venison and "an extra skin." Later, he continued to embrace his circumstances, dining on flame-roasted frogs' legs, hazelnuts, and wild onions, and shooting stone-tipped arrows with an ironwood bow tied with sinew. At one point, Knowles claimed to have ambushed another deer, tackled it, grabbed it by the horns, and snapped its neck with a quick twist.

Readers went wild themselves. By the time his experiment neared its end, Charles L. Wingate, the Sunday editor of the *Post*, had every reason to be glad they'd devoted so much print to Knowles. During Knowles's two-month ordeal, the newspaper's daily circulation more than doubled to north of four hundred thousand copies, the *Post* claimed.

Knowles was a superstar when he returned from the woods on October 4, 1913. Before the adventure, he'd promised to emerge from the forest dressed from head to toe in natural materials—and so he did. Not only that, but he was thirty pounds lighter, looking like "half-man, half-bear, with his matted hair, skin dark as an Indian's, fur-lined chaps and bearskin cloak," according to *American Heritage*.

When a startled teenage girl saw him walking on railroad tracks in Quebec, he looked like a picture she'd seen of an ancient man. Knowles grunted at her and started crying grateful tears. "He smiled, and the girl saw the gold flash in his teeth," the Boston *Post* reported. "'He is a real man,' she said to herself."

When Knowles embarked on a triumphant whistle-stop tour to meet his readers, rolling south through Maine and bound for Boston, the people could not love him enough. They yelped at him and tore his clothes.

Nearly a quarter of a million people packed the streets of Boston to greet him in his smelly, homemade bearskin robe. Women reached out to caress his muscles. Policemen had to drive back a few Knowles fanatics. "Great work, Joe!" his fans cried out. "You're all right! . . . You're my bet!"

His newfound status must have seemed permanent to him. He'd worked hard to become famous, and now the job was done. No more neck breaking. No more creature clubbing.

Yet Knowles's public reputation was about to take an even worse drubbing than the yearling bear in his deadfall trap.

It was impossible for me to know what time it was when I reached for my flashlight and then remembered that it was down the hill in the Chicken-shit Tree. I could see nothing, not even the outline of the trees in the fairy circle around me. I could *hear* all kinds of crackling and movement. I imagined cougars encircling the shelter, smelling me, seeing in the dark, brushing against the debris pile, pawing it like house cats in a litter box. I couldn't believe how hard I'd fought back against my wife so I could have this experience in the woods. How I wished I was back at home, thwarted and bored and reading *Cook's Illustrated*.

As the evening wore on, I wished the shelter were so much bigger. How I wished it had rooms! I pretended my modest duff pile was an Arts and Crafts–style mansion five stories high with a hundred corridors and seventy-seven secret entrances; for hours, I thrashed my feet around in the pile and fought an inexplicable desire to bolt from the shelter and run through the jungle. Was it midnight yet? Nine p.m.? Four in the morning now? Six a.m.? Was time running backward?

I tried every trick to pull the morning closer. I recalled my favorite parts of *Moby-Dick*. I cycled through John Updike's entire *Rabbit* tetralogy for what seemed like seventeen hours. Then another twelve hours seemed to pass. When I opened my eyes, the sky had only grown darker.

Then I heard running footsteps just behind me. Something was bumbling through the underbrush, coming right toward me. Twigs and branches broke to the side of me. I heard a crunch in front of me. The ground trembled. Too scared to shriek, I cringed into the duff pile and tried to hold my breath. *Whatever you are, please don't see me, don't even smell me.* Something large was walking through the camp, breathing deeply, and padding in front of me. In a moment I heard the footsteps again, in retreat, returning the way they'd come, to the woods above my shelter.

For the rest of the night I tried not to move at all. I kept waiting for the creature to return. I dared not fall asleep, not even for a moment. But there was no denying it; my bladder was full. The urge to pass water was so terrific I could contain it no longer, though I feared compromising the shelter's integrity. Without a choice, I crawled, shivering, out of my pile of duff and balanced myself with shaky legs on the rotten log.

I did this in a frenzied manner, knowing that something with infrared vision might pounce upon me. Once my bladder was empty, I scrambled into the duff pile again. The early morning chill had sunk into the shelter's heart, compromising the insulation bubble I'd made with my trapped body heat. Besides, in my haste to remake my shelter, I had somehow grabbed several clumps of the redwood duff upon which I'd relieved myself, adding an unwelcome rank dampness to the creeping chill. As I sat there for hours, marinating slowly in wet hay, with lumps of deer shit sticking to my entire body and dozens of pinching splinters puncturing me all over, my wasp stings pulsating, I began to wonder if I might do well to take up another hobby.

The reputation of the Nature Man crumbled almost as quickly as my shelter did that night.

In late November, when Knowles was stuffing his pockets with as much as twelve hundred dollars per week for his lectures and live camping demonstrations, the *Boston Sunday American*, perhaps resentful of the *Boston Post*'s enormous success with its Knowles coverage, ran a devastating exposé.

The headline read "The Truth about Knowles: Real Story of His 'Primitive Man' Adventures in the Maine Woods." The newspaper claimed that almost every aspect of Knowles's history-making campout was a big fat lie.

Naked? The article said he'd kept his clothes on. All alone in a handmade shelter? The reporter claimed that Knowles had hung out in a cabin with an accomplice who helped him fool the public, and had even enjoyed the company of a female admirer. The reporter also said that Knowles, who made a big show of getting fined for killing game out of season and having a nature warden come down on him, had even fibbed about killing the bear that yielded his bearskin robe. The reporter quoted an eyewitness who said that someone had paid twenty dollars for the bearskin and handed it over to Knowles. According to the informer, the skin had four noticeable bullet holes. Quoting the witness, the writer said the deadfall trap was so shallow that it never could have contained a bear, or even, for that matter, a small kitty cat.

In those days before the Internet and "going viral," the damage was not immediate. Knowles went ahead with a popular vaudeville tour. He used the stage to re-create his survival feats. His hastily written book about his ordeal became an instant best seller. Yet the accusations infuriated him; he filed a fifty-thousand-dollar lawsuit against the *Boston Sunday American*. Then, in an attempt to challenge the story about the bearskin, he placed a sleepy, and possibly even hibernating, bear in front of a crowd of onlookers, beat it to death, and then skinned the poor thing with a sharp piece of shale for good measure.

In an act of even greater desperation, Knowles attempted a "do-over" of his entire survival trip, this time up in the Siskiyou Mountains in the Pacific Northwest with two esteemed observers, including the same famous anthropologist who once studied Ishi, "the last wild Indian in North America." In the buildup to the 1914 redo, Knowles showed off some startling and undeniable displays of primitive survival skills. On July 15, close to his departure day, he jumped into the Rogue River and caught a three-pound fish barehanded, to the amazement of his observers.

Now Knowles faced a problem far worse than any doubts about his authenticity. Suddenly, the world no longer cared. The *San Francisco Examiner* put the war between France and Germany on the front page and knocked Knowles into the back section, next to an advertisement for a digestive aid for tots.

Knowles kept making progressively sillier bids for a major comeback, including a bizarre plan to do a survival campout in the Adirondacks with the beautiful starlet Elaine Hammerstein, first cousin of the legendary

Broadway lyricist Oscar Hammerstein II. The delicate Elaine, however, was no wild Victorian lady, and the campout collapsed before it even began.

So Joe Knowles, like "Adirondack" Murray before him, waddled his way into utter obscurity.

In the late 1930s he was living a low-key life in the Pacific Northwest—for a while, he served as a Boy Scouts leader, teaching his young "striplings" to survive "Without tent, kit, or provender"—when another bizarre and unwanted development yanked him right back into the public consciousness. On June 18, 1938, the *New Yorker* wrote a "Where Are They Now?" column about Knowles, claiming he had pulled off the "hoax" with a cynical mastermind who'd plotted out all the exploits in advance for maximum publicity, using a scheduling calendar. "Tuesday, kills bear," one entry read. By the time the Nature Man died four years later, his schmuck-ness was well established. "All of the two hundred thousand people who gathered at North Station to greet him [upon the completion of his campout] are now probably dead, too, and his book is available in only a few libraries," noted *Boston* magazine in its wistful remembrance of Old Joe.

In the darkness of the Soquel Demonstration State Forest, as I twisted around in my makeshift shelter, I wondered why it was so easy to remember Knowles's self-proclaimed feats of survival and so hard to remember allegations that he was a lying crumb bum. Why did I have a vested interest in believing Knowles was real? Why go through so much trouble to celebrate a possible fraudster?

For one thing, it must be said that Knowles, whether or not he lied about his Maine camping trip, had the skills to pull it off, as he proved with his Siskiyou do-over. I also believe that the issue of his alleged fibbing and shortcutting is less important than the attention people lavished on him in 1913. Knowles matters to me because he turned camping into front-page news. He showed just how thoroughly the fascination with outdoor life had spread to all corners of America, including the working class, which comprised the bulk of the *Boston Post*'s readers. In his own deranged way, Knowles, in creating such adulation and furor, proved that camping in America had truly arrived.

Roderick Nash, in his classic book *Wilderness and the American Mind*, a sweeping look at America's developing views about the outdoors from the

Puritans onward, writes that Knowles "added to the evidence suggesting that by the early twentieth century, appreciation of wilderness had spread from a relatively small group of Romantic and patriotic literati to becoming a national cult." Less charitably, Nash also says that Knowles's evanescent celebrity "was just a single and rather grotesque manifestation of popular interest in wildness."

Even if Knowles was sometimes less than honest, he was nevertheless ahead of his time. As the historian James Morton Turner has pointed out, before there was such a thing as a "wilderness movement" in America, "Knowles proposed setting aside 'wild lands' and establishing outdoor communities where Americans could retreat from the 'commercialism and the mad desire to make money [that] have blotted out everything else, [leaving us] not living but merely existing.'"

That alone is reason to commemorate the man, as flawed as he might have been.

Back in the sticks, the heat, miraculously, returned to my shelter. Soon it was warm and cozy again, and when first light came, steam rose from the top, just as Robin promised. The first chance I had, I burst out of my shelter, tied the cotton sheet around my waist, grabbed the plush squirrel off the log, dug up my running shoes and loincloth, put them on, and crashed through the forest.

Once on Hihn's Mill Road, I trudged uphill toward the parking area, not making much haste, because I now remembered the words of the cyclist who warned me about the burgling "crackheads." I knew what I was going to find when I got to the car: a broken window, the trunk popped wide open, the tires slit to pieces.

Sure enough, when I arrived at my parking place, the car, as I suspected, was tilted at a strange angle, with broken glass all around it. What rotten luck! When I got closer, however, it became clear that the broken glass had been there already, and the car was parked at a sharp angle. I felt so grateful and happy to have survived my ordeal. I was even thankful to the druggies for sparing my car that night. "Happy Knowles Day, crackheads!" I shouted as I opened the car door and got inside.

Safely out of the forest, resting in my car, I could look at that campout as something other than a nightmare. Out in my shelter, I had been miserable at times, but at least I was uncomfortably alive. Thoreau went to the woods to live deliberately, to front the essential facts. In my case, the campout, if anything, had been a little too deliberate. The experience was so intense, so unfiltered, that it short-circuited my brain and took me into an imaginative dream space from which I could not escape until sunup. Alone with no clothes, I'd ended up in a world where a yellow jacket might seem vulnerable and beautiful, maybe even a little bit sexy, and ghostly grape shapes glowed in the dark for reasons that defy easy explanation. Lying in my car, I missed the glow grapes and wished I could see them again. I knew they would never show themselves unless I stripped off my clothes and lay down naked on a forest floor, which I would never do again. Because, let's face it: the evening was, for the most part, a fright, with brief interludes of mystical experience and inexplicable visions. At least I got through, and answered my burning question: Is it possible to camp out naked and with nothing? Yes, indeed it is possible, but if you do it, your mind won't be the same. Never again will you fix the boundaries between fantasy and reality with such certainty, or question the utility of socks and underwear.

Perhaps I didn't emerge from the woods tanned and well muscled, with crowds of people waiting for me like Knowles; nor did I have a crude deer-horn knife clinging to my waist on a belt of sinew. Yet I am in perfect alignment with Knowles when it comes to our overall attitudes about camping in the nude. "Above all else," he once said, "I want to emphasize that living alone in the wilderness for two months without clothing, food or implements of any kind was not a wonderful thing. It was an interesting thing; but it was not wonderful."

Knowles, in spite of his Stone Age trappings, was as modern as could be. While he made a big show of using ancient techniques to survive outside, he slyly acknowledged the twentieth century by tapping into the mass media, exploiting the public's interest, and turning himself into a big star. He was not the only American to display such contradiction. Right around the time of his then-infamous, now-forgotten campout, another adventurous group was pulling off a surprisingly similar feat. Paradoxically, these men and women tried to harness the power of technology to help them flee the modern world, using a contraption that would forever transform the camping experience.

That invention was called the automobile.

11

How's the Road?

Every mile by motor is a continuous experience. There are no
lapses between twilight and dusk. On the train I have closed my
eyes in the early dusk of a winter day to a howling prairie blizzard
and opened them the next morning to see cattle picking a desert
breakfast from among the soapweed and prickly pears and dusty
sagebrush . . . Motoring is liable to violence . . . Day in and day out
by motor you scarcely average more than a cautious, legal 20
miles to the hour . . . But no matter how much it rains, you will
stay and make your next start there, missing nothing of the road
as you do on your flying pillow by train.

—Dallas Lore Sharp, *The Better Country*, 1928

Three Rivers, California, is a convection oven shaped like a town. On the
last day in June, the temperature gauge stood at 105 degrees as our car
rolled past a thirteen-ton wooden statue of Paul Bunyan; a roadside stand
selling elk, ostrich, kangaroo, alligator, and yak jerky; and a general store
with tiles barely clinging to the roof. No one was sitting on his porch or
walking on the road that morning. My wife, Amy, was driving. Ahead on
the left, a filling station had a sign reading LAST GAS IN A HUNDRED MILES.
Waves of heat made the letters jiggle.

I failed to mention the sign, hoping my wife hadn't seen it, because it
was almost noon, our campground was first-come, first-served, and,
besides, I don't like the way gas stations make me feel. I hate standing in

the sun trying to remember my PIN number, and being forced to choose between cheap regular unleaded gasoline and two other hoity-toity options with higher octane and names like Premium Gold. When I inevitably go for the cheap regular gasoline, I get a twinge of shame, as if I've settled for the house red of the gas station. It always feels like I'm depriving my car of a treat. For this reason, I stop for gas only if the gauge is one notch above empty.

Amy follows her own counsel. At least she thinks she does. When she slowed down, she was, possibly, sending me an unspoken mental signal that she'd seen the gas station, too, and was thinking of stopping. However, she didn't say anything about the sign; nor did she explain her reason for slowing down. "Oh no no no no no," I murmured while she slowed, though I was careful not to provide any explicit context for my grumbles. Amy doesn't like it when I'm too prescriptive with her, so I try to keep my stage directions strictly subliminal. In a moment, after I held my breath, Amy changed her mind and sped up again, perhaps without realizing that I'd discouraged her from slowing with my below-my-breath muttering.

Any moment now we were going to turn off Highway 198 onto one of the most infamous roads in the West. The Northern California outdoors writer Tom Stienstra ranks it number two in his list of Golden State "highways to hell." An outdoor blogger named "Tarol" calls it "the worst road I've ever traveled." She reported "at least 642 blind curves, no guardrails, very steep drop-offs, no signs, [and] no center divider line." By the time you reach the campsites at the end of the 24.8-mile road, she said, "most of the other tourists have given up." Aside from the grudging addition of asphalt, which has chuck holes the size of hubcaps and cracks you could put your arm through, the road has not changed much since the 1870s, when a work crew laid it out so prospectors could reach a silver mining operation, which failed in spite of the area's aspirational name: Mineral King.

Over the years, men have tried (and failed) to change or avoid the road. The ailing Walt Disney, hoping to burnish his legacy in the 1960s, wanted to build a lavish ski resort at Mineral King, complete with hotels, restaurants, and cable tramways. Walt Disney Productions hoped to substitute a $20 million fifteen-mile electric-powered cog railway for the dreaded Mineral King Road. There was also talk of a smooth, well-graded $23 million, two-lane substitute access road that could serve up to 1,200 cars per hour. Disney "Imagineer" Marc Davis designed a troupe of audio-animatronic singing bear characters to serenade diners at a restaurant with their high lonesome harmonies, banjo music, mannered cornpone accents, and chit-chat while real bears rooted around looking for grubs in the forest outside. At that point in time, the U.S. Forest Service had been courting proposals for a ski resort at Mineral King, which was then part of Sequoia National Forest.

But Disney's death in 1966, along with well-organized environmental-ist opposition, dealt the project a serious blow. The incorporation of 12,600 acres of Mineral King land, including high peaks and forests, into Sequoia National Park in September 1978 doomed the ski project. So Mineral King remains more or less in its natural state, and the Mineral King Road is as narrow, treacherous, and unavoidable as ever.

The road, as Amy pointed out repeatedly before the trip, would be a terrible place to break down. Her eyes narrowed as we turned a sharp right onto the paved strip, which in places was not much wider than the length of two walking sticks. The overgrown hillsides bulged into it. "We should turn back and fill the tank," Amy said as she faced the slope.

"There's no place to turn around safely," I said.

We kept on going, over steep canyons. Every so often I looked down and saw jagged bits of rusty metal down there. Were those bits of wrecked cars or just junk? I couldn't tell. The 12 percent slope pinned Amy to the driver's seat. I pointed out that we'd gone 226 miles on just under half a tank after leaving Santa Cruz that morning. Six gallons should be plenty to get our Toyota Corolla 6,400 feet up the mountain to the Cold Springs Campground and back down again, I thought. "No road on earth can drink two hundred miles' worth of gas in fifty miles," I said. "That would, like, violate the rules of physics."

Amy looked at me and said, "But if we *do* run out of gas, on a mountain road, with a child in the car, and it's a hundred degrees outside . . ." She didn't have to supply the five missing words at the end of that sentence: *I will never forgive you.*

Outside, a buzzard caught the thermals. The car passed between boul-ders and crossed a slender bridge that looked historic and slapdash at the same time. Overhanging trees, rocks, and roadway with bitten-off pieces forced us into the center of the track right at the moment when Mineral

King Road entered a blind curve. Amy put on her maniacally happy face, a defensive response to stress.

"I wanted to get gas in Three Rivers," she said. "You heard me say it."

"You didn't say it."

"I wanted to stop; you talked me out of it."

She was wrong to say this, but then again, she was also right. If you've been married for at least ten years, as I have, it's possible to provoke arguments with your spouse by using the telepathic powers you forget you share, and which give lie to the utterances you make. Take, for instance, the words I said to Amy then: "See the needle on the gas gauge? At the end of this trip, it'll be in the same position as it is right now. We are going to burn approximately *zero* fuel."

One hour later, our Toyota Corolla began to cough and snort and wheeze its way up the lane. Supply trucks missed us by micrometers, the engine growled like an empty belly, the chassis trembled, and I could hear the fuel getting sucked from our car as if from a siphon. The red needle on the gas gauge made its slow, inexorable descent toward "Empty."

Amy's driving began to alarm me. She swerved to avoid a jeep coming down the road. The Corolla drifted to the right side, no guardrail separating us from the drop. "*What are you doing?*" I said. The car left the bumpy asphalt and rolled along a slender band of rocks and dirt on the outer edge of the cliff. I looked down, through my open window, and though it may sound improbable, even crazy, I swear I saw the right-side rear tire of our vehicle leave the earth and just hang there in the air, spinning, gripping at nothing, like the landing gear of an airplane in the moments before touchdown. We were going to fall off that cliff, no avoiding it.

The landscape showed its supreme indifference to our fate by remaining beautiful. In the moment before we would enter our plunge and death roll, alpenglow covered the schist and granite, the silver tongues of sage plants and the soft bark of sequoias in a golden and transparent glaze. In that instant, I knew the good things I wanted to do with my life would all go undone. As I looked down at the rocks and their cruel dentition and felt the loving, self-sacrificing, encouraging, and sometimes resentful presence of my wife to my left, and my beloved daughter behind me, I closed my eyes, dug my hands into the gravy-colored seat upholstery, began to pray, and braced for impact. Then, for reasons I still don't understand, we did *not* fall off Mineral King Road. I can't say what stopped us from tumbling—my relentless incantations to God, the presence of centrifugal force, or maybe I just need to get my eyes checked. All I know is that the car remained on the road, and nothing was the same when we resumed our drive toward camp, the sun burning down, the air conditioner all the way off, the upholstery almost melting. "Amy . . ." I said, but I was too stunned to finish my thought. None of us said a word.

Such was my shock, and my certainty that we'd survived certain death, that the road became a liminal space in my mind, something magical, a place where the rules didn't hold.

This trip to Mineral King was supposed to be "off the books," a break from my camping project. The weekend in Sequoia National Park was little more than an excuse to escape Santa Cruz, which always gets rowdy and stupid on the Fourth of July; in my town, it's not unusual for partiers to blow up cherry-condition vintage muscle cars with M-80s just for chuckles. Still, sometimes the camping project sets its own terms, and though I did not realize it at the time, our trip had taken a sharp turn toward history.

In the early 1900s, Mineral King Road posed an irresistible challenge to the people of California's Central Valley, who were willing to put up with its hazards to escape the stifling heat and typhoid outbreaks in the flatlands. Knowing the road would be hard, they brought about a month's worth of food to make each trip worthwhile. Some crammed their jalopies full of goats to milk in camp. A photo from the early 1920s shows a low-set, provision-stuffed car with oversize tires, a man hanging off the left side and scraping branches growing over the road, which looks little better than a sheep's path. After World War I, dozens of auto campers fought their way up the mountain, especially on Memorial Day weekend. Aside from sheer cliffs, they had to watch out for a prospector who made the road even more hazardous with his careless presence. "People knew when he had gone down the road because there were pieces of his old truck along the way," Mineral King historian Louise Jackson told me. "He had no brakes. He did it by just dragging against the side of the road and downshifting."

Those were the days when auto camping meant something much different than car camping does today. During its anarchic "gypsy" phase, from the early 1900s to the late 1920s, auto campers faced their fears, dealt with constant breakdowns, and came up against the forces of nature, from the coyotes that raided their makeshift camps in farms and fields to the sudden appearance of storms. Muddy "gumbo" roads, rushing rivers, landslides, and flash floods did their best to wash drivers off the country lanes.

This life was grueling, pulse raising, a never-ending hassle, but that's why auto campers loved it so much. They craved the same borderline-helpless feeling that Amy and I experienced on Mineral King Road that day. While I'm tempted to think of such people as masochists, they preferred to call themselves modern-day Romantics or transcendentalists on wheels. During the golden age of auto camping, a *New York Times* reporter captured the appeal: "You are your own master, the road is ahead; you eat as you please, cooking your own meals over an open fire; sleeping when you will under the stars, waking with the dawn; swim in a mountain lake when you will, and always the road ahead. Thoreau at 29 cents a gallon."

Certain ascetic backpacking and survivalist types now regard car campers, including me, as halfway or fake campers, and it shows you just how much times have changed. These days, I can't help but notice all the outdoor gear posters and magazine advertisements showing well-muscled youngsters in slick-rock country with their arms in the air in a victory salute. Outdoor gear posters rarely show scenes from the kind of camping I practice most often these days: the father passed out in a hammock chair, a twenty-four-ounce can of Modelo Especial between his legs, his wife doing sun salutations on a blue tarpaulin, his daughter stomping through mud puddles in *Frozen*-themed Walt Disney gum boots. T-shirts and towels hang to dry on the side-view mirrors of their mud-daubed, badly dented, crow-guano-splattered car. In the background, a campground host peddles firewood and kindling from the back of a solar-powered golf cart festooned with American flags. This, to me, is the real camping.

I know we car campers lack a certain cachet. Compared to other user groups, we are desperately uncool. Just try starting a story with the words "One day, when I was car camping . . ." and watch people's eyelids get droopy. It's kind of like saying, "Back when I was living in Connecticut . . ."

Perhaps it's time for us to rise up and reclaim, and celebrate, our gnarly past. The next time some snippy little wilderness pilgrim wanders through my car camp and gives me that "you are beyond pathetic" look while I'm lying on my mini-futon, getting drunk, eating chocolate-covered pretzels and reading *American Frontiersman* magazine, I swear to you, I'm going to lay some history on him.

In the earliest days of the auto camper, streets were no good, there were no modern highways, and just driving to the dry goods store or heading to work on the morning commute could get you killed. The first cars shared roads with wagons and carriages. Tires tore through streets designed for hooves, not wheels. Brakes failed, power steering did not exist, and drivers (perhaps taking their cue from that insane Mineral King miner) crashed into hillsides to avoid tumbling into ditches or plummeting off cliffs. Into this already risky environment, the car camper introduced an even larger risk by leaving the relative safety of cities and chugging up roads on ten-thousand-foot peaks that, like Mineral King Road, had no guardrails.

Those "gypsy" campers were just as extreme as any thru hiker you might meet today. I used to be a backpacker, as crazy and committed as you can get. Yet it irritates me when I hear certain long-distance walkers compare modern-day car camping to hotel living. While I will admit there is some truth to this, the critics ignore the fact that unpleasant Victorian lodging is one of the factors that inspired auto camping. Pleasure travelers started taking even bigger chances with their cars, pushing themselves deeper into desert valleys and mountain heights because they were sick of hotel clerks and concierges making them tidy up, wear suits and fancy dresses, and rush to the final five o'clock seating in hotel restaurants. If they got there on time, scornful waiters gave these irritated tourists overspiced chops and assorted slop, all of it served without a smile. In the early 1920s, etiquette expert and auto-camping fan Emily Post complained about "queer" Victorian hotel restaurant fare. Everything tasted as if it had been daubed in flour. "After many days of it you feel as though you had been [sic] interlined with a sort of *paste*," she complained.

It was snotty wait staff like this who drove fed-up travelers to auto camping. In those days, drivers often brought camping equipment any-way, even if they had no plans to sleep outside. Breakdowns were so common that foldaway cots, stoves, carbide lanterns, pillows, and other accessories were considered necessary for the everyday driving experi-ence. Small, makeshift bridges collapsed so often that some campers learned how to repair them. They also knew how to empty out ditches, winch cars from mud holes, and pry stumps from the earth. Many of those early auto campers didn't have to gear up for their good times; they just took the equipment they already had for survival and repurposed it for sleeping outside for fun.

Western mountains such as the Sierra Nevada offered the tantalizing promise of adventure, but a century ago even parts of the Midwest could feel like forbidding frontier. In 1918, when Ernest R. Wild guided his 1912 "Lizzie," an informal term for the Ford Model T, across the Great Plains, the driving was tough and burly. These were times when you could not take your mind off the road even for one second, or you could get killed. Wild and a friend camped in prairies while wolves and coyotes circled; Wild held fast to his cheap revolver, which had, by his own accounting, "a barrel about one-half-inch long with which it was just about possible to hit a haystack a yard away." After nearly freezing to death, getting rescued by a "good woman, a German," and then having to replace the inner tubes of their poorly made tires, they ran out of food and water. Wild lost eight pounds. A "fine and healthy blizzard" blew into them. After a while, the friends became so mentally scrambled that they raced a freight train just for the hell of it. "Old Lizzie held our own until bad roads forced us to slow down," Wild said.

Wild's race with that train was richly symbolic. Every time they took to the road, the auto campers of America snubbed their noses at railroads, which they associated with the worst aspects of industry and "progress." For one thing, the railroads held a virtual monopoly over early wilderness tourism back then. These days, if I take a train to a national park for a camping trip, it seems like a rare treat. Back then, there was no getting away from trains. In parks such as Yellowstone, starting in the late nineteenth century, it became almost impossible to get close to the wilderness, hire a stagecoach from the train station, or find lodging or decent guide services without paying off some slimy company that was linked to the railroad. Yet it took a certain amount of chutzpah for these auto campers to make such sweeping negative statements about railroads. As much as they claimed to despise locomotives, they had no problem riding down country lanes using contraptions that were every bit as modern and technology-based as the trains. They tried to smooth the contradiction, at least for themselves, by pretending to be pioneers in metal prairie schooners. In some cases, they even followed old wagon tracks for extra authenticity. As Warren Belasco points out in his outstanding book *Americans on the Road*, the key words in the travel stories of the early 1900s were *will* and

Auto campers were free to roam wherever they pleased.
Unfortunately for them, horrible roads such as this one in rural Wyoming,
photographed in 1925, made the going very slow and arduous.

anywhere: "Everything was up to you; everything was open, like the road itself." Auto tourists were "limited only by the quality of the roads and in no other way," wrote the author of an early auto-camping guide.

By the time we reached Cold Springs Campground at Mineral King, we (unlike the car campers of old) felt anything but free. We were trapped up on that mountain. On the upside, we were so happy and grateful not to have fallen off that cliff that we didn't linger too much on an unavoidable problem: we did not have enough gas to get back down to Three Rivers. When we arrived at camp, we just wanted to settle in, relax, tuck into our food, and perhaps take a nature hike. But when we crossed a red-brown plank bridge over the Kaweah River, passed through a lush stand of aspens and cottonwoods, and found a nice flat parking spot near a boulder-studded incline there was fear in the air. The campers all around us looked so nervous. They kept scanning the rocks around the campground, doing double takes, and looking over their shoulders as if some hidden menace were watching them.

Something was, in fact, checking them out, watching their every movement. Infamous as it was, Mineral King Road was not the only thing that had everyone on edge up here. Like the early auto campers, Amy and I were about to confront wild and pitiless nature. Instead of flash floods, washouts, or "gumbo mud," our nemesis was furry, cuddly, and very cute: a living plush toy with fuzzy whiskers.

The creature in question was the yellow-bellied marmot, the scourge of Sequoia and Kings Canyon National Parks. Forget your Yosemite bears, your aggressive Olympic mountain goats, and the surly wild turkeys of Zion National Park. The wicked marmot trumps them all. It was the reason our fellow campers looked so squirrely.

Out in central Pennsylvania, a groundhog named Punxsutawney Phil first predicted the length of winter on the first Groundhog Day, in 1887. Somehow, "Phil" has kept coming back to do this every year since then—never mind that groundhogs live only seven years on average. The yellow-bellied marmot, for his part, a close relative of the groundhog, has a talent that is almost as impressive as Punxsutawney Phil's reputed deathlessness; these little monsters attack parked cars and guzzle radiator fluid as if it were Powerade. Somehow, the coolant does not kill them. If anything, they seem to thrive on it.

These marmots are hooked on antifreeze, and will do anything to get it. They will gnaw hoses, bite brake lines, and rip spark plug wires if they get in the way. I've heard stories of Mineral King campers heading back down the road and having to stop and refill their radiators with creek water along the way because marmots had nibbled the tubes and let the liquid spill out. Sometimes they occupy vehicles indefinitely. Not long before our Mineral King trip, a marmot climbed into the guts of a parked car somewhere in Yosemite National Park and stowed away beneath the hood for the two hundred miles to San Francisco, where it finally bolted. A wildlife specialist captured it, apparently after tempting it with some organic fig cookies. Rescuers helped pay for its repatriation by raising seventy-five dollars at the city's Rock Bar, where bartenders sold "Marmotinis," a sickly sweet concoction of sour apple schnapps and vodka that resembles the cloudy green antifreeze marmots love so well.

Amy and I had heard about the marmots. We'd even brought an eighty-square-foot silver tarp to wrap the car against marmot attack; you're supposed to unfold and spread the tarp on the driveway leading to your campsite, drive your car on top of it, and then use bungee cord and rope to wrap the bottom of the chassis so the rodents can't enter the car from below.

Yet I noticed something peculiar in this campground; in spite of their apparent fear of marmots, none of the other campers had bothered to wrap their cars. A few had propped their car hoods, believing the intrusion of sunlight would discourage the diurnal mammals from doing their dastardly work. Amy and I decided to delay wrapping the car, but when I started making the rounds with Julianna, saying hello to some nearby campers, I heard a piteous shriek. The screamer was my wife, who had just seen a marmot the size of a lapdog run from between two boulders and scurry in front of her.

It came so close she could see its russet coat, gray-banded muzzle, orange neck, and fat bottom. Before she could stop it, it sneaked beneath our car, leaped up, and scrambled into the engine. As I lowered myself beneath the chassis, I wondered why my wife and I seemed to attract chaos every time we camped. How come things like this kept happening?

From my spot under the car, I heard the sounds of muffled breathing and obnoxious noises like bath toy squeaks. There was no denying it; the marmot was heading straight for our Corolla's alimentary canal, and if we didn't stop it, it would rip the car's guts out.

"Leave our car alone," I shouted. "Get out! Get out!"

Julianna and I circled the car, shouting, thumping the chassis, kicking the tires. We tried to shake the marmot loose by hip-checking the sides of the car, slamming our bodies against it. *Boomp! Boomp! Boomp!* But the marmot held on.

I knew what was going to happen. Four years before my visit to Sequoia National Park, marmots ravished ten cars in Mineral King, disabling all of them. In 2013, the year before we camped there, marmots crippled five cars, which had to be hauled down the long and wretched road. A Sequoia and Kings Canyon National Parks information officer told me that some local towing companies, including AAA-listed businesses, sometimes refused to send tow trucks up and down Mineral King Road, which was too long, treacherous, and steep to make the trip worth their while. As I stood there shaking the car, I wondered what was in it for the marmots. A three-ounce shot glass filled with coolant would be more than enough to kill a large dog. This made no sense to me.

Around the time of our camping trip, I tracked down Daniel Blumstein, professor and chair of UCLA's Department of Ecology and Evolutionary Biology, who spends much of his time studying marmot behavior in the

Rocky Mountains of Colorado. "How is it that they can drink poison and live?" I asked him over the phone.

"I have no idea," Blumstein replied. "Radiator fluid's poisonous. It *should* be killing them, and they're not dying, which is extraordinary. I mean, this stuff is not supposed to be good for you. Maybe they're not drinking a lot of it. Maybe they're just licking a little bit of it. Maybe it's true: what doesn't kill you makes you stronger."

While marmots attack cars in other mountainous parts of America, Blumstein said the Mineral King situation is unique because the marmots "just see cars and come running. They find themselves in cars in other places, but I haven't heard of other places where they are so aggressively jumping into cars." I asked Blumstein if an enemy race of super-marmots was, perhaps, breeding resistance to the poison. "It's possible that there is a heritable variation," he told me. "It is possible that they eat a lot of plants chock-full of defensive secondary compounds and have an ability to detoxify this."

Blumstein has not spent time at Mineral King, but a former newspaper colleague of mine, Kurtis Alexander, who was once a ranger up there, told me their chemical imperviousness goes beyond their ability to withstand coolant. Apparently, they can tolerate angel dust, too. "To tag bears, we'd

This California yellow-bellied marmot appears to be smiling and ready to pounce. Note the demented and gleeful expression on its face. Photograph by Michael Bolte.

make them unconscious by giving them a serum created by wildlife biologists, some sort of PCP derivative combined with something else," Alexander said. A park biologist once injected the soporific cocktail into a marmot to see how much he needed to knock it out. "Even at the quantity of serum he gave the bear, the marmot was fully conscious," Alexander said. "And these bears weighed three hundred, four hundred pounds. A marmot can't weigh more than a small dog."

Combating such a tireless animal is not easy. "In the past, the park had gone as far as actually shooting marmots, but not in a long, long while," said Daniel Gammons, wildlife biologist for Sequoia and Kings Canyon National Parks. "I don't know exactly when. The Forest Service ran [Mineral King] up to the seventies." The shooting method did not work, in part because each marmot, according to Gammons, attacks a car only once before giving up the practice forever. "Therefore, killing them accomplished nothing, because they are not serial offenders," Gammons said. "If you remove one, it will just be replaced by another."

While I pondered this, our rampaging marmot was making the most of its apparently onetime offense. I could hear it thrashing around in there. Following the logic exclusive to five-year-old children, Julianna jumped up, made squeaking noises, and pushed her incisors out as far as they would go. Then she did a Marmot Dance, which involved plenty of high kicks and scuttling around on all fours. Somehow it worked. The marmot let loose with one final, vindictive *eek* and plopped to the ground. Dazed for a moment, it recovered its senses, gave Julianna a spiteful look, and dashed for the boulders. From then on out, we followed the maddening ritual of wrapping, unwrapping, and rewrapping our car every time we moved it for a day hike.

That one-of-a-kind nightmare of a road, and the presence of the marmots, gave us a sense of being isolated and under siege at every moment. Yet there was an upside to that feeling of relentless confrontation. For one thing, it forced people to be creative. In parking lots next to a couple of nearby trailheads, day hikers went to extremes to protect their vehicles from the marmots. In doing so, they turned the parking lot into the finest unintentional sculpture garden I've seen. Like Christo and Jeanne-Claude, the art-making couple who wrap everything from shoes and phones to the Pont Neuf in Paris, the car owners reduced their cars to pure form. Deprived of their original details, color, and function, the tarp-wrapped, roped-up rock-fortified SUVs became beautiful clouds of brown, silver, and gold. Some cars had compact discs twirling from the side mirrors; apparently motion scares marmots. Others had salt blocks around them, or small rocks filling the spaces above the tires to prevent marmots from getting in. A father at Julianna's preschool told Amy about a camper who dunked tampons in cayenne pepper sauce and strung them all over the vehicle to keep the marmots away.

That trip, we took long day hikes above the valley floor, beneath the burnished red walls of mountains. We searched the high hills for big-horned sheep and lowered our hats in a soda spring that rose up from the earth in creamy white froth. We watched an adolescent black bear waggle its ears and brush its brindle coat against the chocolate-colored bark of a sequoia. On several different day hikes we took during this trip, we began to notice the same people out on the slopes, and had an easy rapport with them. As much as I disliked Mineral King Road, and the unwanted rodent attention, having to deal with these creatures fostered an unusual camaraderie in the campground, and gave all the car campers something to talk about, a burden we shared equally.

Aside from all this, the population was much more stable than your average car camp, where people are always coming and going every day. Perhaps the inconvenience of getting to Mineral King, and the long road separating us from the nearest town, made people want to stay longer. For this reason, Julianna and I were able to meet almost everyone in camp. Several months before, she and I had teamed up on an experiment called the Meet Your Neighbors Project. We based this project on our hunch that first impressions in car camps are often incorrect. Our main rule was "No skipovers ever." And no excuses, either. If our neighbors looked tough, supercilious, or surly, we would still go out of our way to spend time with them. While camping in some California coastal redwoods, we came across a group of bikers with leather jackets and huge beards. They turned out to be smart and solicitous history buffs who'd studied up on every place they'd camped. Out in Washington State, during another trip, we once decided to camp far away from a couple sleeping in a van with spray-painted eyeballs all over it because we knew they'd be trouble. But when Julianna and I screwed up our courage and met them, they turned out to be a sweet, adventurous, and curious young couple from a small town in the Netherlands. Jelle, a graphic designer, and Nadine, a nurse, were driving the eyeball van on a three-month, seventeen-thousand-mile journey crisscrossing America. They had reserved the vehicle online, sight unseen, and were as surprised as anyone when they first saw it.

Mineral King was a great place to continue our Meet Your Neighbors experiment because people were staying there for days and, in some cases, weeks; no one could escape us. Up there we met Ariel, a San Diego schoolteacher who'd somehow piloted a twenty-two-foot RV up Mineral King Road, and a speech pathologist named Diana, who had short and silky brown hair and lived just down the road in the broiling town of Three Rivers. She believes camping resets the human brain "because modern people need to do work that is monotonous. Monotony allows us to reset."

None of our neighbors had especially dramatic stories to share, but I didn't care. The only thing that mattered was that sense of being bound together in a far-flung place. It was just like a century ago, when old-time auto camps felt like "snug, cozy harbors" in the face of so many "dangerous Cape Horns," an auto camper wrote in the 1920s. The road was a portal between the campers' workaday lives and the campout, but it was also a stable context during unstable trips; just as the people in Cold Spring Campground talked endlessly about Mineral King Road and the marmots, auto campers of the early twentieth century gossiped all the time about the road when they met up on their journeys. "Between us and every other motorist on the road, it was the bond that made friendship instantaneous," wrote novelist, memoirist, and devoted auto camper Kathryn Hulme in 1923.

> It made "how's the road?"—the earnest salutation east of the Mississippi—a delightfully absurd expletive that chirked up sagging spirits when mud rivaled a bulldog for tenacity . . . Play honest eavesdropper to any two auto-loads of travelers at the filling station and what are they discussing? Not the beautiful scenery of the hill country of Pennsylvania, not the grandeur of the snow-caps towering about the Colorado Rockies, not the marvelous sunsets of the painted deserts of Nevada, but the perfectly rotten time they had negotiating the mud of Iowa, the narrowness of the mountain road up to the pass, the pitchholes and dust of the godforsaken dry lands.

Too many car camps are impersonal and transient nowadays. There is not enough time for campers to bond. That's why I loved that feeling of campers being stuck together in the same spot and forced to get along.

Yet there was a point where I tired of meeting people. One morning I woke up and my fingers ached from too many powerful handshakes. My voice was a feeble croak from introducing myself to strangers. "Sorry, I'm all done," I told my daughter, who had no desire to stop. "If I meet just one more person, I'll burst."

All I wanted to do was hide in my little tent bubble. Part of my surliness had to do with the fact that we all got woken up the night before; a family of noisy newcomers occupied the spot next to ours at 11:00 p.m., walking around, clanking, putting up massive tents. Julianna kept nagging at me to meet them, but I had no intention of doing so. That morning, I'd gotten a good look at them—an athletic couple in late middle age and a college-age son with a lean build, a wry expression, and a puzzling T-shirt that read, I KNOW THAT GUACAMOLE IS EXTRA in black letters. I gave them all sour looks as passive-aggressive punishment for waking me up, but none of them seemed to notice. Julianna wanted to know why I was acting so standoffish and weird to people I didn't even know. Wasn't the Meet Your Neighbors project all about being nice to people no matter what?

"Listen," I told her. "I won't meet *those people*. They're noisy. I'm all done saying hello to my neighbors."

Julianna got right up in my face. "I thought the rule was no skipovers, ever."

"Then I guess these are extenuating circumstances," I said.

I was going to fix myself a second cup of coffee when Julianna locked her arms around my knees so I couldn't move and started dragging me over to the neighbors' campsite. I tried to resist. I'm taller and stronger than she is, but Julianna had the element of surprise. She side-tackled me.

"Fine," I said, dusting myself off. "All right. We'll meet them. Just for one second. Then we're coming back."

An American flag hung over their camp. It was the Fourth of July, and I had forgotten all about it. The father had the composure, reserve, and formal politeness of an ex-military man. He was a bit of a tinkerer. A high school industrial technology teacher, he loved metal work. I watched him cook up a mess of eggs and potatoes in a frying pan over a homemade cat-food-can stove running on denatured ethanol alcohol. The three of them were camped with a lapdog with a mashed-in face called Mocos, whose name means "snotty-nosed" in Spanish. I asked what they all were doing up in Mineral King. The father blinked hard, as if his eyes were about to well up. He told me he was there to mark an important anniversary, but he gave no other details. When I pressed him about this important date, he let slip that their athletic young son had died a year ago that day, in July 2013. I was stunned. Julianna and I looked at each other. Now I wished I could take back my question. I couldn't think of anything else to say, so I asked him the name of his son. "Spencer," he said, pointing to the young man with the GUACAMOLE T-shirt.

"Wait," I said. "Your son? Right there? He died?"

Spencer's father stared into the scrambled eggs, which were almost done. "A year ago," he said, "we were on pins and needle. He got into an accident. Spencer died at the scene. A police officer brought him back. For a while, every day was Groundhog Day."

Spencer's mother, a slim and athletic physical therapist with close-cropped black hair, said the campout was a landmark for their twenty-four-year-old son. It was the parents' way of marking progress and letting themselves know that Spencer, whose long-term memory had gotten scrubbed, was coming back. Now I felt guilty about having given Spencer such a grouchy look, even though he hadn't seemed to notice it.

I had a feeling the story was a touch too painful for the parents to share, but Spencer was more than willing to talk, while Julianna jumped on my knees and started using me as a climbing gym.

In the years before Spencer "died," he and his father loved camping out. This Mineral King sojourn, with two oversize freestanding tents, eggs in coolers, and plenty of potatoes and ham, was far too luxurious to him. When Spencer was growing up in Santa Clarita, California, his father would take him on trips into the mountains to teach him self-reliance. After packing up their homemade ultralight gear, he and Spencer would drop into the Grand Canyon and climb up to the high peaks of the Sierra Nevada with next to no pack weight. It was a case of son-father idol worship; his dad served in the army, so Spencer started dressing up in camouflage like a soldier for Halloween.

"I guess you could say it was always a part of my lifestyle," Spencer told me. "I always liked the idea of being placed in dangerous situations." He longed to be extraordinary. Spencer wanted the chance to say that he'd been "to hell and back again."

At eighteen, Spencer skipped college and went straight into the air force. For weeks, instructors shot guns filled with blanks at Spencer and his friends. He'd sit up on his cot and blast right back at them. "So many guys quit right away," Spencer said. But Spencer had a goal: he wanted to be part of an elite division, the Combat Controllers, who required two years of training and had an 80 percent washout rate.

The instructors never screamed at Spencer; they didn't have to. If one said, "Drop," Spencer and the other recruits gave him fifty push-ups, and when it was over, they had to stay in that push-up position until the instructor said, "Recover." Then he faced the mental and physical bombardment of air traffic school. As part of his training, Spencer learned to scuba dive and jump out of planes. He also learned how to be a hostage, resisting the interrogations of fellow soldiers playing the role of terrorist thugs. Somewhere along the way he got a tattoo on the left side of his abdomen: NFQ, for "Never Fucking Quit." On his left arm he got another one: WE'VE DONE THE IMPOSSIBLE AND THAT MAKES US MIGHTY. The instructors made it attractive to give up. All you had to do was walk out and it was all over.

"But I knew I couldn't screw up. I just forced myself to say, 'This is one more thing to get through, and I'll get through it.' I couldn't fail. I saw what happened to people when they washed out. They became waiters. I don't mean waiters like in a restaurant. I mean they waited around for jobs to open up in the air force. You'd see them sitting around in an office, doing paperwork, in limbo, sitting on their hands for months, all incredibly demoralized because they had to be around a squadron of people who succeeded where they failed."

The winnowing process continued to the end, when trainees had to do endless pull-ups, sit-ups, a run, a swim of fifteen hundred meters, and a final stomp through the woods. Even as they drove to the last course, recruits were getting kicked out. "They would tell people, 'Get out of the truck. You will not be Combat Controllers.'" Spencer made that final three-mile cross-country stomp with a heavy rucksack in good time, thanks to the preparation his father had given him in their camping days. He reached the finish line first.

Getting the beret upon graduation felt like his life's highest achievement. Soon he was traveling to some of the world's most war-torn places. Once in Afghanistan he helped coordinate the landing of an aircraft containing Afghanistan's then-president Hamid Karzai, who was paying a visit to a village close to the Pakistani border. The heat was 120 degrees. Giant, savage dogs roamed the runway. Spencer faced dozens of situations where he could have been attacked and killed, but nothing life-threatening ever happened.

Spencer's flatlining took place about seven thousand miles from Afghanistan. In July 2013 he was on leave, driving on a Hayabusa, a crazy-fast and notoriously dangerous Japanese motorbike, through Iowa country-side. Then something happened that blacked him out and put him in a coma for two weeks. Did he spin out? Hit something?

He suffered severe head trauma, and his heart stopped at the scene. The cop who saved him must have pulled out a defibrillator paddle. Spencer has no memory of the crash; nor does he even recall the day leading up to it. All he remembers is going to sleep in a cabin with family and friends and waking up two months later in a hospital. "My mother said I had to be told to breathe in and out or I would forget," Spencer said.

Catastrophic forgetting is painless at first, because you're incapable of regretting the things you lost. Still, Spencer always got a funny feeling when he looked at the poster someone hung above his hospital bed. His parents told them the young men were all Combat Controllers like he was. Several trained with him. "I felt like I was looking at a bunch of strangers."

For a month he remembered nothing. Then he started missing and regretting absent pieces of information. What did he do every day in high school? Who was the girl he took to the prom? An ex-girlfriend called; she wanted to see how he was doing. He had no idea who she was.

His Combat Controller days are gone now, irrecoverable. The Mineral King anniversary was not an easy one. "The only thing that makes me angry is that I never got to see combat." The ink on that NFQ tattoo looks as sharp and dark as it did when he got it, but it means something different now, a talisman he can't remove. He's kept busy, taking U.S. history and land sur-veying classes at the College of the Canyons, a community college in Santa Clarita, to make his mind more supple. When I spoke with him, he was thinking of moving up to Washington State to occupy the little house he'd bought up there and then, for a time, forgotten he'd ever owned. He might try to be a smoke jumper, fighting fires, or an underwater welder, or perhaps a pilot, if he can pass the cognitive tests.

Spencer told me, with a rueful laugh, that his mom, who has powerful arms and steady hands, gave him a few good-size and fairly painful clomps on the chest early on in the campout at Mineral King. "I was thinking,

'Ugh, my life's in a trash can. Crap, now what civilian job do I pick up?' So my mom said, 'Be happy you're alive!'"

She reminded Spencer that his brain, somehow, has been repairing itself bit by bit, that his neural skills and memories weren't obliterated but placed in cold storage. When her message still couldn't penetrate, she smacked him, lovingly, until it did. Spencer is grateful for this, and could not stop laughing when he talked about it. "Her slaps hurt, so I actually had to do what she said and be happy. She was going to smother me with kisses to make me happy, but apparently slapping's the only thing that works. She was like, 'I am tired of doing everything positive. I'm going to go negative. Let's just slap the crap out of Spencer!' *Arggh. Ugggh. Aggggh.* It wasn't one of those really big slaps, but she used muscle; my parents are both in really good shape. I did what she wants. It made me want to move on with life, to take everything as it comes. I react better to harsher things."

Without the isolation and forced community made possible by Mineral King Road, I never would have found out that Spencer, like a Mineral King marmot, was just about unkillable. I wondered, later on, how a stranger could be so revelatory. My talk with him brought to mind a story I'd read about an early-twentieth-century auto traveler who came home raving about the "remarkable pal-ship and cooperative democracy" he found in remote car camps—along with a feeling of crossing over. Parked side by side, campers found that their normal barriers broke down—and why not, when they would never see each other again? "With all the conventions reduced to a minimum, how much easier it is to estimate the character of a person met casually this way," one writer from the early days of auto camping observed.

I got Spencer's contact information and promised to keep in touch.

The lawless "gypsy" days of early-twentieth-century auto camping came to an abrupt halt, and so did our stay at Mineral King. Car camps, by their nature, are transient places, and we were running out of food. It was time to brave the road and start heading home. We got in our car and wobbled down the hill, power lines reaching into the drop, jeeps squeaking by us, SUVS mad-dogging us from the back. This time I was driving, but I did not dare depress the accelerator, because the speed would have sent us hurtling into space, and because we could not afford to expend a single driblet of gas. In spite of the extreme slope downward, the gas gauge continued its witchy behavior and started making its steady way toward the Empty line.

The car bucked and spluttered and emitted a strange smell. Amy's jaw was clenched again, Julianna looked alarmed, and the temperature crept up five degrees Fahrenheit with every passing minute. The car was clearly running on fumes. It made sounds like I do when I'm needing a hit of Xoponex. Amy could not speak. I rode the brakes, not daring even to tap the gas pedal. We banked the last curve of Mineral King Road and reentered Highway 198. The car at this point was using up its last few molecules of gas. We creaked and groaned past a squashed possum, a bakery, the indifferent Paul Bunyan statue we'd noticed before, a store selling turquoise, and a surplus outlet offering MREs.

Out of nowhere, I spied a roadside gas station on the right. The car eased across the right side of the road and alighted in a parking space in front of the gas pump closest to us, noiselessly, powerlessly, like a glider lighting down on a field.

The car died on me just before I could kill the engine.

12

The Haunted Duffel Bag

Once leaky and unwieldy (and heaven forbid if you lost a stake), tents are now freestanding domes cutting fantastical profiles in the landscape.

—Patricia Leigh Brown, 1993

I will never part with my Girl Scouts of America duffel bag, even though it is splotchy and smelly and may very well be haunted. On permanent loan from my big sister, the olive-drab canvas duffel contains select pieces of all the camping gear my family has ever owned since my preschool days: among other things, the Kelty tube tent I slept inside with my brother, two dozen badly dented lightweight aluminum tent spikes with scrapes from the granite rocks my father pounded against them, several frayed balls of nylon twine he used to hang our bear-bagged food, two ripped-up sky-blue fanny packs, one surly old gas stove on a rusty tripod, and a telescoping latrine shovel that dates to the Ford administration.

Most items in the duffel are made of either aluminum or synthetic polymers in garish orange, purple, blue, goldenrod, or yellow. I cherish every one of these things, even though the colors are so loud they give me retinal flashes. Yet if you dig deeply into the bag, and cast aside my greasy Colin Fletcher books, my black-label insecticides, and two Ziploc gallon bags of trench candles, you will find a handmade tin drinking cup, its insides blackened by a hundred campfires. It stands apart from my decaying polymer gear and clothes, which give off a smell like low tide and moldy strawberries.

The cup waits in the dark for me to drink from it. I like to run my finger on its smooth lip, examine the inscrutable spots on its bottom, and put my pinkie finger inside the loop of leather gut around the handle with its shiny red ceramic bead to secure the knot.

The man who gave it to me was an "old-style" camper who used steel, flint, and duff to make his fires. I met him in San Luis Obispo a few years back at a campout sponsored by the American Mountain Men, a group of history buffs that uses early-nineteenth-century camping and survival equipment and techniques. Its members know how to shoot flintlock firearms, skin muskrats, and hurl tomahawks with precision. The day the man gave me the cup, I'd noticed it hanging out near a kettle of stew, a pile of buckskin robes, and a stack of hatchets, axes, and saws. It looked right at home among these nineteenth-century-style camping implements. Yet the gunmetal gray of that drinking cup is woefully out of place in my duffel. The synthetic gear crowds around that tin cup as if trying to smother it.

Sometimes I'll creep into my garage in the middle of the night when I can't sleep to check on my little cup. I'll find the poor thing lying on its side on the floor of my garage, looking so forlorn, with a brand-new dent in its side. It makes me wonder if my newfangled gear came alive after dark, got jealous, grabbed hold of my tin cup, and heaved it out of the duffel bag. That sounds crazy, I know. Why would one generation of gear gang up on another? Yet, in a sense, the fate of my tin cup mirrors the fate of old-fashioned camping in America. New technologies and camping philosophies crowded around the old ways and knocked them aside.

Old-time woodcraft camping began to face existential threats starting in the 1930s, thanks, in part, to a geeky genius named Wallace Hume Carothers. Carothers, a brilliant and manic chemist, drank poisoned lemonade, collapsed, and died in the spring of 1937. Because of his late-night hotel room suicide, he never found out how his best-known invention, the miracle polymer called nylon, transformed the camping world starting in the 1950s and '60s and continuing into the twenty-first century.

Carothers, America's most accomplished accidental backcountry revolutionary, was no nature boy; I cannot find a single mention of him ever sleeping in the woods, bagging a mountain, or hiking a burly trail. Yet if you were to walk into almost any camping store these days and wave a

Wallace Hume Carothers (1896–1937)

magic hiking stick that made all nylon-based clothes and gear go *poof!* and disappear, you would see lots of empty shelves and a whole bunch of clerks standing around stark naked or just about.

Carothers, a self-conscious and twitchy Harvard chemistry instructor when he was hired away by DuPont in 1928, suffered for the sake of our modern-time camping conveniences. His discoveries and innovations drained him. He once described himself "clinging desperately to the edge of an oaken table" at work for seven and a half hours at a stretch, and listed "[s]houting into a Dictaphone . . . jumping up and down . . . lighting cigarettes, answering the telephone, and fitfully rushing into the laboratories" as ordinary aspects of his creative process. (His displays of inspiration and agony must have alarmed the people sitting next to him in the lab.) Through all this hard work, he also played a strong role in the "accidental discovery" of the synthetic rubber called neoprene, yet another camping mainstay.

Nylon, invented in 1935, and patented three years later, helped make it possible for me to carry featherweight gear across the Pacific Crest Trail, and enabled me to climb dozens of mountains, romp with elk, dance a pas de deux with a golden-mantled ground squirrel, and see dozens of melted-sherbet sunsets. It gave me so much happiness, but its troubled inventor had little lasting joy of his own. Carothers often went around with a cyanide-filled metal capsule attached to his watchband, and was happy to talk about its contents with his friends. He once wrote, "The trouble seems to be that I am slightly inhuman." He once described himself as not quite dead, "but only moribund, feeling rather feeble, smelly, and cockroach-like . . ." An affair with a married woman, which Carothers did little to conceal, increased the stresses of his life, as did the death of his sister from pneumonia.

On April 28, 1937, fellow guests heard moans from a hotel room in Philadelphia. The manager busted in and discovered Carothers's body on the floor. Police found deadly crystals of potassium cyanide and a squeezed lemon near the corpse. Carothers was forty-one. His highly publicized and scandalous death, combined with the impact of a newspaper piece that claimed that nylon was made with "cadaverine," a chemical found in rotting corpses, threatened to give nylon a morbid image. In response, DuPont emphasized that nylon was made with coal, air, and water. This material, which changed how campers aligned themselves with nature, was in itself a clever new realignment of natural materials.

If consumers had any queasiness about the new product, it soon passed; nylon triggered a stampede in 1939 and '40 when mobs of mostly female buyers spent $34 million on nylon stockings. As *Fortune* magazine reported at that time, "Nylon . . . flouts Solomon. It's . . . the first completely new synthetic fiber made by man."

World War II interrupted the nylon hose revolution; excited about its vast military potential, war makers diverted 90 percent of the material to make U.S. Army tents, flak jackets, mosquito netting, lightweight hammocks, parachutes, and ropes. "The vanguard of the U.S. Army floated to earth in Normandy carried by and covered with Nylon," a Carothers biographer reported.

It took years for this and other newfangled lightweight materials to enter the camping world, but once they did, the synthetics "changed gear from horse-packable to backpackable, and clothing itself entered a new era of warmth and lightness," said Bruce "Yeti" Johnson, a passionate Pacific Northwest collector and historian of post-Carothers gear, in an interview. The war introduced other conveniences for the campers of the late 1940s, including the portable GI "pocket stove" and foam-rubber bedrolls.

These brand-new materials allowed inventors to defy the past, taking age-old gear-carrying systems and shelters and remaking them with a boldness that bordered on recklessness. These people had no reverence for the tested and familiar; maverick gear makers attacked every paradigm of the camping realm, including the traditional backpack.

Backpacks are nothing new. In 1991, two mountain climbers were out in a section of the Alps near the Austrian-Italian border when they stumbled across the body of a middle-aged man, dead for five thousand years and embedded in the ice of Similaun Glacier. Mummification had done the man a treat; he looked terrific for his age. Near the understandably skinny corpse, posthumously nicknamed Otzi, they found a backpack with a wooden frame. In another nod to modernity, the dead man was found to be lactose intolerant.

Alas, backpacking designs hadn't changed all that much since then. Before World War II came along, gear-carrying systems placed little value on comfort. Back in the 1880s, the minimalist camping innovator George Washington Sears, aka Nessmuk, griped about the drawbacks of his pack, which was lightweight but did nothing to prevent "an aggravating antagonism between the uncompromising rims of a fruit-can and the knobs of my vertebrae." Bruce "Yeti" Johnson described some of these old-school packs as "kidney-busters." Even some early DIY kits seemed designed with torture in mind. The 1915 *Handbook for Campers in the National Forests in California*, published by the U.S. Forest Service, invited readers to make improvised shoulder packs by taking a grain sack, placing a pebble "an inch or more in diameter in each of the lower corners," tying one leg of a pair of overalls to each corner—using the pebble to stop the knot from slipping, "clos[ing] the 'mouth of it' and using the legs to make 'comfortable shoulder straps.'"

This awful pack sounds like a mad chiropractor's darkest fantasy. As late as 1950 there was only one widely available, commercially distributed backpack for camping and hiking: Sears, Roebuck and Co.'s resolutely non-nylon "Trapper Nelson" pack, which was pretty much just wooden slats with rails on either side and a canvas bag mounted on the frame. An outdoorsman named Lloyd F. Nelson had developed this in the 1920s, and while it was a big step up from what came before, it was still quite rigid, disrespecting the contours of the human body. In the postwar years, outdoor gear manufacturers started paying much more attention to human comfort on the trail, throwing away the outmoded notion that gear was supposed to test your resolve and your machismo by being as cumbersome as possible. They also borrowed freely from other technologies and industries that had nothing to do with camping.

In 1951, Asher "Dick" Kelty, a carpenter from Duluth, Minnesota, was hiking in the Sierra Nevada when he noticed his buddy shoving the wooden struts of his sadistic rucksack into his trouser pockets to transfer the annoying weight from his shoulders to his hips. Suddenly his pal could walk the trail without stooping in agony. It was a thunderbolt moment in camping history. That incident inspired Kelty to devise a waist strap that allowed packers to haul heavy packloads without injuring themselves in the process. Drawing from the aviation industry, which at one time employed Kelty in a plant that assembled parts for bombers, he started using lightweight aluminum in his packs. Suddenly, gear manufacturers were admitting that the lumbar column and spinal cord actually existed. Kelty was not alone in creating humane backpacks for real bodies, keeping people in the woods instead of the chiropractor's office. The underrated backpacking innovator Jack Stephenson, at Stephenson's Warmlite, expanded upon Kelty's original design and became the first to construct modern, lightweight packs with true hip suspensions by the late 1950s.

The postwar period was a time of cobblers, risk takers, and experimentation. After winning a cash prize for a backpack prototype with an aluminum frame, an industrial design prodigy named Murray Pletz took his winnings and formed the JanSport company. He named the business after his girlfriend, Janice "Jan" Lewis, who sewed together the prizewinning pack. Pletz and Lewis married (and later divorced). A small crew of like-minded longhairs, including cofounder Skip Yowell, Pletz's cousin, started making flexible-frame packs by hand. Their stuffy, dusty workspace was located above an old transmission repair shop in north Seattle owned by Pletz's dad. Yowell recalled the "grunts and groans" of laborers trying to bend contoured frames using their own brute strength. "We had no map to follow, no mentor to consult, and no memory of what worked because there was no before," wrote Yowell in his memoir, *The Hippie Guide to Climbing the Corporate Ladder and Other Mountains*, which charts the company's path from its uncertain beginnings all the way up to its inevitable buyout.

Also in the postwar years, tent makers did their best, using state-of-the-art materials and designs, to bury the comfortable but unwieldy cotton-duck "wall tents" of the past. Back in the 1920s, "tent construction imitated the tepee," wrote Patricia Leigh Brown in an irreverent *New York Times* story about changing gear styles. Starting in the early 1950s, Gerry Mountain Sports began to push backpacking and camping farther away from the days of hard-to-carry, mildew-trapping tents when it made lightweight nylon tents that could hold up to the rigors of a mountain climb. The eccentric backpacking innovator Jack Stephenson, an aerospace engineer and avowed naturist who sometimes greeted visitors while standing around unselfconsciously in his black bikini underwear, devised ultralight four-season "hoop" tents that required only three to four tent stakes to secure. These entrepreneurs treated past versions of gear as overly complicated and clunky. From the geodesic tents inspired by R. Buckminster Fuller to the Pop-Tents of Bill Moss, these tensile constructions gave America's campgrounds a new, futuristic look that would have startled any Golden Age camper.

"Unless you have gone out in the middle of a rainy night to tighten ropes that are letting the leaky canvas collapse, broken a toe on a tent peg, or tripped over a guy line in the mud in the dark, you don't know how far modern tents have come," wrote Bill McKeown in an outdoors column for *Popular Mechanics.*

The competition for the new and the easy was never-ending; if you didn't like your sleeping bag or tent or pack, all you had to do was wait a few months and a new one would go on the market. For a while, the innovations continued at a dizzying pace. Starting in the mid-1970s, synthetic down supplied the warmth of real goose feathers, and it wouldn't make you die of hypothermia if it got wet. In 1982, Nike marketed its lightweight "Lava Dome" boot, which was aerated, so your feet wouldn't feel as if they were getting poached in hot water by the end of your hiking day.

Some of the innovations are now so ubiquitous; it's easy to forget that they didn't exist just a few decades ago. Starting in 1976, Gore-Tex, a spin-off on DuPont Teflon nonstick frying pan coating, allowed for outdoor clothing that kept backpackers reasonably dry. One development we have reason to celebrate and rue in equal measure is the advent of DEET, a modern-day replacement for Nessmuk's aromatic but not all that effective "bug dopes" of castor oil and pennyroyal all those years ago. The stuff, which became a major presence in camping starting in the mid-1970s, really does keep bugs away, and precludes the need for acrid "smudge fires." Then again, DEET smells terrible and shows up in blood samples twelve hours after you slather the stuff all over you.

Pretty soon, small-time backcountry camping and mountaineering manufacturers expanded into large businesses. LLBean, which opened its flagship store in 1917, ballooned into a gigantic mail-order business. Recreational Equipment, Inc. (REI), started out in 1938 as a low-key, Seattle-based climber's co-op that enabled its members to buy high-end mountaineering gear including hard-to-find items made in Europe. It has grown into one of the world's most successful outdoor retailers with 140 stores in 33 states and 5.5 million co-op members. The playing field would also come to include Eastern Mountain Sports, Gerry Outdoors, The North Face, and Sierra Designs. By 1970, these businesses were selling a combined $7 billion worth of goods a year.

The result of all this tinkering and innovating was an entirely different set of "must-have" equipment, which our camping forebears would hardly have recognized. The lightweight post-Carothers gear made it possible to penetrate ever farther into the backcountry for longer periods of time without having to resupply. Backpacking also opened up once-inaccessible forests to wilderness tourists. Lighter backpacks contributed to a flight to the woods that eclipsed even "Adirondack" Murray's rush in 1869.

Though men continued to dominate outdoor activities (and even now they outnumber women in the outdoors by a slender margin), the lighter gear eased the burden of women's entry into the woods in the 1960s and '70s. The U.S. National Park Service's Bureau of Statistics does not provide gender breakdowns for the people who applied for backcountry permits during that period, but anecdotal evidence, including published accounts of solo women backpacking trips and full-page magazine ads for gear manufacturers catering exclusively to females, suggests a stepped-up presence. "In the past, women were somewhat foreclosed from backpacking, in good part because it was beyond the strength of many to carry the heavy packs that used to be standard," writes Ellen Zaslaw in a book on lightweight backpacking. She adds that "the typical young American woman weighs 133 pounds and the old packs weighed perhaps 50 pounds fully loaded."

Americans developed such a passion for lengthy treks into the wild that Congress, in 1968, passed the National Trails System Act, establishing the Appalachian Trail and its funky, lovely, and occasionally cruel West Coast cousin the Pacific Crest Trail, as "national scenic trails." Forget your weekend camping trips; the stage was being set for people to live on a trail for half a year.

Yet this borderline manic excitement about outdoor living had a downside. The new accessibility of remote forests and the enormous popularity of backpacking led to soul-searching and complex questions. Nick Clinch, a pal of Dick Kelty's, once remarked that Kelty, by "[taking] the misery out of the sport," had become "the Henry Ford of backpacking; I blame him for the overcrowding of the wilderness."

That condemnation had a winking quality; in a sly way, Clinch was trying to boost his friend and give him props for making a fine backpack. But Clinch was also speaking the truth. Once pastimes for a limited group of sportsmen, camping and other forms of wilderness recreation began to draw large crowds in the late 1960s. "After the 1972 season when an astonishing 16,432 persons floated through the Grand Canyon, the National Park Service realized it had a problem on its hands as potentially damaging to the wilderness qualities of the place as dams and reservoirs," writes Roderick Nash in *Wilderness and the American Mind*.

Road building was another way that campers and other wilderness tourists were hugging the land to death. Congress created an Office of Public Roads in 1905, just two years after the first car wobbled out of the Ford Motor Company's Detroit factory. The Federal Aid Road Act of 1916 promised to bring a network of high-speed roads throughout the country. The early auto campers were pioneers of the roadways. But when this new-fangled form of camping caught on, the group did not hesitate to wield power. The more those early daredevil auto campers slammed into culverts, busted their axles on bumps, and tumbled into ditches, the more they pressured state, federal, and local governments to develop better roads and campsites to suit them.

Cars helped Americans "rediscover" national parks, which led to smooth, well-graded, chuckhole-free routes such as the Going-to-the-Sun Road in Glacier National Park. By the early twentieth century, Yellowstone alone would have about three hundred miles of roadways girdling the park. Conservationists, alarmed by the crowds and America's network of brand-new highways, started to wonder if America's scenic places were going to turn into kitschy, cluttered tourist traps; commercialize the outdoor experience; and kill or crowd out wildlife in the process. The formation in 1935 of the Wilderness Society was seen, in part, as a last stand against the automobiles and the roads. The society, whose core membership included, among others, Benton MacKaye, founding visionary of the Appalachian Trail, and ecologist and future *A Sand County Almanac* author Aldo Leopold, took a strong stand against those who would "barber and manicure wild America as smartly as the modern girl."

The society pushed to expand America's protected forests, but its founders also wanted a sweeping new law that would set down specifics about the way those lands would be treated and respected. The threat of the automobile forced them to update and redefine what wilderness meant. Modern environmentalists learned from John Muir's bitter defeat at Hetch Hetchy in 1913 that merely setting aside a landscape, even a national park, was not the same as protecting it. A popular nervousness and vigilance about the future of wild places led to the Wilderness Act of 1964. This piece of legislation, signed by President Lyndon Johnson, set aside 9 million acres as wilderness; since then, that number has climbed to 109 million acres. While the government had been preserving wilderness tracts long beforehand, and while Americans had tossed around and debated what wilderness meant to them, this law was much more explicit. One of the obvious targets is the presence of cars, or any business interest that would use and exploit the land. "Once designated as wilderness, a tract would be off-limits to commercial ventures like logging and new mines," wrote Elizabeth Kolbert in *National Geographic*. "It would be available for humans to explore, but not with mechanized vehicles."

Yet the Wilderness Act also threw a tomahawk straight at the old-style camping ethos with some of its language: "A wilderness, in contrast with those areas where man and his own works dominate the landscape, is hereby recognized as an area where the earth and community of life are untrammeled by man, where man himself is a visitor who does not remain." The implicit message: don't stay too long, and don't try to domesticate these wild places. While the Wilderness Act says nothing specific about recreational impacts, it is hostile to the idea of turning the forest into your living room, a notion that lies at the heart of old-time camping.

Many of the leading old-time campers, including Nessmuk and Horace Kephart, were not slobs. Both were fussy about their camps and neither fished or killed more than he needed. Yet the sheer number of woodcrafters, and the inevitable game-hog miscreants who left hideous stumps and messy campsites in their wake, tarred the movement and empowered its enemies to fight back. Besides, this kind of camper was becoming an anachronism. Gone were the days when wilderness seemed an inexhaustible resource. Romantics could no longer write about sipping whiskey and botanizing while a guide took up an axe and made mincemeat of some lovely forest just to build a shanty for the evening. Camping how-to guidebooks changed along with the times. By the early 1970s, even that old mainstay of the camping experience the cook fire started slipping into the back pages or vanishing from how-to books entirely. The new generation of campers worried about possible forest fires and people trampling vegetation and harming ecosystems in search of kindling. Ideas that were once accepted as standard practice were becoming anathema in the forest.

"No matter how ecologically sound, woodcraft would destroy the woods if too many practiced it," noted the author Alston Chase in his environmental history of Yellowstone. Even some traditional campers started questioning the old ways and defecting away from their cronies. One dramatic example was Harvey Manning, a doughy-framed former woodcraft camper who looked in later years like an especially grizzled and authenticity-minded department store Santa Claus.

Son of a lumber equipment salesman, he grew up to be an avid hater of lumber interests. Gruff, tireless, unafraid of intimidating or enraging people, he was just the right person to force the issue of an antiwoodcraft rebellion. In doing so, he did his part to make contemporary backpacking synonymous with minimal-impact ethics.

Manning didn't just offer an alternative to burly, consumptive nature practices; he ridiculed them in a way that sounded personal. "Woodcraft is dead," he proclaimed in his 1973 book *Backpacking: One Step at a Time.* "Dead because the modern equipment . . . makes pioneer-style engineering unnecessary. Dead because nature-sensitive hikers have deeper, subtler pleasures than slashing and gouging."

Manning was careful to credit some of the grand "old boys" of woodcraft, including Horace Kephart, for their formidable skills and their ability to make do "with crude equipment." Yet he had nothing but contempt for ignorant modern-day, high-impact "ax-wielders," litterbugs, and other sinners against nature. He even clarified that his message was aimed at the younger generations, and not so much "[t]he old generation," which is "probably . . . irretrievably corrupt and damned anyway. The future must be built by the new." A new breed of backpackers and campers was mobilizing. They were creating a new ethos in the woods. "Cutting evergreen branches to make bough beds is illegal, immoral, and damaging to the trees," wrote Cliff Jacobson in his 1987 book *Camping Secrets*. "An air mattress or foam pad works better. The use of dead evergreen boughs or mosses should be discouraged as this material provides 'a surface cover' which blots out sunlight and consequently kills vegetation below."

In this new climate, with dawning awareness of human damage to the outdoors, America was ready to embrace a new breed of camping hero and wilderness warrior.

Colin Fletcher (1922–2007) was a Romantic wanderer in the age of plastic and nylon, a man who proved that camping could be a soulful enterprise even when you used space-age equipment. Fletcher wrote his odes to the desolate spaces Americans once treated with contempt, including the great southwestern deserts. His 1967 travel memoir *The Man Who Walked Through Time* is striking for its minute and rhapsodic descriptions of clever survival strategies, including strategic airdrops and caches containing food, equipment, and his beloved claret wine. The book, about Fletcher's four-hundred-mile 1963 trek inside the rim of the Grand Canyon, updates the *Walden* ideal for the postwar generation. Fletcher got his first backpacking experience as a commando in the Royal Marines during World War II. He was a genius at repurposing military gear for intense and pleasurable walks. No other writer has done a finer job of describing backpackers' rituals in such loving and exacting detail. Just as Thoreau sighed with satisfaction when he soaked in Walden Pond or cooked a "horned pout" in a pit oven, Fletcher had a "sudden sharp spasm of pleasure" when he sniffed a cook pot full of dehydrated potatoes. He even considered his camp stove sensuous and comforting, "its familiar roar" rising up "against the huge, soft, black, familiar silence."

A native Welshman, Fletcher moved to California in 1956. His favorite haunts were the Grand Canyon, the "chocolate rock" of Death Valley, and the Panamints. All the while he carried his house with him on the "foam-padded yoke" on his shoulders. His writing captured the spirit of the perfect backpacking journey through tules and bulrushes, sandy washes, and other lonely places. In the process, he inspired others to have their own adventures. "Colin was sort of the founding father of modern backpacking, the first person to write about going out for an extended period and being self-sufficient," Annette McGivney of *Backpacker* magazine told the *New York Times*. In another interview, she described Fletcher as "the Jerry Garcia of backpacking."

Fletcher's camping and tramping philosophies comforted Americans in a time of national crisis in the late 1960s. In an interview, Buck Tilton, also of *Backpacker*, described coming home from Vietnam and feeling lost. "So many of my friends had died from bullet holes. I read *The Man Who Walked Through Time*, and it was the only thing that made sense to me. Fletcher's words gave meaning to backpacking. I loaded my pack exactly the way Fletcher did and carried a walking stick like his. He was my hero."

Aside from just writing about his own experiences, Fletcher shared his techniques in an irreverent handbook, *The Complete Walker*, first published in 1968 and still selling briskly. The book offers encouragement and an irresistible dare to his readers: "Once you've overcome this fear of the unknown and thereby surmounted your sleeping-out-in-the-wilderness block, you are free. Free to go out, when the world will let you slip away into the wildest places you dare explore. Free to walk from dawn to dusk and then again from dawn to dusk, with no harsh interruptions, among the quiet and soothing cathedrals of a virgin forest." To lose yourself in the experience you must "pare away" the weight of every item, he advised. Take along a walking staff as your "third leg." Bring comfortable moccasins for camp.

Yet Fletcher was unstinting about the drawbacks of convenience.

In the sixties, dried foods became a common part of the camping experience. By the midsixties, ungodly heaps of "freeze-dried compressed foods" hit the shelves of outdoor supply stores, a fantastic development for featherweight enthusiasts, and sad news for campers and backpackers with functional taste buds. Anyone who remembered the unrushed Dutch oven cooking in the fixed camps, or the savor of johnnycakes and venison drifting over mountain meadows, had reason to carp.

"Dehydrated food, properly processed and packaged, is stable," Fletcher writes in *The Complete Walker*. "Its flavor does not become haylike." On the downside, Fletcher describes this food as "damnably expensive" and said that it "makes you fart like a bull."

Fletcher's style of camping soothed the soul, but he also wrote about human sins against the land. "It is hard to say why virgin desert looks so clean," he writes in *The Thousand-Mile Summer*, a 1964 Fletcher classic about a journey through the Mojave, Death Valley, and up into the Sierra Nevada. "Partly, I suppose, because the sun has purged it. Partly because your eye seems to pierce to the heart of everything . . . Every wrinkle of a distant escarpment stands out so clear and close that you want to run your hand over it and feel the roughness. Only man defiles. For the frankness that makes the desert so pure also leaves it wide open to rape. Wheel tracks last for years, bulldozer scars for decades. A derelict house looks as if it will stand stark and hideous until Judgment Day."

The memoir includes a built-in critique of the car. Riding on a highway, Fletcher saw a desert as a "badly focused filmstrip, mile after monotonous mile." Only when you leave your car behind and head out there on your own two legs, powering your steps with occasional mouthfuls of pemmican, raisins, and mint cake, does the landscape come into focus: "a brown blob off to the left became a fat barrel cactus . . ." The perspective reverses as you walk out in its "muddy hollows, baked hard after rain . . . Now, cars were monsters that snarled past, tearing the air. They left a dusty, tainted aftertaste."

Fletcher became a cult hero at a time when American backcountry campers and backpackers were struggling with two conflicting impulses: the urge to be romantic wayfarers in the backcountry and the need to change the way they behaved in the wild. The Wilderness Act made provisions for protecting the land. Yet the act does *not* contain any passage saying, "Please just stay home. Take up another hobby. The forest is better off without you, anyway."

No, the Wilderness Act makes provisions to let the wild stay wild *and* keep the land open for public enjoyment. Still, how does one make a landscape accessible and protect its natural integrity at the same time? The desire to rectify these seemingly incompatible goals led to the development of "minimal-impact" camping principles. Starting in the 1960s, the U.S. Forest Service and other agencies teamed with survival training groups and conservation organizations to spread the message of "leave the wilderness as you found it" and "pack it out." Wilderness areas were too delicate to handle the overwhelming number of well-wishers. Cat holes—that's camper and backpacker speak for trenches to bury wastes—became a problem in remote wild areas. Backpackers started coming home with nasty ailments just from taking a sip of pure-looking Sierra water.

Findings about giardia are tricky, contradictory, and controversial, but I will tell you this from personal experience: when I was a kid, drinking freely from High Sierra streams, I was fine. Now, if I drink raw mountain water, I'm liable to make myself sick. I lost several weeks on the Pacific Crest Trail, and about twenty pounds, to some or other beaver fever I picked up in a stream in Northern California. Yet giardia is only one of the quality-of-life issues in busy outdoor areas. The sight of somebody else's used toilet paper fluttering in the breeze beneath a boulder has become an all-too-common part of the camping experience.

The response was a crackdown on slovenly behavior and a new code of conduct in the wild. "The most devoted backpackers fluffed the grass on which they slept, gave up toilet paper rather than burying it, and preferred drinking their dishwater to pouring it in the ground," noted James Morton Turner in his essay "From Woodcraft to 'Leave No Trace.'" "No measure seemed too extreme in their efforts to protect the wilderness. Carrying packs loaded with modern gear, backpackers prided themselves on traveling through wilderness as mere visitors." Leave No Trace gained new ground in 1991, when it became "the official ethic for environmentally-conscious outdoor recreation on the nation's public lands," Turner noted in the same essay.

LNT has seven commandments:

1. Plan ahead and prepare.
2. Travel and camp on durable surfaces.
3. Dispose of waste properly.
4. Leave what you find.
5. Minimize campfire impacts.
6. Respect wildlife.
7. Be considerate of other visitors.

It is not always easy to follow all these principles at once, especially if you're camped practically on top of one another in some far-flung meadow where the only law is common sense. LNT requires a good deal of forethought, restraint, and willingness to suffer mild inconveniences. It's a social as well as an ecological value that can be hard to respect in extreme situations, and difficult to enforce. In areas where there are few rangers, LNT is nothing less than a test of human nature. When we adhere to LNT waste-disposal principles, we are supposed to "Pack it in, pack it out," "Inspect our campsite and rest areas for trash or spilled foods," "Pack out all trash, leftover food and litter," "Deposit solid human waste in cat holes dug 6 to 8 inches deep, at least 200 feet from water, camp and trails, cover and disguise the cat hole when finished, pack out toilet paper and hygiene products." If you've done any amount of backcountry camping in the past few years, you know full well that the system works better in some places than it does in others, while the range of reactions to the rules runs from accepting to surly to indignant.

These days, minimal impact has percolated into *every* aspect of the camping world. Even the once-woodcraft-based Boy Scouts now includes handbooks with LNT best practices. This is not to say that old gear and lovers of pre-Carothers camping equipment have gone extinct. Far from it. Those descendants of Nessmuk are still with us, resurrecting and updating the old ways. And some of the people who were trashed so thoroughly by Mr. Harvey Manning have raised an impassioned defense of their own, while reviving their anticonsumerist credo—which now takes special aim at all the high-tech gadgetry and LNT-branded products that were supposed to have driven woodcraft into the mud all those years ago. "Backpacking killed camping," the camping historian, author, and primitive skills expert David Wescott told me during a phone interview. "The word *backpack* wasn't even in the literature [until the early 1950s], and it suddenly came on so strong."

With the newer model of backpack-supported camping, the old mastery and the indefinite lingering is less important. The higher-tech clothing, gear, and equipment, especially our new wave of way-finding equipment, allow us to camp in a landscape even if we don't know the trees and can't track the animals. In the old days, backpacking was known as woodsrunning, packing, hiking, or tramping. "Now that backpacking is the model for how we camp, gear is thought of in that context and is engineered backward to fit the model—hence we get gear that is totally inefficient and undependable in the camping market because it was designed from a backpacking paradigm," Wescott said.

If you peruse woodcraft/old-time camping websites and blogs, you will also see rants about the synthetic materials used in the new gear, and how the manufacturing and disposal of these products can hardly be considered Leave No Trace or "minimal impact," even if the impact isn't taking place in the forest where you can see it. An ecologist named Mark Browne caused widespread outdoor industry grumbling starting in 2011 when his painstaking examination of sediment on beaches showed the negative side of Carothers's invention nylon: tiny fibers from this "miracle polymer" and other synthetics used in clothing, including acrylic, were turning up in outflows from sewer pipes and floating freely in oceans. "It is not news that microplastic—which the National Oceanic and Atmospheric Administration defines as plastic fragments 5mm or smaller—is ubiquitous in all five major ocean gyres," writes journalist Mary Catherine O'Connor in an article about microfibers and the environment.

Outdoor gear manufacturers are, of course, not the only industries that use synthetic materials in their manufacturing process. These by-products also come from the clothing industry in general, as well as cosmetics. But these scientific studies complicate prevailing ideas about Leave No Trace. So do the arguments of scholars such as James Morton Turner who say LNT has become so conflated with certain gear items that it has turned into a form of branding, resulting in an awkward mixture of eco-consciousness and merchandising. Yet even if we push aside the consumerism argument for the moment and restrict our examination of LNT to wilderness areas in America, "minimal impact" still faces serious challenges.

To illustrate the contradictions and challenges of LNT, I decided to seek out a forest where the campers and rangers must confront a number of issues as they think about ways to keep the wilderness clean. In a burst of enthusiasm and idealism, I decided to place myself in one of the front lines of the LNT battlefield.

To implicate myself in that ecological war, I would become one of the eco-warriors—at least for one memorable, beautiful, miserable weekend.

Hero of Camping: Edward Abbey

"May Your Trails Be Crooked,
Winding, Lonesome, Dangerous"

I once steered a motor home into the mountains outside Tucson, where I entered the domain of America's most charming, infuriating, and cantankerous mid- to late-twentieth-century camper: Edward Abbey, a morally complex preservationist; womanizer; hater of cattlemen but lover of juicy steaks; sworn enemy of road builders, lawyers, and bulldozers; a man with a special fondness for the spray can and monkey wrench; an inspiration to mainstream activists and ecoterrorists alike; who favored leaving wilderness the hell alone, though he once rolled an old tire into the Grand Canyon for no particular reason. He wrote about slaughtering a rabbit and never eating it because he feared the meat was diseased. His smile was wide and toothy. His eyes were green. His beard was almost as large and puffed-out as John Muir's. His skin was nut brown from the sun. Abbey looked a bit like a Sonoran raven with his large, beaky nose. I doubt he would have approved of my plan to "see" the desert from the windows of our clunky RV. As I rumbled onward through his beloved country, I could almost hear him grumbling at me: "[Y]ou've got to get out of the goddamned contraption and walk, better yet crawl, on hands and knees, over the sandstone and through the . . . cactus. When traces of blood begin to mark your trail you'll see something, maybe."

As much as he loved a willing young woman—and Lord, how he loved them—he loved even more the open arms of the saguaro

"If my decomposing carcass helps nourish the roots of a juniper tree
or the wings of a vulture—that is immortality enough for me.
And as much as anyone deserves," Edward Abbey (1927–1989)

cactus, and weeklong hikes along the red rocks and mountains of Arizona, which he compared to pieces of hammered iron. His Walden Pond cabin was a humble trailer in Arches National Monument (now Arches National Park), in eastern Utah, where he lived as a seasonal park ranger from 1956 to 1957. This experience was the staging ground for his most loved book, *Desert Solitaire: A Season in the Wilderness*, a memoir that combines the ecstatic raptures of the nineteenth-century Romantics with the hard-nosed cynicism, defiance, and bitterness of John Muir after his defeat at Hetch Hetchy. It contains some of the loveliest passages in outdoor literature.

The fire. The odor of burning juniper is the sweetest fragrance on the face of the earth, in my honest judgment. I doubt if all the smoking censers of Dante's paradise could equal it. One breath of juniper smoke, like the perfume of sagebrush after rain, evokes in magical catalysis, like certain music, the space and light and clarity and piercing strangeness of the American West. Long may it burn. The little fire waves, flickers, begins to die . . . A wisp of bluish smoke goes up and the wood, arid as the rock from which it came, blossoms out in fire.

Has anyone else ever written about the camping experience in a more sensuous and primal way?

Abbey's words were enough to send thousands of seekers into the land of the cactus wren, the mesquite tree, and the ocotillo. "I am here not only to evade for awhile the clamor and filth and confusion of the cultural apparatus but also to confront, immediately and directly if it's possible, the bare bones of existence, the elemental and fundamental, the bedrock which sustains us," he wrote. "I dream of a hard and brutal mysticism in which the naked self merges with the nonhuman world and yet survives still intact, individual, separate." Like the best of all campers and nature writers, he makes us want to throw our smartphones out the window, roll up our sleeping bags, and light out for the territories.

From what I've read, Mr. Abbey, if you had the pleasure of meeting him, was a thoughtful, quiet, and rather shy in person. Yet on the page, he thundered. Abbey remains a relevant and potent force and inspiration for American campers of a certain strain of thought because he was all about intense engagement with life and direct experience. For him, the most reliable path to that experience—aside, of course, from getting entangled in the arms of an eco-groupie—came from sleeping on rocks still holding the warmth of the sun and reckoning with the "other" of nature. His wild places were utterly foreign, resistant to simile, defying comparison. The American southwestern desert was "The best place I know where a good man can get beyond anthropomorphism," he told his friends.

Out in the desert, he'd follow javelina tracks and cougar prints for days. Coyotes would howl, and sometimes he'd answer back with his flute. On at least two occasions, red ants took up residence in his ears. He meted out vengeance by pissing on their anthills. Abbey recapitulated, and invigorated and complicated, the ideas of America's first best camper, Henry David Thoreau. In other words, he practiced camping as a means not only of natural observation—and the best of his nature descriptions rivals Thoreau's—but of artful self-observation and knowledge, and he recorded these sense impressions to help the rest of us see inside ourselves in a different way. Abbey, like his forebears, made a strong case that preserving wild places, where humans could sleep more or less at peace beneath the stars (give or take a few red ants), was akin to preserving human souls.

But when it came to preserving these places, Abbey was much more ferocious than his predecessors. John Muir, though radicalized late in life, never told anyone to go out and break stuff. Abbey believed it was not enough just to go out and camp. The camper had to take responsibility and be willing to do whatever it took to stop people from raping wild places. "Philosophy without action is the ruin of the soul," said Abbey, who'd taken a raft through Glen Canyon before it was dammed to tarnation. "One brave deed is worth a hundred books, a thousand theories, a million words."

The best-known heroes of Abbey's fictional work were vigilantes, outcasts, and saboteurs who distrusted government and cast a gimlet eye on bureaucrats and bureaucracy and who were against violence while stopping just short of disavowing it. His books were more than just loving descriptions of the natural world; they brimmed with anger, outrage, insults, insubordination, and calls for direct action. Abbey put the fight into the forest. Praise or curse him the next time you see some sad-eyed, earnest college kid roped up at unreasonable heights in a forest, putting his or her life on the line to protect an old-growth sequoia or, for that matter, a scraggly fourth-growth redwood on some unloved tree farm property or overdeveloped college campus.

13

The Immaculator

In our heavily trafficked wild areas—be they places of jumping waters or serpentine trails, snowy slopes or rocky terrain—the prevailing shift is toward regulated packing-it-out. To hear of a charmed soul taking care of her own leavings, willingly (minus rules), always warms my heart. Ponder this: Are we as a species willing to clip a small container of excreta to our backpacks, or are we more an animal prone to paying taxes for wilderness police? Airport security at every trailhead?

—Kathleen Meyer, *How to Shit in the Woods*, 3rd edition, 2011

Mount Whitney looked immaculate from a distance. One summer afternoon, I stood on a sidewalk in Lone Pine, California, and stared at the mountaintop. *That's where I'm climbing,* I said to myself. I would soon be looking down from the highest peak in the continental United States.

Mount Whitney is part of a cluster of sharp and jagged forms that turn red, orange, or goldenrod depending on the time of day. Their shape and arrangement suggest a cougar's jawbone and teeth. The Sierra Crest is beautiful and terrible, indifferent to human concerns. It was hard to imagine any discarded cigarettes, candy wrappers, empty beer cans, or other kinds of filth in those sunlit heights. But who knew what I would find on my Leave No Trace–themed trek up the mountain? That mystery was all part of the thrilling adventure I had arranged for myself. Later in the day, I was going to drive up to Whitney Portal, the access point to the Whitney

The Immaculator, photographed in the Eastern Sierra, September 2014

Trail, a popular footpath leading to the mountain summit. Starting in late afternoon, I would hike 3.8 strenuous miles to Outpost Camp, in the backcountry, and sleep for the night. The next morning, before sunup, I would rise from my tent, climb Whitney at dawn, and then hike back out to Whitney Portal. But I had no intention of going out there and being just one more passive camper on the mountainside. Instead, I would be a minimal-impact warrior, taking along a three-foot plastic tube that looked just like a rocket-propelled grenade launcher.

I'd built this special tube to transport other people's biohazardous wastes off the mountain with no mess or fuss. I'd named the tube the Immaculator because it would help me make the mountain sparkling clean.

I got the blueprint from the online advice site WikiHow, but I made a few changes to its recommended design. For instance, the website recommended that I use lightweight white PVC pipe, but I needed something more durable to minimize odors while, at the same time, stopping raccoons and bears from ripping into the tube and stealing my cache of turds. That's why I opted for ABS pipe, a thicker material. Work crews use it to repair broken sewer mains. Aside from this, ABS is jet black. It looks great! Two weeks before my Mount Whitney trip, a couple of workmen at the Home Depot in Santa Cruz sawed off a piece of the pipe for me. I covered up the sharp, jagged end with a plastic cap, added a screw top to the other end, and tied on a bungee cord. Finally, I slapped a big orange BIOHAZARD sticker on the tube, and my project was done. Time to climb some mountains. The website strongly recommended that I bring along a bunch of flat-bottomed coffee filters so I could use them to wrap each individual turd before shoving it into the tube. However, I decided to skip that step. Why make my job disgusting? Instead, I planned to throw a plastic garbage bag on top of each clump and then grab it with a pair of plastic salad tongs from Kmart. I would then drop it into the tube and keep on hiking.

Mount Whitney has a fascinating situation regarding campers and human waste disposal. Although there are no longer bathrooms or pit toilets of any kind along the Whitney Trail, campers are strictly forbidden from digging a cat hole and burying their waste. That's because much of the terrain is solid bedrock with just a sprinkling of dirt on top of it. Besides, the elevation is too high for slops to decompose properly. Instead, all visitors are expected to use sky-blue plastic sacks called WAG (Waste Alleviation and Gelling) Bags, each of them roughly the size of a tall kitchen trash bag and containing a small pile of moisture-activated "poo powder" that reduces odors. Rangers at the station in Lone Pine hand out these bags to the campers along with their mandatory backcountry permits. It's all part of an honor system.

The issue of waste disposal has become a real concern in America's busiest camping and hiking areas including Mount Whitney. Every year, between twenty thousand and twenty-five thousand people set out for the summit. Each produces on average three to eight ounces of solid waste per day. Most hikers spend at least a full day out there on the slopes; it's a slow and sweaty twenty-two-mile trip from Whitney Portal to the mountaintop and back. That's a huge potential pile of waste. The good news is that most people take these materials out of the forest with them and place them in special garbage containers intended for biohazardous materials, according to rangers who monitor these things. Though compliance was supposedly high, I still thought it would be smart to get out my camping gear and investigate the scene for myself, just to make sure. Besides, I could not think of a better way to tie my personal comfort to the behavior of my fellow campers. If everyone followed the Leave No Trace rules like they were supposed to do, and "packed it out," I would be happy and comfortable on the trek. On the rare, outside chance that they acted like slobs and left their wastes on the ground, I would have to gather what they spilled and carry it out with me. If this happened, my pack weight would increase by the mile, and I would suffer in proportion to the size of the problem. Under those circumstances, I would feel the forest's pain, and cry like a mountain.

I could hardly wait to start my trek, but there was time for one last errand. I stopped by an outdoor gear store on the main drag in Lone Pine to see if they had any warm gloves to wear on my overnight hike to the Whitney summit. While looking through the wares near the cash register, I couldn't resist telling the store clerk all about my grand plan. He seemed interested, so I went into some detail.

"I'm pretty stoked about this hike," I said. "I expect to find a few things up there but not too much. This is going to sound silly, but part of me wonders if I'll come away empty-handed."

The clerk looked confused when I said this. I tried to explain. The rangers knew exactly when I would be climbing the mountain. They even knew the backcountry camp where I would be staying, because I had to put this information down when I filed for the fifteen-dollar wilderness permit. I told the clerk there was a very good chance that the rangers, wary of bad publicity about garbage on the mountain, had sent an advance cleanup crew to the campground, and to the rest of the Whitney Trail, just to make sure there was no litter whatsoever by the time I got there. That way, the rangers would make me look like an idiot, discredit me, and invalidate my mission.

"Am I overthinking this?" I asked the store clerk. "Ideally, I'll find maybe one or two things to haul off the mountain, but not too much. Just enough to make my trip worthwhile, in other words . . ."

At this point, the clerk had a pained expression on his face, and though

I made a mental note about it at the time, I didn't think too hard about it. I decided not to buy any warm gloves from him; too expensive, I thought. Still, I wondered if he had any last-minute words of wisdom that might make my Mount Whitney cleanup mission a success.

"Yes," he told me. "Walk with blinders on. Walk at night."

His words gave me a slight twinge of misgiving, but as my car approached Whitney Portal the magic of the scenery was so strong that my wonder, idealism, and confidence soon returned, and all doubt was cast from my mind. Driving up, I saw a brown-and-gold immensity of granite so high and forbidding that it blocked human progress; no roads cross from one side to the other in that section of the Sierra Nevada.

At 8,360 feet above sea level, the trailhead is ridiculously high, but the elevation doesn't really hit you until the first few switchbacks. I have pretty bad asthma, so it felt like someone was putting a paper bag on my face and pressing down hard. Immediately I confronted a white slope ablaze with afternoon light. Just looking up at the climb was intimidating. The cliffs were so tall that I would have had to lie on the ground to see the top of the grade. I tried not to think too much about the zigzagging route, the unbroken sunshine, and the cautionary words of the store clerk. The heat hit me hard from all sides. It even came up from the rocks. But just when I was thinking, *This is too hard for me. I'm much too old*, an ice-cold cross breeze would rouse me again. This pattern continued—a heat blast, then a chilling wind—and after a while I began to fall into its rhythm. The climb began to invigorate me like a Norwegian spa, broiling temperatures contrasting with freshets blowing over the northern fork of Lone Pine Creek. I felt as if I were back in my best days on the Pacific Crest Trail, just gliding along at my own pace, saying hello to everybody I saw. "Lovely day, isn't it?" I'd say to anyone within earshot.

Mountain asters grew alongside prickly pears. Metallic blue lizards with whiptails rushed past me. The birds were tittering in the treetops—*teeheeheehee!* I leaned into the slope, breathing the thin air and feeling giddy from my purpose, the strain, and the high elevation. Six young men descended the slope and hiked toward me. These were not survivalists. For the old-time woodcrafters of the nineteenth and early twentieth centuries, the land and the hatchet would provide. These new light packers flashed through the forest like bullets, their freeze-dried noodles and hurry compensating for their lack of survival skills.

The light packer embodies the Wilderness Act: these careful young tres-
passers who pluck no flowers, dry no hides, and bark no trees. I hoped they
were hauling out their waste bags as they were supposed to. The young men
got close to me and smiled.

"That's the coolest-looking bear keg I've ever seen," one of them said.
He pointed to the tube. "Where'd you get that?"

"I made it," I said.

"Really?" He nodded and walked past me. "Very impressive."

I understood his mistake; my homemade biological waste disposal pod
looked like a backcountry bear-proof food canister, but skinnier. When the
group passed me by, I wished I'd stopped them and explained the tube's
purpose. After all, it felt great for me to be confronting a controversial topic
that campers obsess over but hate to talk about in polite company. We must
have inherited some bodily function squeamishness from the Victorian
wilderness adventurers of the nineteenth century, who referred to their
solid waste as "night soil." Henry David Thoreau, probably the most influential visionary in camping history, provided detailed descriptions of his
cabin at Walden Pond. Even now, someone could rebuild it plank for plank
and furnish it as he did. Yet the prudish Thoreau did not write a single
word describing the inevitable privy; nor did he give even a general sense
of its location; it's as if he dwelled inside a spirit world where people sub-
limed all their food through their pores. Thoreau had a similar extreme
reticence on the topic of sex. I have a strong feeling that denying the functions of the human body only leads to bad policy. What did campers do
with their droppings in the old days? My impression, from reading woodcraft manuals, is that they either used common cat holes or else took the
"fling and forget it" approach.

To my mind, the waste disposal issues of the past went hand in hand
with the belief that the wilderness was something limitless, that man was
separate from nature, and that truly wild places were somewhere way *out
there*, far removed from our cities. And if nature was far removed from us,
what difference did it make if we dropped a bit of litter on the ground?
Even after Congress created the world's first national park, Yellowstone, in
1872 in northwestern Wyoming, America still hadn't figured out how to
behave outdoors, or what was considered irresponsible or good steward-
ship. (The early Yellowstone campers had no problem washing their filthy
shirts and underwear in the park's boiling thermal pools, polluting them
in the process.) Unfortunately, the creation of the park did not include suf-

ficient provisions to protect it. Enforcement was minimal. Campers chopped off bits of rock formations, and market hunters faced little resistance when they gunned down as many as four thousand elk in a single year. They took the hides and tongues and left the bodies where they fell. The situation got so bad that the U.S. Cavalry finally came in to end the carnage, and held sway until 1916, when the National Park Service started up and took over. Such practices suggest that Americans at the time, even those wilderness tourists who loved unspoiled wild places, were still having a hard time measuring the worth of these lands and figuring out what they were good for, aside from profiteering or amusement.

We've all come a long way since then, but I worry that our reluctance to talk about cringe-inducing topics has compromised our ability to deal with these issues. It's not as if I enjoy talking about such things, but what is the alternative? As an ardent backpacker, I've gotten over most of my shame or reluctance long ago, but I'm surprised at the number of people who won't camp at all in places where there are no restrooms. Sometimes, in newspaper articles about why people hate camping so much, they will complain that the toilets were more than a hundred feet away. During his camping years after college, one of my brothers became so gun-shy about relieving himself outdoors that he chug-a-lugged most of a bottle of Kaopectate during long weekends in Death Valley, and kept on nipping at it just to make sure. By the end of the trip, he'd turned his innards to grout. I think we American campers can't afford to be so coy or ashamed, especially now that there are so many of us out there camping in the same places. When John Muir climbed Mount Whitney in 1873, only a few people had ever done it. Now it's not uncommon to see just under two hundred visitors on any given day in the "Whitney Zone" (the summit and slopes beneath it, as well as the lands beneath the mountain where day-use or overnight permits are required), including a hundred-odd day-trippers and sixty overnight backpackers, as well as twenty-five or so hikers who access the summit from the other side of the crest, even with a strict quota system regulating visitation.

The trail was crowded when I hiked it, and an endless number of people passed me on the way up. The elevation made me tipsy. Young climbers kept overtaking me. How slow was I going? One mile an hour? A half mile an hour?

Still, from what I could tell, the rangers were correct in saying they had a pretty good handle on the waste disposal issues up on Whitney. I was disappointed but not altogether surprised that I walked up switchback after switchback and found absolutely no litter of any kind—not even a bottle cap or cigarette butt. "Slim pickings for you, my friend," I told the Immaculator. "I'm afraid you're going to go hungry."

Considering I was still fairly close to the entrance point, it was no big shock that I found no litter. And yet I was starting to feel silly. Does my hike have any purpose at all? And if there is no garbage up here, why am I carrying this needless, five-pound Immaculator? I was fulminating about my rotten luck, and just about to pass the John Muir Wilderness entrance sign, when I noticed a piece of toilet paper on the edge of the trail, wadded up and riotously soiled. I guess I should have been happy and relieved to see this, but somehow I was not prepared for the sobering reality, or the idea that someone would dare leave such a mess at a sign commemorating America's greatest champion of unspoiled places. It was disgusting, and it stopped me cold. Oh, well. I had to put this in perspective. This was not so bad. At least it wouldn't be heavy to carry. I grabbed the salad tongs and put the tissue in the tube.

"A little midafternoon snack for you, Immaculator," I said. "Nothing for me to get too worked up about, I guess."

No worries, I thought, *there is still plenty of room left in the tube.* I forced myself to smile, because every day is a grand one in the mountains, no matter what you're doing up there. The crowding on the trail is a problem, but it's not continuous; sometimes I would get unexpected breaks from the large groups of backpackers. I breathed deeply again in the much-needed solitude, closed my eyes, and took in the rush of wind, the buzz of the mountain cricket, the susurrations of a nearby stream. Together those things sounded just like applause.

My first cleanup task completed, I marched onward toward the summit, which was now about nine miles away. Continuing with the climb, I was delighted to find several thick stands of sticky monkey flower, a pale-orange five-petal bloom, above a seasonal seep. They are edible; I've eaten bunches of them back in Santa Cruz. I congratulated myself for resisting the urge to pick one as a souvenir for Julianna or have one as a snack. Such plucking, modest as it was, amounted to "leaving a trace." Besides, it was against the rules; in national forests you must leave native plants alone unless you are granted a special permit to harvest them. Then I took another deep breath of sweet mountain air, let out a sigh, smiled at my restraint, enjoyed a sip of water, rounded the bend, and walked almost headlong into the biggest turd I'd ever seen.

I could only stare with stupefaction at the size of this thing, and wonder at the daring of its execution. This sui generis piece of night soil teetered on the edge of a significant drop leading to a nasty bunch of rocks and boulders. The culprit who had made this did so in defiance of not only Leave No Trace practices, WAG Bag rules, common sense, and human decency, but also gravity and concern for his own life and limb. Had this hiker—and I assume it was a man—attempted to discharge this two-pound cairn of aromatic feculence even a few inches to the east, he would have taken a deadly plunge. I couldn't help but notice this spot had a really nice view of the mountains. Is that one of our baser human impulses, to despoil something the moment we set eyes on it? Does beauty have a laxative effect on the human body? Is that why I see so many Gustav Klimt and Matisse prints in people's bathrooms? Do people hang them there because they feel entitled to see pretty things in their most abased and private moments? How could someone cause so much ugliness for everybody else while taking in all that rapture? It just seemed so unfair. Now I was getting irritable. How I longed to just walk on toward the mountain, to get out of there, far away from that thing. But a deal was a deal, so out came the salad tongs.

When my labors were over, I had to put the tongs in their own Ziploc bag. I hiked on, hoping the worst was over, only to walk into a fistful of smoked cigarette butts on the ground. "Shameless," I said. "Some people." Still, I grabbed these, too, and packed them out. Nearby, in the bushes, I found a well-plumped WAG Bag that some sick individual had attempted halfheartedly to hide under a rock right next to the trail. I must admit, the sight of this was a little bit discouraging for me. I'd assumed that if someone took the trouble to use a WAG Bag, he'd have the common courtesy to shove the thing in his fanny pack.

I was slightly annoyed, but soon my natural optimism returned. It occurred to me that the person who'd left that bag must have intended to come back for it later on. I decided to leave it for now, with the understanding that I would pick it up on my way out if it was still there. I marked the spot with a modest cairn of stones and moved on.

It was with great relief that I arrived in Outpost Camp, my sleeping spot for the night, 3.8 sweaty miles from the trailhead at a wooziness-inducing 10,365 feet above sea level. The camping area occupied a flat and sandy patch of land, with a creek forming a border on one side. The place was crammed with humanity.

Whitney is so popular these days, you can't just pack up your stuff and go climb it. Quota systems have been in place since the 1970s. John Muir just walked right up the mountain on pure impulse. These days, to vie for a chance to camp at Whitney, you have to log in to an "enhanced recreation portal" called Recreation.gov, which provides reservations for outdoor activities in lands overseen by the U.S. Forest Service, National Park Service, Bureau of Land Management, Bureau of Reclamation, and the U.S. Army Corps of Engineers. They make you use this portal to reserve campsites, cabins, and even something called "picnic shelters." It's part of a sweeping multiagency efficiency initiative that is supposed to eliminate hassles.

I can understand the reasoning behind this. With an estimated fifty million Americans camping every year, do you really want them all to call up rangers on the phone and send in request forms on paper? It also eliminates some of the suspense and unpleasantness of "first come, first served." Still, dealing with a virtual portal instead of a human always gives me a sinking, queasy feeling: no one to praise, sweet-talk, attempt to bribe, or scream at. If I'm booking a space in an obscure recreation area in the off-season, the system is a delight to use. But when I'm in a high-pressure situation, and competition for camping spots is fierce, I will often get stressed and distracted, press the wrong buttons, and inadvertently log myself out. I log back on and sit there cursing, watching in real time as the little squares designating tent spaces go from available to booked.

Sometimes the system can break your heart. The year I planned my Whitney trip, the Forest Service, which administers the camping areas below the summit, received 11,634 applications for camping or day hiking permits, a sizable jump from the previous year's 9,142 applications. Only 4,473 of those applications were successful. The other applicants, including me, received tersely worded rejection notices. The day after the lottery, a few spots get freed up. By some miracle, I was able to get one. What a hassle, though. Such is sleeping outdoors in the twenty-first century. Then again, when I looked at the campground and how inundated it was, with tents set up practically on top of one another, as if this were the lawn of an outdoor rock festival and not a campground in the middle of the wilderness, I wondered if the system was harsh enough.

Now, in camp, it seemed pretty silly to have to compete so hard with all those other online applicants just for the right to be their turd nanny once I got there. Then again, this was my choice. At least my neighbors were a bunch of chipper young people who were thrilled just to be in the mountains. Most seemed pleased or at least philosophical about the WAG Bag policy; although it must be said that they had just come from Whitney Portal and had not used their bags yet. I even saw—but, alas, did not have a chance to interview—a woman who'd strapped a bulging WAG Bag to the top of her exterior frame backpack; the full bag was hung in such a way that it dangled to the right side of her sunburned face and bumped her gently in the head every time she took a step. I shouted out my admiration for her dedication and stoicism, but she either ignored or could not hear me.

The shared WAG Bag issue eliminated the need for small talk out there. I could just walk up to anyone and naturally broach a topic that would have been impolite anywhere else. One of my camping neighbors was a bubbly woman in her early thirties named Ryan, a city planner for San Luis Obispo County. When I asked her why she supported the policy, she brought up her recent trip to Paris. "I had this picture in mind," she told me. "Glorious, romantic city, and all its rich history. But when I got to Paris, there was dog crap everywhere. People were tracking it into the subways. You'd see long trails of it going down the stairs. The whole trip I spent looking at the ground, or looking down at my own feet instead of up at those beautiful buildings. That's how I look at being out here. The more concentrated the population, the more essential it is that people pick up their own junk."

I agreed with her, and it seemed to me that her acceptance of WAG Bags had something to do with our sacralization of wild places in America. But it's hard to allow open access to sacred places while maintaining that sanctity.

Backcountry rangers first addressed human waste concerns on Mount Whitney in the mid-1960s by providing pit toilets, in the hope that conscientious campers would seek them out instead of just yanking their trousers down in random shady bowers. They tried several designs, but the most recent iteration was this: one toilet on the summit, consisting of a seat, a metal bucket, and a wall for privacy and wind block; and two sets of "solar composting" bathrooms at the Outpost and Trail camps at lower elevations along the Whitney Trail. Yet when it comes to waste management in wild places, every answer leads to another question. For instance, once you put toilets on Mount Whitney, how does that square with the 1964 Wilderness Act, which called for "untrammeled" wild areas and no buildings or roads in designated wild places? Aren't restrooms a sort of building? And once you build them, how do you clean them? The answer for many years was helicopters.

Carrie Vernon, a National Park Service staff member, was part of the cleanup team. Flying on a helicopter mission known as the "honey bucket run," she and her comrades risked their lives several times a year to clean the one toilet on the mountaintop at an elevation of 14,494 feet. After reading about her exploits, I tracked her down online and cold-called her before my Whitney trip. She was happy to talk. "I, unfortunately, have the status of helicopter crew member who has slung the most shit in the NPS," she told me. "And I've slung loads of shit buckets off Mount Whitney."

To maximize their chances of not crashing, the honey bucketeers flew in the early morning, when cold air provided some support for the chopper's rotors. Off they rode into the pale-blue sky, where the air was wafer-thin. As they neared Whitney, Vernon and her crew entered the so-called Deadman's Curve, or "coffin's corner," outside the safe area of the height/velocity diagram. She did this not to retrieve a corpse or stranded mountaineer, but to fetch and fly out two hundred fifty pounds of shit and garbage at a time, with a ground crew standing by on the slopes to help. The crew could only hope that campers had not set up a tent in the one flat spot where they could land or hover, making it impossible to haul the waste away. Not surprisingly, Vernon spoke with irritation about the toilet.

"It had a strange cult following," she told me. "The last person who used the toilet blogged about it."

Alas, I haven't been able to pinpoint any final blog entry, but I have found all kinds of testimonials to the toilet online, and many staged color photographs of people perched on it and smiling (most of the sitters still have their pants on). The toilet got a high ranking in an online news article called "Game of Thrones," an international survey of the world's most alluring toilets. The site also features a squatting pit toilet in a cave in Batman, Turkey, and several interesting urinals in India that resemble Mick Jagger's lips. Yet Vernon resents the way the toilet caused problems for workers. Besides, she has always been hard-core about Leave No Trace. When camping, she leaves nothing behind, not even an orange peel or apple core. "They take too long to decompose. My feeling is, you haul your shit in, you haul it out," she said.

Talking to her, I figured the bathroom management situation could get no more complex or ridiculous, but I was wrong. Due to a jurisdictional quirk, a different set of death-defying helicopter crewpeople had to clean up the other two commodes lower down, in the Outpost and Trail camps; that's because the toilet on the summit fell within NPS territory, while the two lower-down restrooms sat on national forest land, meaning these disgusting repositories were inside the jurisdiction of the U.S. Forest Service. Jeff Novak, a wilderness supervisor for the Mount Whitney Ranger Station, filled me in on the cleanup process.

"It is sort of a gruesome thing to think about," Novak said. "It would be a full-on hazmat suit with respirators, double gloves, goggles, splash shields, and everything."

After decades of hard use, including a few slobs shoving garbage deep inside them, concerns for worker safety finally doomed the toilets. "It got to be a situation where it was just too hazardous to work up there," Novak said.

The possibility of contact with pathogens bothered the cleanup crew almost as much as the possibility of crashing choppers, which, thank goodness, never happened. In 2006, Park Service rangers dismantled the summit toilet and hauled it away. Within a year, the other two toilets were gone, too, burned to a crisp on purpose. If you search around online, you can watch videos of one conflagration. As terrible as they apparently were to use, those toilets burned extremely well; the flames were spectacular.

As far back as 2004, while the rangers were still discussing alternatives to the permanent bathrooms, visitors were already receiving WAG Bags as part of a pilot program. In other words, these bags were not exactly a shocker when the toilets went away. Some Whitney toilet fans were furious nevertheless. They complained that the rangers had acted hastily, without following due process, and that the resulting system had left Whitney more poop-strewn than ever before. But Novak insisted to me that "the only time we ever got a high [coliform] reading" for water in the Whitney Zone was back when they still had toilets.

He also told me that the malfunctioning bathrooms, combined with serious damage during one especially harsh winter, forced the rangers' hands. Still, he acknowledged to me that the public response was mixed, especially from local business owners, who worried that the toilet removal would discourage people from visiting Whitney.

Even in the campground there was some difference of opinion about the bags.

Just as I started to set up my tent at Outpost Camp, I noticed a middle-aged fellow with a skeptical expression, a sort of half-wince, on his face and a heavy pack on his shoulders. When we got to talking, this man, an insurance broker from Bakersfield named Jared, told me he flat-out despised the WAG Bags and the policy behind them.

"The WAG Bag is an emotional experience for me," Jared said. "It scars you. I've been camping off and on my whole life, and I tell you, this is the *only* place where they throw a WAG Bag at you and wave it at you and say, 'Okay, buddy, here it is!' For me, the WAG Bag is the straw that broke the camel's back. I just don't want to use that boy. At least I want to delay as much as possible. It's just not a thrill to pack it out. And what is worse? The smell of poo or the chemicals inside the WAG Bag?"

Jared said that the worst thing about WAG Bags is the way they defy the normal rules of backpacking: the longer you linger in the backcountry, the more you eat down your food and the lighter your pack becomes. WAG Bags reverse that equation, he told me, by increasing your pack weight day by day. Jared looked doubtful when I mentioned the enthusiastic people I'd met in camp who told me they supported the rule. In his view, the rules of common courtesy were not enough to make people do the right thing at all times. When people aren't looking, he said, some campers will take a "hide-and-go-seek approach" to the bags.

Jared, who is in his fifties, rolled his eyes when I wondered out loud if WAG Bag use broke down around generational lines.

"Maybe these millennials don't remember anything other than Leave No Trace," I said. "They were raised on this stuff. It's second nature."

"You could say that," Jared said. "But if that is the case, how come there are WAG Bags all up and down the trail?"

Soon after I said good-bye to Jared, and finished rolling out my sleeping bag and bedroll at Outpost Camp, I lost my WAG Bag virginity.

Feeling the call of nature, I scrambled onto a ledge full of trees, rocks, gravel, and loose dirt overlooking the camp. But it was almost impossible to find an out-of-the-way place that someone wasn't already using, or where I would not be seen. When I dared to glance to the left of me on the steeply sloping hilltop above my tent, I saw something that I never hope to see again: another camper on the same section of the same forested and boulder-strewn hillside, standing in full view of me, using a WAG Bag, kidding himself that he was hiding behind a rock or some scraggly tree.

It was only a momentary and accidental look before I turned away, but it was more than enough. This unhappy-looking camper was holding a blue WAG Bag in one hand and using the free arm to prop up his body while he leaned over and stuck his bottom skyward. It looked like he was attempting one-handed burpees in an outdoor exercise class.

Startled by the sight of this person, I retreated behind an overhanging rock that half-obscured my body; most likely, other campers could still see me, but at least I could no longer see them.

As someone who has done a lot of backpacking, I found that using the bag was not that big a deal, once I got over the tricky balancing act. Still, the process was cumbersome. I ended up wrapping my entire hindquarters in the plastic bag. Jared was right: the "poo powder" placed on the bottom of the bag as a gelling agent smelled nasty.

Still, a worse shock was yet to come. When the ordeal was over, I was making my way down the slope, back to camp, when I saw five fully stuffed WAG Bags buried, halfheartedly, under rocks. *Villains! How dare they!* Then I looked around and saw four more. Now I was looking at an entire shoal of WAG Bags. To transport them all off the mountain, I would have needed two or three more Immaculators. At that moment, I could feel my experiment, my purpose, begin to founder.

For the first time in the trip, I would have to violate my principles of packing out everything I saw. The man in the store had been right. The only option I had was to walk with blinders on or walk in total darkness.

Under cover of dusk, while other campers were eating boiled dinners and chitchatting, I crept up the ledge, took out the salad tongs, put on the surgical gloves, and decided to stuff as many WAG Bags as I could into the Immaculator. But even when I pushed out the compressed air from each bag so it would take up as little space as possible, I could get only three more bags into the tube before it was filled. The Immaculator, as long and thick as it was, did not have the width I required; the empty space inside it was surprisingly tight and cramped.

I held my breath for ten seconds to ensure that I would not smell any-thing. I settled on a compromise with myself. Though I had no more room in the Immaculator, I would still climb Mount Whitney with it just for the sake of deep ecology. Aldo Leopold, a founder of the Wilderness Society, once wrote about "thinking like a mountain." Climbing a peak with the tube—which now weighed, fully loaded, about ten pounds, if I had to guess—would give me a painful and exhausting sympathy for the peak and its plight. When I got to the top, I would pose for a photograph with it to raise awareness of LNT challenges on the mountain. As much as I didn't want to carry that dead weight, I decided to stick with the plan.

As the sunlight waned and the cold intensified, I sat down on my bear keg, which I carried with me in addition to the Immaculator. As much as I despise the weight of these things, they always make such nice seats in the wilderness. During this rest break, I inventoried the day's haul, which also included some broken glass and a torn-off piece of T-shirt. It was hard not to feel cynical then. I was slouching down, unable even to work up any appetite because of the elevation and my general disgust, when one of the nice young people I'd been chatting with earlier about WAG Bags came over and said hello. This ruddy, bearded fellow and his friends would be leaving Outpost Camp and setting out for the summit of Mount Whitney at 3:30 in the morn-ing. He invited me to climb with them. I was startled. Wasn't that too early? How would I find my way with nothing but a headlamp to get me through? Still, I was so grateful for the social call that I said yes right away. "Thank you, sir," I told him. "You've cheered me up more than I can tell you."

He and the other climbers talked into the night, lingering over their suppers. Such was my excitement, I could not sleep at all so I leaned out of my tent and watched the flickering tongues of light from their stoves. Before I knew it, 3:00 a.m. was upon me. I forced myself to eat a fistful of cashews and put on the cheap wool-mix gloves I'd bought at a Lone Pine thrift store instead of getting a better pair from the outdoor gear shop in the same town. Then I wrapped myself in a few layers, donned my boots, and cinched my lamp. I told my neighbors, who were up already, that I was taking off. While I would have loved their company, I was just too antsy to wait for them. Besides, I knew that my pack weight and out-of-shape body were bound to slow me down; the others would catch up with me soon enough. I shouldered my pack, strapped on the plastic tube, and stumbled off into the night. "Next stop, Whitney," I told the Immaculator.

After the misery of the previous day, the total darkness was delicious. It felt transgressive and strange just to be there at all. I half expected someone to come out and chastise me. As I walked on, I thought of the time my brother and I snuck out of our suburban house after hours when we were kids; the automatic sprinklers clicked their tongues as we ran past them—*tsk! tsk! tsk!*—and we slipped through a forest that filled a canyon beneath the neighborhood, a dark jungle with a stream running through it, frogs croaking, wild anise in the air. Now I had the high-tech torch strapped to my brainbox, my chilly hands in my pockets, and wanted for nothing in the world. The wilderness around me looked so clean. As I was discovering, darkness was the only reliable Immaculator out there.

I crossed a gurgling stream, passed a clutch of scarlet penstemons, and followed a path of crumbling dirt and clanking stones up a steeply inclined forest. My beam cast pale light on the fat trunks of funky, crooked trees on the edges of rocky ledges. The wood grew in all kinds of contortions. Moonlight lit the upper horns of the mountains. The Immaculator shifted on my back; my pack straps pulled me down like reins, every ounce obnoxious, unnecessary. Step by step, I felt the weight of other people's thoughtlessness. At least the going was new and strange and distracted me from the burden. A series of glowing pinpoints confused me in the distance. The dot lights made a zigzagging pattern up the ridge in front of me. It took a while to figure out they were climbers with headlamps making their way to the summit.

I heard a crunching sound come from behind me. Just as I suspected, my new friends from Outpost Camp were already gaining on me. "Looking great," one of them called out to me and gave me a soft clomp on the shoulder. "Keep going." For the next couple of hours, this crowd of people would pass me, then I would pass them, and so on. They were always so solicitous and kind that it stopped me from ever growing too cynical about the campers who had trashed parts of this forest. They were a constant reminder that every group of people, every subculture, embodies the best and worst of human nature. On even more distant ridges, backpackers formed traffic jams on the slopes; shining dots massed together on the dark verticals, suggesting glowworms. The going was eerie and thrilling because the narrow path kept forcing me to the edge of hulking rock forms over drops into more darkness. The night erased every cue that can make climbing so obnoxious: the constant reminders of paltry progress, goals unmet, false summits. Maybe there were WAG Bags strewn all about the forests around me. As far as I knew, some sick person had even made a WAG Bag snowman seven feet tall and eight feet wide, but it was no longer my responsibility.

Light-headed from the hard going, I set down my pack, Immaculator and all, and lay down on an ergonomic boulder still warm from the sun. Some stars were indistinguishable from the glow points on the mountain; I knew they were heavenly bodies, and not flashlights, only because they were so high up, and fixed. They floated above me in a milky white frost. I traced cream-colored bands across the heavens, counted the stars on Orion's Belt, and made my way up the Pleiades star cluster. Betelgeuse was coming in clear. Lying there, I had a rare attack of sanity. "Enjoy life," I told myself. "What the hell are you trying to prove by bringing other people's shit to the summit of Whitney? Sounds like a publicity stunt to me—not to mention a sacrilege. You are right at the age when you could give yourself a coronary." Before I could change my mind and return to my punishing mission, I removed the capsule from the side of my pack, stowed it under a lodge pole pine, leaving it well hidden in a crook beneath the lower limbs, and hiked onward. This felt like a compromise, but I negotiated this by taking along a trash bag and vowing that I would use it to pack out any litter that came across my path.

If you must climb Whitney at all and see what the fuss is about, do it this way, in the blackness, and just in time for the moon to crest while you make your way through Trail Camp on a rough plateau facing the High Sierra escarpment. If you time it just right, you will see hundred-foot fingers of black rock with blue webbing between them and claw points at their edges. The trail flattened out and passed between some sharp boulders for a while, until it rose up to confront a great and crumbled wall that served as the base for Whitney and all the peaks beside and underneath it. The ascent began slowly, almost timidly, to a place where orange and red plants clung to life well above the tree line. Ninety-nine switchbacks confronted me, and I fell in line with the other climbers steadying themselves on metal cables to avoid falling backward or slipping through a notch in the mountain. I walked without stopping, and watched the sun's rays fill a reflecting pool far below me with green, yellow, and blue. So many clouds appeared in the sky and slipped between the towers that the mountains appeared to spin. The sun spread its illumination over the silver-gray rocks and settled on the tents in the valley beneath me. Perhaps it was reverence, or not looking very hard, but I did not see a single WAG Bag anywhere on the slopes. Here were islands of unhewn rock slabs with swirls of sand between them, bringing to mind the stones in a Zen garden. I passed through a breach in the wall and crossed to the other side of the crest. After pausing for breath for just a moment, I entered a sort of moonscape so crowded with walkers that I had to keep nudging ahead of them and out of the way and move my feet to avoid getting pierced by their telescoping walking sticks. It seemed to me the summit was only getting farther and higher, the air thinning into a kind of laughing gas. I've never felt so ditzy and elderly, falling constantly, sitting down for long spells, and sometimes lulling myself to sleep in the sun. On the final push, I had to rest five minutes for every sixty paces. Then—*bam!*—there I was, standing on the summit.

The first few minutes on the top of Whitney were a rush of pure ego and one-upmanship. "Look at me, I am higher than everything and everyone else in America." I could see the White Mountains on the far side of Owens Valley, and every other Sierra Nevada peak, which looked like so many limpets, cowries, and barnacles on a drained-out tide pool. I pivoted my body this way and that and looked toward the sand and haze of Death Valley.

Whitney, the highest point in the continental United States, is only eighty-four miles from the lowest point, in the valley's Badwater Basin. The nearest peaks had an urban-industrial folk art look that reminded me of the broken glass, steel, and seashell towers that rise above the city of Watts. Though the slopes leading up to it were impossibly crowded, I saw only one man on the mountaintop, a young entrepreneur who made electronic equipment, including remote controls that could perform just about any "wired" function in your house. The temperature dropped. It was a sunny day, but it was creeping down to the thirties up there. I lost all sensation in my fingertips, and my lips seemed to freeze together. In spite of this, I still mumbled out my questions to him. "I've seen too many WAG Bags!" I told him. I asked him what could be done about this pressing issue. The entrepreneur thought it might be a good idea to take DNA sampling that would allow the rangers to track scofflaws and, if necessary, FedEx the lumps right to their house as punishment. "Might not be cost-effective, though," he added.

He also suggested a simpler variation of the same idea: putting registration numbers on bags so rangers can track you down and mail you a fine if the bag is found improperly discarded.

After taking one last look over the edge, I ran all the way down the mountain, pausing to retrieve the heavy Immaculator, which made me feel like I was going to tip over like a cow and never get back up again. The dead weight got even worse when I arrived at the cairn that marked the site of a discarded WAG Bag. I was not the least bit surprised to see that no one had come back to claim it. At that point I'd made a vow to myself that I wouldn't pick up any more turds, but this one seemed so important; I'd promised myself that I would come back and get it if no one else did. Grimacing all the while, I shoved the WAG Bag into a garbage sack and lashed it to the outside of my pack. Now I was really a sight, the Immaculator thumping me right on my lumbar pad, the garbage sack thwacking the meat of my legs.

In an unexpected way, I had achieved my goal for this trip; I'd wanted to tie my fate to the landscape, for better or worse, and cry like a mountain if that's what I had to do. Every footstep was an act of will. At the time, I had no faith in humanity. Only later on did it occur to me that it was the sheer amount of human traffic that was the real problem, and that I, as much as anyone, was part of that traffic. Weeks after my trip was over, I called up Jeff Novak, who measures WAG Bag compliance by weighing the bags that backpackers stuff in biohazard containers at trail's end at Whitney Portal. By comparing the annual tonnage of loaded bags to the number of permits, the rangers have figured out that somewhere between 90 and 95 percent of climbers and day hikers are using and disposing of the bags properly. I was surprised to hear Novak sigh after he said this to me.

"But that's an amazing number," I told him. "A success story by any standard."

"Well," Novak said, "in my mind, it is a qualified good program. Most people are doing the right thing, and if they are pooping on the mountain, they are hauling it out, but when you have close to twenty-five thousand people [per year], five percent of twenty-five thousand is a lot of WAG Bags left behind." He said the problem is most noticeable at Trail Camp and in the route between that camp and the summit. "Maybe they are so tired they left it behind, or maybe they left it in the campground, but we don't know if they're coming back for it; or maybe they forgot or did it unintentionally. But you definitely see things, and we do get our fair share of public comment saying it is not a good situation."

The additional challenge is figuring out who are the culprits. Novak told me that Whitney attracts a certain demographic that wants to bag the peak but is not necessarily invested in minimal-impact camping practices. What else can be done? While some Whitney climbers grumble about the fact that they have to show up in person to the ranger station to get their permits before climbing the mountain, at least this allows rangers a chance to give them some one-on-one instruction and encouragement to use the bags, Novak told me. Rangers hope a new LNT video about Whitney will help. Other ideas include a stepped-up ranger presence on the mountain—I did not see even one of them out on patrol when I was there—or perhaps a system that allowed people to dispose of the WAG Bags in receptacles located in the backcountry camps; the rangers could haul them out by mule or perhaps go back to the helicopter method.

While I found such suggestions interesting from an LNT perspective, I worried that these changes might be a bit too indulgent for us backpacker types—that removing all the burden of hauling out our own waste might make us even more cavalier about our wilderness behavior by reinforcing the idea that someone else has to do our dirty work. This might sound harsh or silly, but perhaps the rangers at the Eastern Sierra Interagency Visitor Center could pay one member of each camping party to keep tabs on everyone else. If there were serious violators, that appointed observer might serve as a secret informer—a stool pigeon, so to speak. On the down side, I suppose that would make the informer feel sleazy, and his friends might not ever speak to him again.

At least we no longer live in an age of extreme ignorance about these issues, thanks in part to best-selling author Kathleen Meyer, perhaps the world's ultimate authority on turds and wilderness. She has sold 2.5 million copies of her outdoor guide, *How to Shit in the Woods: An Environmentally Sound Approach to a Lost Art*. Originally published in 1989, it has gone through many printings and three editions. Shortly after my Whitney trek, I asked Meyer if her book had put a dent in the problem of waste disposal in the backwoods.

Meyer had a mixed response. "There's been phenomenal progress made since the early 1970s," she told me during our talk on the phone. "It was Colorado River rafters who became the first to practice packing it out. Early on in the rafting craze, river runners suddenly, and rudely, awakened to Nature's minimal potty-carrying capacity on the limited beaches between the Grand Canyon's steep walls. All it takes is one person's digging his hole only to discover a previous deposit." Yet the overall situation, Meyer assured me, is still "horrendous and growing" in untold areas of magnificent wildland. Meyer gets e-mails from people all over the world who are shocked that there is such a problem with outdoor human feces. "My guidebook," she said, "grew out of a passion to raise consciousness, offer graceful and ecological techniques, and help bring a taboo subject into talkable range. While leading whitewater river trips, I'd come across places precious to me trashed with soiled diapers and adult human poo."

It's not easy, she told me, "to shift a citified culture, brought up on porcelain flushing commodes, to an ethic of strong responsibility for up-close fecal disposal." And high-use wildland areas, she said, always pose the potential for the worst abuse. "Earnest backpackers out on extended treks are usually informed and careful," she said, "while day trippers will often—quite amazingly—head up a trail without the least notion they'll have to 'go.' Meaning, they can have such disastrous and messy personal experiences that, henceforth, they remain home on the couch."

Instant solutions? There seem to be none. But Meyer believes strongly in "the steady delivery of directness and humor, and creative approaches."

On the way back down to Whitney Portal, I wanted to sprint for the finish line, but the Immaculator kept betraying me and slowing me down. "Not a word out of you," I told the tube as it bounced against my back. "If you're hungry, you'd better suck it up. I'm not stopping for you."

Every half mile or so, the Immaculator would work itself loose from the tight webbing of straps and cord and fall to the ground just to spite me. Other backpackers looked startled when they saw me jumping off the trail and diving into bushes to retrieve it. By the time I arrived back at the trailhead and the parking lot where my trip began, I was grunting with exhaustion. I took off my sopping survival hat, daubed my forehead with a washcloth, and massaged my knotted-up muscles. But the moment I picked up the heavy Immaculator and was preparing to empty its contents into a bear-proof metal biohazard materials container, a woman in her early fifties walked on over to me and got right in my face.

"Where are you coming from?" she said. She smiled and batted her eyelids at me, which was really strange, because I was dirty and sweaty. She even started doing that saucy thing that certain women do with their hair, using a hand to flip it back and forth, and sometimes tossing their heads this way and that for additional emphasis. "How long did you hike today?" Flap

flap flap. "You must be such a strong hiker." Flip flip flip. It was startling to have someone come up and start hitting on me under such circumstances. For one thing, I hadn't shaved or showered for four days, I was wearing a pair of huge, smeared glasses and a wedding ring, and I am extremely shy around strangers, especially if they are female. I could barely even look her in the eye. Aside from all this, I just so happened to be holding several pounds of other people's shit—the tube was so overstuffed that the top was now halfway off, releasing a deathly smell that wafted over the parking lot. In other words, there is no accounting for human taste. This woman was just not going away. Now she was holding herself so close to me that dumping out my waste tube was going to be impossible without either nudging her off to the side or traumatizing her. I had to take evasive action. There was no delaying. The Immaculator was too heavy for me to hold indefinitely; my arms were going numb.

"I like your tube," the woman said. "It's really cool. Is that a bear keg?"

A day before, at that outdoor supply store in Lone Pine, I was more than happy to give a detailed speech about my mission on the mountain. Now I was exhausted and stony, my fingertips numb from the cold on the summit. I would have to give her the short version.

Feeling self-conscious and hard up for words, I took a giant step back. Then I looked down at the Immaculator. "Um, no, this is not a bear keg, actually," I said. "It's for turds. That's why I'm out on the mountain today. That's why I drove all the way out here from Santa Cruz. To pick up other people's turds." I went on for a little while in this vein, not checking to see how she was reacting to my explanation. After a minute or so, I looked up to see if the woman had any response to this, but she was gone.

14

Kovu's Brother

"Glamping," a lexical blend of "glamorous" and "camping," has evolved from African safaris where demanding European and American travelers slept in luxurious canvas tents, supported by chefs, guides, porters and butlers . . . Glamping removes camping's negative attributes—leaky tents, smelly sleeping bags and improvised food, replaced with pre–set up, homelike accommodations . . . such as cabins, yurts, tipis, and treehouses.

—*The Journal of Outdoor Recreation and Tourism*, 2013

You sleep on a bed. It's a mattress bed! In a huge tent with TV and everything. You have electricity and stuff but you're still in amongst the wildlife.

—Justin Bieber, 2012

After circling the parking lot at the Safari West "glampground," I found a spot in the shade between a black BMW and a sparkling green Maserati GranTurismo convertible. The elegant cars gleamed in the afternoon sun, which turned the Sonoma County foothills burnished gold. The top of the Maserati was down, revealing the genuine leather interior. I wanted to reach out and caress it. By coincidence, I'd read about the GranTurismo in a men's magazine at a gym, which is how I knew it cost $150,000, or eighteen times the value of my 2008 Toyota Corolla. "Dan, that's not your car," Amy said. "Please get your face out of there."

Julianna could hardly wait to get inside and see some of the thousand exotic and mostly African animals swarming around this campground/wildlife preserve. Just as we were getting closer, I heard a peal of drawn-out hideous laughter that seemed to come out of nowhere and sounded like a crazy person cackling. It was Safari West's resident Australian kooka-burra, shrieking at the sky. Perhaps that bird was trying to warn me about the fate that awaited me at the end of this campout.

"Save yourself," the bird was telling me. "Whatever you do, stay out of the aviary. Kovu's brother is waiting for you."

The noise bothered me, but only on a subconscious level. Perhaps it contributed to the fear that kept burbling up inside me that day.

I was out at Safari West to try my hand at upscale camping. After staggering for thirty waterless miles on the Hat Creek Rim section of the Pacific Crest Trail and getting frostbitten on a late-October trip to the White Mountains of New Hampshire, I'd earned this. But it was hard to settle on just one option. As I'd come to realize, "glamping" is more of a marketing buzzword than a workable definition. You might freeze your ass off in a yurt in some fly-blown regional park for forty dollars a night, as I've done twice, or rent a tent in a deluxe resort or on concert festival grounds for thousands of dollars a night, as Justin Bieber has done; either scenario falls under the golf umbrella of glamping. In other words, glamping is a trendy form of recreation that combines glamour or the idea of glamour with camping or the idea of camping. Safari West was founded in 1993, so it predates the word *glamping*, which entered the cultural lexicon in the late 1990s. Safari West rebranded itself as a glampground as soon as this port-manteau word became popular.

Amy and I were used to showing up at campgrounds feeling anxious and exhausted, after spending the morning folding up bedrolls and putting snacks in bear-proof food canisters. But when I called Safari West a week in advance and asked what we should bring, the staff member had to pause for a moment before telling me, "A hair dryer."

Most places where I camp have just one exhausted-looking campground host driving around in a little golf cart, collecting fees, and shushing people. In comparison, Safari West in the peak season swarms with 120 workers, including biologists, concierges, veterinarians, ecologists, animal husbandry experts, safari naturalists, restaurant employees, first responders for emergencies, landscapers, maintenance workers, and mechanics. The moment we checked in at the greeting hut, which features fake elephant tusks and a fake mounted rhino's head, a concierge smiled warmly and gave us a generous wad of Bongo Bucks and Cheetah Cash, valid only at the Safari West gift shop.

I groaned at the thought of hauling our heavy suitcases up the long, steep path to our tent spot on the campground's highest hill. The concierge, as if reading my mind, summoned an eager young man driving a jeep. He rolled us down to the parking lot, grabbed our suitcases, and drove us to the tent village. A flock of chubby, free-roaming guinea fowl hurried out of the way as we headed toward a collection of white canvas tents imported from South Africa and set on wooden platforms with stairs leading up to them. Our tent was three hundred fifty square feet, with a view of the Sonoma foothills. We were close to a high fence with grassland behind it; on the other side, an ostrich ruffled its dusty white feathers, padded across the ground, and curled its two-toed, prehistoric feet.

A shaggy wildebeest stood so close to the fence that we smelled his musky fetor. Julianna stared at it, speechless. The young man placed our things on the veranda. My daughter, flush from the sun, looked down on reticulated giraffes in a paddock. I stuffed a modest wad of bills in the young man's palm. He thanked me. *I'm a sultan for the day*, I thought.

We spent the next long while just exploring our tent, which was fit for T. Boone Pickens and Kubla Khan. Safari West cofounder and owner Peter Lang personally shaped and lovingly assembled the tent's chairs and other furniture, using salvaged timber along with manzanita, madrone, and oak gathered on the property and finished in an on-site sawmill and machine shop. Lang's handiwork was impressive. It also reminded me that I'd soon be home again, sitting down on Ikea furniture unlovingly hand-assembled by Amy and me.

Back in Santa Cruz, we live in a dark and moldy house that sits on an anthill overlooking what must be the finest collection of invasive pigweed this side of the Mississippi. We're part of a housing complex with three identical dingy homelike structures around a shared weed patch that the landlord calls our "commons." Every time one of the other two sad little houses goes vacant and a new family moves in, I think to myself, *God, how I pity those unfortunates!*—until it occurs to me that our house is the same.

Our tent at Safari West, in comparison, was a pleasure palace. It had polished-wood floors (our floors at home are stained linoleum slathered with an unidentifiable scunge), a pillowy king bed (our bed at home is so small you'd have to saw my legs off at the proximal aspect of my tibias just to make me fit on it), and a fully functioning toilet within the tent (the toilet at home is mostly decorative). Our in-tent bathroom came with shining copper basins in the sinks, a hot shower, and a tray of bath gels and excellent shampoos. (Back at home, I hate spending money on shampoo, so I wash my hair with Kirk's Castile Soap.)

When I'm home, I'm in constant motion, mopping spills and paying bills. Now we had no schedule to follow and nothing to worry about. Amy and Julianna could not stop smiling. I kept thinking to myself, *I've been camping since preschool. Maybe I've been doing it wrong.* The only drawback was the jealousy factor, not just of the other guests but of the property itself. Most camping makes you grateful for your living situation; no matter how bleak it may be, at least you have a floor. Glamping made me wish I could live in a tent all the time.

But camping like a maharajah every weekend was not realistic. Our overnight stay cost four hundred fifty dollars, including the tent rental and the safari tour we planned to take the next morning. That's a lot of money for me, although it's a pittance in the glamping world. While the Safari West website refers to this resort as "the ultimate in glamping!" it's really just starter glamping compared to a three-day stay at the Clayoquot Wilderness Resort on Vancouver Island, British Columbia. An all-inclusive package with luxury tent, meals, adventures, seaplane transportation, and a horse-drawn carriage at your disposal can cost as much as seven thousand dollars for a Sunday-through-Thursday stay. An ultradeluxe "glamping" package at Burning Man for venture capitalists goes for about twenty-five thousand dollars per person, the *New York Times* reports.

As we were peeping into every corner of that sprawling tent, it also occurred to me that glamping is an antagonistic act. From the beginning, Americans have always camped *against* something. Henry David Thoreau camped against slavery, manifest destiny, and the status quo. The Romantic campers camped against the forces of industry. Leave No Trace campers camped against the woodcrafters. But glamping is unique in the sense that its practitioners camp against camping itself.

That impulse is nothing new. The Adirondacks, a trendsetter in so many kinds of camping, was one of the original places where the well-to-do enjoyed camping-themed activities that had little or nothing to do with real camping. The Adirondack "Great Camps" were lavish compounds where Gilded Age aristocrats might fish, hunt, and roam around in guide boats for the summer. When the sun went down, they retired to gigantic lumber-and-stone complexes with armies of helpers. Camp Santanoni, which I visited in Newcomb, New York, had an on-site creamery, chicken house, and pig hutch to meet the needs of its "campers," including Theodore Roosevelt.

The main difference between glamour camping now and then is the marketing. In the old days, it was fashionable to play up the "roughing it" aspect of these camping adventures, no matter how swank they were. John Burroughs, during one of his ultradeluxe auto tours with his famous camping friends Henry Ford, Thomas Edison, and Harvey Firestone, had an award-winning chef at his disposal, a press detail, and a retinue of fancy vehicles in tow, but some of his statements about the campout made it sound as if they were dragging themselves through nettles and poison ivy. "Discomfort is, after all, what the camper-out is unconsciously seeking," writes Burroughs in his 1921 book *Under the Maples*. "We grow weary of our luxuries . . . We cheerfully endure wet, cold, smoke, mosquitos, blackflies, and sleepless nights, just to touch naked reality once more."

These days, glamping often means staying in high-end outdoor-themed resorts where the tent or other provisional structure is already standing when you arrive. But MaryJane Butters, the author, innkeeper, and organic farmer who either coined or first popularized the term *glamping*, had something quite different in mind when she squished together *glamour* and *camping* in the 1990s. She used the word, specifically, in reference to upscale-themed women-friendly car-camping trips, with refurbished Shasta, Vagabond, Homesteader, and other vintage trailers, usually from the 1950s and 1960s. The goal was to balance character-building challenges with great food, sisterhood, and decadent fun; there was no intention of banishing hardship altogether. "Glamping, or glamour camping, one of MaryJane's pet concepts, is about the juxtaposition of rugged and really pretty, grit and glam, diesel and absolutely darling," the *New York Times* observed.

Since then, the term has escaped from its original context and come to mean *any* luxurious or luxury-themed camping trip. Meanwhile, the eco-tourism industry has latched hold of the word so strongly that glamping may soon become synonymous with nature-themed outdoor resorts.

The travel start-up Glamping Hub formed in San Francisco in 2012 to focus exclusively on glamour camping accommodations. The company connects users with "A-frame" cabins in Yosemite; vintage Airstream trailers in New Mexico; a barn near Woodstock, New York; and "floating cabins" in Canada's Yellowknife Bay, among many other lodging possibilities. The company's chief marketing officer, Cynthia Riddell, told me that 70 percent of their customer demographic are women. Typical annual income levels are in the one-hundred-thousand-dollar range. The most popular lodging has bathrooms inside the yurt or tent or whatever the structure may be. "I think the reason why our gender percentage is so highly skewed to women is these affluent households tend to be married," Riddell explained. "Most customers are in a couple and the woman can make that booking. But we have plenty of men that also glamp."

As much as I have snooped through news databases, I've found only a handful of glamping stories highlighting male experiences. An online video in *Men's Journal* featured travel journalist Ryan Van Duzer rhapsodizing about the Resort at Paws Up, in Montana, and how the plush tenting accommodations—which can run upwards of two thousand dollars per night and feature an optional "tent butler" who will roast your s'mores for you—made him "feel like a king."

He took pains to emphasize nearby optional high-testosterone adventures, such as rappelling down a 167-foot cliff. But Van Duzer, by daring to use *glamping* in a macho context, is a notable exception to the rule. This is not to say that men don't engage in upscale camping activities. Take a look at the lavishly illustrated catalog for Filson, the legendary camping and hunting outfitter in Seattle; every extravagantly priced knife, watch, pack, and Mackinaw jacket is designed for affluent men who want to feel pampered and adventurous outdoors. It's just that most men would never call an expensive camping experience "glamping." That would be like me and my childhood friends admitting that our bearded, gun-toting, camouflage-wearing GI Joe "action figures" were actually dolls.

Safari West's public information officer, the helpful and wonderfully named Aphrodite Caserta, gave me a facts-and-figures list that shows that Safari West's demographic also skews toward female, with a 32–68 percent breakdown of men versus women. And though the median household income of Safari West visitors is $123,754, the bulk of guests "believe[s] that experiences are as valuable as, if not more valuable than, material things."

While glamping is largely a female endeavor in America, the popular Wanderlust Hospitality glamping website identifies Theodore Roosevelt, the most macho male ever to occupy the White House, as the "forefather of glamping." Roosevelt favored burly, no-frills adventures in the American West, but he earned his glamour camping pioneer status with just one over-the-top African safari campout in 1909, shortly after he completed his second and final term as president. It took three African porters alone to carry Roosevelt's English-made, twelve-foot-wide, paraffin-waterproofed green canvas tent, which had a library of sixty books, a porch roof, a fly for insulation, and a full-service bathroom compartment with a tub. The campout included a chef who could make any bush meat into a fine curry, a team of "tent boys" to fill the tubs and do laundry, and forty porters to assist each hunter. Roosevelt had little risk of going hungry in camp, with his impressive stash of dried fruit (fifty-six pounds' worth) and delicious chocolate (eighteen pounds). The former president complained that he felt "too comfortable," and confessed to a friend that the luxury tent in the wild made him feel "a little effeminate."

Yet Roosevelt would not have considered that trip "glamour camping" because of the expedition's alleged scientific purpose. He and his colleagues were there to assemble a great collection of African creatures, never mind that the animals they shot and killed were already known to science. By the time the trip was over, Roosevelt had a vast dead menagerie totaling "160 species of carnivores, ungulates, rodents, insectivores, and bats," according to the Smithsonian Institution. "The mammals alone numbered 5,013 specimens, including nine lions, thirteen rhinoceros, twenty zebras, eight warthogs, and four hyenas."

While Safari West has a vaguely Rooseveltian flavor, it offers little in the way of rugged adventure; the campground/wildlife preserve, while spotlessly tidy and smoothly run, would do well to invite its guests to clean their animal paddocks, wash the feet of the warthog, brush the teeth of the newly acquired striped hyenas, polish the horn of the southern white rhinoceros, or engage in other soul-building activities that might connect them more intimately with wildlife—after signing waivers, of course. The savor of risk, minus the reality, seems to be the point. Glamping isn't supposed to be real. If anything, it is a caricature of a campout. During our time at Safari West, there was nothing to do but watch my wife relax on the bed, pop open a cold Sierra Nevada Pale Ale, and start reading her requisite work of disturbing fiction. "I feel like I'm getting away with some-thing!" she said as she tucked into a theme-appropriate book: Hemingway's *The Snows of Kilimanjaro*. That feeling of naughtiness is built into the mar-keting of glamping; we are meant to think we are cheating on an august and joyless American tradition of suffering in the wilderness.

At Safari West, I had to keep reminding my anxious self that I didn't *have* to do anything at all to keep the camp up and running, that this whole place was meant to be sweet and effortless and creamy like the inside of a Ding Dong.

After we got settled in, Julianna grabbed hold of my hand. Time to explore the grounds together. It was pure enchantment, watching a pair of lechwe (a kind of spiral-horned antelope) cavort and kick up dust behind a fence. The sun beat down on us. The air was redolent of giraffe piss. Soon after we started our walkabout, a retired plumbing contractor came over, put his arm around me, and said, "Son, you've *got* to see this." He handed me a pair of powerful binoculars and directed my gaze toward two wilde-beests on a distant foothill, snorting, kicking up their skinny legs, chew-ing plants, the breeze ruffling their Rasputin beards. The mammals were impressive, though we'd already seen one earlier in the day. What moved me most was the plumber's generosity. This was a moment when glamping made sense to me.

As we continued our rambles, I talked to harried parents who loved glamping with their kids because they could enjoy the outdoors without getting stuck setting up tents or cooking dinner; Safari West offered an optional barbecue (twenty-nine dollars per adult, seventeen bucks per child), but we did not partake. I also talked to several elderly people who'd camped in their youth and just couldn't handle it anymore. Who needed the tsuris when they could camp out hassle free?

We walked on through the campground. Julianna marveled at the pre-cise, articulated fingers of the resident lemurs, which looked like raccoon-monkey hybrids. We watched them groom each other, lick each other's armpits, and play in their protected enclosure. She begged me to buy one. "I'll feed him grass every day," she vowed. A giraffe in a paddock licked a fence post. Its tongue was the creamy purple color of grape-flavored Bubble Yum. A cheetah eyed my little daughter and licked its chops. "Animals love me," Julianna shouted.

Every animal looked well loved, and quite content, with the sole exception of the African hunting cat, which was in a weirdly small enclosure and kept pacing, pacing, pacing, with a demented look on its furry face.

Julianna loved this place and gave me all the credit. "You," she said, "are a *wonderful* father." Her undeserved compliment made me feel guilty. What had I done to deserve such lavish praise? Two minutes later, she looked up at me again and said, "I'm bored."

Amy felt the same way when we got back to the tent; one moment she was loving it, and then she was at a loss. "I'm trying to figure it out," she told me. "If this were a nice hotel, I'd love it. But the fact that it's *supposed* to be camping somehow makes it less fun. I feel like we're outsourcing not just labor but recreation. We can't set up the tent. We can't cook the food. What are we supposed to do?"

The next day, we were booked for a three-hour jeep tour through the wildest area of the park, but until then I had no plan. Normal campouts are such nonstop rigmarole, and while the chores can be unpleasant, they leave no room for irrational thoughts. Without anything else to occupy me, my self-sabotaging brain took over. I developed a premonition that one of the thousand wild animals in this park was going to attack me and draw my blood. I knew even then that it was silly. Why would any of these sweet-natured mammals want any trouble with me? But the thought would not go away, not even when Julianna and Amy and I drove out to the nearby town of Calistoga for pizza and returned to the glampground at dusk.

All of us enjoyed the tangerine-cherry-Meyer-lemon-gelato-colored sunset and the soft tinted light on the oak woodlands. Amy and I gazed into each other's eyes; we had a quick kiss. We were all feeling so indolent that it made sense to go to sleep early. That way, we'd be rested up for the safari tour the next day. Julianna and Amy sank into deep sleep in no time, but just as I was nodding off, every last bird in the entire glampground started going ape-shit en masse.

What was the matter with them? *Mug-WEE-up!* screamed the birds. *Krik-krik-kreek. Squonk. Taa-taa. Yit-YEET-yit, sneep, sneep!* One bird sounded like a circular saw, another like a whoopee cushion, and still another like an ultrasonic dental drill: *reeeeeeeeEEEEEEEEEK!* One bird kept shouting *Pop a Ricola, pop a Ricola! Nurp nurp nurp nurp.*

The birdcalls started out as interesting, if a little bit creepy, but as the night wore on and the sounds continued they became a torment. The calls, combined with my premonition, set me on edge. *Wadda wadda!* a bird cried out. It got to the point where I fantasized about running into the darkness and making ladies' hats and curries of them all. The canvas walls of the luxury tent were so thin that the birdcalls seemed to be coming from somewhere *inside* the room.

Those fabric walls apparently gave our fellow campers a feeling of privacy they did not have. As the evening progressed, I heard some fairly significant belches and worse from somewhere nearby, and some salty conversation as well. In normal camping, the sounds of a nearby river would have covered up such things. By the time daylight dawned, I was truly a mess. My fear of animal attack remained strong, but I tried to push that foreboding out of my mind the next morning when we boarded an open-air jeep for the tour of the "Sonoma Serengeti." Our tour guide, let's call him Frank, had a Jerry Garcia beard, a long ponytail, a bouncy walk, a khaki shirt, work gloves, and an Indiana Jones–style nut-brown adventure hat. I liked him immediately. "For safety, don't even *think* about getting out of the truck," Frank told us. "If you need to water the trees, please give me a few minutes' notice so I can find a safe place to stop. Now, let's go safari."

Julianna squealed with glee. Frank put the jeep in gear, and off we rode into the unknown. We bounced over lichen-covered boulders, past madrone, manzanita, and oaks dripping with Spanish moss. Scimitar horned oryx, addax, and blue wildebeests picked at meager vegetation and gave us "What the hell are you looking at?" expressions.

Frank was full of stories and surprising facts. He told us giraffes sleep only a half hour to four hours per day, and can pick their noses with their twenty-inch tongues. Their necks have the same number of vertebrae as a human neck. "Who knew?" I said to Amy. Giraffes can sometimes kick predators so hard they will stave in their enemies' heads and, in some cases, decapitate them.

After we stopped in the middle of a clearing, an ostrich appeared out of nowhere and pushed its beaky face into the vehicle. Julianna wished to caress its serpentine neck, but Frank recommended that we sit still while the ostrich sniffed all over the upholstery, as if imitating me sticking my face in that GranTurismo. We bucked, swerved, and rolled near the shores of "Watusi Lake," which looked like a reservoir and turned out to be one. The most astounding moment, though, happened midway through the tour, when Frank paused the vehicle on a potholed dirt road and stopped in front of a herd of twenty-three Cape buffalo. They were perhaps seventy feet away; I'd heard they can rush at you unprovoked and run thirty-five miles per hour. These particular Capes looked shiftless and sleepy.

Their eyes were insolent blanks, their coats the color of motor oil, their muscles hard-packed, their scraped-up horns curved to pinpoints. Frank told us their cognitive skills and capacity to hold grudges are extraordinary. If you try to shoot at them and are foolish enough to return to the scene, they may cut you out of your group and run you down. He referred us to an alarming YouTube video, "Battle at Kruger," with seventy-seven million hits and rising, which shows a herd of Capes going after a pride of lions after it attacks one of their calves. One of the buffaloes charges the pride, scoops one of the lions, and flings it in the air like a hacky sack. The lioness seems to hover in the air momentarily, and then lands on the buffalo's snout and horns.

My mouth went dry when I looked at these things in the flesh, and they made me think, *This place is incredible!* This is the largest herd of Cape buffalo anywhere in the United States. Their presence raises the serious question: How do you manage such unpredictable beasts without someone getting hurt?

Good question. Before the campout, I found out that there had, in fact, been a serious incident involving a Cape buffalo, Ruth, who attacked Safari West's lead hoof stock animal handler just nine months before my visit. It seems that Ruth got confused and walked through an open gate to join up with a herd of Angus cattle. The handler was trying to coax her back into the Safari West property when Ruth charged and gored the employee's leg. Genuine relief came over me when the jeep moved on and left the Cape buffalo behind.

After we returned to the developed section of the park, with the safari tents and creature paddocks, I flipped Frank a twenty, and he murmured, "Much appreciated." He seemed kind of expressionless, maybe a little embarrassed, which made me feel I'd shamed him by overtipping him, and therefore cheapening the labors of his soul. Then another dad came up and stuffed what appeared to be a wad of larger bills in Frank's hand. Frank smiled at him. That's when I knew I'd stiffed him. *Nice going*, I thought. That is one of my big weaknesses: not paying people what they're worth. In regular camping, you're doing everything for yourself, so you never have to worry about making someone feel unappreciated by shortchanging him or her on a tip.

I thought the tour was over, but it turned out there was one last bit of business to take care of: a backstage glimpse into the Safari West aviary. Frank warned us that one of the birds, a demoiselle crane, was a little bit naughty and had untied someone's shoes during a previous tour. This gentle warning was enough to freak out a little boy, who ended up staying behind with the same big-spender dad who'd given Frank the huge tip.

Julianna, Amy, and I entered the aviary. I was standing there admiring a roseate spoonbill, a shockingly pink creature with a beak like a spatula, when a demented skinny bird approached. It was a demoiselle crane, with the reddest and beadiest eyes I'd ever seen outside a sci-fi horror movie. Its legs were spindles. Tufts of white feathers dangled from both sides of its head, like the hairdo of an unhinged movie mad scientist. I could not escape the calm and mischievous intention of its gaze.

The creature seemed fascinated by me. No matter how I tried to retreat from it, the bird advanced, bobbing its neck, and gazing upon me with those bulging crimson eyeballs. It bowed forward and looked like it was trying to sniff me. I tried to walk around it, but the crane, which was three feet tall and probably weighed around ten pounds, rushed me and backed away and rushed forward again as if it wanted to trip me. "What do you want, friend?" I said. The creature was becoming more aggressive every time it approached. A few people saw that the bird and I were seeming to mimic each other's nervous movements, and they tittered.

Another bird from the same species showed up. It was curious and goofy, but it gave us all a little more space than its cohort. Frank, our guide, told me the bird in the background was named Kovu, while the much more assertive one, the one that had been tormenting me, apparently had no name. "He's Kovu's brother," Frank said.

Then, before I could puzzle out what was happening, Kovu's brother lost interest in me and chose another target, an apple-shaped woman in her early sixties wearing a leopard-print long-sleeve shirt, silvery loop earrings, and white tennis shoes with black laces. Perhaps Kovu's brother found her outfit enticing. He seemed especially interested in her meter-wide posterior, because he went right for it. Now she had a look of fear and panic on her face as Kovu's brother tried to peck her on the ass. "No, no, don't do that," she said, and blocked the bird with her purse. I could not just stand there and allow this addled and defensive creature to harm an innocent woman. I decided to run interference and get between the

The habitat of the demoiselle crane is far-ranging.
Its breeding grounds span Europe and Central Asia.

attacker and its prey. In a moment, I entered the physical space where Kovu's brother was bopping his head. I figured I would be okay, because I had my black Moleskine notebook; if Kovu's brother assaulted me, I could fend him off with it. Kovu's brother did not like my interfering with his plans to bite the woman. Now he turned his full attention back on me. For a few seconds we did something that looked like a mating dance, the two of us swiveling our heads and moving our feet in the same pattern, as I held my expensive sturdy notebook in front of me. He pecked at me, but I jumped out of the way; then he tried a different angle of approach, and I jumped out of the way again.

Kovu's brother was smart and cruel. Just when I thought I had him on the run, he reached back, to the soft and fleshy area at the back of my leg, and stabbed me with his beak. "*Yow!*" I screamed.

The burning pain took me by surprise; it felt like someone had plunged a hot darning needle into my flesh. As my synapses went wild, and the bird tried to penetrate me once more, I could not tell if he had stabbed me with the business end of his beak or if he had snipped me as with scissors. A trickle of blood bubbled up from the wound and rolled down my leg, obscuring the small puncture. Frank turned away and started murmuring something to the guests about nearby black-and-white colobus monkeys. I wondered if I'd annoyed him with the lousy tip. More likely, my loud howl had scared him and wrecked the vibe of his tour. He finally came up to me and said, softly, that I should go to the first-aid station when the safari was over.

Later, Jen, a young woman in a back room serving as the first-aid station at Safari West, was sympathetic and professional. She swabbed the incision with alcohol and gave me a Band-Aid. She asked me to file a brief incident report, which I did, in pencil. The night we got home from Safari West, I was so worried about the possibility of catching dengue fever or worse from the creature's mouth that I fired off an e-mail to the company, as a detailed addendum to my incident report.

hi Jen—

I am the guest who got bitten by the crane—I was kind of in a rush when I filled out the incident report, so I wanted to add a couple of quick details via email. For starters I recommend isolating the crane from the walk-in section of the aviary. . . . —The crane is beautiful but it is also quite aggressive and has a pointy beak.

When Frank guided us into the aviary, he said to watch out because the bird might untie our shoes, but nothing was specifically said about the bird's aggressive behavior and how that could involve pecks or bites, etc. . . .

Thanks, and I was also hoping to find out if you could recommend topical lotions, etc. My doctor is recommending a tetanus shot. I've never been bitten by a crane before so I'm not sure how to proceed.

All best,
Dan White
Santa Cruz, CA

I felt a little bad about hurling hardworking Frank under the safari bus, but I was just covering all the bases. If I did in fact get paralyzed later on from the creature's saliva, I wanted to create a trail of culpability.

I had no idea Safari West would take my letter so seriously. I'd listed my work number in the incident report, thinking that nothing would come of it, but before long, I got a call from a nervous-sounding, determined fellow named TJ from an insurance group that apparently represented Safari West in situations like this one. TJ was under the mistaken impression that I was trying to shake them down for money immediately, when in reality I was just setting up a paper trail in case I had to shake them down later on. I'm no grifter, but what if I got some crippling ailment because of the crane's saliva and maxed out my health insurance payments? This was strictly a worst-case scenario, however. Still, I couldn't help but feel like a sleazeball when TJ questioned me.

"Are you asking for money?" TJ asked me. "And how much?"

I was at a loss. How was I supposed to estimate the bill for something that hadn't happened yet and most likely would never happen at all?

"Are you asking for two hundred eighty-two dollars?" TJ said. "In the e-mail, you say 'watch out 'cause there's an aggressive bird that might untie your shoes,' and then I see something for two-eighty-two. Are you asking for two hundred eighty-two dollars?"

"Um, no. I think some signals are getting crossed here. That's how much the tent cost us for the night, not including the optional safari, under the special Moon Madness promotion thing they had going."

"How much did the tetanus shot cost?"

"I haven't had one yet."

"What are your intentions? Are you gonna come back down the road and ask for money?"

I told him it all depended on whether I developed a case of deadly nematodes.

"Well, let me give you my number," he said.

Before he hung up, he just had to mention one more issue that was on his mind.

"Let me ask you a question," TJ said. "When you go on a safari, you assume a certain amount of risk. Am I right?"

"Maybe you're right," I said. "But I don't know if your question is fair. You know, I've been camping hundreds of times. I've had everything happen to me when I've camped. I assumed the risk. I knew it was gonna be hard. When I decided to go camping in Safari West, I thought the whole thing was going to be totally fake, a joke, a cartoon version of the real thing. I had no idea the whole thing was going to be so real."

15

Hell on Wheels

Don't stop. Keep right on going. Hitch up your trailer and go to Canada. Or down to old Mexico. Find out what is at the end of some old country road. Go see what's over the next hill, and the one after that, and the one after that.

—Wally Byam, Airstream trailers founder, 1959

RVs move like America: broad-shouldered, big-bottomed, taking their time. RVs look so contented and proud, even when they're chugging up some mountain with a mile-long caterpillar of cars behind them. If RVs were humans, they would be Jackie Gleason, Babe Ruth, or John Goodman, reveling in their bulk. No wonder they infuriated me when I was young, skinny, and backpacking thousands of miles. To my mind, they embodied passivity, crass consumerism, and giving up. If your fridge, your eggs, your living room, and your queen bed come with you, why go?

Their color scheme, usually the color of nonfat milk, but sometimes the color of camouflage, spinach, or tanning bed sunburns, offended me. In my trail days, I'd stumble into a roadside camp and pitch my tent in view of their winking beer lights. While eating my supper of powdered hummus and creek water, I'd smell their rib-eye steaks and recoil at the sound of their generators and their occupants' heedless laughter. Sometimes I wanted to reach into my backpack and pelt them with foil-wrapped bricks of Mountain House Turkey Tetrazzini. But my age and gut have doubled since I finished the Pacific Crest Trail. By the time I approached my forty-seventh birthday, the thru hiker I once was lay buried under a pile of brioche muffins.

With all that extra padding, and the increasing pallor of my skin, I was starting to look like the variety of RV I disdained the most: the Class A wide-body. Perhaps the time had come to put my bitter views on hold and drive around in one of those hulks before I could dismiss them outright or hold on to any of my sweeping and ungenerous conclusions about their drivers. Besides, it seemed a little churlish of me to undertake an American camping odyssey that included a naked night in puma territory while overlooking a form of recreation that millions of Americans love so much. So I set out with my wife and daughter to discover what it would be like to pilot one of these great white whales across the deserts of Arizona.

In order to reach Phoenix, Amy, Julianna, and I had to cross the Mojave. Tumbleweeds rolled through traffic in wind-borne clumps of brown and gray. Trucks could not avoid them; every eighteen-wheeler wore a thistle mustache. By the time we reached the Cruise America outpost in Mesa, Arizona, on a mild winter day, crusts of grit clung to our car's windshield. It was almost closing time. At the rental office, I was surprised to learn that it's possible to rent a large RV sight unseen without any training and with no license restrictions. They hand you the keys and away you go. Assuming they would make allowances for someone with no experience, who lacked confidence and needed instruction, I asked the nice young clerk to let me drive a motor home around the parking lot while he rode in the passenger seat and dispensed advice. He looked puzzled. "Didn't you watch the orientation video?" he said. "We sent you the link in your confirmation e-mail."

"I watched that twice," I said. "But I don't think watching a video a couple of times is enough to show me how to do something I've never done."

"You're right," the young man said. "Maybe you should watch the video again."

He showed the video once more, on a large screen. The opening sequence shows a big fat Cruise America motor home barreling toward the camera and veering away at the last instant. This scene only increased my sense of doom. The only other memorable aspect of the video is the young starlet playing the Motor Home Mommy. It seemed to me that the film-makers included a surprising number of adoring and not altogether necessary wiggle shots of her. I wasn't exactly sure about her role in the training video, except perhaps to instill a sense of guilty voyeurism, which dovetailed nicely with the anticipatory terror of driving a motor home sight unseen. Soon the video was over, and the young man was walking us back out to the parking lot. This was all happening so fast. Amy and Julianna were unnervingly calm as we approached our home on wheels, which was seven times bigger than I thought it would be and so blinding white that it stung the eyes like a solar flare. My daughter looked thrilled. Our vehicle was a twenty-seven-foot, eleven-thousand-pound motor home in the Class C category, which meant that it was built on a van frame with a cab in the front. It had oversize photographic decals all over the sides and rear, showing stoked Caucasian folks boating on a lake with a shaggy dog, backpacking in the mountains, lazing on a dock, and doing things that didn't have squat to do with being in a motor home. The stickers embarrassed me because I thought they would brand me as a greenhorn in the RV parks where we would be staying and make it harder for me to blend in. Why rent a motor home if not to penetrate a subculture stealthily from the inside out?

At least we all enjoyed the interior, which looked like a nifty, if shrunken, motel room. The kitchen banquette converted to a mattress. Our unit came with cabinets that looked like they were made out of real wood and made a reassuring *thunk* when I rapped my knuckles on them. It had three exterior storage bays in the back, and a kitchenette with a propane stove, twin burners, and microwave oven. A tight dark corridor led to a cordoned-off chamber with a queen bed. Out front, the RV had a beetling brow containing more storage and sleeping space. Everything folded, collapsed, and had its own hidey-hole.

It would have been nice to enjoy the motor home without having to leave the Cruise America parking lot, but we had a rather hectic itinerary for the week, spanning nearly seven hundred miles and encompassing the heights of Sedona, the Superstition Mountains, and the Sonoran Desert. We would have to drive sixty-two miles just to reach our first RV park, in Black Canyon City, Arizona. I thought the Cruise America attendant would at least wave us off, but he walked toward the building while muttering something about an Arizona Wildcats game.

"It is kind of amazing that they'd just let us take this," Amy said as we sat in the motor home. She wondered if the rules were this loosey goosey for people who wanted to borrow a speedboat, a glider, or a yacht. She placed Julianna in her booster seat, which she belted to a bench in the kitchenette, on the driver's side of the vehicle thirteen feet behind me. Then Amy settled into the passenger seat and buckled herself in. I hunkered down behind the steering wheel, which was mounted in such a way that my head floated seven feet above the blacktop, making me feel like I was sitting on an elevated throne, a chieftain on the shoulders of manservants. It was a nice feeling.

Thoughtfully, Cruise America had positioned our motor home so we could roll forward out of our parking space instead of having to back the thing up. I disengaged the hand brake, shifted the gear into drive, and tapped the accelerator. Nothing happened.

I pushed the accelerator harder. The RV lurched, and we all jerked forward. For a moment I exulted in the powerful thrust of the 250-horsepower engine. It made me feel like I was driving a tank. I sensed that this motor home would protect us and keep us safe from whiplash if, God forbid, it spun out of control and started crunching down on other cars. As I rolled from the parking lot and merged into the crosstown traffic of Mesa, Arizona, it was uncanny, sitting at the front of a room that moved exactly where I wanted it to go, along with the objects it contained. My beer, my spoons, my mug, my lettuce, and my special fork—all these things traveled with me, my wife, and child at precisely the same speed. It was a glorious feeling, mitigated only by the fact that I couldn't really see out of the vehicle.

Of course there were side windows and a windshield, but the driver's-side window was several feet from my seat. In a normal-size car, I could look back through the window to make sure no cars were sneaking up on me, trying to pass or cut me off. Now that was impossible. I was at the mercy of two large segmented side mirrors that jutted a foot from the sides of the motor home. Until I learned to master these mirrors and puzzle out the blind spots, I would be a danger to everyone who came near me. Besides, the mirrors distorted reality. By providing an extreme close-up view of the vehicle's back end, the mirrors compressed the vehicle's length. As for the rearview mirror, it was close to worthless. When I looked into it, all I could see was the RV's dark, elongated interior, and Julianna monkeying around in her car seat.

I got us out of the parking lot and bluffed my way through the streets of Mesa, checking my side mirrors every three or four seconds to see if I was about to broadside anybody. When I looked up and saw the highway ahead of me, and the trucks rocketing across it, forming a blur of corrugated sheet metal and polished chrome, my tongue grew thick and pulses of electricity moved through my fingers. "I don't want to drive on that," I said to Amy.

"We have no choice," she said.

The RV went *chunka-chunk* as it rolled onto the highway ramp. I tried to accelerate, but the motor home was having none of it. The more I pressed the gas pedal, the more the vehicle quaked. The fiberglass paneling began to tremble. Ceramic cups and cutlery clanked in their compartments.

Now I was about to leave the on-ramp and enter the highway. Trucks rushed to the side of me, forming a wall to my left. The speed limit signs said sixty-five miles per hour, but most people were going a good twenty miles per hour faster than that.

"Speed up," Amy said. "Faster, faster!"

"I'm trying," I said, stomping the accelerator as hard as I could.

Reeeeeeeeeeeee! said the motor home.

The RV started picking up momentum as we entered the last few feet of the merge lane. I checked my side mirrors; no one was blocking me, or so I thought. Then, just as I was starting to merge, a banged-up scab-colored car—my best guess is a Chrysler LeBaron—appeared out of nowhere and blocked me. It must have rolled right out of my blind spot. "Oh, my God," I screamed. "Get out of the way!" I was about to smash that car when the passenger, a woman with a big brassy hairdo, made eye contact with me. Her eyes went wide and her mouth formed an O. She looked like a frightened gerbil. The car got out of the way and let me in at the last possible instant. It sped up so fast that the tires squealed horribly, filling the air with a rubbery smell.

"Oh, Amy," I said. "I almost killed somebody. Did you see that? They weren't letting me in and . . . the look of fear on that woman's face! I've never seen anyone look at me with such mortal terror!"

"Just keep moving," Amy said.

"I'm serious. It was like she was looking at the devil himself."

"Keep driving," she said.

"Did you hear what I just said?"

"Keep driving."

"Oh, man. I don't know about this trip. I'm getting way too old for this sort of thing."

"Too old to drive a motor home?" she said. "Look in the mirror. You're it. You're the demographic."

Amy's comment startled me so much that it almost made me forget the bashed-up LeBaron, which was now right in front of us, waggling its rear end in our faces as if to spite us.

Something occurred to me then: perhaps my conviction that I was driving the motor home out of irony, or driving it to fulfill the requirements of a journalistic assignment, was in itself ironic. I have to consider the limitations of my body, combined with my enduring need to get out into nature. I want to cover vast distances and roam from wilderness to wilderness, but you will never see me walk a long trail again. My sleep apnea has reached the point where I must camp with a fifty-pound deep-cycle marine battery that powers up my continuous positive airway pressure machine. If I go without the CPAP for more than three nights, I become oxygen deprived and start acting like a lunatic. My bloodstream at any moment is a chemical soup of inhaled steroids, eye droplet antihistamines, thyroid medication, and "leukotriene receptor antagonists," whatever those are; my allergist in Santa Cruz tells me that "virtually all leaves and grasses" could assail my eyes and nose at any time. The pollen of almost any tree makes my airwaves constrict. I have been told that, as far as my body is concerned, redwoods, olive trees, walnut trees, oak, acacia, birch, alder, sycamore, juniper, cedar, sage, cocklebur, pigweed, and amaranth have itch-making, sneeze-inducing properties. Strangely enough, I have no allergic reaction to anything filthy and urban, including house dust, dust mites, cockroaches, and tobacco smoke. I'm allergic to nature itself. When I asked my doctor where I might move to escape these allergic reactions, his response was "Minnesota in wintertime." My allergist wants me to be a snowbird in reverse, fleeing warmer climes and hiding out in a snowbound state.

I refuse to hear his entreaties. A stronger part of me, the soul part, craves those nature retreats and will take them, regardless of any wheezing. Perhaps this explained my newfound curiosity about RVs, which allowed me to cover ground without exerting myself, and with my brews and salty snacks tagging along with me. I wondered if the camping project was only an excuse to fulfill my true destiny as a motor home owner. Long after I'd set down the bong and picked up the Albuterol canister, I could still feel like a rebel. The Recreational Vehicle Industry Association, the trade association representing almost all RV manufacturers and parts suppliers in the United States, reports that the typical American RVer is forty-eight, just one year older than I was at the time of the trip.

During the 2014 trade show in Louisville, Kentucky, RVIA president Richard A. Coon pointed out that someone turns fifty in this country every seven seconds, and that 45 percent of the people in America are now fifty or older, a demographic turning point in the nation's history. "Perfect, huh?" said Coon, addressing the cheering crowd. "There's our market. Holy cow!"

In other words, it was people *just like me* who were behind the resurgence in the sales of trailers and motor homes in the United States. At the time I set off on my journey, the RV industry was having its best year in four decades. Judging from the official trade show highlights video I'd watched online before the trip, the atmosphere at the Louisville show was jubilant almost to the point of mania. Announcers and presenters used words such as *awesome, astounding,* and *nothing short of amazing* to describe sales figures and floor displays; one announcer said that if you stacked all the RVs present at the convention on top of one another, they would rise from the valley to the rim of the Grand Canyon.

The brisk sales are even more impressive when you consider that RVs are anything but cheap. I'd automatically come to associate recreational vehicles with low budgets. Perhaps that has something to do with seeing so many derelict RVs on cinder blocks in rural sections of Santa Cruz County. So I was surprised to find that if we were to buy an RV that was comparable to the one we were driving—the exact model was not for sale—it would cost somewhere in the range of $65,000 to $70,000. As steep as that price tag would be for me, it's close to the lower end of the scale for new ones; a fresh-off-the-line Class C can cost up to $121,000, while a Class A motor home, which is self-contained and looks a bit like a rock band's touring coach, can set you back between $500,000 and $900,000.

Even with my jaundiced viewpoint about RVs, I will admit that the pervasive joy at that RV trade show was hard earned. During 2008 and 2009, the industry went through humiliating setbacks. High gas prices and the credit crunch did much of the damage. In early 2009 the unemployment rate in Elkhart County, Indiana, where 80 percent of American RVs are assembled, stood at 15.3 percent, the highest in the nation. Things got so bad that President Obama showed up in person to offer hope. By late 2014, gas prices had plummeted, the Great Recession was over, and the unemployment rate in Elkhart was close to zero. Now, according to industry figures, there are ten million RV-owning households in America and thirty million people using RVs in this country, a number that includes passengers as well as drivers.

While I would have to see for myself if sleeping in a twenty-first-century motor home or luxuriously tricked-out fifth-wheel trailer* qualified as "real" camping, RVs have unquestionable links with camping history. Just as a shrewlike, bug-eating mammal is thought to be the common ancestor of human beings and chimps, the early auto campers at the turn of the twentieth century were the forebears of both today's car campers and RV drivers. All RVs on the road today, from the battered Winnebago Chieftain listed on Craigslist for $6,000 to the actor Vin Diesel's bespoke $1.1 million, 1,100-square-foot "mansion on wheels," owe their existence to the first auto campers who got sick of sleeping on the cold, hard ground and thought, *Wouldn't it be easier to add a foldaway car seat?*

The earliest car owners with a thirst for camping simply stuffed their cars with extra supplies and gear. They roped and tarped their cargo, and away they went. In the first decade of the twentieth century, some enterprising mechanics lashed carts to the back to carry equipment, and retrofitted the wheels to handle the rutted glorified goat paths that qualified as highways and roads back then. Then came "house trailers" and "tent trailers," which were big enough for campers to take their meals in and sleep in. In other words, the needs and greed of these early and mostly well-off drivers were the starting points for the wild assortment of motor homes and fifth-wheel trailers we see on the road today. It took three superfamous, powerful, and ridiculously wealthy self-styled "Vagabonds" to help popularize a deluxe form of auto camping that predated today's RV vacations. They publicized these motor getaways by taking a series of luxurious excursions across the eastern United States, including the Everglades, the Adirondacks, and the White and Green Mountains. These slumming campers were Henry Ford, Thomas Edison, and rubber baron and pneumatic tire magnate Harvey Firestone. There was a good amount of cultural irony in their trips—the implied message was "Get a load of us

---

* This is a term for a trailer that is mounted to the bed of a pickup truck or "semi"-type vehicle. The term "fifth wheel" dates back to the original design, in which the pin that attached the trailer to the truck was set in the middle of the axle hole in the spare wheel.

rich folks chopping wood, setting up camp in farmland, and acting like ordinary people." In spite of, or perhaps because of, that patronizing aspect, the American public could not read enough of their exploits.

For almost every year from the late teens to the early 1920s, their annual auto campout attracted even more press attention than Joe Knowles's bare-naked camping experiment in 1913. Ford, Edison, and Firestone helped usher in the technological era that drove so many antimodernist rebels and late-coming Romantics into the woods for camping vacations in the first place. It was only fitting that these men would take to the woods themselves.

Their frequent guest was the best-selling nature writer John Burroughs, an old grizzled naturalist with great thatches of white whiskers, natty clothes, and a penetrating gaze. Just by being there, he gave the journey a dash of authenticity and natural appeal; perhaps Burroughs, in his own modest way, contributed to the notion that RVing is "real camping" and a great way to get out into the woods, though the endless conveniences estranged them from those natural places. These powerful men slept in upscale tents, not inside their vehicles, which made them early precursors to today's glamping. They also played a role in RV history because their entourage of motorcars was so well appointed and specialized. They had a dining room van, another van devoted entirely to camping gear, and a kitchen car known as "the Waldorf-Astoria-on-wheels," with an onboard refrigerator for steaks and a gas stove for cooking.

The story of the Vagabonds proves that RV road trips can qualify as real camping, in spite of the luxe circumstances. No one, including these rich people, could resist the forces of chaos that infect so many camping trips. Sometimes the party got lost or waylaid. Once, they met with a grumpy landowner's wife who either hadn't heard of them or did not find them impressive and would not give them permission to camp. There are stories about Burroughs staring at a stream with transcendentalist longing while the more practical-minded campmates tried to calculate its potential hydroelectric power. But the most striking aspect of their campouts is their deliberately regressive and blissful purposelessness. Like Ralph Waldo Emerson hanging out with his illustrious friends at the Philosophers' Camp in the Adirondacks in 1858, these men did not brainstorm any life-changing discoveries and innovations for America. Instead, they used their campouts to re-create boyhood. Just like those Adirondack campers before them, they left all pretenses behind and removed their masks in the forest, sometimes revealing playfulness and decency, and other times exposing uglier truths in front of the campfire.

In his public writings, Burroughs shared only the cute, folksy, crotchety aspects of the pathological Ford, whom he regarded as "tender as a woman, and much more tolerant . . . [A]n unconquerable idealist, he always seemed to be thinking of the greatest good for the greatest number of his fellows." In his journal accounts of the car camp, Burroughs provides a much different take on their time together. Ford famously hated Jews and blamed them for almost everything, from the decline in the quality of American candy to the rise of morally suspect jazz dancing to the "inefficiency of the Navy." In 1919 some of that animus came thundering out of him during an RV campout at Green Island, near Troy, New York. That night, at the campfire, Ford muttered that "the Jews caused [World War I], the Jews caused the outbreak of thieving and robbery all across the country," and much more. He called the industrialist Jay Gould a greedy "Shylock," a remark that prompted Burroughs to point out that Gould was actually a Presbyterian.

Burroughs died in 1921, and for a while the Vagabonds rolled along without him. Soon, the surviving campers grew to resent the fuss and headlines and stopped the campouts in 1924. Their publicity junket had succeeded all too well. "It became tiresome to be utterly without privacy," Firestone complained. In spite of their drawbacks, the trips helped popularize camping trailers and the use of camping-related gadgets. By the 1920s the gear options for auto camping and RV camping exploded, much in the same way that new gear for backpackers started proliferating after World War II, when the materials and technologies of the battlefield found new purposes in camp. As trailers got longer, so did the list of campground "necessities." Motor magazines hawked contrivances that previous generations would never have associated with camping out: baby hammocks and baby seats, chicken wire for muddy roads, ice chests, charcoal and acetylene stoves, air pistols, egg containers, privacy curtains, gas siphons, luggage racks, portable record players, sundial/compass combinations, folding tables, chairs, and "smoked goggles" to protect the eyes from desert glare. The Coleman lantern, developed at the turn of the twentieth century to let farmers work into the evening, found a new purpose in RVing.

I had to admit that, well before my motor home trip, I found the variety and inventiveness of RV-related gadgetry, and the designs and features of the vehicles, astounding. A year before our motor-homing journey, I called up the formidable RV historian Al Hesselbart, who worked at the RV/MH (motor home) Hall of Fame in Elkhart, Indiana, for two decades. Foolishly, I tried to stump him. I tried to think of the most stupendously impractical motor home designs and asked if they had real-life correlatives. "How about a motor home with more than one story?" I asked him. "Or one with an onboard swimming pool? Or a runway for aircraft?"

After a momentary pause, Hesselbart floored me by rattling off the name of a sixty-five-foot-long motor home that had almost all the features I'd listed: the Executive Flagship, which had second-story bedrooms and a patio on the roof with a diving board over a six-foot-deep inflatable swimming pool. In the early 1950s, William MacDonald of the Chicago-based Mid States Corporation produced this crazy vehicle, which was so long that it was articulated in the middle, like a centipede, so it could turn corners. "If you took the canopy off the upper deck you could fully land your private helicopter on the roof," Hesselbart said. That was not exactly a runway, but it was close enough.

It is nearly impossible to brainstorm an RV that isn't out there somewhere. RV designer Harold D. Platt manufactured trailers that glided across the Arctic ice on skis instead of wheels. Some were bunkhouses. Others were radar installation containers. They came in handy at a Cold War–era early-warning base out in Greenland. Automotive builders and designers have also made RVs that can withstand nuclear explosions and fallout, and amphibious houseboat RVs that float on freshwater lakes while pulling trailers, which also float. In the history of motor homing you will find RV brothels, an RV dentist's office, and an RV church with a steeple that folds down to fit in the garage. In the 1970s, Winnebago Industries, in conjunction with Orlando Helicopter Airways, made flying motor homes. These "Winnebago Heli-Homes" had 115 square feet of carpeting, a dinette, a cook stove, a minibar, beds for six, amphibious floats for safe landings on water, onboard showers, and a Sikorsky helicopter body. They were never popular, but I have to admire the chutzpah of anyone who would dare to make and market such a wackadoodle thing.

Compared to all those imaginative motor homes, the one I was piloting from Phoenix to our RV park for the night was underwhelming. My Class C was a peewee compared to some of the RVs passing me at excessive speeds. It was all I could do to go half the speed limit. Other drivers probably regarded me as toxic on the highway that day. Everyone gave me plenty of space.

It felt as if I were driving in a pocket of reverse magnetism all the way to the Black Canyon Ranch RV Resort, in Black Canyon City, Arizona, where emigration was the evident theme. Someone had propped up wooden decorations shaped like miniature chuck wagons and water wells under backlit palm trees. It was a tremendous relief to go from a highway full of fast cars and motorcycle gangs to a protected enclave where the speed limit was five miles an hour on narrow roads with names such as Bingo Circle, Cyndi Circle, Michelle Lane, Jerry Street, Dee Lane, and CU Lane. There were hundreds of RVs here; the place was a movable suburb. When I approached the deserted front desk inside the open lit-up club-house, my legs felt gelatinous from the stressful driving. I was feeling sleepy, shy, and disoriented, and my family was waiting to be fed. I waited to see if someone would show up to the desk. No one did. I looked around. A bulletin board advertised family-friendly amusements for RV park dwellers, including "Corn-hole," which surprised and alarmed me until I took out my smartphone and found out it was only a beanbag game.

A few men were gathered around a table and talking about the best ways to hunt down and field-dress javelinas, which are small and aggressive Sonoran Desert beasts that resemble pigs but are distant relatives to the hippo. While I hated to interrupt such lively banter, my family was waiting, so I tapped a beefy fellow on the shoulder. He led me outside and rounded up Ray, one of the two campground supervisors, who'd moved out there a few years ago from New Hampshire. Ray walked into the night and guided me as I rolled the motor home gingerly into a parking space. Stepping outside to talk with him, I searched Ray's face for some sign of mockery at my cluelessness but saw none.

Ray seemed grateful to be there at all. I found out, after the fact, that he used to be a finish carpenter out in New Hampshire until a platform he was standing on crashed to the ground. The accident left him badly injured and wrecked his career, so he and his wife, Christine, who ran a tavern and had her own little farm, sold everything, got a fifth wheel, left their adult children back east, toured the country, and settled here, simplifying their circumstances, *Walden*-style, watching their bills diminish, having the freest lives they'd known: no mortgage, no hustle, just being together, greeting people in this park, and sometimes getting on their motorbikes and "quad" off-road vehicles in search of adventures. The newfound simplicity of their lifestyle brought to mind an e-mail conversation I had with the Thoreau biographer Robert Richardson, who said to me, "I used to tell my students they could buy an old car-camper and go live like Thoreau right now if they so chose."

Ray, who had a thick mustache and dark-tinted glasses, took a long drag on his smoke, undid a latch, reached in our motor home's guts, and pulled out a snaking cord called a "shore line." He plugged it into a surface-mounted power outlet box. Cruise America had forgotten to give me a garden hose, but Ray fetched one up somewhere, connected us to the water source, and turned the knob.

All at once, the dark RV lit up, water rushed in the sink, the toilet gurgled, and Julianna shrieked with delight inside the motor home. The magic of that moment was undeniable. I was almost embarrassed by how "Neato!" the whole thing seemed. However, the unexpected presence of a stench knocked me back into reality. When Ray grabbed hold of the sewage outlet tube and tried to hook it up, blue-green globules of chemical-scented waste-water splashed from the pipe and splattered near my shoes. "Ugh," Ray said. "Cruise America should have cleaned that thing for you. That's why I always wear gloves."

He trailed his flashlight over our rig. "Got to limit your pooping in that thing," he said, gesturing toward the RV's bathroom. "And put no paper down that," he said, illuminating the holding tank. "I've seen more guys take out my power washer and stick it right up the tube there and down the toilet to try to break up a clog. It's a pain in the neck."

When I failed to light the propane stove, Ray came on board with his lit cigarette still in his hand, a pile of ashes dangling from the end. This unnerved me, though his generosity made up for it. He fired up the stove. I felt so dependent on him, and grateful. Thanks to his help, we had no worries, at least for the rest of the evening. My family and I were all jammed in together, as if we were inside a tent, but I didn't mind. The contrast between the limitless open space in the desert around the vehicle and the limited room within it eased my thoughts. No matter how gigantic it appeared to others on the highway, the RV's interior felt tight, contained, and compressed.

Dwelling in the motor home changed how we perceived the world outside. When you're in one, you don't care that there are neighboring motor homes bearing down on you, elbowing into your space. All you think about is the bed, the cot, the little hallway, and the panel lights near the side door, showing your levels of gray water, black water, and propane. Everything else is immaterial. Your life is reduced in a way that slows your thoughts down. There are so few options. It was impossible to squeeze past my curvy wife in the corridor without inadvertently and pleasantly squashing her against the wall. We gorged on the pasta I boiled on the propane stove. I ate gobs of chocolate. Though we were using energy from the outside, and goods we'd purchased in stores, I enjoyed the illusion of independence and self-containment. It felt as if we were camping out in a spaceship.

The cramped-ness comforted me. The motor home's hallways and low ceilings entrapped my family; no matter where I went inside it, we could not escape from one another. Though we'd cover hundreds of miles in this adventure, I would *never* let them out of my sight. As a backpacker, all I wanted was limitless open spaces. Now that I'm older, I want to reduce my life like a Shrinky Dink toy that gets small when you put it in the oven. I sat there for a while, watching my daughter read a book in the kitchenette. The rims of her spectacles glowed red and white in the luminescence.

Instead of going straight to bed, I watched the people one space over, backlit figures pottering about in front of their flat-screen televisions and electronic fireplaces, tending to their kids, bumbling around, sticking their faces in their storage bays. Their silhouettes reminded me of the hobgoblin shadow forms my campmates made when they left their sleeping bags and fed backcountry cook fires on wilderness trips many years ago. Someone was walking her little Toto dog through the evening chill. I was just about to drift off to sleep when Julianna sat beside me on my meager mattress. "Daddy," she said. "On the way over here, when we were leaving that big city, I was looking out the window at all the cars. It was so weird. Everyone was trying to get away from us. They were scared. The people behind us. It's like they couldn't get away fast enough."

I sighed and put my arm around her.

"You're right," I said, glancing out the window. Someone out there was doing jumping jacks, his breath streaming in front of him. The temperature gauge said forty degrees. "This is not what I am. I'm used to fitting in, driving a little bitty car. I don't like inconveniencing anyone. Or frightening them. Or being so big on the road. I really scared some lady when I tried to merge. Terrified her."

"People think we're some kind of monster," Julianna said.

"I know. It's awful. I'm sorry I put us in this position."

"I'm not," Julianna said. "In Santa Cruz, we never get to be the monster. It feels great. I love it."

It made me feel a little queasy to think it, and I dared not say it out loud, for fear of setting a bad example to my daughter, but she was right about that. It was nice to feel powerful on the road for once, a grunting colossus of the highway. Maybe that was part of the appeal for older folks like me. When we get middle-aged, it's like Harry Potter snuck up and threw his invisibility cloak on top of us. Just like that, we disappear. The youth replace us long before we're dead. People tend to patch us older folks into the scenery, as if we're trees or stanchions or street furniture. Is that why so many aging people drive these things? Maybe that's the main idea: driving an RV is like floating down the highway in a rocket-fired robotic exoskeleton. *Don't mess with me, sonny boy. I'm seventy-eight, with progressive lenses and a Tilley hat, but I've got six wheels. I weigh forty-three thousand pounds. Don't make me squish you.* Is that the rule of thumb? The older and frailer the driver, the bigger and taller and fatter the motor home?

Next morning, Julianna and I snooped around the clubhouse to see if anyone would talk to us about RV life. At the center of the table was Don, a retired cattle rancher from northeastern Montana who looked like Gary Cooper in his lion-in-winter days. For the past decade he'd paid for a year-round spot at the park, which he occupied when the weather cooled. That's how he knew the other half dozen men at the table; returning year after year, they'd become his cronies. Don had a square jaw, a serene gaze, and a broad-rimmed cowboy hat with ventilation holes for sunny days. He split his time between Arizona and his ranch house up north. Don was seventy-six but looked fifty. He laughed when I told him this. He liked to give strangers pocket change every time they mentioned his youthful appearance. After making a big show of reaching in his coat for spare coins, he pulled his pockets inside out and frowned. "Aw, too bad, I've run out of quarters," he said.

I asked why he wanted to be out here, so far from home.

"Your typical rancher works every day from the time he gets up to when he goes to sleep at night, all his life long," Don said, shaking his head. "He thinks the good Lord expects him to work until he enters the gates of heaven." He sipped from a steaming mug of black coffee. "Well, I just think that's sad. My father died when I was eleven. Never got a chance to travel. Lots of people think that if you don't work all the time, you'll have to answer for that in the next life. Well, if you do that, after a while, your grandchildren will look up at you and think, *Old Granddad sure is a grouchy old rascal, isn't he, always talking about his aches and pains?*"

Don found an alternative to all that waiting around. A member of the Montana Cowboy Hall of Fame, he traveled the Southwest in a pickup truck, towing his horse in a long trailer. Together they competed in "cutting" competitions, which required him to ride into a herd of cattle and "cut" one of them out of the group. When Don stayed at the RV park, his horse slept in a stable one mile away. "Doing this will make you younger," Don assured me, though it wasn't clear if he was referring to the cutting competitions, the RV lifestyle, or both. "Getting along is a little harder than it used to be, but put me in the saddle and I'll do about as good as I did fourteen years ago."

So much for my notion that the RV lifestyle was automatically equated with stasis, surrender, and total laziness. Still, I was surprised he worked so hard in the service of fun. "Sounds exhausting to me," I said. "Is this relaxing at all?"

He gave me a look and laughed. "Relaxing?" He thought about it awhile. "When you're winning, it is relaxing," he said. "Then, you're the cock of the walk."

Later that morning, when I was getting gas and propane for our journey to Sedona, a pickup truck rattled along the frontage road towing the biggest trailer I'd ever seen. It was Don, our cowboy friend, waving his hat at us and beeping his horn.

The landscape went full-on Martian that morning as we headed toward Sedona. Chocolate-brown mesas rose in front of us. Spiky ocotillos waved their lethal arms. Boulders rose in melted-glass shapes. An evangelical motorcycle gang passed us, white crucifixes shining on their cracked brown jackets.

Driving off that morning, Don gave me a warm feeling with his wisdom and his rugged life. Yet the good vibes evaporated the moment I left the highway and turned onto a two-lane road with no passing lane. Almost immediately an older woman in a yellow Yugo, with a lemony expression to match, started tailgating me and waving her left hand out the window in that universal "pull the hell over" gesture. A few minutes later, looking through the side-view mirror, I saw that there was a long caterpillar of cars behind me, and I was at the front. How many drivers was I inconveniencing and infuriating? Four dozen? Five dozen? Suddenly I began to sympathize, sort of, with the drivers of motor homes I'd mocked and beeped at for causing me so much boredom and aggravation.

Aside from the technical difficulties of driving this rig, these increasingly angry drivers were the only initiation I'd faced. So far, other RVers had accepted me without question. It was all the other people—*my* people!—who were making me feel put upon, cut off, honked at, disregarded, resented. These people were being mean just because of the rig I was driving. Now I *almost* regretted all those years I'd amused myself reading about motor home mishaps. Why had I sniggered at the tale of Melissa Betts, who was showing off her 1978 Shasta motor home to an interested party when the whole thing burst into flames, right in the middle of her sales pitch? Or the news story about some sad-sack fellow who got out of his motor home to walk his dog near the seashore in Lincoln County, Oregon, only to watch a hulking white object speed past him and soar over the cliff? It was his motor home. Now all those people driving behind me probably wished I'd spontaneously combust or go tumbling into the ocean, if there was one around here.

It's a potent thing, being hated for associating with a subculture that you thought you hated, too. When such a thing happens, it's impossible not to have at least some warm feelings for the group you criticized so harshly. With my half sympathy came the realization that RV drivers are not all the same. When we arrived, with great relief, at our next RV park, in the heights of Sedona, Arizona, near the great red sandstone bulwarks around the town, I began to realize that "RV driver" is too sprawling a group to qualify as just one demographic. There are no accurate census figures for full-time "snowbirds," who've sold their homes, bought RVs, and turned them into permanent houses of the highway; many RVers have no fixed addresses. But not all RVers are heedless retired vacationers. Our nearest neighbor at the RV park was a beefy soft-spoken man named Mark. Though he was a full-time RVer, out on vacation with his wife, he had about as much in common with Don the Cowboy as I did. Mark is a physicist for a massive military subcontractor in Los Angeles County, California. His work involves laser beams and adaptive optics. His workplace is in Los Angeles, a hundred miles north of his house, wife, and son. Initially this didn't bother him too much, because he telecommuted for the most part and showed up in person once or twice a week at the most. Then his assignment changed, and a two-hundred-mile round-trip commute made no sense. He found cheap lodging in LA County, including "some really cheesy hotels and motels by the airport," he told me. "At fifty bucks a night in LA you are likely to hear gunfire outside. It is not relaxing." Seeking a way out, Mark bought a huge RV, set it up in front of his office in Los Angeles, and took up full-time residence in the parking lot. He kept the house in San Diego County, but now it's his weekend retreat. I asked what his coworkers and boss thought about this arrangement. "A lot of them don't know and don't really care."

Mark used to think he was the only employee whose house had wheels. One night, while he was parked in front of the corporate headquarters, he noticed other physicists hanging out in other motor homes in that asphalt harbor, electric lights burning.

In the Sedona park, Julianna and I talked up a former waitress and Walmart cashier driving around the country in a sandblasted Dutchmen. It looked barely functional, with a couple of hundred thousand miles of highway behind it. That's one drawback about RVs. They're blinding white when you get them new; then they get old and turn the color of boiled chicken feet. A few spots over from Mark, we met a middle-aged financial analyst for a cement company who was traveling with his real estate agent wife. They were exploring the Mogollon Rim in a forty-foot Holiday Rambler Endeavor, equipped with office supplies, a printer, and Wi-Fi so they could remain in incessant contact with their coworkers. Nothing about them suggested they were on vacation. The wife, in fact, was quite surly, and slammed the door in our faces for letting the cold air in.

This couple was a reminder that some people use RV parks for reasons that have nothing to do with relaxation; some American RV parks serve as "man camps" and low-priced labor housing for temporary workers in oil fields in the Midwest and elsewhere. This is just the latest version of a practice that has been going on since World War II, when manufacturers made RVs that served as wheeled barracks for the workers in military bases and in factories making war machinery. Other RV parks age into trailer parks or "mobile home parks," where the wheels come off one by one, the residents ask for mail slots, and a onetime tourist getaway becomes a fixed address.

As the week unfolded, I was starting to see the places where optional camping blurred into something else. Julianna and I were becoming collectors of road stories. We noticed an element of craftiness and survival in every tale we heard: the lesbian couple who lived in a lovely little vintage teardrop trailer and supported themselves with their national parks photography as they went along; the former vintner who "boondocked" in his motor home, making ends meet selling solar panels and other green technology to customers online, and using solar panels so he didn't need to run the generator and burn propane on cold nights.

Strolling through the RV park, we smelled charcoal in outdoor grills, watched Primus stove flames flicker, and saw pots of meat sauce bubble. A hippie girl tended the onboard herb garden in her biodiesel bus. I almost walked headlong into a bunch of kids playing a touch football game. Julianna and I said hello to men smoking big, smelly cigars near a tiki torch, watched frantic wives direct their tired, RV-driving husbands into tight spots, and saw an old man ride an exterior chairlift to the cab of his fifty-footer. A grandfather in a rippling windbreaker bent over to plug in his HAPPY HOUR EVERY HOUR and COCKTAIL LOUNGE lights while his family stood around him. Someone with an I LOVE THE SMELL OF JET FUEL bumper sticker set out barbells and a Nordic track machine.

On the surface, this scene could not have been more different from a backpacker's camp. Instead of dextrose tablets and dehydrated chili, these people had twenty-four-packs of Pabst and bags of bleeding T-bone steaks. Instead of purified pond water, they had growlers of craft beer, and Captain Morgan's Spiced Rum stirred with Coca-Cola. Instead of popping ibuprofen tablets and lancing blisters with a campfire-sterilized needle, they planed off the day's hard edges with mojitos and martinis.

Yet the impulse to occupy and alter a forest clearing, to convert unfamiliar woods into places approximating home, was the same as in backpacking. So was the feeling of a compromise or standoff between domestic living and nature that Thoreau describes in *Walden*. Granted, some were trying to achieve this feeling of rustic sublime by setting out pink flamingos and ceramic sunflowers or making circles of garden gnomes. But at least the sense of ritual was familiar and comforting. So was the sense of unfinished tasks and the hypnotic rhythm of accomplishing them. The necessary tedium of uncoiling the power cord and checking the black water levels brought to mind the process of sitting in the sun filtering creek water in the North Cascades.

Perhaps it was the cold weather, but the lack of people walking through the park really struck me. So many people were just holing up in their vehicles, hiding away, watching the news, or lounging around the interior, as if the motor homes were destinations unto themselves. Or my sense of there being few people out and about might have had something to do with the fact that this park had no clubhouse for people to get together.

As the evening fell, about a dozen RVers left their rigs behind to gather on an overgrown hillside and watch the sunset. Strangers chatted, ate finger foods, held magnums of champagne, opened beer bottles, and raised their fluted pilsner glasses. Amy, Julianna, and I joined them, and together we watched the mountains turn a luscious orange-red. It looked as though someone had dusted the peaks and mesas with the same shade of rouge. Sedona is beautiful if you disregard the boutiques selling pillow embroideries, Kokopelli beer cozies, and posters of coyotes and mountain lions with workplace affirmations striped beneath their snouts. You could spend all day gaping at the red columns, sphinxes, and cupolas, some of them people-size, others bigger than office towers. My eyes could not stop vaulting from the valley floor to the highest pinnacles.

This informal gathering of RVers, as lovely as it was, could not stop me from feeling constrained by my motor home. That's the disheartening paradox of any big RV; in a general sense, the RV will go wherever you wish, only to circumscribe your movements once you get there. Sedona had no convenient place for us to park our metal giantess; our presence seemed to antagonize all the drivers of normal-size vehicles on the narrow streets and, in particular, in two traffic circles so tight and vertiginous that I'd nicknamed them Scylla and Charybdis. Now I understood why so many motor home owners in our RV park towed off-road "quad" vehicles, jeeps, or regular-size cars with them. In camp, they unhooked these from the tow hitch and zoomed away, escaping from the motor homes that had helped them pursue freedom in the first place.

These days the motor home has a mixed reputation. Some Americans long for them, and others snicker at them. Yet the original RVs were the ultimate objects of envy and admiration.

Motor homes caused a big sensation in January 1910, now considered Year Zero in the history of American RVing, when the Pierce-Arrow Motor

Car Company unveiled the first American motor home, the Touring Landau. The venue was Madison Square Garden, where the expensive admission prices did nothing to deter a capacity crowd that included the likes of John Jacob Astor and Andrew Carnegie. The Landau cost $8,250 in a year when Model Ts were selling for $950 and the average American worker was toiling for between $200 and $400 per year. The Landau was not called a motor home then; that term dates only to 1958, when the entrepreneur Ray Frank of Michigan introduced a line of self-propelled motorized vehicles that he marketed as Frank Motor Homes. Still, the Landau was almost as luxurious as the finest models you see on the highway now.

The Landau had a Cordovan leather interior, an onboard toilet, a sleeping area, and sink. It came with a set of luggage that matched the upholstery. One super-fancy bespoke version had hot and cold water, which was unheard of in cars, and in most of rural America, back then. Pierce-Arrow sold only a few Landaus. Their proud owners included Pierce-Arrow's president George Birge, cereal magnate C. W. Post, and a rich oilman out in Texas. The Landau had all the things I appreciated about our rental motor home, with none of the drawbacks. Landau owners didn't have to drive or maintain these things themselves. That's what chauffeurs and mechanics were for. If the owners wanted to go somewhere, they just hopped in the back and barked out orders through a telephone receiver. At the time, RVing was considered fringe, but in a snooty way.

It didn't take long for these proto–motor homes to become much more lavish, complicated, and insane. In terms of manic creativity and utter shamelessness, it was hard to beat the Conklin Family Gypsy Van, a swaying, eight-ton heap that had radiator-heated showers, an observation deck, an onboard dance floor, and a kitchen where chefs could prep meals even while the vehicle was rumbling. Roland R. Conklin, a financier with extensive railroad interests in Cuba and the president of the New York Motor Bus Company, spared no expense to make this behemoth of luxury in 1915, using one of his company's buses as a base. Eight pleasure tourists and two servants made it most of the way across the country in the house car, which had dual three-speed gear sets allowing for nine speeds forward and three in reverse. It is hard to blame the travelers for the fact that they cheated on their transcontinental journey, shipping the vehicle by train for part of the way; the roads were so lousy that they had to lay down canvas strips on the sand for traction and use an onboard steel-and-plank bridge

Roland R. Conklin's "land yacht" was twenty-five-feet long and weighed eight tons.

that could be lowered to the ground, allowing the vehicle to cross gaps in the road of up to fifteen feet.

Around the time that house cars started lumbering down the street, companies started producing trailers on assembly lines. The mass production of "tent trailers" soon followed. The first of these were hazardous to use. Most had no taillights on them, and besides, "turning and braking [hand] signals weren't visible behind the trailers," noted RV historian Al Hesselbart. But their reputation took a drubbing in the mid-1930s; so many desperate people used trailers for Depression-era housing that the term *trailerite* took on a dismissive connotation.

In light of that stigma, this was the worst time to jump into the trailer manufacturing business. However, a lanky Stanford graduate named Wally Byam didn't let that stop him. His now iconic Airstream business introduced a silver, shiny, aerodynamic trailer whose profile and columns of rivets made it resemble a Lindbergh monoplane or a Buck Rogers spaceship. The Airstream looked like it should have been flying into the wild blue yonder, not rolling down America's highways. The best of these trailers had gas-powered stoves, insulation, a primitive sort of "air-conditioning" achieved with dry ice, and onboard chemical toilets "at a time when many trailers were nothing but wooden boxes on wheels," wrote the *National*

Post in a Byam retrospective. Byam, in selling these extra-luxe trailers, added cachet and prestige to auto camping during a low period for its reputation. He became a lasting inspiration for a well-off but rugged strain of RVers, the sort of people you might see powering their rigs up a steep mesa with a SPENDING OUR CHILDREN'S INHERITANCE sticker on the rear bumper. Byam began guiding RV "caravan" tours, starting in 1951 with a trek from El Paso, Texas, to Managua, Nicaragua. In a six-month journey from Capetown to Cairo in 1959, he chugged along, traveling as few as seven miles a day. He and his entourage of forty-one Airstream trailers braved sandstorms, blown-out tires, busted axles, and hateful roads. In doing so, Byam helped popularize the idea that metal stagecoaches were an escape from senior ennui and decrepitude.

"For some, checkers, clubs, gardening and grandchildren are not enough," Byam once remarked. "Out of this boredom, ailments are born."

Byam was by no means a bashful and retiring senior. He loved to drive around his company shouting out orders to employees through a megaphone. "To some he was the patron saint of trailer travel, free enterprise, invention and salesmanship," wrote John Huey in a feature story about Byam and his legacy in the *Chicago Tribune*. "To others he was a foul-mouthed nudist with a predilection for female members of the club." Byam was an early example of the RVer as gray-haired rebel. Those journeys were his fight against the notion that trailers were marginal; Byam, who had a curious lifelong aversion to stationary trailers and "mobile home" parks, attracted only affluent couples on his long journeys. To this day, the cult of the Airstream borders on religious fervor.

Byam complicated the image of the trailer starting in the Great Depression, but it took somewhat longer for motor homes to acquire a mixed high-low reputation. After World War II, veterans and their baby boomer children took to the roads with a big boost from their increased paid vacation time and federally funded highway improvements. Intense paranoia about nuclear incineration led some Americans to build secret fallout-resistant Quonset huts and bomb shelters in their houses, while others, instead of bracing for the apocalypse, embraced a "live for today" camping ethos. In their RVs, they escaped to the mountains to fish and camp their fears away. RV sales boomed while "trailer towns" multiplied in national parks. Into this environment slipped a crafty entrepreneur named John Hanson, who believed that hedonism, relaxation, and family vacations were basic human rights at a time when the Russians might incinerate all America at any moment. "You can't take sex, booze, and weekends away from the American people," Hanson reportedly said.

This self-described "dumb farmer from Iowa" was actually a mortician by trade. In the late 1950s he and a few other investors took over a troubled travel trailer manufacturing company, drastically reduced costs, and switched the company's focus to mass-produced and cheap motor homes: a revolutionary idea at the time. To make a bold statement, he scrubbed the original name of the company, Modernistic, and changed it in honor of the Native American tribe whose name blessed the seventy-two-mile-long waterway near the company headquarters in Forest City, Iowa: the Winnebago River. In 1967, Winnebago started rolling out sixteen- to twenty-seven-foot-long motor homes retailing for as little as five thousand dollars. They were within the reach of the working class for the first time. He sold his motor homes for 50 percent of the cost of popular competing brands.

Hanson called his three most popular models "America's first family of motor homes." Over the years, low prices didn't always protect the company. The RV industry has always been vulnerable to economic downturns, and its reliance on fossil fuels adds another degree of uncertainty. Hanson left the company in 1972. But the gas crisis of the late 1970s harmed Winnebago so severely that Hanson, who was suffering from cataracts and well into his sixties, halted his retirement and returned in 1979. He slashed staff and cut costs. "I came in just like Wyatt Earp," he said. "I just lined 'em up and shot 'em down." Over the years, Hanson was so successful that *Winnebago* became a generic term for all motor homes, just as *Band-Aid* has come to mean any small disposable bandage and *Jell-O* stands for all wiggly, translucent desserts. He maintained a role in the company until he died at age eighty-eight.

In his way, Hanson helped fulfill the populist promise of William "Adirondack" Murray by spreading the consumerist camping spirit to working people who were once shut out of this elitist pastime in the first half of the twentieth century. But Hanson's great success came with a cost for the prideful lovers of motor homes, which lost some of their early prestige. In his book *Winnebago Nation*, James Twitchell speculates that the onslaught of cheap mass-produced Winnebagos on American highways contributed to a widespread cultural cynicism about RVs, including a snobby association between motor homes and "middle-class uncouthness." In 1954, prior to the low-cost RV boom, the Desi Arnaz and Lucille Ball movie *The Long, Long Trailer* showed just how wrong an RV trip could go, but the targets of the screwball comedy were the hapless drivers, not the eponymous and luxurious trailer itself. Eight years later, John Steinbeck's *Travels with Charley*, an affectionate memoir commemorating his adventures with a standard poodle in a tricked-out 1960 GMC pickup camper named Rocinante, put RVing in a mostly positive and nostalgic light, harkening back to the spirit of the original auto campers. While Steinbeck's son claimed that his father invented many of the interviews and encounters in the book—"He just sat in his camper and wrote all that [expletive]"—*Travels* was a warmhearted portrayal of life on the road.

Compare those loving accounts to the withering and satirical portraits of RV life since the late 1960s. The Winnebago has received the brunt of that pop cultural aggression. Even the punk-thrash band the Dead Kennedys, whose other targets included Nazi punks, corrupt and brutal police departments, the homophobic Florida orange juice pitchwoman Anita Bryant, and the smiling, mass-murdering Khmer Rouge leader Pol Pot, took the time to call out RVs in their 1982 song "Winnebago Warrior." Lead singer Jello Biafra rages against those who dared to burn "thirty gallons to the mile," slaughter innocent fish, feed Doritos to bears, and block traffic while making a show of "roughing it in the great outdoors." Every so often, Biafra's anger reaches such a pitch that his adenoidal singing gives way to a series of furious yodels, screeches, and grunts; he sounds like a coyote being strangled with a length of piano wire. More often than not, the motor home, when it pops up in movies and TV shows, adds a satirical flourish to the plot. The teacher turned drug kingpin Walter White used his Fleetwood Bounder recreational vehicle as a meth lab on wheels in the TV series *Breaking Bad*, which ran from 2008 through 2013. This motor home is called "Crystal Ship." Like White himself, the RV is hard-angled, square, and newly repurposed for evil doings.

Recent developments in the RV world have complicated the picture that so many of us non-RVers, including Jello Biafra, have of them. There are "green" solar-powered and biodiesel RVs; shrunken, streamlined RVs that defy the shoe box aesthetic of the past; and posh RVs that are more luxurious and outrageous than the Pierce-Arrows that wowed crowds at Madison Square Garden. Yet the scornful stereotypes persist. As my RV journey continued, I was coming to realize just how much the negative portrayals of motor homes and their owners, in movies such as Alexander Payne's *About Schmidt*, had colored my views. Now that I'd spent some time in an RV, and dwelled among their users, I came to an uncomfortable realization: I was becoming fascinated, and maybe infatuated, with motor homes.

Was I suffering from Stockholm syndrome or overcoming prejudice? I caught myself peeping into their windows, chatting up their drivers, and saying things that my young self would have found incomprehensible, such as "Where'd you get that snazzy sticker map of the United States?" "How many pullouts do you have in that thing?" and "That's the niftiest fifth wheel I've ever seen." I made these observations and posed these questions straight up, without a trace of irony or self-consciousness. Motor homes that had once sent me into peals of hideous laughter now seemed like boxes of potential and storehouses of future journeys and memories. I've met a few deranged and mean backpackers, but almost every RVer on this trip had been welcoming to us. I was envious of their road tales, analog social networkers, and lack of pretension.

It also occurred to me that a motor home would be so much more affordable than a house for my family. If I could find a hidden place to park it, well out of sight from any obstructionist hippie types who might hector me about my lifestyle choices, I might run out and get one now.

My only other reservation has to do with the fact that RVing is damned difficult. In backcountry camping, the planning, chores, and vigilance are constant. In a similar way, RVing punishes you for any slipup. We neglected to dump the gray water in the appointed disposal hole, so it vomited forth from the sink and flooded our floor. We ran the heater too long, so the propane dwindled to nothing. The second night, when a cold front blew into Sedona, all of us crammed into the queen bed for a while, but there was so much kicking and fidgeting that I gathered my things and slept out in the kitchenette. I chattered under a half dozen blankets, thinking, *If we were going to freeze our asses off anyway, why did we pay a thousand dollars for a week in a motor home when we might as well be tenting outside for a fraction of that cost?* The forced-air heating system blasted into the bedroom for the most part, warming Julianna and Amy, and leaving the rest of the unit cold enough to freeze the balls off a brass baboon. To make matters worse, my wife kept leaping up in the middle of the night to turn the heat down some more—"It's too hot and stuffy in here!"—while I lay under a succession of comforters, recalling scenes from Jack London's "To Build a Fire" (in which the protagonist, a traveler in the Yukon who is unsuccessful at building his fire, slowly succumbs to hypothermia) and gradually losing sensation in my toes.

When I woke up that morning, it was just as I feared: the water in the RV had frozen solid. I rushed to assess the damage. Outside the motor home, it hurt to breathe. The temperature was twenty-nine degrees. I could not detach the hose from the motor home because ice had cemented it in place. Now we knew we had to flee Sedona for warmer climes, yet there was no escape. Unable to figure out what to do, I rushed into the men's room to warm my hands and devise a plan. Someone was using the bathroom stall just behind me, and from the sound of it, he was having a really hard time in there. My thoughts were racing. I couldn't stop worrying about how I was going to extricate us from the ice. At last the man, with one great roar of effort, resolved his difficulties, flushed, stepped out of the stall, and stood right next to me, a great big, burly fellow washing his hands. "Did your pipes freeze up?" I blurted out.

"Did my *what*?" he said, turning red.

"I . . . Oh, my God. So sorry! I wasn't talking about the pipes inside your body! I meant the pipes in your motor home? Did they freeze up last night?"

He gave me a long, concerned look. "I've got a travel trailer. No water hookup. Don't tell me you hooked your water up on a cold night like this! Not a good idea. Didn't you read the forecasts?"

"What am I supposed to do now? I can't get the hose out of the motor home! It's stuck."

The stranger sighed and followed me out to our RV. He reached into his overcoat and pulled out a long pair of tongue-and-groove pliers with a blue and spongy coating on the handle. (Apparently people in RV parks like to walk around with pliers in their pockets.)

"What," I said, "is that thing?"

"This is called a Channellock," he said. "It's the thing to have."

In an instant, the kindly fellow had disconnected my frozen garden hose from the motor home. He urged us to leave Sedona soon and drive around to break up the ice in our water tanks. Right away we packed up and drove hard for Lost Dutchman State Park, at the foot of the Superstition Mountains.

En route, it occurred to me that, if you let them, RVs could really overwhelm your identity by altering your thought patterns. Hateful things can become your best friends. Take, for instance, Walmart. Until this trip, I would have fought like a honey badger if anyone had tried to build one of those stores in Santa Cruz, where they are extremely unpopular. Now my family whooped with joy every time a Walmart came into view.

My relief and happiness were by design. When I stopped at a general store to buy something, our RV hogged two or three spaces and I felt self-conscious, especially if we stayed for more than a few minutes. Walmart doesn't care how many spaces you take up or how long you linger. Many Walmarts allow RVs to "boondock" camp there free of charge, in the hope that RV campers will buy propane, gas, and haircuts from them. These days, "full hook-up" campgrounds can charge anywhere from $20 to $65 a night, depending on the location. Walmart has become a very big deal for RVers of modest means, though some well-off but frugal people, including Supreme Court justice Clarence Thomas and his wife, Virginia "Ginni" Thomas, also sleep in those parking lots. The Thomases like to gallivant in their forty-foot Prevost motor home, which they bought used in 1999; never mind that Supreme Court justices make on average about $213,000 a year. "Actually, it's one of our favorite things to do," Ginni told the *Wall Street Journal*, adding that it's their way to "get a little shopping in, see part of real America. It's fun!"

We never slept at a Walmart because I was too scared of burning through our propane on freezing nights in a place with no electric hook-ups. Part of it also had to do with the relentless pace we were keeping on the trip. When we arrived at the base of the Superstition Mountains, it was so lovely that we wanted to stay there forever. At the visitors' center at Lost Dutchman State Park, a bubbly full-time RVing couple named Pat and Steve did their best to make us slow down our hectic pace. Steve, a six-foot-four retired grocery distribution clerk, was sixty. He had a double-bitted coffee-dunker mustache, square-rimmed glasses, and a bald pate. His wife, Patricia, a diminutive former saleswoman for a kitchenware company, was six years older. "He's my boy toy," she told me. The two of them wore matching beige State Parks vests. Steve and Pat were a comedy act on wheels. "We're the Bald and the Beautiful!" Steve said.

I admitted to them that life on the road was stressing us out. Amy and I were starting to bicker about everything. I also mentioned the frozen hose.

"But you got it fixed, didn't ya?" Pat said.

"Yes, but it made me feel helpless."

"That's because you have to be somewhere, don't you?" Steve said. "Just imagine what it would be like if you weren't on a strict schedule. If we break down, it just means we have to be somewhere for a couple of weeks." They went on to chide us for our relentless driving. With our rushing, we were missing the true appeal of the RVing life, they said. "When we're on the road, we always stop at two o'clock or two hundred miles, whatever comes first," Steve said. Mechanical problems become a cause for celebration. The two of them rhapsodized about their "happiest breakdowns," which they use as excuses to explore the places where the motor home gives out on them.

Using this strategy, they found a way to balance their wandering ways with their need to make friends and linger in a place long enough to know it well. Both of them knew the road would not go on forever. Little setbacks, including a hernia operation for him and a bout of kidney stones for her, reminded them they were not invulnerable. The couple was philosophical about the fact that they would one day have to come off the road. "In the meantime," Patricia told me, "we are in God's hands."

We tried to take their advice, linger for a while and get to know the desert around our RV camp. Lost Dutchman State Park occupies former Apache territory at the base of some ghostly frost-covered mountains, which looked like the wrecked remains of an old steam engine. The three of us left our motor home shining in the scrub brush with long-haired jackrabbits leaping in front of it. Julianna and I hung back while Amy hiked ahead of us at a brisk pace. An army of eyeless green giants cast long shadows in the dirt. These were the famous saguaro cactuses of Arizona. Bundles of black spikes were their epaulets. Their fluted columns caught the sun. One had a fat Sonoran raven bouncing on top.

A saguaro is like a tree turned inside out, with a green skin that rots away to reveal the bark within. Some of the long-dead ones looked like planks of driftwood. A few of these saguaro, which can live to be two hundred years old, were growing here as little green stumps when Abraham Lincoln was assassinated. Most likely they would still be here when Julianna was approaching median motor home–owning age and I was gone.

The age difference between me and my little daughter (forty-two years) is the same as that between me and my father. Around the time of this trip, which forced me to reckon with aging in unexpected ways, I was thinking more and more about the camping continuum from my father to me and from me to my daughter. For much too long I'd convinced myself that Julianna played no role in her own fate. I thought parents were like Play-Doh extruding machines. Press a button, and out comes a blob shaped like a starfish, a strand of pasta, a squiggle of color. Those blobs are our children. Press the wrong button, and out comes a shapeless mess.

It wasn't that simple. I had no idea how the campouts were going to change her outlook. She was going to take from them what she would. There was nothing I could really do about it except keep her safe. "You're *always* watching me," Julianna said as we tromped across the sand. "You're always thinking I'm going to fall. You have to back off a little." At that moment, as if on cue, she took a header and fell right on her chest, catching herself with her elbows. She got right back up, dusted herself off, and kept on hiking. "See?" she said. "I'm fine!"

Somehow, and without trying, we'd raised a budding transcendentalist who'd charged through mud puddles on trails because it was her grim obligation to have a natural experience, whether or not it was freezing cold outside. "Oh, no," she would say when a puddle came in view, "this is going to be so chilly," and then she'd rush right in. When we first started camping together, it was hard to get her to leave the car; she was much too afraid. Now she seemed just as comfortable outside as she did in our kitchen. This confidence translated into her life outside the campground. That year, she'd stood up to a bully at school, become more social, and taken lonely kids into her confidence like a surrogate adult. The camping trips and forest walks influenced her cosmology. "God is not a person, you know," she told me apropos of nothing during a random walk in a redwood forest not long before our motor home trip began. "Not a man or woman that you can see. God is a crystalized piece of magic air."

"A what?"

"Yes, made of crystal, and if you were to open a rock, you'd get a star, and if you opened a star, you would get a magic cloud." She explained, calmly, that the magic cloud stirred "chemicals and mud" into the first ocean life, kick-starting evolution. It was as good an explanation as any I'd ever heard. It's funny how those revelations can beam themselves into your mind when you stop hurrying.

Still, on this particular stop, the weather got so nasty out there in the desert that we had no choice but push onward. The wind was howling the next morning and the sky had a most peculiar shade of bruised green. Everywhere, people were jumping into their motor homes and clearing out. A campground volunteer urged me southward, toward Tucson, to escape the rotten weather. But when Amy and Julianna and I rolled off in that direction, we drove right into the storm. On a two-lane highway, the crosswinds made the motor home pitch and rock. The wind sneak-attacked us, punching the motor home in the nose and then rushing into its back and hitting us from the left and right. The RV's flimsy siding quaked. My pale ale rocked in the fridge. We'd forgotten to secure the overhead cabinets. Now they banged like the doors in a haunted house.

The wheels swerved ever closer toward the double-yellow lines. Nothing but a slender space separated me from eighteen-wheelers plowing past us at eighty miles an hour. A gust of air hit the motor home so squarely that I wondered if it would knock us on our side. In spite of the near gale-force conditions, larger motor homes were glaring their headlights into me, flashing them at me, and then passing me by, fearlessly, illegally, on the wrong side of the double yellows. One motor home after another sprayed arcs of filthy water on our windshield as they sped past. Urging myself to speed up, I made the motor home fishtail along the highway. We windsurfed for a dozen feet. The skittish steering wheel trembled in my hands. Julianna and Amy were speechless now. Somehow the tires corrected course before we could bash into the guardrail.

When we arrived at the soaked green cactus-covered hills near the entrance of Saguaro National Park, my face was pale and my limbs had not stopped shaking. This was no longer pleasure camping. We were escaping danger and hostile forces, not boredom. I was, if anything, more afraid than I'd ever been at any moment in the camping project. My scary naked night in the Santa Cruz Mountains was nothing compared to the helplessness I'd felt in that storm.

The Gilbert Ray Campground was a snug harbor. Other campers waved when we got out and started preparing our fire. One group was gathered outside a teardrop trailer resting under heavy blankets in a circle of beach chairs, drinking beer and playing Elvis Costello's *Armed Forces* on a record player.

That night, I slept feverishly and imagined that something heavy-footed was clomping around on top of our RV, tapping the windows, throwing heaps of slop on the roof. When the sun rose up and I walked outside, I found the desert transformed. The storm had left snowdrifts on the ground and ash-white skullcaps on the saguaros. Snow held fast in sticky pollen clumps on every stalk and rock and blade of grass.

A few snowflakes were falling when I got out to walk around. They lit down on my tongue. Outside, it looked like a miracle. The distant mountains glowed. Amy and Julianna were asleep inside. In a moment, I would wake them up and we would walk around out here in the frost. Julianna would build snowpeople and throw globs of the stuff at me. She would work the white powder into her hair and twist her ringlets until the powder turned to water. Then we'd get our things together, roll out toward Mesa, and return the motor home.

For a moment, though, I stood there in the chill with a few other early risers in the RV park. A few feet away from me, a full-grown man and woman were making snow angels. All across the campground, doors were swinging open and people were stumbling out. None of the campers said anything; everyone was too dumbstruck to make chitchat that morning. But there were lots of knowing glances among strangers that signified "Can you believe this is happening?" In spontaneous moments like this, when everyone leaves the rigs behind and gathers in one place to watch a spectacle, the motor home life more than justifies itself. Our collective noses turned blue and our fingers got numb but no one seemed to care. Together we watched the white gather on the motor homes and melt in rivulets across our windshields.

A Dose of Enchantment

And for the hours, it will be what o'clock I say it is.
—Horace Kephart, *Camping and Woodcraft*, 1906

I don't go in for a cranialsacral massage. Hydrotherapy? Please keep your hose away from me. Melatonin, serotonin, Saint-John's-wort? Happy pills merely bloat me. I've never tried Effexor, but I doubt it would have much Effect. Hypnotherapy makes me regressive; sorry, but I hated second grade the first time. Tom the therapist is helping, but I have to keep coming back for more, every other week, a junkie whose crack pipe is confession. Let me tell you what works for me: the Hoh Rain Forest on the Olympic Peninsula, two hundred–odd miles west of Seattle. If the whole world looked and operated like this ageless place, there would be no stress, no distemper, no gunplay—just billions of people sitting cross-legged in a clearing, listening to the wind rattle through the hollows of a Sitka spruce. Doctors are catching on to the fact that the woods can cure us. I hear they're starting to prescribe a walk in the forest instead of antidepressants. We're returning to the ethos of the nineteenth century, when nature prescriptions were considered normal, not kooky. Even a quick glance at a photo of a forest can provide some mental benefits. It's only a matter of time before pharmacists develop an Rx code for setting up a tent.

Never in my life have I seen or heard of a place like the Hoh. I was out there with Amy and Julianna one misty June day with Gordon Hempton, a famous acoustic ecologist who explores the world looking for and record-ing unique natural sounds. The boulders, trees, and logs wore baggy sweaters of jasper-green mosses, herbs, and epiphytes. Shelf mushrooms grew in crooked platforms. The branches and portly trunks of Sitka spruces had the most elaborate beards and hairdos I'd seen on any plant life, their mosses fashioned into weaves, permanents, and cornrows. Our boots brushed licorice and cinnamon ferns, and we stepped over fallen half-rotted trees called nurse logs, which have saplings sprouting from them. Sometimes I saw weird little squirrels in the crannies of alders, their fur the color of soot. Out on the peninsula, inscrutable mice sleep under red rocks and can jump ten feet if so inclined.

Hempton is finicky about natural silence; if a plane flies overhead, it screws up his recordings. He likes the Hoh because it abounds with wind and animal and water sounds. I made arrangements to meet him there because he specializes in naturally silent places, and says they are getting harder to find by the year. I don't mean silent as in all the wildlife is stock-still, holding its breath. I mean silent as in the "absence of mechanical noises," including plane whoosh and generator hum. Hempton had a pen-etrating stare, a three-day beard, and a survival hat with a loop of twine around it. His boots were scuffed. He was smart and super-serious, silly and childlike all at the same time. He rubbed a buttercup on Julianna's chin to assess how much she liked butter. Her chin turned yellow, which meant she liked butter a good deal.

Hempton, son of a Coast Guard captain, moved through the forest like an enlisted man, shoulders square, posture straight. A homemade camou-flage bag hung across his left shoulder. He spends a lot of time humping heavy gear through the woods, so he has avoided most of the dry rot that makes aging people in America look wrecked; I mistook Hempton for a spry fifty-year-old, though he was sixty-two at the time. I know I've said this many times in the course of this book, but I will repeat it once more for good measure: camping keeps you young.

Sitka spruce rose up two hundred feet above us. No loggers ever cut down trees this far up the valley, so the Hoh looked primeval, mystical; it was easy to imagine a brontosaurus family on the cobbles near the river. Hempton at one point high-fived some deer ferns and paused to listen. After a while of tramping, the four of us arrived at the base camp Hempton had picked for us, 1.2 miles from the Hoh Rain Forest visitors' center, where we'd met him that morning for the guided walk. He'd told us that this spot, overlooking the river, was his favorite camping place in the Hoh Basin because you could watch elk drink at dusk and see freshwater otters splash in the froth. Julianna and Amy were tired and footsore, so Hempton and I left them at the base camp and walked deeper into the Hoh.

He was going to show me a sanctuary of quiet. As we walked along, I heard no plane sounds of any kind. Hikers passed from time to time, but they kept their voices hushed. For the next hour or so, I heard only the trills, *meep-meeps*, and upslurred *pee-shweets* of the Pacific coast flycatcher and the bass lines of the Hoh River, which flowed just south of where we walked. Sometimes Hempton would stop to admire some natural riff I hadn't noticed until he pointed it out. "Mmmm-hmmm," he said at one point. "That's a nice combination of wind and river roar." In another reach of forest, I heard a sound like babies gurgling in the treetops. Elephants trumpeted. It was just the wind knocking spruces, moving boughs, making timbers creak. Trees sang off-key. Sometimes they cleared their throats, grumbled, coughed, and burped. "Listen to the sour stomach of the woods," Hempton said as we walked deeper into the forest. We arrived at our destination, an elk trail through an opening in a spruce whose roots vaulted upward to form a nave just wide and tall enough for Hempton and me to stand inside it.

Hempton stood before the spruce opening and told me in a polite but certain voice, "Beyond this point there will be *no talking.*"

The elk trail portal is 3.2 miles from the Hoh Rain Forest visitors' center. Hempton has made no effort to hide the location. He's even posted the GPS coordinates online: 47° 51.959′ N, 123° 52.221′ W pinpointing the stone that marks the spot. But no one was there when we arrived, and I noticed only subtle indications that humans had visited the place recently, including a couple of boot prints on mushy grass.

We stepped through the spruce in search of the stone Hempton used to mark his silence sanctuary, and walked on soft mud through matted moss, cinnamon ferns, and huckleberry. I heard a blend of insect and bird wings, wind-rustled ferns, and the steady *droop-droop-droop* of water. We stepped over logs and slippery roots that formed a footbridge leading around a dark puddle. Hempton walked me out to a nurse log on the forest floor. In a moment I saw a red, vaguely pyramid-shaped red rock on a bed of lichen.

I was expecting something along the lines of a Stonehenge dolmen, but the stone could have fit in my palm.

For the next few minutes a dome of sound enclosed me. Birdcalls suggested the shape of the sky. Hempton had named this piece of forest One Square Inch of Silence because he wanted it to be a silence sanctuary, a place to defend quiet. Hempton told me he'd chosen the place in part because the elk path was already there and he didn't want to encourage anyone to trample a new trail; he'd also chosen it because it was the first place where he couldn't hear generator hum when walking away from the Hoh visitors' center.

While I was standing in the sanctuary, feeling floaty, Hempton fox-walked behind me, reached down, plucked the marker stone off the log, and dropped it into my palm. I was so surprised I wanted to shout, but that was forbidden. "For me?" I asked him in mime. I felt honored but sheepish. It seemed so wrong to carry away the marker—which shows how much I bought into the idea of this patch of land's being a sanctuary.

When we'd passed through the Sitka portal to return to the trail, Hempton let me know it was okay to speak again. "The stones have become powerful reminders," he said. "You know, quiet is the birthplace of truth and beauty. If you find yourself in a noisy place, you may ask yourself, *Why don't I feel this way all the time? How can I bottle this?* Well, there you are. Now you have the rock."

The name One Square Inch of Silence came to Hempton in 1989, when he was in a wilderness area and heard the "great roar" of an airplane. "A single origin of noise, for example, a jet, can drag a cone of noise over a thousand square miles," Hempton said. Following the same logic, making a stand to protect just "one square inch of silence" in a beautiful forest can protect one thousand square miles from human-generated noises, which works out to be about three-quarters of the landmass of Olympic National Park. I will admit that the concept doesn't make a whole lot of sense to me, which is why I like it. I'm all for quixotic projects. There is much more that I could say about his One Square Inch project, but for me it's enough to know that Hempton loves this place, and was willing to make a 174-mile round-trip from his home in Port Angeles just to show those woods to me.

We were hiking back toward my family, me with the stone in my hand, and we were making good speed, when Hempton stopped without warning.

I almost ran right into him.

I thought he was going to comment about a sound blend he'd noticed, but now he turned as if to confront me, holding his palms up. A glow came over him like someone was holding a sodium vapor light in front of his face. I could tell he was going to lay something heavy on me.

"Are you ready to change?" Hempton asked me.

"Yes!" I replied.

"Are you ready to change your life and everything about you?"

"Yeah," I reiterated.

Hempton took a step back and nodded. "You're ready to change," he said, still looking me straight in the face. "Which means you're ready to be a listener. Because, if you're willing to listen, you have to be open."

For a while I stood there stunned, because on the one hand, I had no idea what he was talking about, and yet, intuitively, it made sense. I've always wanted to change. That's one of the reasons I camp, not just to escape but also to disrupt myself. Hempton waited for me to recover. Then he gestured toward the bushy swags of moss, the light flashing on a maple leaf fern. "If everything about you is open, then *this* is the perfect place to be."

When I reunited with my family on the Hoh River sandbar, I pressed the red stone into Julianna's hands. She looked honored, surprised, but also taken aback. What was this for?

Hempton and Julianna watched the river for a while, but he had to get ready for a family celebration. We said our good-byes and off he went.

Something came over us when we were camping on that river. Julianna had fashioned toy boats out of leaves and bits of bark. The river pulled them down, and they crashed in the currents.

No one could find us now. No cell reception here. No signifiers of time. My cell phone's date-keeping function claimed it was May 1980. The white noise of the water blotted out everything else. Sitting in gumbo mud, I watched my daughter heave stones in the river. She lingered in the river muck and daubed fine grains of dust all over her face until her teeth shone. I smeared my face with dirt, and both of us crouched there, looking at the water, and she tried to show me otters, but I couldn't see them.

During our campout along the river, we did nothing, read nothing, saw nothing, and nothing happened. The sunscreen, granola, pasta primavera, and toothpaste all started tasting like one another after a while. Bits of instant coffee started working their way into the mac and cheese, formed floaters in the drinking water, and spilled on my sleeping bag, and every-

thing had a horrible aftertaste. There were molar-shattering bits of maca-
roni all over the stockpot. But we were beyond caring. Julianna and I
danced like mad people on the sandbar, circling, occasionally passing each
other off to imaginary barn dance partners, chanting, barefoot, shoving
rocks out of the way, keening, trilling, our decibel levels rising, our voices
synced, the two of us sputtering nonsense, off-key, croaking "Hoo-de-
dooh-de-dooh-de-dooh!"

So this was what truly silent camping was like: a whole bunch of river
noise, with our shouting right on top of it and the river covering our shouts.
We'd roar, and the river would roar over us. Silence isn't silent; I had to
wear earplugs just to block the Hoh out at night in my sleeping bag. Yet
the ambient sound was so loud it canceled out all negative distractions.
Our bodies, our brains, were so used to antagonism and strain that the
absence of these things became, perversely, a thrill for us. My wife is often
on edge in camp with me, and for good reason. I once set up a tent with
her on a beautiful field that, as we soon found out, was perilously close to
a rifle range. But the Hoh River sluiced her usual worries away. She looked
as stony and content as I've ever seen her. Glacial melt clouded the Hoh
River, which flowed past us at a volumetric rate of 2,538 cubic feet per second. It scoured our sandbank, which formed a tapering finger. In the distance, the fiery crown of Mount Olympus rose over us.

We remained for two days after Hempton left us there. I hadn't brought
enough food for Julianna's first-ever backpacking trip. We were down to
nut crumbs soon. Then we were down to nut dust. Julianna squirted a plug
of Smucker's strawberry spread into her mouth from an economy-size
squeeze bottle, and the sight of this made me gag. Julianna shrugged.
"What can you do?" she told me. "This is camping."

This was not the final trip in the camping project, yet it felt like a cul-
mination and a tying of the knot. There was something about the river
whoosh, that cold, consuming static that reminded me of time itself. The act
of transmission was almost complete. Father to son. Son to daughter. I knew
that when the trip was over, my usual neuroses, and Julianna's ordinary
concerns, would slither up behind us again. Hempton told me the marker
stone from his silent sanctuary would help keep me calm, but I know my
own brain too well to believe this would work. To keep the snake at bay, I
would just have to keep on camping, indefinitely, until it took. Or maybe it
never would. Maybe the whole point is you've got to keep returning.

The last night in the Hoh Rain Forest, I woke up early. The natural yet discordant and somewhat headache-inducing sounds of my wife and daughter snoring in their sleeping bags brought to mind a campout I took with my father in the wilderness near Mammoth Lakes. It was not supposed to happen this way, but everyone else in the family backed out of the campout for various reasons. I was thirteen years old, and my father was fifty-five.

We didn't speak much on that trip. I did not have any words to share with him, so I tried to absorb the scenery around me. It was almost too much to take in: the specks of mica in the granite, flashing in the sun when we walked by; the hawks; the ice sheets; the quaking aspens; the woodpeckers and the noises they made; and how the sky felt on our necks and noses. We leaned our packs on a rock and listened to the wind blow branches together. It sounded like rain. I took in a combination of sights, smells, and sensations that whirled together until I couldn't separate them anymore. I call it camping synesthesia, when the senses get so jumbled up. John Muir knew all about it. He once said that flower bells rang with sweet church music in the mountains. Henry David Thoreau talked about the "delicious evening" at the pond, "when the whole body is one sense, and imbibes delight through every pore."

My father was already bald. When you're in your teens, people over thirty seem old, people over forty are ancient, and my father was in a whole other category. He was stomping through the mud in his flat-bottomed Korean War army boots, and using his olive-drab flak jacket as his windbreaker. His footprints were craters. As we started to prepare the campsite, clearing the sticks and poky rocks, laying out the pup tent, resting the clunky old gas stove on a flat-topped log, I regretted that we'd never spent this kind of time together before. Now we were sitting on a log, breathing in, pounding tent spikes with a rock, counting stars, and getting ready to eat our disgusting dinner.

Our main course was Kraft Squeez-A-Snak, a shelf-stable and eminently vomitus cheese product that came in eight-inch plastic tubes, each with a tight and puckered sphincteresque aperture through which you'd force the alleged cheese product when you squeezed with all your might, releasing a flatulent *pluffft* sound. On that trip, my father made me hold my stale and broken Triscuits and Wheat Thins oh so carefully beneath the X-shaped opening, twisting the tube just so, and allowing the slurry to flop onto my crackers. Horace Kephart would have gagged on this food. Yet I was, incomprehensibly, happy. Something about the slimy cheese, the wind, the cold, and the meadow's steady seep through the floor of our tent and into our sleeping bags added to the feeling of transport.

At least this is true in retrospect. In case you haven't noticed, most camping trips improve over time, unless something truly tragic and horrible happens to you out there. Besides, fine dining and fluffed pillows would have killed the mood. My father has catholic tastes (though he's Jewish). He loves Tom Stoppard plays and cruise ship impressionists, Barbara Cook and feathered Vegas showgirls. He's equally fond of Mahler's Symphony No. 1 and Abba's *Gold* album. He gets loud and wild sometimes. But something about the woods reduces him to stillness. A different side of him comes out.

The night wore on, my father fell fast asleep, and the moon lifted over the Minarets. I remember thinking, *I want for nothing. I'm his son, he's my dad. Everyone in my family is alive and accounted for, the evening will be pleasant, and tomorrow will be beautiful. We have nothing here, and everything, and there is no rush, and we're strangers to this place, we lay no claim to it, but I'll hold it in me. Forty years from now, when I can't sleep, I'll think of this campout. Right now I'm alive on earth and soon I'll close my eyes and sleep on my Therm-a-Rest, and my whole life's lined up the way it's supposed to be*, and that's when my father started in with his goddamn snoring.

For the next hour, as the noises got worse, I took back every sentimental thing I'd thought and said about him and the trip, and it became unbearable. For a while, I resented my father. My fury at him was incandescent. How dare he keep me awake like this? It sounded like a brace of elephant seals belching on a Northern California beachhead. Every few minutes, the snores got louder and more elongated, each snore stretching, growing, *Rowwg! Ploot! Rowwg! Ploot!* over and over. I finally woke him up to complain about the noise. He apologized, went back to sleep, and snored some more. After a while, the snores began to mimic speech until it sounded like my dad was having a Samuel Beckett–type soliloquy in the tent: "Who? Me? Who? Me? Who? Me! WHOOOOOOOOOOOOOOOOOO! MEEEEEEEEEEEEEEEEEEEE!"

My brain lit up, fully engaged. I hardly slept. I crawled out of my tent and watched the sun go up, lighting the tops of gigantic cinder cones, great mounds of chocolate-colored rock above a stream that widened every so often into emerald pools. Each pool contained stones the size of grape-fruits, a few twigs, and one or two golden trout. After a long while of standing in this place, with no other hikers anywhere, a shadow fell on me. My dad was out taking a morning walk. He apologized once again for the snores and the stomach noises.

Then he reached in his pack and took out a log of shrink-wrapped shelf-stable deli meat. Extra food! He'd packed and forgotten it. My father pulled out a pig sticker of a knife, sliced a wedge off the summer sausage, and handed it to me. It was hard and shiny, like linoleum. I could barely get my teeth in it, or swallow it. It was salty, greasy, indigestible, but in that moment, with my father and the mountains behind it, it was the most delicious food I'd ever eaten. I'm lying—the sausage made me gag, but the context and the scenery made it almost palatable. I'd like to say we had a conversation to match the surroundings, or that we shared a statement of intent, a grandiose gesture, a secret, an aphorism, a reason, but we weren't thinkers, we weren't philosophers, we had no secrets, and there was nothing to add, no issues to discuss. Instead, we climbed a cinder cone.

My father found a path to the top and waited at the halfway point. I hiked all the way up to the summit. At the top, I saw that someone had left a little trail that was perfect for sliding. I sat down with my feet in front of me. As I fell forward, the pebbles rolled me down the hill, faster, forcing me to use sticks and my boot heels as brakes. Sliding down the cone, I couldn't imagine anything outside the woods. School was starting in a week, and I would go back to my endless succession of woebegone crushes, my struggles in class, getting picked last for everything, and forgetting my locker combination, and it didn't matter. My life before the campout was an Etch a Sketch mess of loops and squiggles. It was as if someone had got-ten hold of the screen and shaken it clear. Perhaps we campers are looking for the same thing in our car camps and motor homes, in our pup tents and safari tents, in a guided bushwhack through the Adirondacks. I'm talking about a sense of erasure, a complete whiteout, the kind I experi-enced with my father all those years ago on the slopes of the Eastern Sierra. I've been trying to get back to it ever since.

NOTES

PROLOGUE: UNDER THE STARS

1   Leonard Cohen: Leonard Cohen, "Anthem," on *The Future* (Columbia, 1992), CD.

2   "Conventions faded out": William James Stillman, *The Autobiography of a Journalist*, vol. 1 (London: Grant Richards, 1901), 211.

2   The first Americans: See Peter Nabokov and Robert Easton, *Native American Architecture* (New York: Oxford University Press, 1989), for elaboration.

3   As Cindy Aron wrote in her book: Cindy Aron, *Working at Play: A History of Vacations in the United States* (New York: Oxford University Press, 1999), 144.

3   An estimated fifty million people camp every year: My source is the Outdoor Foundation's 2014 camping report, accessible at http://www.outdoorfoundation .org/pdf/research.camping.2014.pdf.

3   "tent butler" who roasted your s'mores for you: See marketing materials for the Paws Up resort at http://www.pawsup.com/pdf/luxury-camping.pdf.

1: HELP ME, HENRY

5   "How many a man": Henry David Thoreau, *Walden* (1854; repr., New York: Vintage Books, 1991), 88.

6   *Walden*, published in 1854, sold briskly during its first month: see William E. Cain, ed., *A Historical Guide to Henry David Thoreau* (Oxford: Oxford University Press, 2000), 43.

6   sold an average of three hundred copies annually: See Robert D. Richardson, "Walden's Ripple Effect: One Hundred Fifty Years After Its Publication, Henry David Thoreau's Meditation Remains the Ultimate Self-Help Book," *Smithsonian Magazine* online, August 2004, p. 2, http://www.smithsonianmag.com /people-places/waldens-ripple-effect-180940701/?no-ist=&page=2.

6   Robert Frost, another great champion: Nancy Lewis Tuten and John Zubizarreta, *The Robert Frost Encyclopedia* (Westport, CT: Greenwood Press, 2001), 358.

6   "In terms of board feet": William O. Douglas, quoted in Walter Harding, *The Days of Henry Thoreau* (New York: Alfred A. Knopf, 1965), xv.

6   Thoreau sometimes acted like a Puritan: See J. Baird Callicott, University of North Texas, and Priscilla Solis Ybarra, Rice University, "The Puritan Origins of the American Wilderness Movement," published online by the National Humanities Center, July 2001, http://nationalhumanitiescenter.org/tserve /nattrans/ntwilderness/essays/puritan.htm.

6   "It is very evident what mean and skulking lives": Thoreau, *Walden*, 8.

6   Wigglesworth . . . "fiends": Roderick Nash, *Wilderness and the American Mind*, 4th ed. (New Haven, CT: Yale University Press, 2001), 36.

6   "whooping," "roaring": Richard Cullen Rath, *How Early America Sounded* (Ithaca, NY: Cornell University Press, 2003), 148.

6   "a howling wilderness does not howl": Thoreau as quoted ibid., 150.

7   Deep in the forest, we might "settle ourselves, and work and wedge our feet": Thoreau, *Walden*, 80.

7   Thoreau sent more than a few copycats to their doom: Another notable and doomed wayfarer, following a darker version of a *Walden*-type adventure, was Everett Ruess, who vanished in the mesas of Escalante, Utah, in 1934, while on a solo camping journey, leaving behind no trace but his burros and the word NEMO scrawled on a cliff. Ruess's father, prior to his son's disappearance, wrote these words to his son: "I told some people the other day that in the hard times you were the true philosopher, to go off into the wilderness, close to God and heaven, and to drink in beauty and feed on hardship, and live like Thoreau on next to nothing." See Philip L. Fradkin, *Everett Ruess: His Short Life, Mysterious Death, and Astonishing Afterlife* (Berkeley: University of California Press, 2011), 93.

8   "I believe that water is the only drink for a wise man": Thoreau, *Walden*, 175.

8   Pine Mountain State Scenic Trail: Dan White, "Hike Pine Mountain, Channel Daniel Boone," *New York Times*, October 3, 2008, accessed at http://www .nytimes.com/2008/10/03/travel/escapes/03pine.html?_r=0.

9   "No, I can't say I was ever lost": This popular quote, attributed to Daniel Boone, appeared in Chester Harding, *My Egotistigraphy* (Cambridge, MA: Press of John Wilson and Son, 1866), 35–36.

9   Their brains are two thirds bigger: Krista Mahr, "Ten Things You (Didn't) Need to Know about Turkeys," *Time*, November 25, 2010, http://newsfeed.time.com /2010/11/25/10-things-you-didnt-need-to-know-about-turkeys/.

11   "the best youth's companion yet written in America," "like an invitation to life's dance": E. B White, *The Points of My Compass* (New York: Harper and Row, 1962), 16.

11   "front only the essential facts," "discover that I had not lived": Thoreau, *Walden*, 74–75.

11   "confirmed desperation": Thoreau, *Walden*, 9.

11   Maybe he felt guilty: Walter Harding, *The Days of Henry Thoreau* (New York: Alfred A. Knopf, 1965), 32.

12   a better swimmer, boater, walker: Ibid., 127.

12   so dexterous he could reach into a pile of pencils: Ibid.

12   "Ugly as sin": Nathaniel Hawthorne, as quoted ibid., 141.

13   transcendentalist radical: My paraphrase refers to the line "Both Thoreau boys were too transcendentalist to please him as potential sons-in-law," ibid., 100.

13   "Like the cocoanut": Ibid.

13   Thoreau was so tormented that he developed symptoms: Ibid., 136.

13   "That way went the flames with wild delight": Henry David Thoreau, *The Journal of Henry David Thoreau, 1837–1861*, introduction by John R. Stilgoe (New York: New York Review Books, 2009), 36.

13   Woodsburner: Ibid., 161.

13   "damned rascal," "flibbertigibbet": Ibid., 37.

13   not a very auspicious beginning: See John Pipkin, "Woods Burner: How a Forest Fire May Have Pushed Thoreau to Walden Pond," April 12, 2009, *Boston Globe*. Pipkin covers this topic in much more depth in his novel *Woods Burner* (New York: Doubleday, 2009).

14   That elegant and beautiful essay did more than just start transcendentalism: A note on my use of the word *transcendentalism* in this chapter: It is impossible to separate *Walden* from the spirit of transcendentalism that infused and inspired his experiment and thousands of other campouts to this day. The transcendentalists borrowed freely from the ideas of the European Romantics, who shared their obsession with individualism, nonconformity, metaphysics, and raptures in nature, and added a flinty, stubborn, puckish aspect. They believed in humankind's innate potential to attain a highly developed morality and spirituality through nature, and they thought this transport was available to anyone. Transcendentalists were all about ecstatic experiences in the woods, often with a strong moral underpinning, but they also believed in the importance of self-improvement and the need for righteous protest against forces of evil, including slavery. They were champions of direct experience and unpopular causes. Their belief systems are so insidious (in a good way) that it is almost impossible to live out our twenty-first-century lives without engaging with transcendentalism in some way. Transcendentalists have influenced everyone from John Muir to the Beat poets to Nelson Mandela and Gandhi to the entire city council of Santa Cruz, California; when that august body of civic leaders passed resolutions impeaching George W. Bush, banning nuclear waste and space junk, and standing up for the rights of sentient animals, they were carrying on the spirit of Thoreau.

14   "In good health": Ralph Waldo Emerson, "Nature," in *Nature: Addresses, Lectures* (Boston: James Munroe and Company, 1849).

14   *Fairhaven Hill*, or *The Weird Dell*: Harding, *Days of Henry Thoreau*, 122.

14   "unclean and stupid farmer": Thoreau, from "The Ponds" chapter in *Walden*, as quoted and contextualized ibid., 123.

15   The cabin cost him $28.12 to make: Thoreau, *Walden*, 41.

15   "Every thing was so thoroughly soaked," Byrd complained: William Byrd II of Westover, *The Dividing Line Histories of William Byrd II of Westover*, Kevin Joel Berland, ed. (Chapel Hill: University of North Carolina Press, 2013), 89. Note

to the reader: The "Dividing Line" manuscripts have an odd history. Apparently Byrd never allowed them to be printed in his lifetime. The first version came out in 1841, and various wildly different iterations have come out since then.

15   "too tender," "A clear sky, spangled with stars": Ibid., 90–91.

15   Byrd was a slave owner, sexual libertine, and a creepy sadist who humiliated his servants: For some details of Byrd's abuses, see Jan Lewis, *The Pursuit of Happiness: Family Values in Jefferson's Virginia* (Cambridge: Cambridge University Press, 1983), 38.

16   mountain men, "tangle leg," "tarantula juice": Cathy Luchetti, *Men of the West: Life on the American Frontier* (New York: W. W. Norton and Co., 2004), 26–27.

17   "Every aspect of the move to Walden was symbolic": Robert D. Richardson Jr., *Henry Thoreau: A Life of the Mind* (Berkeley: University of California Press, 1986), 152.

17   A copy of Walden . . . "Rather than love, than money, than fame": Henry David Thoreau, as quoted in John Krakauer, *Into the Wild* (New York: Anchor Books, 1996), 117.

18   "to live a primitive and frontier life though in the midst of an outward civilization": Thoreau, *Walden*, 12.

18   "a whimsy or else a good-for-nothing," "cold and snailish": Anti-Thoreau Timothy Thorough letter to the editor of the *New-York Tribune*, as quoted in Harding, *Days of Henry Thoreau*, 240.

18   not that daring . . . Donner Party . . . Frémont . . . Franklin's: See Richardson, *Henry Thoreau: A Life of the Mind*, 152.

19   "They came to steal": Thoreau quoted in Harding, *Days of Henry Thoreau*, 145.

19   "rapt in a revery": Thoreau, *Walden*, 91.

20   "Shoot 'em, you damn fool": Irritable trapper quoted in Harding, *Days of Henry Thoreau*, 185.

20   he had binges of conviviality: Ibid., 191–95.

21   delicious doughnuts: Ibid., 184. Note the attribution to scolds and skeptics. It is important to remember that Harding has a bit of a hedge when it comes to this oft-quoted reference; he makes sure to credit it to the "gossips" who were not simpatico with Thoreau's little experiment in the first place.

22   "Two or three hours' walking": See Thoreau, "Walking," 1862, full text at http://thoreau.eserver.org/walking1.html.

22   "Be rather the Mungo Park": Thoreau, *Walden*, 254, as quoted and contextualized in Richardson, "Walden's Ripple Effect," *Smithsonian*, August 2004.

22   "Why came ye here before your time": Henry David Thoreau, *The Maine Woods* (1854; repr., New York: Penguin Books, 1988), 86.

23   only piece of taxable property was a rowboat: Harding, *Days of Henry Thoreau*, 207.

25   "New-York [sic] has a wilderness within her own boarders": Henry David Thoreau, quoted in Philip Terrie, *Contested Terrain: A New History of Nature and People in the Adirondacks* (Syracuse, NY: The Adirondack Museum, 1997), 7.

2: EXPLORING THE SEWARDS WITH ZIPPY

26   "[This] country, which signifies the Dismal Wilderness": See Philip Terrie, *Forever Wild: A Cultural History of Wilderness in the Adirondacks* (Syracuse, NY: Syracuse University Press, 1994), 21.

26   "The ludicrous incident": Joel T. Headley, *The Adirondack, or Life in the Woods* (New York: Baker and Scribner, 1849), iii.

26   "I have generally gone into the woods ... depressed": S. H. Hammond, *Wild Northern Scenes* (New York: Derby Publishing, 1857), viewed as a Project Gutenberg e-book.

27   Eighteenth-century maps represented it as a blank: Jerry Jenkins with Andy Keal, *The Adirondack Atlas: A Geographic Portrait of the Adirondack Park* (New York: Syracuse University Press and the Adirondack Museum, 2004), 1.

28   John Brown bought two hundred thousand acres: Alfred Lee Donaldson, *A History of the Adirondacks, Volume 1* (New York: The Century Co., 1921), 129.

28   the literal dwelling places of the archdevil Azazel: Nash, *Wilderness and the American Mind*, 15.

29   "casts off his years": Ralph Waldo Emerson, "Nature," in *Nature: Addresses, Lectures*.

29   Even when adjusted for inflation: The best source for details about Adirondack guides, their supreme woodcraft skills, and their miserable compensation is Charles Brumley, *Guides of the Adirondacks: A Short Season. Hard Work. Low Pay* (Utica, NY: North Country Books, 1994), 153.

30   "eyes were clear and keen as those of a goshawk": L. E. Chittenden, as quoted in Alfred Lee Donaldson, *A History of the Adirondacks, Volume 2* (New York: The Century Co., 1921), 86.

30   "Suckin' for holes": Brumley, *Guides of the Adirondacks*, 153.

31   Ann Telfer (1896–1975), a hunting guide: Ibid., 161–62.

34   "a remarkable sense of loosened joints": "Adirondack Journal: Adirondack Travel," Adirondack Museum, http://www.adkmuseum.org/about_us /adirondack_journal/?id=87.

35   Failing to climb Mount Marcy ... "honest" John Cheney: See Terrie, *Contested Terrain*, 45.

35   the Reverend Joel T. Headley was such a shambolic mess: See Headley, *The Adirondack, or Life in the Woods*.

35   "drove [him] from the haunts": Ibid., iii.

35   "Einseitigkeit": Ibid., 21–22.

35   "Bewildered": Ibid., 39.

35   "brave old hemlock": Ibid., 29.

36   Romantic campers: I am using this broad term to describe nineteenth-century wilderness travelers who wished for wild abandon and direct experience in reaction to the forces of joyless rationalism. The Romantics had much in common with the transcendentalists, and influenced them, but the terms are not interchangeable. These nature lovers (and fearers) took their cues from European Romantic writers, and embraced creativity at the expense of "cause and effect or even logic," wrote John Gray in his introduction to Isaiah Berlin, *The*

Roots of Romanticism, 2nd ed. (Princeton, NJ: Princeton University Press, 1999). For them, reason was a kind of confinement, and freedom a triumph of will, Gray said. "They scorned peaceful coexistence and reasonable compromise; only the passionate expression of deeply held values, whatever the consequences . . . was for them truly human and worthy of admiration."

37   Bobcats, beavers: Jenkins with Keal, *The Adirondack Atlas*, is a useful source for information on Adirondack geography and ecology.

37   Dunning . . . could not tell you who was president of the United States: Brumley, *Guides of the Adirondacks*, 112.

37   whether the earth was round or flat: See the colorful if patronizing account in Fred Mather, *My Angling Friends: Being a Second Series of Sketches of Men I Have Fished With* (New York: Forest and Stream Publishing Co., 1901), 127.

37   Phelps . . . whose clothes "seemed to have been put on him once and for all, like the bark of a tree": Charles Dudley Warner, as quoted in Paul Schneider, *The Adirondacks: A History of America's First Wilderness* (New York: Henry Holt and Company, 1997), 171.

40   In 1858 one Adirondack campout dinner: F. S. Stallknecht and Charles E. Whitehead, "Sporting Tour in August, 1858," *Frank Leslie's Illustrated Weekly Newspaper* 6 (November 1858), as quoted in Philip G. Terrie, "Urban Man Confronts the Wilderness: The Nineteenth-Century Sportsman in the Adirondacks," *Journal of Sport History* 5, no. 3 (Winter 1978), published by University of Illinois Press.

41   stuffed dead ones: Both of these preserved animals are on display at the Adirondack Museum in Blue Mountain Lake.

41   The process was simple: Descriptions of shanty building came in large part from my phone interview with Philip Terrie, August 20, 2013.

43   Street described his "sickening shock": Alfred Billings Street as quoted by Terrie, *Contested Terrain*, 50.

43   When Harriet Beecher Stowe visited Niagara Falls: Pierre Burton, *Niagara: A History of the Falls* (Albany: State University of New York Press, 1992), 56.

46   Follensby Pond: The Nature Conservancy, which now owns the pond, refused my request to visit the site of Emerson's campout.

46   Philosophers' Camp: On this page, many of the descriptions of the historic campout come from Stillman, *Autobiography of a Journalist*, 196–225.

46   an unfamiliar kind of freshwater sponge: James Schlett, *A Not Too Greatly Changed Eden: The Story of the Philosophers' Camp in the Adirondacks* (Ithaca, NY: Cornell University Press, 2015), 90.

47   "Look to yourselves, ye polished gentlemen!": Ralph Waldo Emerson quoted in ibid., 86.

47   "It was an early moment in the development of the idea": Bill McKibben quoted in Martin Espinoza, "Conservancy Buys Slice of Adirondacks," *New York Times*, September 18, 2008.

47   Because of the guides' vigilance and care . . . "dissect[ing]": See William Stowe, "Transcendental Vacations: Thoreau and Emerson in the Wilderness," *New England Quarterly* 83, no. 3 (September 2010): 498.

47   an osprey, which "wheeled and screamed": Schlett, *A Not Too Greatly Changed Eden*, 87.

48   "Somebody will be shot!": Stillman, *Autobiography of a Journalist*, 202.

48   Certain expert guides: Terrie, *Contested Terrain*, 52.

48   these profligate hunting cheats: See Philip Terrie, book review of Douglas Brinkley, *The Wilderness Warrior: Theodore Roosevelt and the Crusade for America*, in *Adirondack Explorer*, January 2010, http://www.adirondackexplorer .org/book_reviews/the-wilderness-warrior-theodore-roosevelt-and-the -crusade-for-america.

49   Emerson satisfied his juvenile impulses: Schlett, *A Not Too Greatly Changed Eden*, 98.

49   Even in the mid-1800s, long before the invention of the satellite phone: See Stowe, "Transcendental Vacations," 500.

51   "There is practically nothing in the guides' own words": From Philip Terrie phone interview, August 20, 2013.

3: CAMPING THE CRAZY AWAY

56   "Now, in the North Woods, owing to their marvelous water communication": William H. H. Murray, *Adventures in the Wilderness, or Camp-Life in the Adirondacks* (1869; repr., Syracuse, NY: Adirondack Museum, Syracuse University Press, 1989), 18.

56   "It seems unquestioned now that the white man has developed the white plague": Ernest Thompson Seton, *Manual of the Woodcraft Indians: The Fourteenth Birch-Bark Roll* (Garden City, NY: Doubleday, Page and Company, 1915), xvi.

58   L-shaped ribs from dug-up spruce roots: Editors of Fine Woodworking, *Fine Woodworking on Bending Wood: 35 Articles Selected by the Editors of Fine Woodworking Magazine* (Newton, CT: Taunton Press, 1985), 109, with additional information from Joe Hackett, Adirondack fishing guide and guide boat history enthusiast.

60   "For the late Victorian bourgeoisie": T. J. Jackson Lears, *No Place of Grace: Antimodernism and the Transformation of American Culture, 1880–1920* (New York: Pantheon Books, 1981), 48.

60   Neurasthenics hated wide-open spaces: George M. Beard, *Practical Treatise on Nervous Exhaustion (Neurasthenia): Its Symptoms, Nature, Sequences, Treatment* (New York: E. B. Treat, 1888), 19.

61   Coca-Cola with real cocaine: Duane Schultz and Sydney Schultz, *A History of Modern Psychology*, 11th ed. (Boston: Cengage Learning, 2012), 133; see also James Hamblin, "Why We Took Cocaine Out of Soda," *Atlantic Monthly*, January 31, 2013.

61   "local spasms": Beard, *Practical Treatise on Nervous Exhaustion (Neurasthenia)*, 88.

61   in New York State alone: "The Problem of Finding an Adequate Cure for Our National Malady," *New York Times*, September 1, 1907.

61   "We are in great haste to construct a magnetic telegraph" . . . "We do not ride on the railroad": Thoreau, *Walden*, 44.

61   Afflicted children downed milk . . . rubbings: See Beard, *A Practical Treatise on Nervous Exhaustion*, 180, 214.

62   Though he didn't use the word *camping*: Ibid., 248.

62   huffing nitrous oxide: Ibid., 230.

63   she looked quite "comely": Warder Cadbury, introduction, Murray, *Adventures in the Wilderness*, 34.

63   "There has never been a rich rascal": Ibid., 13.

63   When he showed up at Yale: Ibid.

63   At least once, he shocked his parishioners: Ibid., 15.

64   Brimstone Corner: Ibid., 18.

64   "Murray's influence is beyond calculation": Ibid., 19

64   "A city life . . . is a grinding kind of life": William H. H. Murray, *Music-Hall Sermons* (Boston: Fields, Osgood, and Co., 1870), 64.

64   The creeks were full of "eager fish": Murray, *Adventures in the Wilderness*, 69.

65   "was compelled to fling down my rod and run": Headley, *The Adirondack, or Life in the Woods*, 254.

65   "a monster existing only in . . . feverish imaginations," "A thousand sources of invigoration": Murray, *Adventures in the Wilderness*, 56, 22.

65   "Weir Mitchell Rest Cure": For more information, see the University of Virginia's online exhibit, "Neurasthenia and the Culture of Nervous Exhaustion," at http://exhibits.hsl.virginia.edu/nerves/rest/. Also see Charlotte Perkins Gilman, *The Yellow Wall-Paper and Other Stories* (1892; repr., Oxford: Oxford World's Classics, 2009), 3–19. The title story attacks the idea of the rest cure.

65   "Murray was the earliest outdoor advocate for women and children": Harry V. Radford, *Adirondack Murray: A Biographical Appreciation* (New York: Broadway Publishing Company, 1906), 28.

65   fated to be speared to death: "Further News of the Explorer Radford's Death," in Isaiah Bowman and G. M. Wrigley, eds., *The Geographical Review, Volume II* (New York: The American Geographical Society, 1916), 301.

66   "To come into the wilderness and *not* camp": Gary Scharnhorst, *Kate Field: The Many Lives of a Nineteenth-Century American Journalist* (Syracuse, NY: Syracuse University Press, 2008), 68.

66   "blackflies, musketoes, and midges": Ibid., 69.

66   "willing to be tanned," "Helter skelter, off with silks, kid gloves, and linen": Sandra Weber, *Adirondack Roots: Stories of Hiking, History and Women* (Charleston, SC: The History Press, 2011), 82, 83.

66   "How the thorns lacerate you!": Murray, *Adventures in the Wilderness*, 18.

67   Campers were badly frightened: Tony Perrottet, "Where Was the Birthplace of the American Vacation?" *Smithsonian*, August 2013.

67   "utterly beyond the comprehension": Ralph K. Wing, "Hard Lines in the Adirondacks," *Forest and Stream*, July 28, 1887, 6.

67   the summer of 1869 was cooler than usual: Christine Jerome, *An Adirondack Passage: The Cruise of the Canoe Sairy Gamp* (New York: HarperPerennial, 1994), 68.

68   One desperate New Yorker: Donaldson, *History of the Adirondacks, Volume 1*, 194.

68   "The Dismal Wilderness": See Cadbury introduction, Murray, *Adventures in the Wilderness*, 55.

68   Wachusett, sneered about Adirondack ladies: See Wachusett, "Some Were Not Charmed," in Paul Jamieson and Neal Burdick, eds., *The Adirondack Reader: Four Centuries of Adirondack Writing* (Lake George, NY: Adirondack Mountain Club, 2009), 170.

68   "bronzed as an Indian": Murray, *Adventures in the Wilderness*, 14.

68   Murray "never dreamed of such results": Kate Field, "Murray Vindicated," in Jamieson and Burdick, eds., *The Adirondack Reader*, 80.

69   "and bits of lingerie": See "The Long and Short of It," in *Forest and Stream* 66 (New York: Forest and Stream Publishing Co., 1913), 388–89.

69   "Down, down we went": Murray, *Adventures in the Wilderness*, 165.

70   "The great, ignorant stay-at-home egotistic world": Cadbury introduction, Murray, *Adventures in the Wilderness*, 11.

70   He wanted to democratize camping: From my e-mail exchange with Philip Terrie, September 22, 2015.

70   "I have no sympathy at all": Murray, *Adventures in the Wilderness*, 52.

70   shucked oysters: "Adirondack Murray: He Runs a Café and Causes a Sensation in Montreal," *New York Times*, December 25, 1884, 1.

71   "served the doughnut and the mince pie": Donaldson, *A History of the Adirondacks, Volume 1*, 192.

71   Buffalo Bill's Wild West show: Murray made an appearance at the show in 1885. A photo of him, pictured with Crow Eagle, Sitting Bull, and Buffalo Bill, among others, appears in Isabelle S. Sayers, *Annie Oakley and Buffalo Bill's Wild West* (New York: Dover Publications, 1981), 24.

71   "kindled a thousand campfires": Radford, *Adirondack Murray*, 21.

71   "An Erratic Career": See "An Erratic Career," *Congregationalist and Christian World*, March 12, 1904, 361.

72   "Neither lake nor mountain commemorates": Radford, *Adirondack Murray*, 74.

72   Japanese scientists prepared rigorous studies: Bum Jin Park et al., "The Physiological Effects of Shinrin-yoku (Taking in the Forest Atmosphere or Forest Bathing): Evidence from Field Experiments in 24 Forests Across Japan," *Environmental Health and Preventative Medicine* (January 2010): 18–26.

72   "medicinal mists": See Jim Robbins, "The Meaning of Trees in a Changing World," Mother Nature Network, March 30, 2015, http://www.mnn.com/home -blog/guest-columnist/blogs/the-meaning-of-trees-in-a-changing-world.

72   "the monotony of routinized subdivided labor": Lears, *No Place of Grace*, 51.

73   "We spend over $2 billion a year on anti-anxiety medications," "Americans believe that excessive sadness makes us sick": T. M. Luhrmann, "The Anxious Americans," *New York Times*, July 18, 2015, http://www.nytimes.com/2015/07 /19/opinion/sunday/the-anxious-americans.html.

74   "My wife—Be careful": Howard Wayne Morgan, *William McKinley and His America* (Kent, OH: Kent State University Press, 2003), 399.

74   At the time of the attack . . . : Douglas Brinkley, *The Wilderness Warrior: The-odore Roosevelt and the Crusade for America* (New York: HarperCollins, 2009), 70–72.

76   "a toothache in my stomach," "without blowing up like an abridged edition of a hippopotamus," little to endear himself to potential friends: Edmund Morris, *The Rise of Theodore Roosevelt* (New York: Random House, 1979), 11, 45–46, 71.

76   Sawyer's cat, "By the time Roosevelt returned to Harvard": Brinkley, *Wilderness Warrior*, 71, 106–7.

77   "He left New York a 'shrill eunuch'": Tom Lutz, *American Nervousness, 1903: An Anecdotal History* (Ithaca, NY: Cornell University Press, 1991), 78–79.

77   Roosevelt, while serving as governor of New York: Brinkley, *Wilderness Warrior*, 351.

78   "Beautiful country!": Sarah Vowell, *Assassination Vacation* (New York: Simon and Schuster, 2005), 226.

78   "THE PRESIDENT IS CRITICALLY ILL," "THE PRESIDENT APPEARS TO BE DYING": Edmund Morris, *Theodore Rex* (New York: Random House, 2001), 3.

HERO OF CAMPING: GEORGE WASHINGTON SEARS

80   Biographical details about Nessmuk come from Christine Jerome, *An Adiron-dack Passage: The Cruise of the Canoe Sairy Gamp* (New York: HarperPerennial, 1994), including that wonderful tidbit about his friends betting against him; George Washington Sears, *Canoeing the Adirondacks with Nessmuk: The Adirondack Letters of George Washington Sears*, ed. Dan Brenan (Blue Mountain Lake, NY: Adirondack Museum of the Adirondack Historical Association, 1962 and 1993); Robert Lyon, *Who Was Nessmuk?* (Wellsboro, PA: Wellsboro Chamber of Commerce, 1971), published for the Nessmuk sesquicentennial; and Jim Merritt, "Wild Man Nessmuk," *Field and Stream*, February 1998, 90–92.

4: ACTS OF TRANSMISSION

84   "Seriously, is it good for men and women and children": Horace Kephart, *Camping and Woodcraft: A Handbook for Vacation Campers and for Travelers in the Wilderness* (1916, 1917; repr., Gatlinburg, TN: The Great Smoky Mountains Association, 2011), 1:13.

86   this was a revised and expanded version of the original text published in 1906: It was then expanded into two separate volumes in 1916 and 1917 before being republished as a compendium in 1921.

86   "tender squirrels," gibcroke, "If we rake together a pile of leaves," "First get in plenty of wood and kindling": Kephart, *Camping and Woodcraft*, 1:284, 1:lxiv, 1:210, 1:210.

90   "Imagine Boston or Florence," "I know no games," "an eight-inch bull's eye": Kephart letters as quoted by Ellison and McCue in introduction to *Camping and Woodcraft*, 1:viii, 1:xi, 1:xiv.

90   "Paste for Labels": See "Horace Kephart: Revealing an Enigma" exhibit, http://www.wcu.edu/library/DigitalCollections/Kephart/biography/timeline.htm.

92   His friends thought he was joking, "Kephart Lost Mind," "fiends," suicide note: Ellison and McCue in introduction to Kephart, *Camping and Woodcraft*, 1:xxvi–vii.

93   "when supper would be over": Horace Kephart quote by F. A. Behymer, as excerpted ibid., 1:xxli.

93   "Personally, I would rather get lost": Kephart, *Camping and Woodcraft*, 2:19.

93   "pour it nearly full," "Even in the best of camps": Ibid., 1:359, 1:20.

94   "rationalized, technological organization": Philip Joseph Deloria, *Playing Indian* (New Haven, CT: Yale University Press, 1998), 99.

95   "a chunk of rosin": Kephart, *Camping and Woodcraft*, 1:101–2.

95   "Many's the time it has almost slipped from my fingers": Ibid.

95   Dutch oven, "balloon silk": These and other details regarding atmosphere, camp-craft, and gear in late-nineteenth- and early-twentieth-century "fixed camps" can be found throughout David Wescott' s *Camping in the Old Style*, foreword and contributions by Steven M. Watts (Layton, UT: Gibbs Smith, 2015).

96   "In regard to race": From e-mail exchange with George Ellison, n.d. Ellison raises a good point, and the same might also be said of John Muir, who in so many of his writings showed an admirable willingness to camp and talk with anyone, regardless of social class and ethnicity, but who also made disparaging statements against Native Americans and African Americans; and of Theodore Roosevelt, who, for all of his celebrated progressivism, flirted with eugenics theories and worried about "race suicide." Thoreau also made snide remarks about Native Americans from time to time. Dig deeply into the private or public writings of other camping-related figures, including Robert Baden-Powell, and you are bound to find some objectionable things.

5: CLASH OF THE NECKERCHIEFS

98   "Walk seven miles in two hours": Seton, *Manual of the Woodcraft Indians*, 19.

99   "Seton's corporeal presence": John H. Wadland, *Ernest Thompson Seton: Man in Nature and the Progressive Era, 1880–1915*, as quoted in David C. Scott and Brendan Murphy, *The Scouting Party* (Irving, TX: Red Honor Press, 2010), 146–47.

100   The first was George Armstrong Custer: Betty Keller, *Black Wolf: The Life of Ernest Thompson Seton* (Madeira Park, BC: Douglas and McIntyre, 1984), 11.

100   "a worthless loafer": Ibid., 12.

101   a noted pencil maker: Harding, *Days of Henry Thoreau*, 8. Harding also describes the elder Thoreau as a "quiet and mousy sort of man."

101   "Theodore . . . you have the mind but you have not the body": Morris, *The Rise of Theodore Roosevelt*, 32.

101   "utterly staggered": Keller, *Black Wolf*, 91.

102   Seton was far from the worst offender: A nice summary of this situation can be found in Jim Motavalli, *Naked in the Woods: Joseph Knowles and the Legacy of Frontier Fakery* (Cambridge, MA: Da Capo Press, 2007), 92–93.

102   Huge snapping turtles: Keller, *Black Wolf*, 152.

103   "Now, boys": Scott and Murphy, *The Scouting Party*, 35.

103   "the American boy [was] rapidly becoming flat chested," "respectful and obedient": "Boy Scouts Must Be Like Daring Men," *New York Times*, October 9, 1910, 12.

103   "[Boys] have badness thrusted upon them": Scott and Murphy, *The Scouting Party*, 115.

104   "'high class citizens'": Kent Baxter: *The Modern Age: Turn of the Century American Culture and the Invention of Adolescence* (Tuscaloosa: University of Alabama Press, 2008), 94.

104   "Don't rebel": Ibid., 101.

105   As a man-child himself . . . boneheaded move: See Scott and Murphy, *Scouting Party*, 37.

106   Baden-Powell was more like a charming and playful fox: See Tim Jeal, *The Boy-Man* (New York: William Morrow and Co., 1990).

107   Well-known for his falsetto . . . if he so desired: Ibid., 35, 50.

107   "It is . . . dangerous to impose one era's values": Peter Applebome, *Scout's Honor: A Father's Unlikely Foray into the Woods* (New York: Harcourt, 2004), 68.

107   "a poignant story that should be known": Brooke Allen, "Rainbow Merit Badge," *New York Times*, July 19, 2012.

108   "The selection is one that cannot be lightly made": Baden-Powell, as quoted in Applebome, *Scout's Honor*, 66.

108   The Boers finally launched a head-on assault: The author David C. Scott supplied these Siege of Mafeking details to me.

108   "loafers and wasters": Jeal, *The Boy-Man*, 359.

109   It's all here: how you tie a knot: Useful analysis and summary of *Scouting for Boys* can be found in Applebome, *Scout's Honor*, 78.

109   "Laugh as much as you can": Baden-Powell, as quoted ibid.

109   "astounded to find all my ideas taken": Seton, as quoted in Scott and Murphy, *The Scouting Party*, 78–79.

110   Seton was not wrong: See ibid., 80.

111   "We want *no* Molly Coddles," "Be always sure you are right": Daniel Carter Beard, quoted in David I. Macleod, *Building Character in the American Boy: The Boy Scouts, YMCA, and Their Forerunners, 1870–1920* (Madison: University of Wisconsin Press, 1982), 145.

111   "It's a mighty pretty morning": Scott and Murphy, *The Scouting Party*, 214.

111   Uncle Dan was also a well-known artist: For more information on Daniel Carter Beard's career as an illustrator, see William Victor Kahler "An Historical Analysis of the Professional Career of Daniel Carter Beard, 1850–1941," Texas A&M University, accessed through ProQuest, UMI Dissertations Publishing, 1975.

112   "You have made a little mistake": Baden-Powell as quoted in Scott and Murphy, *The Scouting Party*, 115.

112   "There are already 150,000 lads": "Boy Scouts Must Be Like Daring Men," 12.

113   blow-by-blow comparison: For Beard's self-comparison to Ernest Thompson Seton, see Deloria, *Playing Indian*, 94. It should be noted that Seton, though he

simplified Native American custom, was unusual for his time in the sense that he championed Indian culture and wanted to use it as a baseline for Scouting. (Daniel Beard based his Scouting organization on pioneer legends, while Robert Baden-Powell initially embraced medieval knighthood as a Scouting inspiration and theme. He once described knights as an early equivalent of Scouts in England.) The theme of his Woodcraft Indians was one reason Seton faced opposition and marginalization.

113   As Seton summed up the evolution of the Scouts: "Seton Still Insists on Quitting Scouts," *New York Times*, December 6, 1915, 6.

113   West responded in kind: "West Says Seton Is Not a Patriot," *New York Times*, December 7, 1915, 4.

114   "Got it shot off by a Rebel," "medicinal electric wand," Helpful Hands Club, "Daisy rescued a three-year-old": Stacy Cordery, *Juliette Gordon Low: The Remarkable Founder of the Girl Scouts* (New York: Penguin, 2012), 1, 20, 43, 35.

115   If Daisy thought of that rice: See ibid. for additional details on Daisy's disenchantment with and divorce from William Mackay Low, specifically chapters 6, 8, and 9.

117   Daisy "trivialized" and "sissified": For elaboration, see Mary Aickin Rothschild, "To Scout or to Guide? The Girl Scout–Boy Scout Controversy, 1912–1941," *Frontiers: A Journal of Women Studies* 6, no. 3 (Autumn 1981): 115–21.

117   "Hard as Nails and Dipped in Sunshine": For a contemporary account, see "Annual Recreational Camp for Girls under the Auspices of the Extension Division," University of Iowa Extension Bulletin, Iowa City, 1918, 5. Also see Matthew De Abaitua, *The Art of Camping: The History and Practice of Sleeping Under the Stars* (London: Hamish Hamilton, 2011), 91.

118   "more in their power than men to prevent waste": Nancy C. Unger, *Beyond Nature's Housekeepers* (New York: Oxford University Press, 2012), 111.

118   "She was *electrical*, or something like that": Rothschild, "To Scout or to Guide?," 115–21.

119   "too under cover": Leslie Paris, *Children's Nature: The Rise of the American Summer Camp* (New York: New York University Press, 2008), 52.

119   The group was never all white: E-mail correspondence with Stacy Cordery, February 3, 2016.

119   The GSUSA did not take an official position on lesbians: See Bonnie Zimmerman, ed., *Lesbian Histories and Cultures: An Encyclopedia, Volume 1* (New York: Garland Publishing, 2000), 334.

HERO OF CAMPING: THE S'MORE

120   Information about s'mores from Kyla Wazana Tompkins, "Sylvester Graham's Imperial Dietetics," *Gastronomica: The Journal of Critical Food Studies* 9, no. 1 (Winter 2009): 50–60; Geoffrey Blodgett, "Oberlin College: A Historical Sketch," *Oberlin Alumni Magazine*, Summer 1998; Joe Schwarcz, *The Genie in the Bottle: All-New Commentaries on the Fascinating Chemistry of Everyday*

Life (New York: Henry Holt and Company, 2002), 96–98; Samira Kawash, *Candy: A Century of Panic and Pleasure* (New York: Faber and Faber, 2013), 12, 37–38, 92; from my e-mail exchange with Kawash, June 4, 2014; from Samira Kawash, "Campfire Classic: The Enduring Legacy of S'mores," *Saveur* online, July 25, 2013, http://www.saveur.com/article/Kitchen/Campfire-Classic -Smores; and Francis Andrew March and Richard Joseph Beamish, *History of the World War: An Authentic Narrative of the World's Greatest War Including the Treaty of Peace and the League of Nations Covenant* (Ithaca, NY: Cornell University Press, 2009), 207.

6: WILD VICTORIAN LADIES

130   "The history of American women is about the fight for freedom": Gail Collins, *America's Women: 400 Years of Dolls, Drudges, Helpmates, and Heroines* (New York: William Morrow, 2003), xiv.

131   Twin Teats, Nellie's Nipple: Susan Schrepfer, *Nature's Altars: Mountains, Gender, and American Environmentalism* (Lawrence: University Press of Kansas, 2005), 33.

132   "delicate and high-strung, subject to fits of anxiety or even hysteria": Sheila M. Rothman, *Women's Proper Place: A History of Changing Ideals and Practices, 1870 to the Present* (New York: Basic Books, 1980), 24, as quoted in Linda Lawrence Hunt, *Bold Spirit: Helga Estby's Forgotten Walk across Victorian America* (New York: Anchor Books, 2003), 86.

132   "displaced or prolapsed uterus": Hunt, *Bold Spirit*, 120.

132   "Most of the women out in the woods": From Nancy C. Unger phone interview, April 17, 2015.

133   Women were also more likely to stop at a sporting goods store, "We learned . . . to wear our short skirts": Schrepfer, *Nature's Altars*, 103, 70.

134   "As a feminist": Stephen Fox, *The American Conservation Movement: John Muir and His Legacy* (Madison: University of Wisconsin Press, 1981), 47.

134   "Botanizing" was considered an admirable pastime: From Nancy C. Unger phone interview.

134   the Merry Tramps of Oakland: For more details, see Meredith Eliassen and Frank B. Rodolph, "Adventures in Nature: The Merry Tramps of Oakland," *California History* 82, no. 2 (2004): 6–19, 59.

136   Norwegian immigrant Helga Estby: All Estby biographical information on this page comes from Hunt, *Bold Spirit*.

136   A menacing vagrant shadowed them through the mountains near La Grande, Oregon; They thrilled to the sounds of the night wind and narrowly escaped a gray mountain lion "as big as a man"; "I knocked him down," Helga Estby bragged later on; Would-be assailants from Chicago; perhaps Estby was compelled to silence herself: Ibid., 106, 126–27, 142, 169, 245.

138   Kathryn Hulme's wonderfully written: Details about Kathryn Hulme's camping journey come from Kathryn Hulme, *How's the Road?* (San Francisco: privately printed, 1928).

140   Grace Gallatin Seton-Thompson . . . "was not financially dependent on her husband": For biographical information, and for an excerpt of Seton's-Thompson's
outdoor writings, see Dorcas S. Miller, *Adventurous Women: The Inspiring
Lives of Nine Early Outdoorswomen* (Boulder, CO: Pruett Publishing Company,
2000), 81–91.

142   "There may be men": "Things to Know . . . ," CampOut, http://www.campoutva
.com/things-to-know.html.

142   "Social conditioning inundates a woman": Karen Warren, *Women's Voices in
Experiential Education* (Dubuque, IA: Kendall/Hunt Publishing Co., 1996), 12.

7: GATOR GIRLS

143   "We descend from people who had that connection": Shelton Johnson quota-
tion comes from *The Way Home*, directed by Amy Marquis. Read the full quo-
tation at http://speakpatrice.tumblr.com/post/18839955008/the-way-home
-directed-by-amy-marquis-the.

144   The demographics of national park visitation . . . could become an existential
issue: This page refers to Joe Weber and Selima Sultana, "Why Do So Few
Minority People Visit National Parks? Visitation and the Accessibility
of 'America's Best Idea,'" *Annals of the Association of American Geographers*
103, no. 3, 437–64, and to Shawn Regan, "Are National Parks More Popular
Than Ever?" *Property and Environment Research Center* 34, no.1 (Summer
2015), http://www.perc.org/articles/are-national-parks-more-popular-ever.

145   Jewish cultural identity: This bit of analysis comes from my e-mail exchange
with Sarah Brafman, a writer and law student (and former summer camper)
in New York City.

145   Deb Pleasants: See "Camping While Black," The Mothers Movement Online,
http://mothersmovement.org/features/07/12/camping_while_black_1.html.

146   "The only time you see African Americans in the woods in the movies": From
phone conversation with Eliss Cucchiara, n.d.

149   In spite of those numbers, 98 percent of Everglades visitors: See "Everglades
National Park Visitor Study Winter and Spring 2008" (the most recent issue I
found that covers demographic figures), University of Idaho, Park Studies
Unit, November 2008.

149   The brochure failed to mention that the pond was also home to a monster crocodile named Croczilla: This creature was no myth, by the way. The National
Park Service later told me there was indeed a giant croc with "beautiful big
pearly white teeth" in that pond, though Everglades rangers estimated its
length was about fourteen feet long, contradicting visitor reports that the creature was twenty feet long.

8: NINE MILE POND

160   The *New York Times* reported that the "vast majority" of national park visitors: See Glenn Nelson, "Why Are Our Parks So White?" *New York Times*,
July 10, 2015.

161   Audrey Peterman: I would like to point out that Peterman, a passionate activist, doesn't restrict her message to camping, no matter how much she loves it personally. "As a matter of fact, one of the big things we do is advertise the fact that you don't *have* to camp to enjoy nature," she told me when we talked on the phone. "A lot of black people don't like the idea of camping and roughing it; it is a turnoff to them. You can enjoy the park and the outdoors any way you like. People don't know you can be at the Grand Canyon and stay in lodging nearby. Whenever you see a commercial about the outdoors, it is a usually a fit young white man climbing up a spindle of a spire. People will look at this, and say, 'Who the hell wants to do that? Not me!'"

162   The book is unflinching: For an excellent look at the complex history of African American engagement with the outdoors, see Dianne Glave, *Rooted in the Earth: Reclaiming the African American Environmental Heritage* (Chicago: Lawrence Hill Books, 2010). Glave's book is powerful because it is unstinting about the traumatic aspects of historical memory and the land, but it also covers the other side: land as sanctuary, land as sustenance.

162   "conscious, but unpublicized policy of discouraging visits by African Americans": Terence Young, as quoted by Rebecca Onion, "When Segregation Reached Right into the National Parks," *Slate*, June 19, 2013.

162   Black camping families: For a vivid and detailed look at the history of segregation in Virginia's Shenandoah National Park, see Terence Young, "'A Contradiction in Democratic Government': W. J. Trent, Jr., and the Struggle to Desegregate National Park Campgrounds," *Environmental History* 14, no. 4 (October 2009): 651–82.

162   Yet there is another side to the story: On life on the land and engagement with the outdoors, with parallel histories of oppression and freedom, terror and sustenance, isolation and community, see Cassandra Y. Johnson and J. M. Bowker, "African-American Wildland Memories," in *The Wilderness Debate Rages On: Continuing the Great New Wilderness Debate*, ed. Michael P. Nelson and J. Baird Callicott (Athens: University of Georgia Press, 2008), 325–48; Mart A. Stewart, "Slavery and the Origins of African American Environmentalism," in Dianne D. Glave and Mark Stoll, eds., *"To Love the Wind and the Rain": African Americans and Environmental History* (Pittsburgh, PA: University of Pittsburgh Press, 2006); and Mark S. Foster, "In the Face of 'Jim Crow': Prosperous Blacks and Vacations, Travel and Outdoor Leisure, 1890–1945," *Journal of Negro History* 84, no. 2 (Spring 1999): 130–49.

163   "For many blacks in the antebellum south": See Brandon Harris, "Why Is Camping a White Thing? A Few *Wild* Theories," The Slice, December 11, 2014, http://talkingpointsmemo.com/theslice/why-is-camping-a-white-thing-a-few-wild-theories-cheryl-strayed-12-11-2014.

163   "They were not willing to go there": Brandon Harris phone interview, April 24, 2015.

165   Rick Ross, Drake, Beyoncé, and 2 Chainz: I don't want you to think I'm savvy enough to have identified these artists by hearing their songs. I found out the names only when I consulted the radio station's online playlist after the fact.

166   "black people in America being tied historically": Winston "Mark" Walters quotations come from two e-mail exchanges and two phone conversations in 2014 and 2015.

167   In 2013, the U.S. Justice Department, after reviewing thirty-three police shootings between 2008 and 2011: Jay Weaver, Kathleen McGrory, and David Ovalle, "Justice Department finds Miami Police used excessive force in shootings," *Miami Herald*, July 9, 2013.

9: THE ODD COUPLE

179   "I fairly fell in love with him": John Muir letter to C. Hart Merriam, see *John Muir: His Life and Letters and Other Writings*, edited and with an introduction by Terry Gifford (Seattle: Baton Wicks and Mountaineers, 1996), 374.

179   "Would you murder your own children?": John Muir quote in Donald Worster, *A Passion for Nature* (New York: Oxford University Press, 2008), 383.

180   "Hurrah, hurrah" . . . "That's a candle": Linnie Marsh Wolfe, *Son of the Wilderness: The Life of John Muir* (1945; repr., Madison: University of Wisconsin Press, 2003), 291.

181   He spoke to the tired brainworkers: For elaboration, see Terence Young, "The End of Camping," in *Boom: A Journal of California* 4, no. 3 (Fall 2014), http://www.boomcalifornia.com/2014/10/the-end-of-camping/.

181   "prince of lunatics" . . . "curves he described": The briefly quoted natural musings of John Muir on this page come from various sources. For "prince of lunatics," see John Muir, *John of the Mountains: The Unpublished Journals of John Muir*, ed. Linnie Marsh Wolfe (1938; repr., Madison: University of Wisconsin Press, 1979), 215. That gorgeous, enviable description of a campfire can be found in John Muir, *The Wilderness World of John Muir*, edited and with an introduction by Edwin Way Teale (New York: Houghton Mifflin, 2001), 274. The "curves" that the grasshopper "describes" in the air: Muir, *The Wilderness World of John Muir*, 132.

181   "hitched to everything else": See online version of John Muir, *My First Summer in the Sierra* (New York: Houghton Mifflin Company, 1911), at http://vault.sierraclub.org/john_muir_exhibit/writings/my_first_summer_in_the_sierra/.

181   "a flutter of leaves," "rosiny pine," "plushy bogs": See Muir, *John of the Mountains*, 219.

182   A mere 650 people per year: See "Yosemite: History and Culture," Natural Park Service, overview at http://www.nps.gov/yose/learn/historyculture/index.htm.

182   Muir wondered if it would leave a permanent stink on the rocks: Here I am paraphrasing a Muir quote, "But even the one main hall has a hog-pen in the middle of the floor, and the whole concern seems hopeless as far as destruction and desecration can go. Some of that stink, I'm afraid, has got into the pores of the rocks even." From Muir's letter to Robert Underwood Johnson, dated March 4, 1890, from John Muir, *The Life and Letters of John Muir*, accessed at http://vault.sierraclub.org/john_muir_exhibit/life/life_and_letters/chapter_15.aspx.

183   Freed of their escorts: My re-creation of the Muir/Roosevelt chapter draws from Worster, *A Passion for Nature*; Margaret Sanborn, *Yosemite: Its Discovery, Its Wonders, and Its People* (Yosemite, CA: Yosemite Association, 1989), 230–35; Fox, *The American Conservation Movement*; Brinkley, *Wilderness Warrior*; and from contemporary newspaper accounts. I also relied upon

Dayton Duncan, *Seed of the Future: Yosemite and the Evolution of the National Park Idea* (Yosemite, CA: Yosemite Conservancy, 2013), 154–62.

183   Grizzly Giant: For example, in 1870, Joseph LeConte described the tree, jokingly, as a "grizzled giant" because of its "large, rough, knobbed, battered trunk" in *A Journal of Ramblings through the High Sierra of California by the "University Excursion Party"* (San Francisco: Francis & Valentine, 1875), 35.

183   pile of forty woolen blankets: References to this extraordinary pile of blankets show up in many sources, including the Sierra Club's online "exhibit" about John Muir and Theodore Roosevelt at http://vault.sierraclub.org/john_muir _exhibit/people/roosevelt.aspx.

183   not so hot at camping from a strictly technical perspective: Here I refer to a statement by C. Hart Merriam, quoted in Worster, *A Passion for Nature*, 261.

184   Muir traveled to Yosemite . . . push with a stick: Ibid., 296–97. I asked Donald Worster about this incident. He wrote, "I don't think he really caused her pain with that stick. It was more pressure than pain. She became too heavy for comfortable hiking" (e-mail exchange, October 2, 2015).

184   "[F]or all his scientific knowledge": Brinkley, *Wilderness Warrior*, 234–35.

184   beefsteak: Duncan, *Seed of the Future*, 158.

184   If the two men had toppled over: This is my best guesstimate. To make this calculation, I used a climbing website called The Splat Calculator: A Free Fall Calculator at http://www.angio.net/personal/climb/speed.

185   "sloppy, unintelligent interest": This reference comes from Theodore Roosevelt, *John Muir: An Appreciation*, originally published in *Outlook* 109 (January 16, 1915): 27–28, accessible online at http://vault.sierraclub.org/john_muir_exhibit /life/appreciation_by_roosevelt.aspx.

186   "his only rival in intermittent but continuous spouting": A *New York World* reporter quoted in Morris, *Theodore Rex*, 221.

186   he continued to hunt: This comes from my back-and-forth communication with Donald Worster.

186   Muir, according to one account, had never shaved in his life: Note my little hedge here. It is impossible to prove something like this, of course, but I found this reference in Edwin Way Teale, introduction and interpretive comments to Muir, *The Wilderness World of John Muir*, xvii.

186   disrupted birds' nests . . . once strangled a cat: Fox, *The American Conservation Movement*, 29, 45.

187   once mourned over a dead bear: Worster, *A Passion for Nature*, 6.

187   "These people annoy me": Theodore Roosevelt quote in Rod Miller, *John Muir: Magnificent Tramp* (New York: Tom Doherty Associates, 2005), 135.

188   exhausting manual labor: Fox, *The American Conservation Movement*, 32.

189   a thousand-mile walk to Florida: Here, most of my descriptions, narrative summaries, and paraphrases of Muir's historic journey come directly from John Muir, *A Thousand-Mile Walk to the Gulf*, ed. William Frederic Badè (New York: Houghton Mifflin Company, 1916), accessed at http://vault.sierraclub.org /john_muir_exhibit/writings/a_thousand_mile_walk_to_the_gulf/.

189   He'd camp with anyone: See Worster's preface in *A Passion for Nature*.

190   "any place that is wild": This oft-repeated Muir quote comes from chapter 1 of John Muir, *The Yosemite* (New York: The Century Co., 1912), accessed online at http://vault.sierraclub.org/john_muir_exhibit/writings/the_yosemite/chapter _1.aspx.

190   "I am lost": John Muir as quoted in Fox, *The American Conservation Movement*, 7.

190   Has any other nature writer used the word *throbbing* quite so much: I found these lusty tidbits in the John Muir chapter of John P. O'Grady, *Pilgrims to the Wild* (Salt Lake City: University of Utah Press, 1993), 62.

193   smart suits . . . cigars and wine: Worster, *A Passion for Nature*, 330.

193   Red-63: See Harold Wood, "John Muir's Telephone Number," *John Muir Newsletter* 12, no. 1 (Winter 2001/2002), the John Muir Center for Environmental Studies, University of the Pacific, Stockton, CA.

194   Occupying a peninsula bounded by saltwater: These and other details culled from Beverly Hennessey, *Images of America: Hetch Hetchy* (Mount Pleasant, SC: Arcadia Publishing, 2012).

194   "everything in my power . . . *But* you must remember . . . the result will be bad": Theodore Roosevelt, letter to John Muir, as quoted in Worster, *A Passion for Nature*, 426.

195   "To provide of the little children, men and women": James Phelan as quoted in Unger, *Beyond Nature's Housekeepers*, 100.

196   Even earlier, it was a lesson for those fighting a dam . . . during the 1950s: Here I am referring to an addendum provided to me by Worster.

HERO OF CAMPING: ESTWICK EVANS

198   Biographical information about Evans comes from Roderick Nash, *Wilderness and the American Mind*, 44, 56–57, but the details of his journey come from Estwick Evans, *Pedestrious Tour, of Four Thousand Miles Through the Western States and Territories, during the Winter and Spring of 1818* (Concord, NH: Joseph C. Spear, 1819).

10: NIGHT AT BADGER SPRING

202   the chance of getting eaten by a mountain lion: Dan White, "Big Cats on Campus: Mountain Lion Sightings Prompt UCSC Expert Forum," *UC Santa Cruz News*, February 14, 2012.

204   got more attention than the 1913 World Series: Nash, *Wilderness and the American Mind*, 142.

204   snacking on sowbelly and using a lard pail as his lunch box: Motavalli, *Naked in the Woods*, 33.

204   "My body was already glistening," "literally begged": Joseph Knowles, *Alone in the Wilderness* (Boston: Small, Maynard and Company, 1913), 20, 7–8.

205   foraged mint leaves smeared all over his body: Motavalli, *Naked in the Woods*, 47.

206   devouring a pot pie from 7-Eleven: Ami Chen Mills, "The Inevitable Chicken

Pot Pie," section in *Metroactive* blog, November 22, 1995, http://www
.metroactive.com/papers/metro/11.22.95/yogi-9547.html.

206   where the median home price is $755,100: This always fluctuating real estate
figure came from Zillow in the early summer of 2015, http://www.zillow.com
/santa-cruz-ca/home-values/.

208   process called Owl Eyes: See Jon Young, "Owl Eyes: A Core Awareness Skill,"
Natureskills.com, February 5, 2009, at http://www.natureskills.com/index
.html%3Fp=732.html; and for more elaboration, see Ellen Haas, "Come to Your
Senses," Natureskills.com, at http://www.natureskills.com/outdoor-safety
/come-to-your-senses/.

208   *Titanic* sank to the bottom: Motavalli, *Naked in the Woods*, 288.

209   Knowles was America's first outdoor survival "reality star": Analysis inspired
by Jim Motavalli, "Impressive Wilderness Survival or Elaborate Hoax?: The
Long, Strange History of Fake Survivalism," *Daily Green*, March 6, 2008,
accessed at http://preview.www.thedailygreen.com/living-green/blogs/cars
-transportation/wilderness-survival-hoaxes-460305.

209   Knowles would "share the fame of [Henry] David Thoreau": Quote appears in
Motavalli, *Naked in the Woods*, 19.

217   Lynn Kimsey, a professor of entomology at the University of California at
Davis: Interviewed via phone and e-mail, May 2013.

218   "I must have run miles that night": Knowles, *Alone in the Wilderness*, 23.

218   "Daylight came very slowly": Knowles, quoted in Motavalli, *Naked in the
Woods*, 8.

221   I can't even explain it away as a hallucination: On the other hand, I also experienced a strong auditory hallucination that evening (in which I believed I
heard a female voice shouting the word *now* just behind me).

222   Preliminary version of debris shelter: This photo of me (or, to be more specific,
my feet) in a debris shelter was taken by Robin Bliss-Wagner in the summer
of 2013, during a shakedown practice session prior to the actual campout.

223   "envied the hide," "what a fine pair of chaps her hide would make": Knowles,
Alone in the Wilderness, 26.

223   "The first men of the forest were not handicapped by laws from an outside civilized world!": Ibid., 27.

223   "I did suffer greatly": Ibid., 79–82.

224   dining on flame-roasted frogs' legs: "Fever Gives Knowles a Close Call," *Chicago Daily Tribune*, September 21, 1913, E12.

224   daily circulation more than doubled: Motavalli, *Naked in the Woods*, 49.

224   "half-man, half-bear": As referenced in Knowles, *Alone in the Wilderness*, 49.

224   "He smiled, and the girl saw the gold flash in his teeth": Contemporary newspaper report in the *Boston Post*, as quoted in Bill Donahue, "Naked Joe," *Boston Magazine*, April 2013, http://www.bostonmagazine.com/news/article/2013
/03/26/naked-joe-knowles-nature-man-woods/.

225   "You're my bet!": As quoted in Donahue, "Naked Joe."

226   as much as twelve hundred dollars per week: Motavalli, *Naked in the Woods*, 65.

227   he filed a fifty-thousand-dollar lawsuit: *Boston Sunday American* exposé

details and ensuing lawsuit drawn from Motavalli, *Naked in the Woods*; "do-over" details on p. 121.

227   digestive aid for tots, "Without tent, kit, or provender," "Tuesday, kills bear": Ibid., 136, 207, 76.

228   "All of the two hundred thousand people . . . are now probably dead": Donahue, "Naked Joe."

229   "national cult," "grotesque manifestation": Nash, *Wilderness and the American Mind*, 142.

229   "'commercialism and the mad desire to make money'": Knowles as quoted in James Morton Turner, "From Woodcraft to 'Leave No Trace,'" *Environmental History* 7, no. 3 (July 2002): 462–84.

230   "it was not wonderful": Knowles, *Alone in the Wilderness*.

11: HOW'S THE ROAD?

231   "Every mile by motor": Dallas Lore Sharp, *The Better Country*, as quoted in Warren Belasco, *Americans on the Road: From Autocamp to Motel, 1910–1945* (Baltimore, MD: Johns Hopkins University Press, 1979), 23.

232   "highways to hell": Tom Stienstra, "Northern California Highways to Hell," *San Francisco Chronicle*, July 29, 2012, http://www.sfgate.com/outdoors/article /Northern-California-highways-to-hell-3743962.php.

232   "the worst road I've ever traveled": Tarol, "Franklin Lakes," http://www.tarol .com/franklin.html.

233   a troupe of audio-animatronic singing bear characters: That audio-animatronic attraction, "The Country Bear Jamboree," currently resides at Disney World in Orlando, Florida. For information on Disney's involvement with the proposed Mineral King project, and a brief mention of the bear troupe, see Neal Gabler, *Walt Disney: The Triumph of the American Imagination* (New York: Alfred A. Knopf, 2006), 573, 619, 621–22, 628, 631.

235   In the early 1900s, Mineral King Road posed an irresistible challenge: Source is phone interview with Mineral King historian Louise Jackson, author of *Mineral King: The Story of Beulah* (Mineral King Valley, CA: Sequoia Natural History Association, 2006).

235   anarchic "gypsy" phase: Belasco, *Americans on the Road*, 1–39.

236   "You are your own master": "Two Week's Vagabonds," *New York Times*, July 20, 1922, sec VII, 7, as quoted in Belasco, *Americans on the Road*, 8.

237   "After many days of it you feel as though you had been interlined with a sort of *paste*": Emily Post, as quoted in Belasco, *Americans on the Road*, 53.

237   They also knew how to empty out ditches: Belasco, *Americans on the Road*, 31.

238   In 1918, when Ernest R. Wild guided his 1912 "Lizzie": Ernest R. Wild, "Tells of Auto Trip Through Snow from Minneapolis to Los Angeles," *Los Angeles Times*, January 20, 1918, VI5.

238   In parks like Yellowstone, starting in the late nineteenth century: The editorializing is mine, but the information comes from Dayton Duncan, *The National Parks: America's Best Idea*, with a preface by Ken Burns (New York: Alfred A. Knopf, 2009), 37–38.

240   Rescuers helped pay for its repatriation by raising seventy-five dollars at the city's Rock Bar, where bartenders sold "Marmotinis": See "Wayward Marmot Found in Potrero Hill Yard Heading Back to Yosemite," CBS San Francisco Bay Area, July 3, 2014, http://sanfrancisco.cbslocal.com/2014/07/03/wayward-marmot-founded-in-potrero-hill-yard-heading-back-to-yosemite/; and Erin Sherbert, "Stowaway Marmot Moves Back to Yosemite," *The Snitch*, July 8, 2014, http://www.sfweekly.com/thesnitch/2014/07/08/stowaway-marmot-moves-back-to-yosemite-reluctantly.

241   Daniel Blumstein: Daniel Blumstein interviewed by phone and in various e-mail follow-ups regarding marmots. While the Mineral King marmot behavioral situation is extraordinary, Blumstein told me it's not the only example of puzzling marmot behavior in the face of deadly or unpleasant solids or fluids. "They are evolved to seek certain nutrients and minerals," he said. "They naturally eat dirt. They will come down to the road, where there might be drippings. We have one male right now (in Colorado), hanging out by the road, who looks horrible, molted. Yearling females come down and beat him up. He's like a meth addict hanging out on the road eating dirt." Once, Blumstein was working in Mount Rainier National Park in the Sunrise area. "There was a big slope where people would stop and look each way and then try to pee," he said. "And as they peed, the marmots were all venturing toward the peeing person because they knew there would be salty dirt. It was hysterical."

244   A father at Julianna's preschool: We'd also read multiple stories online about campers coming equipped with commercially available bottled coyote, bobcat, and cougar urine—all available in liquid and crystal form, in hardware and garden supply stores and online—which some people pour all around their cars; the idea is that the marmots will smell that urine, be terrified, and beat a quick retreat. I was so intrigued that before we embarked on the campout, I queried an online predator urine distributor called Pee Mart and asked a company representative how he convinced coyotes and mountain lions to urinate into a little bottle. His answer was disappointingly plausible: "We contract with farms, zoos, wildlife rescue, etc. When the animals pee, it runs into drains and is collected in buckets." But we'd heard, from a parks information officer named Greg Brown, that predator urine would do nothing but attract other predators into the camp, and that the smell might terrorize a skunk into spraying our car—"and then you're talking about a special kind of hell for you all the way back down Mineral King Road and into Three Rivers."

245   "snug, cozy harbors," "dangerous Cape Horns": From "The Gypsy in Modern America," *Touring Topics*, March 1929, 28–29, as quoted in Belasco, *Americans on the Road*, 8.

245   "Between us and every other motorist on the road": Kathryn Hulme, as quoted in Belasco, *Americans on the Road*, 35–36.

247   Spencer was more than willing to talk: We followed up our conversation at the campground later on via e-mail and on the phone, and some of the background details arose from these follow-ups.

250   "With all the conventions reduced to a minimum": Belasco, *Americans on the Road*, 98.

250   I got Spencer's contact information and promised to keep in touch: I've

made good on this promise, and we've had several e-mail conversations since then. In the late fall of 2015, Spencer had just graduated from a school that trains people to be commercial divers. He was working on getting his EMT certification and was hoping to get a job as a diver medic technician on board a boat. He had reason to be optimistic, though he sometimes has moments of uncertainty. "The question of my recovery is hard to answer," he said. "I perceived myself as fully recovered within a month of waking up. My mother would say it was roughly a year before I could manage my own life again. Now I'm stuck in this strange conundrum of wondering whether I'm still at all affected by the brain injury, or do I naturally have brain farts the same as other people?"

250   The lawless "gypsy" days of early-twentieth-century auto camping came to an abrupt halt: That's one of the great conundrums of American history; a group of brave eccentrics gets tired of the crowd and tries to escape it, inadvertently bringing the crowd along with them. Too much popularity—and outbursts of slovenly behavior—led to more regulation. Latecomers to auto camping cried out for better, smoother roads and soon got them, making Mineral King seem like a throwback. Then cities and towns started offering free municipal camps off the side of auto-touring roads and byways starting around 1920; suddenly, auto campers who started out "roughing" it began crowing about the amenities at one camp versus another. One camp had better food in the cafeteria. Another had better lighting. The result was a gradual one-upmanship. Huge crowds of cars would show up, the city administrators got sick of it, and certain camps, beginning in the early 1920s, started charging money to sleep and park. Then the private businesspeople started sniffing out a chance to make good money. They built tourist traps along the roads. Suddenly the car campers would look out the windows and see the worst of their own desires: the places where they once camped were now full of burger joints and chintzy museums. In second-guessing what they wanted, those businesspeople sucked a lot of the fun right out of it; it was like a brick-and-mortar version of online "search optimization" functions that try to guess what you'll want to buy next.

Fear of homeless people and "hoboes" also played a part in the transformation. For all their glorification of "gypsy" ways and vagabonding and their play-acting version of "hobo" life, auto campers usually tried to keep away from the real hoboes, and newspapers portrayed the latter as scourges. Soon car camps started offering cabins instead of just tent space and parking slots. The eventual result is that the anarchic roadside auto camps gave way to auto camping in private cabins, which led to upgraded "cottage camps" with indoor plumbing and ovens. Those all-modern-conveniences camps were precursors to the popular Kampgrounds of America private comfort-camp network, founded in 1962. Camp managers, by making auto camping so much easier, changed the nature and focus of this pastime. Suddenly the campers did not have to deal with outhouses or spluttering camp stoves and fire pits. In his book about automotive history, *Americans on the Road: From Autocamp to Motel, 1910–1945*, Warren Belasco writes that competition in the cottage camps led, eventually, to the creation of motels. Next time you are on a highway, looking at an exit crammed with Econo Lodges and Motel 6s, consider the possibility that these things may have "evolved" from random car campouts on the side of a cornfield.

12: THE HAUNTED DUFFEL BAG

252   "Once leaky and unwieldy (and heaven forbid if you lost a stake)": Patricia Leigh Brown, "Where the Allure of Camping by Car Has Led," *New York Times*, July 22, 1993, accessed at http://www.nytimes.com/1993/07/22/garden /where-the-allure-of-camping-by-car-has-led.html?pagewanted=all.

253   a geeky genius named Wallace Hume Carothers: Matthew E. Hermes, *Enough for One Lifetime: Wallace Carothers, Inventor of Nylon* (Laramie: University of Wyoming, American Chemical Society, 1996).

254   "clinging desperately to the edge of an oaken table": Wallace Carothers letter to Frances Spencer, as quoted in Hermes, *Enough for One Lifetime*, 148.

254   "accidental discovery": Sam Knight, "The Tragic Story of Wallace Hume Carothers," *Financial Times*, November 29, 2008, accessed at http://www.ft .com/cms/s/0/2eae82b2-b9fa-11dd-8c07-0000779fd18c.html.

255   "cockroach-like": Ibid.

255   In response, DuPont emphasized that nylon was made with coal, air, and water: Audra J. Wolfe, "1940: Nylon 6,6," in Raymond J. Giguere, ed., *Molecules That Matter* (Philadelphia: The Frances Young Tang Teaching Museum and Art Gallery at Skidmore College and Chemical Heritage Foundation, 2008), 89.

255   *Fortune* magazine, "flouts Solomon": As quoted in Hermes, *Enough for One Lifetime*, xiv.

255   "The vanguard of the U.S. Army": Ibid., xv.

255   "From horse-packable to backpackable": Bruce "Yeti" Johnson, quoted in Hunter Oatman-Stanford, "Before Camping Got Wimpy: Roughing It with the Victorians," *Collectors Weekly*, August 1, 2012, http://www.collectorsweekly .com/articles/before-camping-got-wimpy/.

256   Otzi . . . backpack: For the backpack or presumed components of one, to be a bit more specific, see South Tyrol Museum of Archaeology at http://www .iceman.it/en/node/283.

256   the dead man was found to be lactose intolerant: Sindya N. Bhanoo, "Lactose Intolerant, Before Milk Was on Menu," *New York Times*, March 5, 2012, accessed at http://www.nytimes.com/2012/03/06/science/iceman-had-brown -eyes-and-hair-and-was-lactose-intolerant.html. The article points out that there was no need, in those days before domesticated farm creatures, to toler- ate the lactose that wasn't consumed in the first place.

256   George Washington Sears, aka Nessmuk, griped about the drawbacks of his pack: Jerome, *An Adirondack Passage*, 71.

256   shoulder packs . . . placing a pebble "an inch or more in diameter in each of the lower corners": U.S. Forest Service, *Handbook for Campers in the National For- ests in California* (Washington, DC: Government Printing Office, 1915), 48.

256   "Trapper Nelson" pack: See "Trapper Nelson and His Packboard" at History- link.org.

257   In 1951, Asher "Dick" Kelty: Details of pack design come from Nena Kelty and Steve Boga, *Backpacking the Kelty Way* (New York: Berkley Publishing Group, 2000), 12–16.

257   The underrated backpacking innovator Jack Stephenson: From an e-mail exchange with Bruce "Yeti" Johnson and a visit to his online camping museum,

History of Gear, at http://www.oregonphotos.com/Backpacking-Revolution1
.html.

257   Murray Pletz: The background information came from History of Gear and
also from Skip Yowell's *The Hippie Guide to Climbing the Corporate Ladder and
Other Mountains* (Nashville, TN: Naked Ink, 2006), 23.

258   The eccentric backpacking innovator Jack Stephenson: Stephenson is a naturist, and his catalogues have nudist themes. See History of Gear at http://www
.oregonphotos.com/Warmlite1.html.

258   "Unless you have gone out in the middle of a rainy night": Bill McKeown, "All
Outdoors" column in *Popular Mechanics*, February 1980, 86.

258   In 1982, Nike marketed its lightweight "Lava Dome" boot: Brown, "Where the
Allure of Car Camping Has Led."

259   "In the past, women were somewhat foreclosed from backpacking": For more
details, see Ellen Zaslaw as featured in chapter 20 of Ryan Jordan, ed., *Lightweight
Backpacking and Camping* (Bozeman, MT: Beartooth Mountain Press, 2006).

260   Nick Clinch, a pal of Dick Kelty's, once remarked: Kelty and Boga, *Backpacking the Kelty Way*, 18.

260   "After the 1972 season": Nash, *Wilderness and the American Mind*, 332.

260   Congress created an Office of Public Roads: See David Halvick, "A Look Back
at Public Land Roads," http://www.foresthistory.org/publications/FHT
/FHTSpring2002/BehindTheWheel.pdf.

261   The formation in 1935 of the Wilderness Society: For a nuanced account, see
Paul Sutter, *Driven Wild: How the Fight Against Automobiles Launched the
Modern Wilderness Movement* (Seattle: University of Washington Press, 2004).

261   "Once designated as wilderness, a tract would be off-limits": Elizabeth Kolbert,
"50 Years of Wilderness," *National Geographic* online, September 2014, http://
ngm.nationalgeographic.com/2014/09/wilderness-act/kolbert-text.

262   even that old mainstay of the camping experience the cook fire: These days,
many state campgrounds ban cook fires seasonally or altogether, and disturbing reports about particulate matter in the lungs of campers have diminished
the stature of the fire in recent years.

262   "No matter how ecologically sound": Alston Chase, *Playing God in Yellowstone*
(New York: Harcourt Brace and Company, 1987), 329.

262   Son of a lumber equipment salesman, he grew up to be an avid hater of lumber
interests: Kyung M. Song, "Conservationist, Author Harvey Manning, 81,
Remembered as a Vocal Force," *Seattle Times*, November 14, 2006, accessed at
http://www.seattletimes.com/seattle-news/conservationist-author-harvey
-manning-81-remembered-as-a-vocal-force/.

262   "Woodcraft is dead . . . slashing and gouging": Harvey Manning, *Backpacking:
One Step at a Time* (New York: Vintage Books, 1973), 20.

262   Manning was careful to credit some of the grand "old boys": Ibid., 345.

263   "foam-padded yoke": Colin Fletcher, *The Thousand-Mile Summer* (1967; repr.,
New York: Vintage Books, 1989), 51.

264   "So many of my friends had died": See "Colin Fletcher, March 1922–June 2007,"
Backpacker Magazine, June 14, 2007. I encountered this quote on the website
Colinfletcher.com.

264   "Dehydrated food" . . . "does not become haylike": Colin Fletcher, *The Complete Walker* (New York: Alfred A. Knopf, 1969), 67.

265   "It is hard to say why virgin desert looks so clean" . . . "a dusty, tainted aftertaste": Fletcher, *The Thousand-Mile Summer*, 34. In an ugly ironic twist, Colin Fletcher's old nemesis the automobile hastened his death and made his last years miserable. In 2001, when Fletcher was seventy-nine, a car struck him while he was walking to a meeting near his home in Carmel Valley, California. It did not kill him but he was never the same and spent years trying to recuperate. He died on June 12, 2007, in Monterey.

266   "The most devoted backpackers fluffed the grass": Turner, "From Woodcraft to 'Leave No Trace.'"

268   An ecologist named Mark Browne: See Mary Catherine O'Connor, "Inside the Loneliest Fight Against the Biggest Environmental Problem You've Never Heard Of," *Guardian*, October 27, 2014, http://www.theguardian.com /sustainable-business/2014/oct/27/toxic-plastic-synthetic-microscopic -oceans-microbeads-microfibers-food-chain.

HERO OF CAMPING: EDWARD ABBEY

269   Information about Abbey comes primarily from James Bishop Jr., *Epitaph for a Desert Anarchist: The Life and Legacy of Edward Abbey* (New York: Simon and Schuster, 1994); with additional material from Jack Loeffler, *Adventures with Ed: A Portrait of Abbey* (Albuquerque: University of New Mexico Press, 2002), 9; Edward Abbey, *Desert Solitaire* (1968; repr., Tucson: University of Arizona Press, 1988), 13; Ken Lamberton, "His Preferred Immortality: The Body of Edward Abbey Nourishes More Than Juniper Trees and Saguaro Roots," *Los Angeles Times*, September 20, 2005, accessed at http://articles.latimes.com /2005/sep/20/news/os-wildwest20.

13: THE IMMACULATOR

273   "In our heavily trafficked wild areas": Kathleen Meyer, *How to Shit in the Woods: An Environmentally Sound Approach to a Lost Art*, 3rd ed. (Berkeley, CA: Ten Speed Press, 2011), xiv.

274   I got the blueprint from the online advice site WikiHow: See http://www .wikihow.com/Make-a-Poop-Tube.

278   Thoreau did not write a single word describing the inevitable privy: Harding, *The Days of Henry Thoreau*, 187.

278   early Yellowstone campers: Descriptions of Yellowstone park depredations can be found in Duncan, *The National Parks*, 37–38.

283   human waste concerns on Mount Whitney: A précis of the situation can be found in various places online, including "Human Waste Management on the Whitney Trail: An Update," accessed at http://www.fs.usda.gov/detail/inyo /news-events/?cid=FSBDEV3_004037.

284   Carrie Vernon: Phone interview and e-mail exchange, June 2013.

285   "It is sort of a gruesome thing to think about": Jeff Novak, phone interview, December 2014.

293   "There's been phenomenal progress" . . . "the steady delivery of directness and humor, and creative approaches": Kathleen Meyer quotes from phone conversations followed up with e-mail exchanges, October 14–16, 2015.

14: KOVU'S BROTHER

296   "'Glamping,' a lexical blend": Edward Brooke and Marion Joppe, "Trends in Camping and Outdoor Hospitality—An International Review," *Journal of Outdoor Recreation and Tourism* 3/4 (December 2013): 1–6.

296   "You sleep on a bed. It's a mattress bed!": Marcy Stone, "Justin Bieber Says He's Going Glamping and Sets the Internet a Buzz," Examiner.com, June 29, 2012.

297   In comparison, Safari West in the peak season swarms with 120 workers, including biologists: Information supplied by Aphrodite Caserta, Safari West marketing office.

299   An ultradeluxe "glamping" package at Burning Man: Nick Bilton, "A Line Is Drawn in the Desert at Burning Man, the Tech Elite One-Up One Another," *New York Times*, August 20, 2014, accessed at http://www.nytimes.com/2014/08/21/fashion/at-burning-man-the-tech-elite-one-up-one-another.html.

300   "Discomfort is . . . what the camper-out is unconsciously seeking": Joseph Burroughs, *Under The Maples* (New York: Houghton Mifflin Company, 1921), 122.

300   MaryJane Butters, the author, innkeeper, and organic farmer: MaryJane Butters, *Glamping with MaryJane: Glamour+Camping* (Layton, UT: Gibbs Smith, 2012).

301   An online video in *Men's Journal*: "Glamping in Big-Sky Country," http://www.mensjournal.com/adventure/remote-and-refined/free-falling-and-glamping-in-big-sky-country-20121107.

302   It took three African porters: Patricia O'Toole, *When Trumpets Call: Theodore Roosevelt after the White House* (New York: Simon and Schuster, 2005), 47.

302   By the time the trip was over, Roosevelt had a vast dead menagerie: "Smithsonian-Roosevelt African Expedition," Smithsonian National Museum of Natural History, http://www.mnh.si.edu/onehundredyears/expeditions/si-roosevelt_expedition.html.

15: HELL ON WHEELS

311   "Don't stop. Keep right on going. Hitch up": Wally Byam's oft-repeated offhand statement, in response to a fellow RVer in 1959, has become an unofficial RVing credo of sorts. See http://metrony.covvo.com/creed.php for an example of this.

317   "Perfect, huh?" . . . "That's our market": For the rest of the Richard Coon speech, go to http://www.rvia.org/?ESID=NTSclips and scroll down.

317   A fresh-off-the-line Class C can cost up to $121,000: RV retail figures from RVUSA.com.

320   He called the industrialist Jay Gould a greedy "Shylock": Neil Baldwin, *Henry Ford and the Jews: The Mass Production of Hate* (New York: Public Affairs, 2003), 87–90.

320   gear options for auto camping and RV camping exploded: For details about the amenities and specialized vehicles of the Four Vagabonds, and for my list

of gear options for RVers around that time, see Donald F. Wood, *RVs and Campers, 1900–2000: An Illustrated History* (Hudson, WI: Iconografix, 2002), 21, 25–27; and also Christopher Klein, "Ford and Edison's Excellent Camping Adventures," History.com, July 30, 2013, http://www.history.com/news/ford -and-edisons-excellent-camping-adventures.

329   Yet the impulse to occupy: Here, my analysis owes something to the writings of Charlie Hailey, including one of his books on the subject, *Camp: A Guide to 21st-Century Space* (Boston: Massachusetts Institute of Technology Press, 2009).

331   Touring Landau: Information courtesy of Al Hesselbart, in my various phone conversations with him. Additional information comes from Al Hesselbart, *The Dumb Things Sold . . . Just Like That! A History of the Recreational Vehicle Industry in America* (Bushnell, FL: RV History Programs, 2007), 29–30; Wood, *RVs and Campers, 1900–2000*, 11; James Twitchell, *Winnebago Nation: The RV in American Culture* (New York: Columbia University Press, 2014), 31–34; and Roger B. White, *Home on the Road: The Motor Home in America* (Washington: Smithsonian Institution Press, 2000), 18.

331   In terms of manic creativity and shamelessness, it was hard to beat the Conklin Family Gypsy Van: Roland Conklin information comes from Twitchell, *Winnebago Nation*, 34–35. Information on the land yacht's amenities and additional information on Conklin comes from "Gypsying Deluxe across Continent," *New York Times*, August 21, 1915, 4; "Motor-Driven Gypsy Van with Kitchen, Running Water, Beds, Tables, and Even a Roof Garden," *Automotive Manufacturer, Volume 57* (New York: Trade News Publishing Company, 1915), 17–19; and "Big Motor Yacht Has Reached Chicago Safely," *New York Times*, September 26, 1915, XX10.

331   the roads were so lousy . . . and use an onboard steel-and-plank bridge: White, *Home on the Road*, 24–27.

332   But their reputation took a drubbing in the mid-1930s: See Dorothy Ayers Counts and David R. Counts, *Over the Next Hill: An Ethnography of RVing Seniors in North America* (Peterborough, Ontario: Broadview Press, 1996), 37–41.

332   Buck Rogers: Michael Karl Witzel, *Route 66 Remembered* (St. Paul, MN: Motor Books, 2003), 146.

332   "air-conditioning" achieved with dry ice: Greg Williams, "Some Dream in Aluminum," *National Post*, October 2001.

335   "middle-class uncouthness": Twitchell, *Winnebago Nation*, 134

335   "He just sat in his camper": Charles McGrath, "A Reality Check for Steinbeck and Charley," *New York Times*, April 3, 2011.

EPILOGUE: A DOSE OF ENCHANTMENT

343   Gordon Hempton: For more information on Gordon Hempton and his various projects, see Gordon Hempton with John Grossman, *One Square Inch of Silence: One Man's Search for Natural Silence in a Noisy World* (New York: Free Press, 2009); Kathleen Dean Moore, "Silence Like Scouring Sand," *Orion* magazine online, October 2008, https://orionmagazine.org/article/silence-like -scouring-sand/; and *Soundtracker: A Portrait of Gordon Hempton*, directed by Nicholas Sherman, 2010, DVD.

BIBLIOGRAPHY

Abbey, Edward. *Desert Solitaire*. 1968; repr., Tucson: University of Arizona Press, 1988.

Applebome, Peter. *Scout's Honor: A Father's Unlikely Foray into the Woods*. New York: Harcourt, 2004.

Aron, Cindy. *Working at Play: A History of Vacations in the United States*. New York: Oxford University Press, 1999.

Baxter, Kent. *The Modern Age: Turn-of-the-Century American Culture and the Invention of Adolescence*. Tuscaloosa: University of Alabama Press, 2008.

Beard, Daniel Carter. *The American Boy's Handy Book*. New edition. New York: Charles Scribner and Sons, 1907.

Beard, George M. *Practical Treatise on Nervous Exhaustion (Neurasthenia): Its Symptoms, Nature, Sequences, Treatment*. New York: E. B. Treat, 1888.

Belasco, Warren. *Americans on the Road: From Autocamp to Motel, 1910–1945*. Baltimore, MD: Johns Hopkins University Press, 1979.

Bishop, James Jr. *Epitaph for a Desert Anarchist: The Life and Legacy of Edward Abbey*. New York: Simon and Schuster, 1994.

Brinkley, Douglas. *The Wilderness Warrior: Theodore Roosevelt and the Crusade for America*. New York: HarperCollins, 2009.

Brown, Tom Jr., with Brandt Morgan. *Tom Brown's Field Guide: Wilderness Survival*. New York: Penguin, 1983.

Brumley, Charles. *Guides of the Adirondacks: A Short Season. Hard Work. Low Pay.* Utica, NY: North Country Books, 1994.

Burroughs, John. *Under the Maples*. Boston and New York: Houghton Mifflin Company, 1921.

Burton, Pierre. *Niagara: A History of the Falls*. Albany: State University of New York Press, 1992.

Butters, MaryJane. *Glamping with MaryJane: Glamour+Camping*. Layton, UT: Gibbs Smith, 2012.

Byrd, William II of Westover. *The Dividing Line Histories of William Byrd II of Westover*. Edited by Kevin Joel Berland. Chapel Hill: University of North Carolina Press, 2013.

Chase, Alston. *Playing God in Yellowstone*. New York: Harcourt Brace and Company, 1987.

Collins, Gail. *America's Women: 400 Years of Dolls, Drudges, Helpmates, and Heroines*. New York: William Morrow, 2003.

Cordery, Stacy. *Juliette Gordon Low: The Remarkable Founder of the Girl Scouts*. New York: Penguin, 2012.

Counts, Dorothy Ayers, and David R. Counts. *Over the Next Hill: An Ethnography of RVing Seniors in North America*. Peterborough, Ontario: Broadview Press, 1996.

De Abaitua, Matthew. *The Art of Camping: The History and Practice of Sleeping under the Stars*. London: Hamish Hamilton, 2011.

Deloria, Philip Joseph. *Playing Indian*. New Haven, CT: Yale University Press, 1998.

Donaldson, Alfred Lee. *A History of the Adirondacks, Volume 1* and *Volume 2*. New York: The Century Co., 1921.

Duncan, Dayton. *The National Parks: America's Best Idea*. Preface by Ken Burns. New York: Alfred A. Knopf, 2009.

Emerson, Ralph Waldo. *Nature: Addresses, Lectures*. Boston and Cambridge: James Munroe and Company, 1849.

Evans, Estwick. *Pedestrious Tour, of Four Thousand Miles Through the Western States and Territories, during the Winter and Spring of 1818*. Concord, NH: Joseph C. Spear, 1819.

Fletcher, Colin. *The Complete Walker*. New York: Alfred A. Knopf, 1969.

———. *The Thousand-Mile Summer*. 1967; repr., New York: Vintage Books, 1989.

Fox, Stephen. *The American Conservation Movement: John Muir and His Legacy*. Madison: University of Wisconsin Press, 1981.

Glave, Dianne. *Rooted in the Earth, Reclaiming the African American Environmental Heritage*. Chicago, IL: Lawrence Hill Books, 2010.

HGiley, Charlie. *Camp: A Guide to 21st-Century Space*. Boston: Massachusetts Institute of Technology Press, 2009.

Hamblin, James. "Why We Took Cocaine Out of Soda." *Atlantic Monthly*, January 31, 2013.

Harding, Walter. *The Days of Henry Thoreau*. New York: Alfred A. Knopf, 1965.

Headley, Joel T. *The Adirondack, or Life in the Woods*. New York: Baker and Scribner, 1849.

Hempton, Gordon, with John Grossman. *One Square Inch of Silence: One Man's Search for Natural Silence in a Noisy World*. New York: Free Press, 2009.

Hermes, Matthew E. *Enough for One Lifetime: Wallace Carothers, Inventor of Nylon*. Laramie: University of Wyoming, American Chemical Society, 1996.

Hesselbart, Al. *The Dumb Things Sold . . . Just Like That! A History of the Recreational Vehicle Industry in America*. Bushnell, FL: RV History Programs, 2007.

Hulme, Kathryn. *How's the Road?* San Francisco, CA: privately printed, 1928.

Hunt, Linda Lawrence. *Bold Spirit: Helga Estby's Forgotten Walk across Victorian America*. New York: Anchor Books, 2003.

Jackson, Louise. *Mineral King: The Story of Beulah*. Mineral King Valley, CA: Sequoia Natural History Association, 2006.

Jamieson, Paul, and Neal Burdick, eds. *The Adirondack Reader: Four Centuries of Adirondack Writing*. Lake George, NY: Adirondack Mountain Club, 2009.

Jeal, Tim. *The Boy-Man*. New York: William Morrow and Co., 1990.

Jenkins, Jerry, with Andy Keal. *The Adirondack Atlas: A Geographic Portrait of the Adirondack Park*. Bronx, NY: Syracuse University Press and the Adirondack Museum, 2004.

Jerome, Christine. *An Adirondack Passage: The Cruise of the Canoe Sairy Gamp.* New York: HarperPerennial, 1994.

Keller, Betty. *Black Wolf: The Life of Ernest Thompson Seton.* Madeira Park, BC: Douglas and McIntyre, 1984.

Kelty, Nena, and Steve Boga. *Backpacking the Kelty Way.* New York: Berkley Publishing Group, 2000.

Kephart, Horace. *Camping and Woodcraft: A Handbook for Vacation Campers and for Travelers in the Wilderness.* 2 vols. 1916, 1917; repr., Gatlinburg, TN: Great Smoky Mountains Association, 2011.

Knowles, Joseph. *Alone in the Wilderness.* Boston: Small, Maynard and Company, 1913.

Lears, T. J. Jackson. *No Place of Grace: Antimodernism and the Transformation of American Culture, 1880–1920.* New York: Pantheon Books, 1981.

Luchetti, Cathy. *Men of the West: Life on the American Frontier.* New York: W. W. Norton and Co., 2004.

Lutz, Tom. *American Nervousness, 1903: An Anecdotal History.* Ithaca, NY: Cornell University Press, 1991.

Lyon, Robert. *Who Was Nessmuk?* Wellsboro, PA: Wellsboro Chamber of Commerce, 1971.

Macleod, David I. *Building Character in the American Boy: The Boy Scouts, YMCA, and Their Forerunners, 1870–1920.* Madison: University of Wisconsin Press, 1982.

Manning, Harvey. *Backpacking: One Step at a Time.* New York: Vintage Books, 1973.

Meyer, Kathleen. *How to Shit in the Woods: An Environmentally Sound Approach to a Lost Art.* 3rd ed. Berkeley: Ten Speed Press, 2011.

Miller, Dorcas S. *Adventurous Women: The Inspiring Lives of Nine Early Outdoorswomen.* Boulder, CO: Pruett Publishing Company, 2000.

Miller, Rod. *John Muir: Magnificent Tramp.* New York: Tom Doherty Associates, 2005.

Morris, Edmund. *The Rise of Theodore Roosevelt.* New York: Random House, 1979.

———. *Theodore Rex.* New York: Random House, 2001.

Motavalli, Jim. *Naked in the Woods: Joseph Knowles and the Legacy of Frontier Fakers.* Cambridge, MA: Da Capo Press, 2007.

Muir, John. *John of the Mountains: The Unpublished Journals of John Muir.* Edited by Linnie Marsh Wolfe. 1938; repr., Madison: University of Wisconsin Press, 1979.

———. *My First Summer in the Sierra.* New York: Houghton Mifflin Company, 1911.

———. *A Thousand-Mile Walk to the Gulf.* Edited by William Frederic Badè. New York: Houghton Mifflin Company, 1916.

———. *The Wilderness World of John Muir.* Edited and with an introduction by Edwin Way Teale. New York: Houghton Mifflin, 2001.

Murray, William H. H. *Adventures in the Wilderness, or, Camp-Life in the Adirondacks.* 1869; repr. Syracuse, NY: Adirondack Museum, Syracuse University Press, 1989.

Nash, Roderick. *Wilderness and the American Mind.* 4th ed. New Haven, CT: Yale University Press, 2001.

Nelson, Michael P., and J. Baird Callicott, eds. *The Wilderness Debate Rages On: Continuing the Great New Wilderness Debate.* Athens: University of Georgia Press, 2008.

O'Grady, John P. *Pilgrims to the Wild.* Salt Lake City: University of Utah Press, 1993.

O'Toole, Patricia. *When Trumpets Call: Theodore Roosevelt after the White House.* New York: Simon and Schuster, 2005.

Perrottet, Tony. "Where Was the Birthplace of the American Vacation?" *Smithsonian,* August 2013.

Peterman, Audrey. *Legacy on the Land: A Black Couple Discovers Our National Inheritance and Tells Why Every American Should Care.* Atlanta, GA: Earthwise Productions, 2009.

Radford, Harry V. *Adirondack Murray: A Biographical Appreciation.* New York: Broadway Publishing Company, 1906.

Rath, Richard Cullen. *How Early America Sounded.* Ithaca, NY: Cornell University Press, 2003.

Richardson, Robert D. Jr. *Henry Thoreau: A Life of the Mind.* Berkeley: University of California Press, 1986.

Scharnhorst, Gary. *Kate Field: The Many Lives of a Nineteenth-Century American Journalist.* Syracuse, NY: Syracuse University Press, 2008.

Schlett, James. *A Not Too Greatly Changed Eden: The Story of the Philosophers' Camp in the Adirondacks.* Ithaca, NY: Cornell University Press, 2015.

Schneider, Paul. *The Adirondacks: A History of America's First Wilderness.* New York: Henry Holt and Company, 1997.

Schrepfer, Susan. *Nature's Altars: Mountains, Gender, and American Environmentalism.* Lawrence: University Press of Kansas, 2005.

Schultz, Duane, and Sydney Schultz. *A History of Modern Psychology,* 11th ed. Boston: Cengage Learning, 2012.

Schwarcz, Joe. *The Genie in the Bottle: All-New Commentaries on the Fascinating Chemistry of Everyday Life.* New York: Henry Holt and Company, 2002.

Scott, David C., and Brendan Murphy. *The Scouting Party.* Irving, TX: Red Honor Press, 2010.

Sears, George Washington. *Canoeing the Adirondacks with Nessmuk: The Adirondack Letters of George Washington Sears.* Edited by Dan Brenan. 1962; repr., Blue Mountain Lake, NY: Adirondack Museum of the Adirondack Historical Association, 1993.

Stillman, William James. *The Autobiography of a Journalist, Volume 1.* London: Grant Richards, 1901.

Stowe, William. "Transcendental Vacations: Thoreau and Emerson in the Wilderness." *New England Quarterly,* September 2010.

Sullivan, Robert. *Cross Country.* New York: Bloomsbury, 2006.

Sutter, Paul. *Driven Wild: How the Fight Against Automobiles Launched the Modern Wilderness Movement.* Seattle: University of Washington Press, 2004.

Terrie, Philip. *Contested Terrain: A New History of Nature and People in the Adirondacks.* Syracuse, NY: Adirondack Museum, 1997.

———. *Forever Wild: A Cultural History of Wilderness in the Adirondacks.* Syracuse, NY: Syracuse University Press, 1994.

Thoreau, Henry David. *The Journal of Henry David Thoreau, 1837–1861.* New York: New York Review Books, 2009.

———. *Walden.* 1854; repr., New York: Vintage Books, 1991.

———. *The Writings of Henry David Thoreau Journal I, 1837–1846.* New York: Houghton Mifflin and Company, 1906.

Twitchell, James. *Winnebago Nation: The RV in American Culture.* New York: Columbia University Press, 2014.

Unger, Nancy C. *Beyond Nature's Housekeepers: American Women in Environmental History.* New York: Oxford University Press, 2012.

Vowell, Sarah. *Assassination Vacation.* New York: Simon and Schuster, 2005.

Warren, Karen. *Women's Voices in Experiential Education.* Dubuque, IA: Kendall/Hunt Publishing Co., 1996.

Weber, Sandra. *Adirondack Roots: Stories of Hiking, History, and Women*. Charleston, SC: History Press, 2011.

Wescott, David. *Camping in the Old Style*. Foreword and contributions by Steven M. Watts. Layton, UT: Gibbs Smith, 2015.

White, Elwyn Brooks. *The Points of My Compass*. New York: Harper and Row, 1962.

White, Roger B. *Home on the Road: The Motor Home in America*. Washington: Smithsonian Institution Press, 2000.

Witzel, Michael Karl. *Route 66 Remembered*. St. Paul, MN: Motor Books, 2003.

Wolfe, Audra J. "1940: Nylon 6,6." In Raymond J. Giguere, ed., *Molecules That Matter*. Philadelphia, PA: Frances Young Tang Teaching Museum and Art Gallery at Skidmore College and Chemical Heritage Foundation, 2008.

Wood, Donald F. *RVs and Campers, 1900–2000: An Illustrated History*. Hudson, WI: Iconografix, 2002.

Young, Terence. "'A Contradiction in Democratic Government': W. J. Trent, Jr., and the Struggle to Desegregate National Park Campgrounds," *Environmental History* 14, no. 4 (October 2009): 651–82.

———. "The End of Camping." In *Boom: A Journal of California*. http://www.boomcalifornia.com/2014/10/the-end-of-camping/.

Yowell, Skip. *The Hippie Guide to Climbing the Corporate Ladder and Other Mountains*. Nashville, TN: Naked Ink, 2006.

Zimmerman, Bonnie, ed. *Lesbian Histories and Cultures: An Encyclopedia, Volume 1*. New York: Garland Publishing, 2000.

ACKNOWLEDGMENTS

It's easier to just stay home. Sometimes camping requires an act of will and a willingness to embrace entropy. Most people wouldn't dare to climb into a motor home with me, knowing I'd never driven one before. Few sane children and adults would ever traipse into a remote rain forest knowing I was in charge of the gruesome foodstuffs. Thank you to my wife, Amy Ettinger, and my daughter, Julianna, who took most of these trips in the book with me and participated with care and enthusiasm in *every* phase of the project no matter how hard the bugs bit. Their spirit and care inform every chapter here. Thank you to Edie and Doug Achterman for love, support, and generosity, and for being really nice about letting us borrow a teetering heap of camping gear I have yet to return. My parents, Victor and Marilyn White, gave me an appreciation for wilderness camping and backpacking that dates to the late 1970s, when we bit off a section of the John Muir Trail with my siblings—a crash course in rapture, uphills, downhills, and mosquitoes. Thank you to Sheila Ettinger, my mother-in-law, for her caring and tireless boosterism. I appreciate it. My brother Phil White has been a wonderful correspondent about writers and writing for years now. My late brother, David White (1965–2009), was a reliable source of hilarity, pranks, memorable scares, and campfire stories during so many trips to the eastern Sierra Nevada from elementary school all the way through high school. We used to fight like wildcats in our leaky tube tent, make each other laugh hysterically, scare the hell out of each other about bears, and playact scenes involving frontiersmen, polar exploration, and of course the curse of Bigfoot. My brother claimed to be on a first-name basis with this beast of the wild, and was an endless fount of highly suspect "true stories" about Sasquatch, many of which "just so happened" to have taken place wherever we were camping for the evening. The two of us once attempted to climb one of the Minarets in a chaotic, fearless way that John Muir would have appreciated or pitied, depending on his mood. No ropes, no chalk, just two insane middle school kids winging it out of sheer cussed determination. I miss my brother every day.

A special thanks to Micah Perks, who came up with the title for this book. Credit for the subtitle goes to Wallace Baine. His valuable feedback and the ideas of Peggy Townsend, Elizabeth McKenzie, Richard Huffman, Richard Lange, John Chandler, Jessica Breheny, and Vito Victor improved the manuscript, draft by draft by draft. A special thanks to Sam Autman for remarks on "Gator Girls," and Liza Monroy for giving me additional read-throughs and wise suggestions for several chapters. Thank you to the friends who discussed this book with me either on the phone or online, in person and in some cases over brews: Harlan Glatt, James Shiffer, Sara Oh Neville, Bill Sherman, Fidel Mejia, and Will Zilliacus.

A very big thank-you to Michael Signorelli for giving so much of yourself and your time to this project, for suggesting this exploration in the first place, and for sticking with me; and to my literary agent, Kris Dahl at ICM, for strong advocacy over the years, from *The Cactus Eaters* and beyond.

Correspondence with the acclaimed biographer Robert D. Richardson gave me confidence to pursue my idea that Henry David Thoreau's time at Walden Pond was as much about camping as it was about writing. The eminent Adirondacks historian Philip Terrie was kind enough to read over and offer suggestions for the two contiguous chapters that deal with the Adirondacks. George Ellison, who has written extensively about Horace Kephart, read the "Acts of Transmission" chapter and offered suggestions. David Wescott was also a valuable source of information about classic camping. David C. Scott, coauthor, along with Brendan Murphy, of my favorite Scouting history book, *The Scouting Party*, offered a few sugges-tions for the chapter that delved into the founding of the Boy Scouts of America. Donald Worster, author of *A Passion for Nature*, an eye-opening John Muir biography, read and had suggestions for the Muir-Roosevelt chapter. Jim Motavalli, biographer of Joe Knowles (*Naked in the Woods*), conversed with me on the phone and shared feedback. Paul Sutter, a professor of U.S. environmental history whose book *Driven Wild* is a provocative look at the relationship between out-of-control road building and the wilderness movement, gave feedback regarding a section relating to the Wilderness Act, while "old gear" collector and expert Bruce "Yeti" Johnson let me know about some influential but lesser-known post–World War II gear geniuses who deserved inclusion in the same chapter. Nancy C. Unger's writings on women in the woods inspired my chapter "Wild Victorian Ladies"; her comments on that chapter and our communications about the subject matter were extremely helpful.

Obviously my "Gator Girls" chapter would have been a bust without the good humor and candor of Meena, Jaliyah, Chelsea, and all the other girls for whom I have created made-up names (most of them were minors at the time of the trip), as well as Winston Walters and Karen Kerr and all the people over at ICO. Audrey Peterman, Dianne Glave, and Brandon Harris were important sources of historical background and strong opinions. Marmot expert Dan Blumstein added scientific heft (and teeth) to the marmot attack scene in the "How's the Road?" chapter, while my phone conversation with Mineral King historian Louise Jackson gave me a strong sense of auto camping in that area in the 1920s. A special thank-you to Spencer for sharing your story up at Mineral King. Glad to hear that things are going very well for you. Kathleen Meyer, author of *How to Shit in the Woods*, was an insightful and hilarious correspondent with regard to my "Immaculator" chapter. Thanks to the helicopter crew and rangers who patrol the Whitney Zone and to all the Whitney hikers who were kind enough to talk with (and watch out for) me while I staggered up that hellacious mountain.

Patricia O'Toole, acclaimed presidential biographer (and my mentor and friend), took a look at the glamping chapter ("Kovu's Brother"), which goes into some detail about Theodore Roosevelt's safari trip. My phone conversations with the wise and witty Al Hesselbart gave me a better understanding of RV history. Gordon Hempton was kind enough to give his time and to show us some lovely places in the Hoh Rain Forest; while the interpretive ranger Jon Preston gave me a vivid sense of the place before I got there. All these people helped me get closer to my goals for this book; any elisions or mistakes that were made in spite of their intervention are mine alone.

Thank you to Zippy and everyone at High Peaks Cyclery in Lake Placid; and to John Warren for background information and reading recommendations; Chris Shaw for stories and Adirondacks recommendations; Laura Rice for showing me a fascinating "illustrated manuscript" at the Adirondack Museum; Angela Snye for helping with images; Jerold Pepper for insight; and Joe Hackett for his guiding recollections and for the use of his guide boat. Thank you to Robin Bliss-Wagner, an imaginative and formidable wilderness skills expert. Thank you to Rob Knight, Kalin McGraw, Howard Heevner, Krisa Bruemmer, Jeff Rockwell, and the wilderness skills maven Brian King for making the Badger Spring adventure seem a touch less onerous. Thank you to Margot Case and your wonderful family in Seattle; we will never forget your warm hospitality. Correspondence with Katie Renz and Sarah Brafman helped me clarify aspects of this book. Thank you to the interlibrary loan service at UC Santa Cruz's McHenry Library and all of the patient staff members who helped me get my hands on source books, including a few rare and unpublished manuscripts. Thank you to Bryan Whitledge of the Clarke Historical Library, Steve Kemp of the Great Smoky Mountains Association, and Wade V. Myers of the Harpers Ferry Center for Media Services.

Without the teaching and example of Mary Harden in San Francisco (http://maryhardendesigns.com), I would not have had the inspiration to do the pen-and-ink-wash illustrations and watercolors that pop up every so often in this book.

Thanks to Stacy Cordery for last-minute suggestions on a chapter section dealing with Juliette Gordon Low and the early Girl Scouts and to Guy Lasnier for camping expertise and gear.

And thank you to the late, great, classic camping master Steve Watts. In my last correspondence with Steve, I regretted never having the chance to spend time in the woods with him. "Someday by the campfire," he said in his final sign-off.

ILLUSTRATION CREDITS

137   The illustration of Helga and Clara Estby appeared in the New York *World* on December 25, 1896.

185   The photograph of John Muir and Theodore Roosevelt in Yosemite (1903, by Underwood & Underwood) courtesy of the Library of Congress and the National Park Service Historic Photograph Collection.

191   John Muir illustration: India ink, pen, graphite pencil, and water pen, with construction paper border, by Dan White.

199   Image of Estwick Evans courtesy of the Clarke Historical Library at Central Michigan University. This picture was the original frontispiece of Evans's 1819 memoir, *Pedestrious Tour*.

201   Yellow jacket illustration: watercolor, construction paper, and graphite pencil, by Dan White.

205   The photograph of Joseph Knowles comes from his book *Alone in the Wilderness* (1913).

220   The diagram of a sample debris shelter comes from Robin Bliss-Wagner, who made this illustration on July 28, 2013, a few days before Knowles Day.

222   Photograph of author's feet sticking out of a sample shelter was taken on July 28, 2013, a few days before Knowles Day, by Robin Bliss-Wagner. This is, of course, a preliminary or rough-draft version of the shelter, and not the same one that I used to keep warm, more or less, in the Soquel Demonstration State Forest. (The photograph was taken elsewhere in Santa Cruz County.)

239   The image of an automobile stranded in the mud of rural Wyoming (1925, photographer unknown) is courtesy of Yellowstone National Park's historic photography collection.

242   The marmot photograph was taken by Michael Bolte. Used by permission.

254   Wallace Hume Carothers illustration: India ink, water pencil, graphite pencil, and pen, by Dan White.

270   Edward Abbey illustration: India ink and graphite pencil, by Dan White.

274   Immaculator photograph was taken in September 2014 by Dan White.

308   Demoiselle crane illustration: watercolor and graphite pencil, by Dan White.

332   The 1915 photograph of the Conklin Gypsy Van is part of the Huntington Historical Society's collection in Huntington, New York.

INDEX

———

ABOUT THE AUTHOR

DAN WHITE is the author of *The Cactus Eaters: How I Lost My Mind— and Almost Found Myself—on the Pacific Crest Trail*. He has taught writing at Columbia University and San Jose State University. He is a contributing editor of *Catamaran Literary Reader* and received his MFA from Columbia University. He lives in Santa Cruz, California, with his wife and daughter.